# SECOND EDITION BUSINESS AND PROFESSIONAL COMMUNICATION

## SECOND EDITION

# BUSINESS AND PROFESSIONAL COMMUNICATION

## KEYS for Workplace Excellence

**KELLY M. QUINTANILLA**

*Texas A&M University–Corpus Christi*

**SHAWN T. WAHL**

*Missouri State University*

Los Angeles | London | New Delhi
Singapore | Washington DC

Los Angeles | London | New Delhi
Singapore | Washington DC

FOR INFORMATION:

SAGE Publications, Inc.
2455 Teller Road
Thousand Oaks, California 91320
E-mail: order@sagepub.com

SAGE Publications Ltd.
1 Oliver's Yard
55 City Road
London, EC1Y 1SP
United Kingdom

SAGE Publications India Pvt. Ltd.
B 1/I 1 Mohan Cooperative Industrial Area
Mathura Road, New Delhi 110 044
India

SAGE Publications Asia-Pacific Pte. Ltd.
3 Church Street
#10-04 Samsung Hub
Singapore 049483

Copyright © 2014 by SAGE Publications, Inc.

Printed in Canada

*Library of Congress Cataloging-in-Publication Data*

Quintanilla, Kelly M.

Business and professional communication : keys for workplace excellence / Kelly M. Quintanilla, Shawn T. Wahl. -- 2nd ed.

p. cm.
Includes bibliographical references and index.

ISBN 978-1-4522-1762-8 (pbk.)

1. Business communication. I. Wahl, Shawn T. II. Title.

HF5718.Q56 2014
658.4'5--dc23          2012037171

Acquisitions Editor:   Matthew Byrnie
Associate Editor:   Nathan Davidson
Editorial Assistant:   Stephanie Palermini
Production Editor:   Brittany Bauhaus
Copy Editor:   Megan Granger
Typesetter:   C&M Digitals (P) Ltd.
Proofreader:   Lawrence W. Baker
Indexer:   Diggs Publication Services, Inc.
Cover Designer:   Janet Kiesel
Marketing Manager:   Liz Thornton
Permissions Editor:   Karen Ehrman

This book is printed on acid-free paper.

13 14 15 16 17 10 9 8 7 6 5 4 3 2 1

# Brief Contents

Preface     xiii

Acknowledgments     xviii

**PART I. BEGINNING COMMUNICATION PRINCIPLES**     1

**CHAPTER 1.** Business and Professional Excellence in the Workplace     3

**CHAPTER 2.** Verbal and Nonverbal Communication     25

**CHAPTER 3.** Listening     49

**PART II. ENTERING THE WORKPLACE**     68

**CHAPTER 4.** Résumés, Interviews, and Negotiation     71

**CHAPTER 5.** Getting to Know Your Diverse Workplace     103

**PART III. DEVELOPING IN THE WORKPLACE**     124

**CHAPTER 6.** Interpersonal Communication at Work     127

**CHAPTER 7.** Strengthening Teams and Conducting Meetings     147

**PART IV. EXCELLING IN THE WORKPLACE**     178

**CHAPTER 8.** Technology in the Workplace     181

**CHAPTER 9.** Business and Professional Writing     203

**CHAPTER 10.** Leadership and Conflict Management     233

**PART V. PRESENTING IN THE WORKPLACE**     264

**CHAPTER 11.** Informing and Persuading     267

**CHAPTER 12.** Speech Design     289

**CHAPTER 13.** Delivering a Speech With Professional Excellence     311

**PART VI. SURVIVING IN THE WORKPLACE**     334

**CHAPTER 14.** Work–Life Balance     337

Epilogue     373

References     375

Glossary     387

Photo Credits     399

Index     401

About the Authors     409

# Detailed Contents

Preface   xiii

Acknowledgments   xviii

## PART I. BEGINNING COMMUNICATION PRINCIPLES   1

**CHAPTER 1.** Business and Professional Excellence in the Workplace   3

Business and Professional Excellence in Context   5

    *Verbal and Nonverbal Communication*   6

    *Listening*   6

    *Résumés, Interviews, and Negotiations*   6

    *Getting to Know the Diverse Workplace*   6

    *Interpersonal Communication at Work*   7

    *Strengthening Teams and Conducting Meetings*   7

    *Technology in the Workplace*   7

    *Business and Professional Writing*   7

    *Leadership and Conflict Management*   8

    *Presentations*   8

    *Work–Life Balance*   8

Understanding the KEYS Process   8

Defining Communication   10

The Importance of Communication   10

Communication: A Complex Process   11

    *Sender and Receiver*   12

    *Message and Feedback*   13

    *Channel*   13

    *Context*   13

    *Noise*   14

Communication Apprehension   15

    *Types of Communication Apprehension*   15

    *Causes of Communication Apprehension*   17

Communication Ethics   17

KEYS for Excellence in the Workplace   19

Executive Summary   22

Discussion Questions   23

Terms to Remember   23

**CHAPTER 2.** Verbal and Nonverbal Communication   25

Verbal Communication   26

Nonverbal Communication   29

Codes of Nonverbal Communication   33
    *Vocal Expression*   33
    *Space*   34
    *Environment*   36
    *Physical Appearance*   37
    *Body Movement*   38
    *Facial Behavior*   39
    *Touch*   40
Forming Relationships With Verbal and Nonverbal Communication   41
    *Verbal and Nonverbal Communication and Their Impact on Professions*   42
KEYS to Excellence in Verbal and Nonverbal Communication   44
Executive Summary   46
Discussion Questions   47
Terms to Remember   47

## CHAPTER 3. Listening   49

Hearing and Listening   51
Barriers to Listening   53
    *Failing to Limit Distractions*   53
    *Failing to Focus on the Message*   55
    *Failing to Be an Active Listener*   57
Listening Styles and Categories   59
Improving Your Listening   60
KEYS to Listening Excellence   62
Executive Summary   64
Discussion Questions   65
Terms to Remember   65

## PART II. ENTERING THE WORKPLACE   68

## CHAPTER 4. Résumés, Interviews, and Negotiation   71

The Job-Seeking Process   73
Stage One: Exploring   73
    *Self-Exploration*   73
    *Career Exploration*   74
Stage Two: Researching   75
    *Researching Openings*   75
    *Researching Potential Employers*   76
Stage Three: Applying   77
    *Developing Résumés*   77
    *Customizing Résumés*   82
    *Developing Electronic and Scannable Résumés and Online Applications*   83
    *Developing Cover Letters*   84
Stage Four: Interviewing   88
    *Before the Interview*   89
    *During the Interview*   95
Stage Five: Following Up   96

Stage Six: Negotiations   97
KEYS to Excellence in the Job-Seeking Process   99
Executive Summary   100
Discussion Questions   101
Terms to Remember   101

**CHAPTER 5.** Getting to Know Your Diverse Workplace   103
Learning Your Workplace Culture   104
Assimilating College Students   107
Diversity in Your Workplace: Some Important Concepts   112
   *Cultural Diversity Awareness and Worldview*   112
   *Cultural Competence*   113
   *Mutual Respect*   114
Examples of Diversity in Professional Contexts   114
   *Gender*   115
   *Ethnicity and Race*   115
   *Language Differences*   116
   *Religion and Spirituality*   118
   *People With Disabilities*   119
KEYS to Excellence in Getting to Know the Diverse Workplace   120
Executive Summary   122
Discussion Questions   123
Terms to Remember   123

**PART III. DEVELOPING IN THE WORKPLACE**   124

**CHAPTER 6.** Interpersonal Communication at Work   127
Exploring Relationship Types at Work   129
   *Superior–Subordinate Relationships*   129
   *Coworker Relationships*   132
   *Customer–Client Relationships*   134
The Line Between Professional and Personal   135
   *Romance in the Workplace*   135
   *Sexual Harassment*   136
   *Communication Privacy Management at Work*   137
Professional Etiquette   139
KEYS to Excellence in Interpersonal Communication   142
Executive Summary   144
Discussion Questions   145
Terms to Remember   145

**CHAPTER 7.** Strengthening Teams and Conducting Meetings   147
How Do Groups Differ From Teams?   148
Conducting Meetings   149
   *Meeting Environment*   150
   *Meeting Topics (Agenda)*   154
   *Meeting Participants*   155
Team Roles   156
Team Norms   156

Problem Solving   158
    *Describing and Analyzing the Problem*   160
    *Generating Possible Solutions*   161
    *Evaluating All Solutions*   162
    *Deciding on the Solution*   163
    *Planning How to Implement the Solution*   165
Cultivating Innovative Thinking   166
    *Explorer*   166
    *Artist*   167
    *Judge*   167
    *Warrior*   168
    *Supporting Each Role*   168
Conflict in Team Meetings   169
    *Need for Conflict*   169
    *Productive Conflict*   172
    *The Unite Approach*   173
KEYS to Excellence in Team Communication   174
Executive Summary   176
Discussion Questions   177
Terms to Remember   177

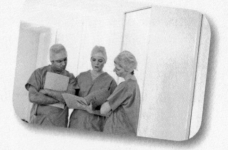

## PART IV. EXCELLING IN THE WORKPLACE   178

**CHAPTER 8.** Technology in the Workplace   181
Communication and Technology: Tools for Professionals   182
    *Maintaining Professional Excellence Online*   184
    *Electronic Communication*   184
Drawbacks of Technology   190
    *Employee Surveillance*   191
    *Time Management*   193
    *Information Overload*   194
    *Electronic Aggression*   196
Professional Etiquette With Technology   197
KEYS to Excellence With Communication and Technology   198
Executive Summary   200
Discussion Questions   201
Terms to Remember   201

**CHAPTER 9.** Business and Professional Writing   203
The Importance of Written Communication   204
    *Striving for Written Communication Excellence*   205
Types of Written Communication   207
    *Business Letters*   207
    *Employee Reviews*   208
    *Recommendation Letters*   209
    *Thank-You Letters*   212
    *Memos*   212
    *Proposals and Reports*   219

*Planning Documents*   220
*Press Releases*   221
*Proactive Media Writing*   227
*E-mail*   228
KEYS to Excellence in Written Communication   229
Executive Summary   230
Discussion Questions   231
Terms to Remember   231

**CHAPTER 10.** Leadership and Conflict Management   233
What Is Leadership?   234
Utilizing Power   236
Improving Communication With Leadership Theories   239
   *Behavioral Theories*   239
   *Situational Leadership Theories*   241
   *Transformational Leadership*   243
Hiring the Right Team   243
   *Developing the New Employee Profile*   243
   *During the Interview*   244
   *After the Interview*   245
Following Up and Following Through   246
Communicating About Your Team   246
Dealing With Difficult People   248
   *Meet Your Organizational Family*   248
   *Leader as Parent*   251
Giving Feedback   251
   *Setting Expectations*   252
   *Providing Feedback Regularly*   252
   *Praising Team Members*   253
   *Holding Team Members Accountable*   253
   *Motivating Through Feedback*   255
   *Enacting Consequences*   256
   *Putting It Together*   257
Managing Your Public Image   259
Keys to Excellence in Leadership   260
Executive Summary   262
Discussion Questions   263
Terms to Remember   263

**PART V. PRESENTING IN THE WORKPLACE**   264

**CHAPTER 11.** Informing and Persuading   267
The Importance of Presenting With Professional Excellence   269
Identifying Presentation Opportunities and Purposes   269
   *Presentation Opportunities*   269
   *General Purpose*   270
   *Specific Purpose*   271
Speaking to Inform   271
   *Ethos*   271

   *Logos*   273

   *Strategies for Informing With Excellence*   276

  Speaking to Persuade   278

   *Types of Reasoning*   279

   *Pathos*   281

   *Strategies for Persuading With Excellence*   282

  KEYS to Excellence in Professional Presentations   283

  Executive Summary   286

  Discussion Questions   287

  Terms to Remember   287

**CHAPTER 12.** Speech Design   289

  Analyzing the Audience   290

  Analyzing the Context   291

  Researching   292

   *Gathering Research*   292

   *Determining What to Include*   295

  Organizing Your Presentation   296

   *Organizing the Body*   296

   *Developing Transitions*   297

  Introductions   299

  Conclusions   301

  Language   304

  KEYS to Excellence in Designing a Speech   305

  Executive Summary   306

  Discussion Questions   307

  Terms to Remember   307

**CHAPTER 13.** Delivering a Speech With Professional Excellence   311

  Delivering the Presentation With Professional Excellence   312

   *The Adrenaline Rush*   312

   *Sense of Play*   315

   *Presenting From an Outline*   315

  PowerPoint and Other Supporting Aids   316

   *Should I Use Supporting Aids?*   318

   *Types of Supporting Aids*   319

  Practice Makes Perfect   326

  Team Presentations   326

  KEYS to Excellence in Professional Presentations   328

  Executive Summary   332

  Discussion Questions   333

  Terms to Remember   333

**PART VI. SURVIVING IN THE WORKPLACE**   334

**CHAPTER 14.** Work–Life Balance   337

  The Importance of Work–Life Balance   338

   *Work–Life Balance Defined*   339

   *Individual Benefits*   341

   *Organizational Benefits*   342

Triggers to Imbalance   343
    *Personality Types*   343
    *The Impact of Difficult People on Work–Life Balance*   345
    *Technologically Blurred Boundaries*   351
    *Life Demands*   352
Strategies for Balance   357
    *Knowing Yourself*   357
    *Developing Emotional Intelligence*   359
    *Developing Time-Management Skills*   363
    *Using the PDA to Maintain Balance*   363
    *Taking a Vacation*   366
KEYS to Excellence With Work–Life Balance   368
Executive Summary   370
Discussion Questions   371
Terms to Remember   371

Epilogue   373

References   375

Glossary   387

Photo Credits   399

Index   401

About the Authors   409

# Preface

As instructors, we must answer many questions when planning a business and professional communication course. First, we must address the broader conceptual questions, such as "What do we want our students to learn?" "How can this information be applied to their current and future professional lives?" "How can we make this material meaningful, useful, and interesting to students with a variety of professional goals and interests?" "How can all important information, skills, and competencies relevant to business and professional communication be covered in one term?"

Next, we must address the nuts-and-bolts questions that emerge about how to organize so much information and how to translate it into accessible language for students. Instructors often grapple with questions such as "Should I require both an individual and team presentation?" "How much time should I put in the schedule for mock interviews?" "How much attention should be given to résumé development?" "How can this course be delivered online?"

We considered many of the same questions and challenges as we made decisions about what content to cover in this text. **Our mission** in writing this book was to focus the research and competencies related to business and professional communication so that it can easily be covered in one term across delivery formats (e.g., traditional, online, hybrid). Further, we wanted to provide a book that speaks directly to the student as a developing professional by focusing on the actual experiences—from the job search to developing workplace relations to managing the challenges of coworker bullies, difficult clients, burnout, and the like. We also wanted to provide a text that is adaptable to a variety of instructional needs—for our colleagues who may need the flexibility to emphasize individual presentations and for others who may focus more on team presentations, not include oral communication at all, or deliver the course online. We recognize the diversity from one college or university to the next.

In response to our goal of focusing directly on the individual student experience related to the development of business and professional excellence, we developed an **organizing feature** (the KEYS process described below), which we believe will help instructors guide students and developing professionals in a variety of professional contexts. The KEYS process fosters the primary theme of this text—one that encourages students, regardless of industry or career, to strive for **professional excellence.** In this text, we provide 14 tightly focused chapters in which the best material—drawn from the research bases of communication, business, leadership, psychology, education, and other disciplines—is explored with relevance to the KEYS process. This book doesn't attempt to cover the entire business and professional world—we've made difficult choices regarding the content, based on our years of communication consulting in the business world, teaching communication in higher education, and experimenting with texts written by our friends and colleagues across the nation. What we ended up with represents the cutting-edge work in the field, including research from a variety of methods as well as popular literature, human resources, corporate consulting, and leadership coaching. **Our goal is to connect students across industries and academic disciplines to both theory and practice by applying information regarding business and professional communication directly to professional life *inside* and *outside* the workplace—without overwhelming them.**

We believe that one of the strengths of this text is that it addresses the challenges we face in today's workplace. In addition to our experience as teacher-scholars in communication, we have worked as consultants designing training and development programs for organizations in a variety of industries. While all these organizations face similar communication challenges, other textbooks merely mention the problems and rarely address solutions. *Business and Professional Communication: KEYS for Workplace Excellence* not only examines workplace problems (e.g., difficult people, negative impacts of technology, work–life balance, corporate health), it also provides students with a communication process that helps them solve problems and continue their professional journeys.

# Organizing Feature: KEYS for Workplace Excellence

We believe that developing an organizing feature lends clarity to a textbook. Further, such a feature helps students apply material directly to their lives. The **organizing feature** running throughout the text is KEYS, a process designed to develop students' critical thinking skills and make them more reflexive communicators with the ability to adapt and continually improve.

The KEYS Process includes the following four phases:

**KEYS:** (**K**now yourself, **E**valuate the professional context, **Y**our communication interaction occurs, **S**tep back and reflect)

1. **K**now yourself: Challenging students to actively assess their skills as communicators and then develop strategies to utilize their strengths and develop their weaknesses

2. **E**valuate the professional context: Teaching students to proactively address the needs of their audience and understand the constraints of the professional communication context, as well as developing their skills for communicating with a variety of audiences and contexts

3. **Y**our communication interaction occurs: Asking students to monitor their own verbal and nonverbal communication in addition to the audience within each interaction

4. **S**tep back and reflect: Examining the effectiveness of verbal and nonverbal messages they convey to others and the overall success of various communication interactions and then taking what they've learned and starting the KEYS process again. Developing the ability to continually adapt and improve using a personalized communication inventory

# Overview of the Book: Strategies for Excelling in the Workplace at Every Stage

The book is organized into five distinct parts. Part I provides an overview of the foundations and key concepts important to the study of business and professional communication and introduces students to central principles related to verbal and nonverbal communication and listening. The next four parts correspond with the stages of experience that come with entering the workplace for the first time, receiving a promotion, or changing careers. **Each chapter includes cutting-edge research, skills, and tips that will help students to advance in the workplace at every stage of their career by honing their communication skills.** Throughout the text, we connect important issues such as cultural diversity, cultural competence, mutual respect, gender, ethnicity and race, religion, people with disabilities, and more to the business and professional context. With each phase of development, students will gain interpersonal competency, enhance their organizational ability, and refine their presentational skills. The final stage of experience, *Surviving in the Workplace*, encourages students to develop strategies for balancing work and life through communication, a topic not covered in most business and professional communication textbooks.

## Features of the Textbook

We provide several unique pedagogical features to help students understand and apply the concepts and theories introduced in the text. The features help reinforce the book's themes and promote critical thinking in readers.

- **Chapter Outlines** detail the organization of each chapter, while **Chapter Objectives** help students prioritize information so that they can learn more efficiently.
- An **opening chapter narrative** connects students to the primary chapter content—a brief example of real world stories to gain attention from readers as they move into a new topic. In all chapters, opening chapter narratives are ripped-from-the-headlines news stories representing actual events and real experiences across business and professional contexts.
- Themes from the narratives appear throughout each chapter and are applied to and evaluated with the KEYS feature in a summary section, called **KEYS for Workplace Excellence**, that appears at the end of each chapter.
- The KEYS organizing theme is also highlighted into four distinct instructional features: **Know Yourself** features self-assessments and inventories for readers to hone their communication skills; **Evaluate the Professional Context** encourages application of knowledge to a variety of professional contexts and situations; **Your Communication Interaction** highlights specific communication interactions and cases that promote critical thinking and class discussion; and **Step Back and Reflect** presents challenges and dilemmas in business and professional contexts, promoting analysis of what went wrong in specific business and professional situations.
- Communication ethics is emphasized in all chapters with a feature called **Ethical Connection**, which connects the topic to an ethical perspective—because it's the foundation of business and professional excellence.

- All chapters also include a feature called **Executive Summary**, designed to promote reading comprehension and serve as a guide to help connect chapter concepts to learning objectives.
- We include **Discussion Questions** that instructors may use as a means of generating class discussions about chapter content, as actual assignments, or as thought-provokers for students to consider on their own time.
- Complete **References** to the research base cited within the text appear at the end of the book and are organized by chapter. Students may find these references useful as they prepare assignments and/or conduct their own research projects. Instructors may use the references to gather additional material for their own research or to supplement instruction.

## New to this Edition

- The text includes **two new chapters**, Chapter 2: Verbal and Nonverbal Communication and Chapter 3: Listening.
- **New chapter-opening vignettes** introduce each chapter with a contemporary example drawn from the real world. **New Executive Summary** concisely reviews key concepts and skills at the end of every chapter.
- **Revised and updated box feature program** now includes four boxes tied directly to the KEYS model: **K**now Yourself, **E**valuate the Professional Context, **Y**our Communication Ineraction, and **S**tep Back and Reflect, as well as a newly expanded **Ethical Connection.** All box features now include discussion questions to promote critical thinking and classroom discussion.
- **New self-assessment feature** entitled **Know Yourself** is included in all chapters.
- Updated photo program throughout every chapter.

# ANCILLARIES

Additional ancillary materials further support and enhance the learning goals of *Business and Professional Communication: KEYS for Workplace Excellence, Second Edition.* These ancillary materials include the following:

## Instructor Teaching Site

### www.sagepub.com/keys2e

The password-protected Instructor Teaching Site gives instructors access to a full complement of resources to support and enhance their course. The following assets are available on the site:

- **Test Bank:** This Word test bank offers a diverse set of test questions and answers for each chapter of the book. Multiple-choice, true/false, short-answer, and essay questions for every chapter help instructors assess students' progress and understanding.

- **PowerPoint® Slides:** Chapter-specific slide presentations offer assistance with lecture and review preparation by highlighting essential content, features, and artwork from the book.
- **Sample Syllabi:** Two sample syllabi—one for a semester class and one a quarter-length class—are provided to help professors structure their courses.
- **Lecture Notes:** Lecture notes for each chapter are provided as a resource for instructors as they lecture or structure their courses.
- **Web Resources:** These links to relevant websites direct both instructors and students to additional resources for further research on important chapter topics.
- **Video Links:** Carefully selected, web-based video resources feature relevant interviews, lectures, personal stories, inquiries, and other content for use in independent or classroom-based explorations of key topics.
- **SAGE Journal Articles:** A "Learning From SAGE Journal Articles" feature provides access to recent, relevant full-text articles from SAGE's leading research journals.

## Student Study Site

### www.sagepub.com/keys2e

The open-access Student Study Site is designed to maximize student comprehension of the material and to promote critical thinking and application. The following resources and study tools are available on the student portion of the book's website:

- **E-flashcards:** These study tools reinforce students' understanding of key terms and concepts that have been outlined in the chapters.
- **Web Quizzes:** Flexible self-quizzes allow students to independently assess their progress in learning course material.
- **Web Resources:** These links to relevant websites direct both instructors and students to additional resources for further research on important chapter topics.
- **Video Links:** Carefully selected, web-based video resources feature relevant interviews, lectures, personal stories, inquiries, and other content for use in independent or classroom-based explorations of key topics.
- **SAGE Journal Articles:** A "Learning From SAGE Journal Articles" feature provides access to recent, relevant full-text articles from SAGE's leading research journals.

# Acknowledgments

This project has been both exciting and challenging. Thus, there are many people we would like to acknowledge. The authors wish to thank the team at SAGE, whom it's been a pleasure to work with, including Matt Byrnie, Nathan Davidson, and Stephanie Palermini, who all offered great assistance, feedback, and encouragement.

We are grateful to our colleagues and friends in the field of communication whose advice and encouragement helped inform our decisions during the review process of this text. We would like to thank all reviewers who worked on this project for both the First and Second Editions.

Reviewers for the Second Edition:

Diane L. Carter, *University of Idaho*

Katherine M. Castle, *University of Nebraska–Lincoln*

Jennifer Karchmer, *Western Washington University*

Alison McCrowell Lietzenmayer, *Old Dominion University*

Amanda Retberg, *Wisconsin Lutheran College*

Astrid Sheil, *California State University, San Bernardino*

Scott Wilson, *Central Ohio Technical College*

Reviewers for the First Edition:

Karla Mason Bergen, *College of Saint Mary, Omaha*

Nicholas F. Burnett, *California State University, Sacramento*

Carolyn Clark, *Salt Lake Community College*

Dale Cyphert, *University of Northern Iowa*

Dale Davis, *University of Texas at San Antonio*

Kristina Drumheller, *West Texas A&M University*

Randy Duncan, *Henderson State University*

Leonard M. Edmonds, *Arizona State University*

Michele Foss-Snowden, *California State University, Sacramento*

Jeffrey Dale Hobbs, *University of Texas at Tyler*

Melody A. Hubbard, *Northwest Missouri State University*

William W. Kenner, *University of Michigan–Flint*

Erika L. Kirby, *Creighton University*

John Ludlum, *Otterbein College*

Marie A. Mater, *Houston Baptist University*

M. Chad McBride, *Creighton University*

Aysel Morin, *East Carolina University*

Laura Umphrey, *Northern Arizona University*

Denise Vrchota, *Iowa State University*

Thanks also to our colleagues, friends, and students at Texas A&M University–Corpus Christi, Angelo State University, and Missouri State University. We are especially grateful to Ashley Billig and Travis Covill for their contributions to the research-gathering process, photographic selections, permissions, and assistance with instructional supplements. We would also like to extend a very special thank you to the always amazing Tara Hall. Her work as a researcher, writer, and editor are second to none.

Finally, we thank our families and friends for their support and belief in this book and its authors. Kelly thanks her mother, Barbara Miller, for instilling in her a love of learning, for always being there, and for proofreading everything she has ever written. She thanks her husband, Anthony Quintanilla, for loving her unconditionally, for always making her laugh, for never letting her win an argument, and for being her biggest fan. And she thanks her daughter, Logan Quintanilla, for being the most wonderful blessing anyone could ever receive. Shawn thanks his mother, Evelyn Wahl, who was always there to listen and provide support during the writing process; his brothers, Larkin Wahl and Shannon Wahl, for their confidence and support; and his dearest friends and mentors Steve Beebe, Dawn O. Braithwaite, Chad Edwards, Autumn Edwards, Phyllis Japp, Ronald Lee, Terry Lewis, Chad McBride, Scott Myers, K. David Roach, Bill Seiler, and Shad Tyra.

—Kelly M. Quintanilla
*Corpus Christi, Texas*

—Shawn T. Wahl
*Springfield, Missouri*

part

# Beginning Communication Principles

Chapter 1: Business and Professional
Excellence in the Workplace

Chapter 2: Verbal and Nonverbal
Communication

Chapter 3: Listening

# Chapter Outline

**Business and Professional Excellence in Context**  5

**Understanding the KEYS Process**  8

**Defining Communication**  10

**The Importance of Communication**  10

**Communication: A Complex Process**  11

**Communication Apprehension**  15

**Communication Ethics**  17

**Keys for Excellence in the Workplace**  19

**Executive Summary**  22

**Discussion Questions**  23

**Terms to Remember**  23

# Chapter Objectives

After studying this chapter, you should be able to:

1. Define professional excellence and communication

2. Identify business and professional communication contexts

3. Understand the components of the communication model

4. Identify and explain the four KEYS to communication in the workplace

5. Discuss communication and professional excellence from an ethical perspective

## chapter 1

# Business and Professional Excellence in the Workplace

**Vicky Oliver believes that new members of the workforce need some guidance about proper etiquette in a professional business setting.** As a career consultant, Oliver criticizes instances of new employees' texting during orientation or playing games on their tablets during business meetings. Another practice Oliver takes issue with is professional etiquette in the elevator. Too often, she notices employees wearing headphones or listening to music in this setting. "'Wearing earplugs is like putting a Do Not Disturb sign on you,' she says. It sends a message to colleagues that you want to be left alone, an unfriendly gesture at best" (Adams, 2010). Oliver discusses these points as part of the greater matter of business and professional excellence in the workplace. Effective and socially appropriate business communication is crucial in presenting yourself as a viable and wanted member of a professional organization.

Standards of business and professional excellence constantly change with the times. With the influx of new gadgets such as smartphones, tablets, and other portable devices, it is important to understand how to use these devices appropriately in a business setting. Spending too much time on your electronic devices can make you appear distant or awkward to your coworkers. Even worse, it can create the perception that you are focusing on something other than the business at hand, leading to labels such as "lazy" or "unfocused." Respecting your colleagues' professional and personal boundaries is also important; barging into someone's office or cubicle unannounced can negatively affect that person's perception of you. Even in an open office, people like to claim "their" space, and respecting that claim is crucial to gaining the respect and appreciation of your coworkers.

Business and professional excellence is an idea that most workers will grapple with throughout their entire careers. There is no concrete formula for achieving workplace excellence, but there are tools available that can help individuals find out on their own what is acceptable in their unique workplaces. In this chapter, we will provide an overview of your study of business and professional excellence, from landing the job to work–life balance.

Reading about Vicky Oliver's experience may have caused you to stop and think for a moment about your own communication and the role communication can and will play in your successes and failures in the workplace. You may ask yourself, "Will I be able to get an interview? Will I be considered for a promotion at work? Will I fit in at my new job? What's the best way to run a meeting? What are the qualities of a professional presentation? How should I respond to negative coworkers?" The preceding questions are commonly asked by people entering the workplace for the first time, as well as by people changing job titles, duties, or careers. It seems that regardless of the position or the industry in which you desire to work, there is one thing that will make or break the experience: communication. So welcome to the world of business and professional communication. As you study business and professional communication over the course of this semester, we encourage you, regardless of your major, to take these principles and objectives to heart. After all, communication is the key to professional excellence, and professional excellence is the key to success.

Let us introduce ourselves as your coauthors. We approach this project with years of experience teaching basic communication courses such as public speaking, business and professional communication, interviewing, teamwork and leadership, organizational communication, and public relations. Balanced with our teaching experience and expert knowledge in the communication field are years of professional consulting and real-world experience in a variety of industries, including retail, manufacturing, shipping, health care, government, education, and more. We know firsthand the communication challenges you will face and the communication skills you will need to succeed. Based on our teaching and professional experience, we wrote this book for you, the student as developing professional.

When designing this text, we talked to professors and students alike, trying to get a sense of their needs. Two themes emerged from those conversations. First, instructors and professors are frustrated because students do not read their books. As a result, class discussions, exam scores, and student learning suffer. On the flipside, students are frustrated because they find most books extremely expensive and full of information they deem unimportant. Repeatedly, students asked, "Why can't professors just put the stuff I need to know on a PowerPoint slide?" Our goal when writing this text is to address both problems/needs. We have tried to develop a text that speaks directly to you as a student who desires success after graduation. We realize that those of you taking this class and reading this text are interested in different professions and are in different stages of your professional lives. Given the array of professional journeys taking place in the lives of you the readers, we have included topics that will be valuable to everyone. The topic areas of the text will focus on *beginning communication principles, entering the workplace, developing in the workplace, excelling in the workplace, presenting in the workplace,* and *surviving challenges in the workplace.* We explore the experiences you will face as you transition from student to professional and, eventually, to leader. You will come to understand the role of communication in successfully handling situations such as job interviewing, providing feedback to supervisors, and working in teams. As an additional feature, this text not only discusses the greatest challenges we all will face in the modern workplace but also provides communication strategies for overcoming those challenges. Issues such as excelling under the pressure of increasingly competitive customer service demands, managing emotions when dealing with irate customers, overcoming stress and burnout, and managing difficult people are just a few of the topics covered. We hope that this approach will engage you as both a student and a reader.

## Business and Professional Excellence in Context

The text's driving theme is **professional excellence**. To demonstrate excellence as a professional, you must demonstrate excellence as a communicator. Excellence does not equate to merely communicating a message effectively or simply demonstrating communication competencies. Professional excellence means being recognized for your skills as a communicator and serving as a role model to others. Before you begin your journey with this important topic, it is important to understand some fundamental areas of communication, such as verbal communication, nonverbal communication, and listening. Additionally, it's important to understand the business and professional contexts that will receive specific attention in this book. The business and professional contexts you will explore are beginning communication principles (i.e., verbal and nonverbal communication and listening), the job-seeking process, workplace culture and diversity, interpersonal communication, team communication, communication and technology, written communication, leadership, presenting as a professional, and work–life balance. These are the contexts that will no doubt shape your experience as a professional. Keep in mind that communication is

When you hear the word *professional*, who or what comes to mind? Do a suit and a tie equate to professional excellence, or is it something more?

at the core of the business and professional contexts you will study in this course. Let's take a look at each one in more detail.

Where would you begin to search for jobs in the industry or profession in which you're interested?

## Verbal and Nonverbal Communication

Chapter 2 explores the importance of verbal and non-verbal communication as the foundation of beginning principles needed to guide your study of business and professional communication across contexts. Verbal communication is both our words and our verbal fillers (e.g., *um*, *like*). Verbal messages are created through language. Effective communication involves accurate interpretations of others' verbal messages as meaning is cocreated. Further, nonverbal communication (sometimes referred to as body language) includes all those ways we communicate without words. Both verbal and nonverbal communication skills are explored in this book using the KEYS process.

## Listening

Chapter 3 connects listening to your study of business and professional communication. Effective listening is central to fostering interpersonal relationships with coworkers, leaders, and clients. Effective listening can impact one's relationship satisfaction and can be a determining factor in whether someone is an effective communicator. Listening, in addition to other communication abilities, is a likely predictor of who gets promoted or who receives other relevant rewards such as status and power. In all, listening is a beginning communication skill or basic principle important to your study of business and professional communication. You will learn the importance of listening across business and professional contexts using the KEYS process.

## Résumés, Interviews, and Negotiations

The context you will study in Chapter 4 is job seeking. Our approach is to provide the information you'll need to conduct a comprehensive job search and know yourself in terms of professional goals and the type of work environment you desire. Job seeking is one context in which business and professional excellence is critical to your success.

## Getting to Know the Diverse Workplace

Once you've landed the job, you'll enter a diverse workplace context. You will no doubt have coworkers whose views of the world and ways of living are different from yours. Further, it can take time to learn the organizational culture in terms of your role and how you fit in. As Chapter 5 explores, getting to know the diverse workplace goes beyond new employee orientation. The diverse workplace context requires professional excellence fostered by careful self-inventory, adjustment, and mutual respect.

## Interpersonal Communication at Work

Central to your personal and professional growth in any career are the relationships and overall rapport you'll have with your boss, coworkers, and clients. Chapter 6 reviews the importance of **interpersonal communication** in common business and professional encounters. While interpersonal communication (also referred to as people skills) helps you build relationships in your personal and professional life, it's critical to be aware of the challenges that these skills can help you survive (e.g., conflict, difficult coworkers and clients).

The handshake is an important example of nonverbal communication experienced in many business and professional situations.

## Strengthening Teams and Conducting Meetings

Another common experience for professionals across industries is working in a team context. You've probably heard other people use terms such as *team player*, *team skills*, and *team building* in reference to job performance. Working in a team context can be both a rewarding and exhausting experience for any professional. Chapter 7 pays specific attention to the team context you'll likely encounter in your professional life, as well as strategies that foster professional excellence in team communication. We will also focus on the skills needed to run effective meetings, a primary tool for team communication.

## Technology in the Workplace

Technology in business and professional contexts is central to communication, planning, marketing, networking, organization, research, and the like. Technology allows you to communicate faster than in years past with the use of e-mail, personal digital assistants, and a host of other devices designed to make the exchange of information in business instant rather than delayed. Chapter 8 examines the impact of communication and technology on business and professional contexts. As technology enables you to excel at work with faster information exchange and interaction, it's important to be aware of the problems and misunderstandings that can occur as the result of various technology-based communication channels. Additionally, we will discuss the role of social media as a professional tool and a professional barrier.

## Business and Professional Writing

Chapter 9 examines written communication as it connects to professional excellence. As you enter business and professional contexts that require you to use written communication, it is important for you to make decisions that will ensure professional excellence. Written communication can challenge professionals in a variety of contexts. How do I select the correct format to get the message out? Is it appropriate for me to send this document via e-mail? What tone should I strive for in this message? These are only a few of the questions about written communication that you may encounter in your career.

### Leadership and Conflict Management

Chapter 10 reviews the role of leadership in business and professional contexts. In order to excel as a leader, you must understand what leadership is and get to know what style of leader you are and if your style works best in the business and professional context in which you're working. Further, this chapter explores the challenges leaders experience, as well as strategies for leading difficult people and managing workplace conflict.

### Presentations

As a professional, you will enter situations that require you to give presentations. The presentation context arises in many forms (e.g., informative, persuasive, motivational, and team presentations). Chapters 11, 12, and 13 explore the presentation skills essential to your professional success. When you're faced with an opportunity to give a formal presentation, pitch a product, present research findings, run a meeting, conduct a morning huddle, acknowledge outstanding employees, or motivate your team in difficult times, view that speaking situation as a chance to communicate professional excellence.

As much as anyone wants to be successful professionally, it's important to think about personal and family life, too. Unfortunately, maintaining balance can be difficult.

### Work–Life Balance

Chapter 14 looks at how the various experiences in your professional and personal life can be in conflict with one another. This tension can present quite a challenge, which can lead to stress and burnout. We emphasize the importance of work–life balance, explore the triggers that cause imbalance, and present communication strategies that enable you to sustain professional excellence and foster meaningful and successful relationships in your personal life.

Present in each of these contexts is the KEYS process.

## Understanding the KEYS Process

You will learn to demonstrate professional excellence by using KEYS, a communication process designed to enhance your ability to critically assess and then improve your communication skills. By following the KEYS process, you will learn to utilize your communication strengths and develop your weaknesses, deliver audience-centered messages, understand the communication context, and reflect on your communication with the intention and ability to improve continually.

Effective business and professional communication is central to your success when entering the workplace for the first time, developing your skills at a job you already have, excelling in your career, or managing challenges that may come your way. But you may be wondering, "How can I master this multifaceted, multidimensional skill? How can I make sense of all this information and really make it useful in my career so I get something practical out of it, something that can enhance my business and professional communication skills and improve my life?" The "how" you are looking for is available to you in this course. Studying communication will enhance your skills as a professional. Doing well in this course will afford you the tools needed for professional excellence. Furthermore, making the KEYS process a part of your communication interactions will continue your development long after this course ends.

What is the KEYS process? The KEYS process (see Figure 1.1) is central to your development as a professional, meaning that we encourage you to personalize it as you continue to expand your understanding of business and professional communication. KEYS is an acronym for **K**now yourself, **E**valuate the professional context, **Y**our communication interaction occurs, and **S**tep back and reflect.

The organizing feature of this text is the KEYS process, a process designed to develop critical thinking skills and make you a more reflexive communicator with the ability to adapt and continually improve. What we strive for in this book is a balance of theory and practice—an approach that emphasizes skill development based on knowledge and understanding. Review Figure 1.1 to familiarize yourself with the KEYS process. We will

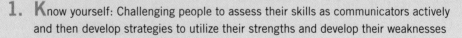

**Figure 1.1 KEYS to Communication in the Workplace**

1. **K**now yourself: Challenging people to assess their skills as communicators actively and then develop strategies to utilize their strengths and develop their weaknesses

2. **E**valuate the professional context: Teaching people to address the needs of their audience proactively and understand the constraints of the professional communication context, as well as developing their skills for communicating with a variety of audiences and contexts

3. **Y**our communication interaction occurs: Asking people to monitor their own verbal and nonverbal cues in addition to the cues of the audience within each communication interaction

4. **S**tep back and reflect: Examining the effectiveness of verbal and nonverbal messages we convey to others and the overall success of various communication interactions and then taking what we've learned and starting the process again; developing the ability to continually adapt and improve

use this feature to personally engage, prepare, and improve human communication in the variety of situations we all have encountered or will encounter in our lives as professionals, regardless of industry.

# Defining Communication

As you begin your study, it's important to define what communication means. Communication has been defined in many ways, but here's the definition we prefer: **Human communication** is the process of understanding our experiences and the experiences of others through the use of verbal and nonverbal messages (Beebe, Beebe, & Ivy, 2007; Ivy & Wahl, 2009; Regenbogen et al., 2012). People come to understand that communication in everyday experiences is the essential process and skill that helps them make sense of things in both personal and professional contexts.

Even if you have some reservations about your communication skills, you probably consider yourself to be a good communicator and good listener. Most people do. After all, it's difficult to admit being bad at something you do all day, every day for your entire life. Because communication is so much a part of our everyday lives, we think of communication as a simple process. Communicating comes so naturally to us that we rarely feel the need to give communication a second thought. When was the last time you really stopped and examined your communication skills? Do you stop and examine your communication regularly? Most people don't.

In some cases, people who fail to reflect on their communication skills trudge through life thinking they are great communicators when they are, in actuality, dreadful communicators. They exemplify a behavior called **communication bravado**—perceiving their communication as effective, while those around them perceive it as ineffective (Quintanilla & Mallard, 2008). Ineffective communicators view communication as simply talking—but truly effective communicators know it is far more complicated than that.

Do you take your communication skills for granted? Are you suffering from communication bravado? Let us assure you that you do indeed have some weaknesses in your communication and listening, simply because everyone does. However, understanding why communication is important and how the communication process works is the first step in overcoming those weaknesses and starting on the road to professional excellence.

# The Importance of Communication

Regardless of your major or the career path you eventually follow, effective communication will be essential to your success in the workplace (Gray, 2010). Your fellow students understand the value and importance of communication in their careers. Of 116 students surveyed at a southwestern university, 97% agreed that communication is a valuable skill and 88% saw themselves using oral presentation skills in their careers (Mallard & Quintanilla, 2007). Further support for the importance of communication in your professional careers comes from business and industry focus groups. In 2008, the U.S. Department

**Table 1.1 Communication Competencies List (U.S. Department of Labor/Business and Industry)**

| | |
|---|---|
| *Personal effectiveness competencies* | • Phone interviews—exhibit personality and people skills<br>• Personal appearance—professionalism<br>• Must come to work and be on time<br>• One-on-one people skills—social skills must be sharp<br>• Sensitivity to diversity in the workplace<br>• Must pass criminal background check<br>• Integrity is critical<br>• Avoid inappropriate phone calls/text messages at work |
| *Teamwork* | • Must be able to work as a team member<br>• Play well with others<br>• Respect others in the workplace |
| *Communication* | • Develop and deliver presentations using appropriate media<br>• Conduct meetings<br>• Interpret nonverbal behaviors to enhance communication<br>• Use politically correct/appropriate language<br>• Share information effectively, small-group communication<br>• Be able to deal with the public<br>• Do not use text messaging–type abbreviations in e-mails and conversation<br>• Phone-answering skills |
| *General skills desired by employers* | • Problem-solving skills<br>• Writing skills<br>• Be willing to work your way to the top<br>• Communication skills |

of Labor reviewed the results and presented a list of important job skills and communication competencies. Take a moment to review Table 1.1, in which we've summarized the competencies. You'll notice that all the competencies listed in the table are connected to your study of business and professional communication in this course.

# Communication: A Complex Process

Communication is a complex process (see Figure 1.2). You see that the communication process consists of a number of elements, all of which are in play every time you communicate. Those who demonstrate professional excellence consider these elements every time they communicate. By the end of this semester, so will you. Let's examine each of these elements in more detail.

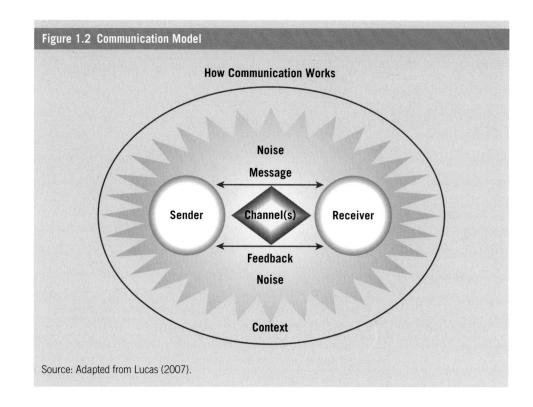

**Figure 1.2 Communication Model**

**How Communication Works**

Sender — Channel(s) — Receiver

Noise
Message

Feedback
Noise

Context

Source: Adapted from Lucas (2007).

## Sender and Receiver

We stated above that, speaking practically, communication involves sending and receiving messages; so it should be no surprise that you take on the roles of sender and receiver when you communicate. When you are acting as the sender, you **encode** your messages with verbal and nonverbal cues to help others understand what you mean. When the receivers of your messages respond or **decode** your message, you find out if your message was successfully transferred. In one sense, this exchange of message and response is a cocreation of meaning, in that both parties play a role in cocreating a meaningful exchange. While the person initiating the exchange (the **sender**) can't control how the listener (or **receiver**) interprets the message, the goal is for the listener to understand the meaning of the message as the sender intended it.

The respective roles of sender and receiver in communication seem fairly clear-cut, but in truth, communication is experienced in a more holistic manner—not as senders and receivers but as communicators. Consider an example: You run into a friend, Pat, while walking to class. Pat says, "Hey, how's it going?" You return the greeting and begin to tell Pat about your plans for the weekend (you are attending a cousin's wedding). At some point during the story you are telling (how your cousin met her fiancé), you notice Pat checking his wristwatch. You cut off your story and say goodbye, and each of you walks to class. In one view of this example, you and Pat switch off as senders and receivers: Pat sends you a greeting, which you receive; you send Pat an explanation of your weekend plans and a story, which Pat receives; then Pat sends you a nonverbal cue that time is short, which you receive by ending the encounter. In another view of this example, you and Pat are both communicators, as you simultaneously send and receive messages.

## Message and Feedback

Implicit in the preceding discussion of senders and receivers is that a **message** is communicated. One principle from the field of communication suggests you cannot *not* communicate.

Professionals send and receive verbal and nonverbal messages in a variety of contexts.

To say that you cannot *not* communicate is *not* to say that everything is communication. Rather, it means that messages have both a verbal and nonverbal component. In the previous example, Pat did not say anything verbally, but he did send a message nonverbally when he checked his watch. What was his message? That is not clear. He may have been giving a nonverbal cue that your wedding story was too long. He may have had an appointment and needed to be on his way. Only Pat knows for sure. The point is, regardless of whether or not Pat intended to provide a message, he did, and you responded in accordance with the meaning you took from that message.

Also included in the communication model is **feedback**. In the model, you will see that feedback is sent from the receiver to the sender. However, since the distinction between sender and receiver is in many ways arbitrary, feedback is the same as the message. As communicators, the notion of feedback reminds us to look for cues from the other person or persons with whom we are communicating.

## Channel

The **channel** is simply the method by which you send your message. With all the technology available today, deciding which channel to use can be a daunting task. When you advance in your career and move into a leadership position, you'll have to evaluate the merits of various communication channels daily. Given the message, should you meet with members of your team one-on-one or call a meeting? Is it better to send a memo or an e-mail? Should you call, or should you text? Each communication channel brings with it a variety of strengths and weaknesses that will be discussed in a later chapter.

## Context

Always and everywhere, communication is contextual. **Context** refers to the location, time, and occasion where communication occurs. Developing professional excellence means beginning to assess your communication context and use that information when developing your message. For instance, consider the context of the business and professional communication course. Virtually everyone in the course is there because they have to be. As a result, if you give a speech in this course, your audience may not be interested or knowledgeable about the topic you select; you might need to educate them and take conscious steps to capture their interest. However, if you are giving a speech to a group of employees about their cost of living and merit raises, they will be hanging on your every word.

## Your Communication Interaction   Advisory Committee

*Read the passage below and then answer the questions. As you read, think about ways the KEYS approach could help you improve **your communication interaction** if you were in Bruce's position.*

Bruce had been an executive with the company for almost 10 years. During that time, he had set up many advisory committees, designed to allow employees on all levels to give feedback regarding important decisions. These committees had been well received, and employees actively sought opportunities to serve on them.

Most recently, Bruce began some advisory search committees. Those serving on the advisory search committees reviewed applications and made a list of the top 20 candidates. Then the list was forwarded to Bruce. He then conducted the interviews by himself and did the hiring. At times, as many as 100 applications had to be reviewed for a single position, so it was a labor-intensive process.

Committee members had asked if they could rank the candidates or give input individually and/or as a group, but Bruce felt that was not necessary since the committee was only advisory. He wanted to avoid conflict between group members over who should be hired. He also wanted to eliminate the possibility of a conflict between his decision and a committee decision. As the executive, he felt it was important for him to make the final decision, so he did not wish to consider their comments. After 6 months, employees stopped volunteering for the search committees.

### Questions to Consider

1. How did eliminating feedback from the communication model impact this interaction?
2. Why are employees not willing to participate anymore?
3. Would you be willing to participate?
4. Using the KEYS process, how should Bruce handle this situation differently?

## Noise

Noise is part of the communication context. **Noise** can be either external or internal. **External noise** includes distractions such as audible talking during a meeting, ruffling of papers, or a cell phone going off in the next cubicle. For our purposes, the definition of external noise is extended to include any external factor that could interfere with a communicator's ability to focus on the message. In a meeting, external noise might also include a team member sending text messages with the sound on or whispering while your boss is talking.

**Internal noise** encompasses any internal condition or state that interferes with the communicator's ability to focus on the message. If your meeting starts at 11:00 a.m., your team members may be looking forward to lunch; if you hold an emergency meeting at 6:00 a.m., your team may be tired. Being tired or hungry creates internal noise. Developing professional excellence includes learning to consider things such as context and noise when making decisions about your communication interactions. Remember that both internal and external noise are doing more than just preventing you from focusing on the message. That is, both types of noise can also interfere with your understanding of the message. You can be focused on a message and still not understand.

# Communication Apprehension

Effective communication skills are essential if you want to excel in leadership. Put simply, to move up the ladder of success, you must develop your communication skills. Unfortunately, communication apprehension is a very real problem that stops many talented individuals from achieving professional excellence. What is communication apprehension?

## Types of Communication Apprehension

According to James C. McCroskey (1982), one of the leading researchers in the communication discipline, **communication apprehension** is "an individual's level of fear or anxiety associated with either real or anticipated communication with another person or persons" (p. 137). You can understand your own communication apprehension by thinking about your communication in particular situations. What types of communication situation increase your apprehension? According to McCroskey (1984), there are at least four types of communication apprehension:

What experiences have you had speaking into a microphone? Did using a microphone increase your communication apprehension?

1. **Trait communication apprehension** means that one possesses a "shy trait." In general, shy people tend not to raise their hands in class a lot, avoid certain social situations, and feel extremely anxious about giving a professional presentation.

2. **Context-based communication apprehension** describes a fear of communicating in certain contexts. A fear of public speaking is a great example of context communication apprehension. For example, a student may not be nervous about meeting new people or participating in small groups, but presenting a speech in front of the class promotes a high degree of apprehension.

3. **Audience-based communication apprehension** explains a person's fear of speaking to certain people or groups. For example, a person may feel comfortable speaking in front of friends in his or her social circle, but speaking in front of colleagues at work makes him or her extremely nervous.

4. **Situational communication apprehension** refers to apprehension to communicate in specific sets of circumstances; everyone at some point in their lives is going to feel apprehensive about communicating something. Think of a person you might want to impress, such as a boss or an interviewer. In general, you are an outgoing person and don't mind presenting in front of people, but someone you want to impress may promote an uneasy or anxious feeling.

## Know Yourself    Personal Report of Communication Apprehension

*The following personal report will help you gain a better understanding of your own communication apprehension. Answer each question thoughtfully and then reflect on the results. How can this knowledge help you be a better communicator?*

## Personal Report of Communication Apprehension (PRCA-24)

The PRCA-24 is the instrument most widely used to measure communication apprehension. The measure permits one to obtain subscores on the contexts of public speaking, dyadic interaction, small groups, and large groups.

This instrument is composed of 24 statements concerning feelings about communicating with others. Please indicate the degree to which each statement applies to you by marking whether you *strongly disagree* = 1; *disagree* = 2; are *neutral* = 3; *agree* = 4; or *strongly agree* = 5.

_____1. I dislike participating in group discussions.
_____2. Generally, I am comfortable while participating in group discussions.
_____3. I am tense and nervous while participating in group discussions.
_____4. I like to get involved in group discussions.
_____5. Engaging in a group discussion with new people makes me tense and nervous.
_____6. I am calm and relaxed while participating in group discussions.
_____7. Generally, I am nervous when I have to participate in a meeting.
_____8. Usually, I am comfortable when I have to participate in a meeting.
_____9. I am very calm and relaxed when I am called on to express an opinion at a meeting.
_____10. I am afraid to express myself at meetings.
_____11. Communicating at meetings usually makes me uncomfortable.
_____12. I am very relaxed when answering questions at a meeting.
_____13. While participating in a conversation with a new acquaintance, I feel very nervous.
_____14. I have no fear of speaking up in conversations.
_____15. Ordinarily, I am very tense and nervous in conversations.
_____16. Ordinarily, I am very calm and relaxed in conversations.
_____17. While conversing with a new acquaintance, I feel very relaxed.
_____18. I'm afraid to speak up in conversations.
_____19. I have no fear of giving a speech.
_____20. Certain parts of my body feel very tense and rigid while giving a speech.
_____21. I feel relaxed while giving a speech.
_____22. My thoughts become confused and jumbled when I am giving a speech.
_____23. I face the prospect of giving a speech with confidence.
_____24. While giving a speech, I get so nervous I forget facts I really know.

## SCORING:

Group discussion: 18 – (scores for Items 2, 4, and 6) + (scores for Items 1, 3, and 5)
Meetings: 18 – (scores for Items 8, 9, and 12) + (scores for Items 7, 10, and 11)
Interpersonal: 18 – (scores for Items 14, 16, and 17) + (scores for Items 13, 15, and 18)
Public speaking: 18 – (scores for Items 19, 21, and 23) + (scores for Items 20, 22, and 24)
Group discussion score: _____
Interpersonal score: _____
Meetings score: _____
Public speaking score: _____
To obtain your total score for the PRCA, simply add your subscores together. _____
Scores can range from 24 to 120. Scores below 51 represent people who have very low communication apprehension. Scores between 51 and 80 represent people with average communication apprehension. Scores above 80 represent people who have high levels of trait communication apprehension.

## Causes of Communication Apprehension

Now that we've reviewed the different types of communication apprehension, let's take a look at some of the causes. Communication scholar Michael Beatty (1988) lists eight causes for communication apprehension. Review the list that follows to see if any of the causes resonate with you personally.

1. *Novelty:* If the type of communication situation, such as giving a speech or running a meeting, is not something you do every day, it can create apprehension until you become familiar with this task or situation.

2. *Formality:* Preparing and organizing something to be in the spotlight can promote the feeling of formality that makes you nervous or apprehensive.

3. *Subordinate status:* If someone in charge of you, such as a manager at work, is evaluating your presentation, his or her higher status and evaluation can cause anxiety.

4. *Peer evaluation:* How are my coworkers going to respond to me? These questions hit some concerns you may have about your peers evaluating you. These concerns can in turn cause apprehension.

5. *Dissimilarity:* Sometimes you may feel different from the audience. Having nothing in common with the audience causes anxiety.

6. *Conspicuousness:* Feeling as though you are in the spotlight and all eyes are on you can certainly cause anxiety.

7. *Lack of attention:* When you feel as though a listener or the audience is bored and uninterested in your message or presentation, you may begin to feel apprehension.

8. *Prior history:* Many people have had a bad experience during a communication interaction, such as an interview, presentation, or meeting. This negative experience can create anxiety the next time you find yourself in a similar situation.

As you can see, there are many different types and causes of communication apprehension. Identifying the types and causes of your communication apprehension is important but not nearly as important as learning the skills that will reduce those fears.

# Communication Ethics

With professional excellence as our goal, we believe that ethical behavior must serve as a foundation for people to be treated with fairness, dignity, and respect. Central to professional excellence is communication ethics. **Ethics** is the general term for the discussion, determination, and deliberation processes that attempt to decide what is right or wrong, what others should or should not do, and what is considered appropriate in our individual, communal, and professional lives (By, Burnes, & Oswick, 2012; Japp, Meister, & Japp, 2005; Johannesen, Valde, & Whedbee, 2008). What considerations or factors help shape our ethical decisions as professionals? **Ethical considerations** are the variety of factors

## Evaluate the Professional Context    John's Presentation Problem

*Read the following passage about John and answer the questions that come after.*

John gave a big presentation today at work. He had spent hours and hours working on his PowerPoint slides. They were loaded with information—lots of statistics and charts. In fact, he had more than 50 slides in his 20-minute speech. When he began speaking, he was a little nervous. Because he had spent most of his time working on the slides, he did not have much time to practice. Still, he had the slides to read, and he thought the presentation went well. However, his audience seemed uninterested when he was speaking, and no one approached him after the speech to praise him for a job well done. Why didn't his preparation pay off for this particular professional presentation context?

### Questions to Consider

1. Given the professional context, what would you have done the same and/or different if you were in John's position?
2. Do you think John accurately evaluated the context? Why or why not?
3. How could the KEYS process help John improve his presentation decision in the future?

Taking part in something as common as office gossip is an ethical consideration. Is the gossip true? Does it show respect for boundaries? What does it say about your integrity?

important for us to consider in any scenario in which we're making a decision, conducting an evaluation, or making a selection (Bok, 1989, 1999; Carter, 1996; Japp et al., 2005; Mathenge, 2011; Tannen, 1998). Ethical considerations vary from person to person, and it is not always as simple as the black-and-white world of right and wrong. For example, you may experience **ethical dilemmas,** situations that do not seem to present clear choices between right and wrong or good and evil. If you are asked to do something illegal, then it may be easy to make a decision. "No, I will not do something illegal." But what if it is not illegal? What if everyone else does it? What if it is just bending the rules a little bit? What follows are five questions we believe you should always consider as an ethical communicator.

Many ethical considerations are connected to our values and virtues. **Values** are moral principles or rules that determine ethical behaviors. Values are often articulated in should or should-not statements. Sometimes values are presented as statements of what a group believes or as lists of rules people intend to honor. Many readers of this text will take jobs in industries that ask all employees to support **organizational values,** specific principles or guidelines such as safety, teamwork, integrity, or ownership that are typically outlined in support of any given organizational mission or goal. For example, some health care systems and private education institutions ask employees to support certain religious values. Regardless of

## Step Back and Reflect   Ethical Considerations

*Throughout this text, you will be given opportunities to step back and reflect on other people's communication interactions. But in this first exercise, we would like you to step back and reflect on your own communication. Read the questions below. When it comes to both your written and verbal communication, can you always answer "yes" to these questions? Can you think of examples for which you could not answer "yes"?*

**Lying:** Are you telling the truth?

**Secrets:** Are you respecting the boundary placed around information by avoiding disclosure to others?

**Integrity:** Are you discerning right from wrong and explaining your reasoning for your decision? In other words, are you vocal about the ethics driving your decision (e.g., care and love, financial, respect for individual rights, equal for all)?

**Aggressive communication:** Are you communicating with others void of power abuse and aggression? Are you communicating with others in a dignified and respectful manner? Are you communicating with mutual respect and open dialogue?

**Plagiarism (cheating):** Are you communicating information that is authentic and not plagiarized? Is the source of information being credited appropriately?

### Step Back and Reflect

1. Have you ever taken part in any of these communication behaviors?

2. If so, did you consider them unethical? Why or why not?

3. Did you consider them unprofessional? Why or why not?

industry, organizational values address both the experience of the people working for the company and the experience of customers with service and product quality. To minimize ethical dilemmas in your professional career, seek employment with organizations that share your values.

Once you've been promoted or elected into a particular position of leadership, you may think, "That's it—job over; I've arrived." We emphasize that leadership is a skill, one that needs to be developed and maintained throughout life. Think about the qualities of excellent leaders. Ethics should be among those qualities. And like all other leadership skills, your ethics must be developed and continually maintained. While not every reader of this book is currently in a leadership position, has the goal of becoming a CEO, or even wants to become a leader, the KEYS process with communication ethics at the foundation drives excellence in professional situations.

# KEYS for Excellence in the Workplace

We opened this chapter with attention to Vicky Oliver's concerns about the lack of professionalism seen in a variety of business contexts today. In response to Vicky's call for workplace excellence, we reviewed fundamental information to begin our study of business and professional communication. We defined human communication and provided a practi-

# Ethical Connection

*Throughout the text, each chapter will touch on particular issues in ethical communication. The topics covered in each chapter are directly related to business and professional excellence. Please read the passage below and answer the questions that follow.*

Tom is a recent college graduate who recently landed a job as an information technology manager at a computer manufacturing plant. Tom never really enjoyed talking to new people, so he made sure his degree involved working with computers so he could minimize his interactions with other coworkers. However, once he began working at his new company, it became obvious that a great deal of his work involved interacting with other people. Because Tom disliked communicating with his coworkers, he was often perceived as grumpy and unfriendly. Management made several attempts to coach Tom on his communication skills, but he still refused to make any effort to work well with others. His lack of communication led to technical problems going unaddressed and sabotaged the company's team-based working environment. Tom was eventually fired from his position and attempted to find another job that did not require him to interact with other employees.

## Questions to Consider

1. What is the ethical issue with Tom refusing to communicate with his coworkers?
2. Is Tom wrong to assume that there are many jobs out there that do not require communication skills?
3. What could Tom have done differently to save his job at that particular company?
4. Using the KEYS process, how could Tom train himself to be a better communicator?

**K**now Yourself

**E**valuate the Professional Context

**Y**our Communication Interaction Occurs

**S**tep Back and Reflect

cal communication model. We defined professional excellence: being recognized for your skills as a communicator, serving as a role model to those around you, recognizing your strengths and developing your weaknesses, being audience centered, understanding the context, and possessing the ability to adapt and continually improve.

Next, we situated our topic of study within the workplace as a communication context and discussed communication apprehension as a common obstacle for professionals. We introduced the KEYS process as a way for professionals to develop their communication. *Knowing yourself* means actively assessing your skills as a communicator and then developing strategies to utilize your strengths and develop your weaknesses. *Evaluating the professional context* entails proactively addressing the needs of your audience and understanding the constraints of the communication situation, as well as developing your skills for communicating with a variety of audiences and situations. *Your communication interaction* requires you to monitor your own verbal and nonverbal cues, in addition to the cues from the audience within each communication interaction. *Stepping back and reflecting* encourages you to examine the effectiveness of verbal and nonverbal messages you convey to others and the overall success of various communication interactions and then take what you've learned and start the process again, developing the ability to adapt and improve continually.

This introductory chapter has provided you with an understanding of some of the basic terminology and the importance of communication excellence. In the second chapter, we explore some of the most important verbal and nonverbal skills needed to enter the workplace or, put simply, how to put the KEYS process in action.

## Executive Summary

Now that you have finished reading this chapter, you can do the following.

Define professional excellence and communication:

- *Professional excellence* means being recognized for your skills as a communicator and serving as a role model to others (p. 5).
- *Human communication* is the process of understanding our experiences and the experiences of others through the use of verbal and nonverbal messages (p. 5).
- Regardless of your major or the career path you eventually follow, effective communication will be essential to your success in the workplace (p. 10).

Identify business and professional communication contexts:

- The *business* and *professional contexts* you will explore are the job-seeking process, workplace culture and diversity, interpersonal communication, team communication, communication and technology, written communication, leadership, presenting as a professional, and work-life balance (p. 5).

Understand the components of the communication model:

- The person initiating the exchange is the *sender*, while the person listening to the exchange is the *receiver* (p. 12).
- Generally speaking, the process of sending and receiving communication is that a *message* is communicated (p. 13).
- When you are acting as the sender, you *encode* your messages with verbal and nonverbal cues to help others understand what you mean (p. 12).
- When the receivers of your messages respond or *decode* your message, you find out if your message was successfully transferred (p. 12).
- *Feedback* is communication sent from the receiver back to the sender (p. 13).
- The *channel* (p. 13) is the method by which you send your message (voice, phone, e-mail, etc.).
- *Context* refers to the location, time, and occasion where communication occurs (p. 13).
- *Noise* can be either external or internal. *External noise* includes distractions such as audible talking during a meeting, ruffling of

papers, or a cell phone going off in the next cubicle. *Internal noise* encompasses any internal condition or state that interferes with the communicator's ability to focus on the message (p. 14).

Define verbal and nonverbal communication.

Identify and explain the four KEYS to communication in the workplace:

- *Know yourself:* challenging people to assess their skills as communicators actively and then develop strategies to utilize their strengths and develop their weaknesses (p. 9).
- *Evaluate the professional context:* teaching people to address the needs of their audience proactively and understand the constraints of the professional communication context, as well as developing their skills for communicating with a variety of audiences and contexts (p. 9).
- *Your communication interaction occurs:* asking people to monitor their own verbal and nonverbal cues in addition to the cues of the audience within each communication interaction (p. 9).
- *Step back and reflect:* examining the effectiveness of verbal and nonverbal messages we convey to others and the overall success of various communication interactions and then taking what we've learned and starting the process again; developing the ability to adapt and improve continually (p. 9).

Discuss communication and professional excellence from an ethical perspective:

- *Ethics* is the general term for the discussion, determination, and deliberation processes that attempt to decide what is right or wrong, what others should or should not do, and what is considered appropriate in our individual, communal, and professional lives (p. 17).
- *Ethical considerations* are the variety of factors important for us to consider in any scenario in which we're making a decision, conducting an evaluation, or making a selection (p. 18).
- *Ethical dilemmas* are situations that do not seem to present clear choices between right and wrong or good and evil (p. 18).

1. What are the contexts for business and professional excellence?

2. Why is it important to study communication?

3. Why must a speaker consider all the elements in the communication model for communication with excellence?

4. Discuss the KEYS process introduced in this chapter. What are the four KEYS features?

5. Work through a personal example—something you either encountered in the past or are presently experiencing—to help you make sense of the KEYS process. Does it help you get more familiar with the situation? Are there changes you need to make considering this particular situation?

**Terms to** Remember

audience-based communication apprehension (p. 15)

channel (p. 13)

communication apprehension (p. 15)

communication bravado (p. 10)

context (p. 13)

context-based communication apprehension (p. 15)

decode (p. 12)

encode (p. 12)

ethical considerations (p. 17)

ethical dilemmas (p. 18)

ethics (p. 17)

external noise (p. 14)

feedback (p. 13)

human communication (p. 10)

internal noise (p. 14)

interpersonal communication (p. 7)

message (p. 13)

noise (p. 14)

organizational values (p. 18)

professional excellence (p. 5)

receiver (p. 12)

sender (p. 12)

situational communication apprehension (p. 15)

trait communication apprehension (p. 15)

values (p. 18)

Visit the Student Study Site at **www.sagepub.com/keys2e** to access the following resources:

- SAGE journal articles
- Video links
- Web resources
- Web quizzes
- eflashcards

## Chapter Outline

Verbal Communication    26

Nonverbal Communication    29

Codes of Nonverbal Communication    33

Forming Relationships With Verbal and
    Nonverbal Communication    41

KEYS to Excellence in Verbal and Nonverbal
    Communication    44

Executive Summary    46

Discussion Questions    47

Terms to Remember    47

## Chapter Objectives

After studying this chapter you should be able to:

1. Define *verbal communication*

2. Define *nonverbal communication*

3. Develop your verbal and nonverbal communication skills

4. Explain the importance of both verbal and nonverbal communication and how they are related

5. Utilize the KEYS approach to conduct yourself with professional excellence through verbal and nonverbal communication in the workplace

## chapter 2

# Verbal and Nonverbal Communication

**Nonverbal cues in the workplace can affect much more than how people perceive one another; they can affect professional decisions and business relationships as well.** Researchers at the University of Michigan have found that nonverbal behavior between medical doctors and patients not only impacts how patients view their relationship with their doctors but also influences the doctors' medical decisions. Dr. Stephen Henry, the lead author of the study, noted that both patients and doctors took nonverbal communication into account when interacting with one another. Patients who perceived their doctor's nonverbal communication as aggressive or hurried reported reduced feelings of comfort and talked less about their illness. Also, the study revealed that physicians incorporate their patients' nonverbal communication, such as body language, eye contact, physical appearance, and tone of voice, into their medical decisions (Dallas, 2011). The findings of the study indicated that a better understanding of nonverbal communication can lead to better interactions between doctors and patients, as well as improve the diagnoses of illnesses.

Although the previous study focuses on doctor–patient relationships, it is important to know that nonverbal communication has a significant impact in any professional working environment. Many of the perceptions that people have of one another can be influenced without a single word being said. From the job interview to the exit interview, your employers, coworkers, and employees all make judgments about you based on your nonverbal cues in communication. However, since many nonverbal gestures are unconscious or unintentional, it is important to be aware of your nonverbal communication at all times and to understand that different gestures carry different meanings to people. What is acceptable in your classroom might not be acceptable in the workplace.

Using nonverbal communication with excellence in the workplace can be an intimidating task; there is no concrete strategy that will work in every situation. However, becoming a critical observer of nonverbal cues in your environment can help you better assess what nonverbal behavior is acceptable or not. In this chapter, you will learn different types of nonverbal cues and how they can affect the workplace based on a variety of factors (e.g., race, gender, environment, ethnicity, etc.).

# Verbal Communication

What is verbal communication? **Verbal communication** encompasses both our words and our verbal fillers (e.g., *um*, *like*). Verbal messages are created through language. Effective communication involves accurate interpretations of others' verbal messages as meaning is cocreated. Otherwise, the meanings of the words you communicate will not be successfully understood. So as a professional, you must make effective use of your language skills and improve your abilities to interpret other people's messages. Robinson and Robinson (1982) concluded that if speakers are to be consistently efficient at conveying verbally their intended meanings to listeners, they must understand that intended meanings may not be fully conveyed by a message and that many factors can lead to a listener's failure to understand what a speaker means.

The symbols communicators use are abstract, vague, and sometimes arbitrary. Because symbols can make things a bit off or fuzzy, we have to interpret the meaning. So we construct meanings as we interact with other people and by processing the information in our own heads (Duck, 1994; Keyton & Beck, 2010). This process of meaning construction is also symbolic, because we use words to think about what things mean (Keyton & Beck, 2010; Wood, 2009).

When you really think about it, it is an absolute miracle that we can communicate with one another at all. Really, think about it for a moment. We have selected a bunch of arbitrary symbols we call words and gestures to represent "things." These can be things we have never seen or never can see, such as feelings. Nevertheless, we use those symbols to express our thoughts, desires, and emotions, and somehow communication does occur. Because of the need for interpretation of meaning, being an audience-centered communicator is a must for professional excellence. It is obvious that communication affects how we are perceived by our audience(s). Still today, some people believe that communication works like a pipeline (i.e., if you send a message, the target will no doubt be reached); if you said something and another person heard it, then effective communication has occurred. We all should know from experience that this simply is not the way it works.

## Step Back and Reflect    Confident Connie

*Read the following passage about Connie and answer the questions that follow.*

Connie works in the accounting department of a manufacturing company. She often complains to her family and friends that her coworkers do not like her and treat her differently than they do the other staff. She is not invited to lunch outings, and she notices that people walk away when she approaches. She considers herself a friendly, outgoing person and cannot figure out what she is doing wrong. Connie believes her coworkers may resent her because she is able to work well with all her clients and is skilled in accounts reconciliations, resulting in company savings of thousands of dollars each month. She is confident in her abilities and speaks proudly in meetings, providing guidance to her teammates about work issues. She enjoys sharing her success stories and has no apprehension about asking questions in meetings. She has been with the company longer than everyone, including her boss, and she often reminds him of the history of why things are done a certain way. Connie is confident that even if her coworkers are jealous of her abilities, her boss recognizes her value as an employee. However, when she receives her performance review, she is shocked by her supervisor's comments:

"Feedback has been shared with Connie several times on her engagement in team meetings. Connie constantly repeats points discussed and closed in meetings, which is a distraction for several analysts. It is evident that Connie is having a hard time following along in meetings, as points and topics are constantly being repeated for her to understand. Feedback has been shared with Connie on staying on point and not drifting off to other tangents. At times, Connie's body language, comments, and tone of voice during meetings seem aggressive and indicate that she disagrees with her manager. This has been shared with Connie and she has been asked to improve."

### Step Back and Reflect

1. What went wrong?
2. How could Connie utilize the KEYS approach to improve her communication interaction?

With little effort, you could give a dozen examples of times when you said something and the listener completely misunderstood the message.

Let's look at an example from the retail industry to illustrate the point. A customer comes into a grocery store and asks for green beans. Trying to provide good customer service, a manager explains, "The green beans are on Aisle 8." Twenty minutes later, the customer is still wandering around the store frustrated. Why? Because canned green beans are on Aisle 8, fresh green beans are on Aisle 1, frozen green beans are on Aisle 14, and the prepared green beans she wanted are in the deli across from Aisle 10. "Green beans" is an arbitrary symbol with various interpretations of meaning.

Verbal communication concerns **communication rules**—shared understanding of what communication means and what constitutes appropriate communication given the context. Two kinds of rules guide communication (Pearce, Cronen, & Conklin, 1979). **Regulative rules** describe when, how, where, and with whom to talk about certain things.

Building relationships in the workplace is vital to being a successful professional. Effective communication is part of this process and involves accurate interpretations of both verbal and nonverbal messages.

These same rules also dictate appropriateness. For instance, it might be appropriate for your boss to call you at home after hours, but would it be appropriate for you to do the same if you had a concern about your travel schedule? What's appropriate for the person with power or control may not be for those serving in a subordinate role. To demonstrate professional and workplace excellence, one must be able to monitor his or her own appropriateness when communicating. In addition, **constitutive rules** define what communication means by prompting us to count certain kinds of communication. In other words, we learn what counts as paying attention (e.g., eye contact), showing affection (e.g., kissing, hugging), as well as what counts as being inappropriate (e.g., interrupting conversations, rolling one's eyes; Duck, 2007; Wood, 2009).

Being aware of oneself can be the difference between losing one's job and nurturing a promising career. We see examples of this in the news headlines and front-page stories of our favorite magazines and newspapers. In early 2012, radio talk show host and political commentator Rush Limbaugh caused controversy after he made inflammatory remarks about Georgetown University law student Sandra Fluke. Despite the fact that his career is based on sharing his opinions, the words he chose on that fateful day resulted in public and sponsor backlash. What factors led to such an outcry? If he had spoken out in disagreement without name calling, would the reaction have been the same? What are the ethical considerations in this situation? What might you take from this story when considering your verbal communication in the workplace? Undoubtedly, the words we say are extremely important. Yet, of equal importance is what we communicate without words.

## Ethical Connection

*Read the following passage about Sheila and David, and then answer the questions. As you read, focus on evaluating the professional context.*

Sheila and David work for an advertising firm and are partners assigned to work on a major advertising campaign. Sheila is a seasoned account manager, while David is a recent college graduate hired as a junior account executive. He is very enthusiastic and has several ideas that he excitedly shares with Sheila via e-mail. Sheila never responds to the e-mail. In a meeting with management to propose their ideas, however, Sheila takes the lead on presenting; as a result of her nonverbal and verbal communication, management concludes that she was responsible for the work. In fact, when commended on the ideas, she accepts the praise and makes no reference to David. David, on the other hand, is afraid to say anything, and his bosses have no clue that the majority of the ideas were his.

### Questions to Consider

1. What are the ethical considerations and dilemmas in this scenario?
2. What did Sheila communicate or not communicate during her presentation and how?
3. What could David have done differently?
4. How would you have handled the situation?
5. Does communicator intent impact the ethics in situations such as this?

# Nonverbal Communication

What is nonverbal communication? Put simply, **nonverbal communication** (also referred to as body language) includes all those ways we communicate without words. A more technical definition for nonverbal communication is "communication other than written or spoken language that creates meaning for someone" (Ivy & Wahl, 2009, p. 3).

The literature provides considerable support for the effectiveness of nonverbal communication as a tool for conveying thoughts, attitudes, perceptions, and meaning. Research indicates that about 55% of interpersonal messages are conveyed nonverbally (Lavan, 2002). This seems logical, because most human beings are visually dominant and live in a society dominated by visual images and are thus more inclined to believe the evidence

This photo illustrates a few examples of nonverbal communication—all the ways we communicate without words. In order to achieve professional excellence, one should become a critical observer of nonverbal cues in any environment.

## Evaluate the Professional Context    A Day With the Chief

*Read the following passage about Mark, and then answer the questions. As you read, focus on evaluating the professional context.*

Mark is a top-performing salesperson at a pharmaceutical supply company. As a reward for his performance, he is treated to a trip to the corporate office in California to meet the chief executive officer, Ms. Mills. Ms. Mills is known around the office as the "Wicked Witch of the West" because of her short and sometimes abrasive demeanor. His coworkers share "horror stories" of their encounters with her, stating that she rarely makes eye contact, never smiles, and dislikes being approached unless she initiates the conversation. Although he is excited to travel, he is also nervous about what he and Ms. Mills might talk about. He prepares by thinking about how he can share his sales strategies and techniques. On the day of the meeting, he waits patiently for her assistant to call him into her office. When he is escorted in to meet her, he is shocked to see a petite woman behind the large desk smiling back at him with kind eyes. He approaches, shakes her hand, and waits for her permission to sit. Ms. Mills is nothing like the horrible person they made her out to be. Ms. Mills asks Mark several thoughtful questions about why he is successful, ways the staff can be supported, and how the company fits in with his professional goals. Mark feels more and more comfortable as she leans forward to listen intently to what he is saying. Mark loosens his tie, crosses his legs, and begins sharing stories of how he feels his immediate supervisor has dropped the ball on more than one occasion and that the team would be better if more money were allocated toward incentives and bonuses. Mark immediately sees Ms. Mills' eyes begin to squint and her brow furrow. She stands up abruptly and says in a gruff voice that their time is up and that her assistant will show him out.

### Questions to Consider

1. Given the professional context, what would you have done the same and/or different if you were in Mark's position?
2. Do you think Mark accurately evaluated the context? Why or why not?
3. What factors led to the change in the chief executive officer's disposition?
4. How could the KEYS process help Mark improve his communication skills?

of the eyes than that of the other senses (Sampson, 1995). In fact, a widely held viewpoint among scholars is that communication is optimized when verbal and nonverbal elements operate in an integrated fashion, producing a coordinated and synchronized effect (Jones & LeBaron, 2002; Laplante & Ambady, 2003). Harrison and Crouch (1975) suggested that verbal communication is only the tip of the communication iceberg and that "nonverbal communication precedes and perhaps structures all subsequent communication" (p. 77).

Nonverbal symbols are everywhere, even though we tend to use verbal forms for our most formal communications. In fact, the nonverbal system accounts for 65% to 93% of the total meaning of communication (Birdwhistell, 1970; Mehrabian, 1981). Nolan (1975) concluded that the many theories of language evolution had one important argument in common: "Nonverbal behavior precedes verbal behavior in the evolution of communication" (p. 101).

What kinds of behavior are included in the term *nonverbal communication*? "Your walk, stance, posture, and footsteps are a form of nonverbal communication. What you wear and how you look, move, and gesture, as well as the facial and eye expressions you make all count as nonverbal communication" (Ivy & Wahl, 2009, p. 3). What are the purposes of nonverbal communication? Why is nonverbal communication important?

Argyle (1988) suggested that nonverbal behavior serves four purposes. The first function is to express emotion. Consider a moment when you may have had a conflict with a friend or family member. When that person asked you what was wrong, you probably responded, "Nothing," but you could not control your facial expressions, which indicated otherwise. Displaying appropriate emotion is vital to professional excellence. One should show passion and drive but also demonstrate resilience and be able to triumph over day-to-day disappointments in the workplace. Could you imagine a classroom environment where students displayed extreme emotion each time they received a grade that was lower than expected? How do you think your productivity would be affected?

The second function of nonverbal communication is to convey interpersonal attitudes. Being skilled in observing and interpreting the nonverbal behavior of others will give you an edge over other professionals. For example, a young woman competing for a promotion with another employee noticed that her coworker would always approach their boss with issues first thing in the morning. The coworker would then complain that he had to repeat himself and that their supervisor seemed to forget what he had been told. The young woman observed that her supervisor always seemed rushed and distracted until he had his coffee and had checked and responded to pressing e-mails. She made sure always to approach him when he seemed more relaxed and focused. When he offered her the promotion, her supervisor said he appreciated her timing and how she always kept him in the loop.

The third function is to present one's personality, such as character, disposition, or temperament. Think about the different work environments you frequent during your week—the bank, the school library, restaurants, etc. What are the character traits of employees at each of these establishments? Do you expect that the librarian will be as outgoing as a server in a crowded bar? Make a list of the top five jobs you have considered, and write down some of the personality traits that might be expected. How might your verbal and nonverbal communication vary between the positions?

Finally, the fourth purpose of nonverbal communication is to accompany verbal communication. Ekman (1965) specified the important ways that verbal and nonverbal behaviors interrelate during human communication. Nonverbal communication can simply *repeat* what is said verbally. It can also *conflict* with what is being said. Verbal and nonverbal communication can be incongruous, or in disagreement. Think of a time at home, work, or school when you experienced someone saying he or she was being truthful yet could not look you in the eye. Did you assume that person was being deceptive? Or think of a time when a loved one said, with a raised voice and tear-filled eyes, that nothing was bothering him or her. When verbal communication carries one message and body language a conflicting message, the result is likely to be communication failure (Jones & LeBaron, 2002; Laplante & Ambady, 2003).

Ekman (1965) also found that nonverbal communication can *complement* or accent a specific part of the verbal message. This can include placing emphasis on certain words by slowing down your speech or changing your tone. Nonverbal behavior can also be a *substitute* for a word or phrase within a verbal message. How many of you have ever nodded instead of saying "yes" when your professor asked you if you understood the curriculum? Or perhaps you have looked away to avoid eye contact instead of saying that you do not want to be called on to answer the question being asked.

In addition to the above, nonverbal communication may also *accent* (amplify) or *moderate* (tone down) parts of the verbal message. As well, nonverbal communication is distinct in its ability to *regulate* verbal behaviors by coordinating our verbal and nonverbal behavior in the production of our messages or those of our communication partner (Ekman, 1965). Imagine the last time you had a conversation with a roommate or friend. How did you determine whose turn it was to speak? Did you use eye contact to end the conversation or to let the other person know you were listening? What hand gestures or sounds might you have made to show your partner that you wanted to speak?

Recall the definition of human communication as presented earlier in the text: the process of understanding our experiences and the experiences of others through the use of verbal and nonverbal messages. In fact, in an effort to categorize the meaning associated with nonverbal behavior, Mehrabian (1981) identified three dimensions that indicate how we use nonverbal communication to make sense of things in both personal and professional contexts:

- *Immediacy*—We react to things by evaluating them as positive or negative, good or bad.
- *Status*—We perceive behaviors that indicate various aspects of status to us, for example, rich or poor, strong or weak, superior or subordinate.
- *Responsiveness*—Our perceptions of activity as being active or passive. This signals the intensity of our feelings about a person or subject.

Remember that our cultural backgrounds can determine how physically close we get to others and how close we let others get to us.

Knapp and Hall (2009) proposed that these three dimensions are basic responses to our environment and are reflected in the way we assign meaning to both verbal and nonverbal behavior.

Now that we have explored the value and importance of nonverbal communication and how we assign meaning, it is crucial that we examine the *components* of nonverbal communication to understand it on a deeper level. Although we focus on these nonverbal communication codes in Western culture, remember that perceptions or reactions to nonverbal communication can vary in other cultures.

# Codes of Nonverbal Communication

The primary categories or **codes** of nonverbal communication include vocal expression; space, environment, and territory; physical appearance; body movement, gestures, and posture; facial and eye expressions; and touch (see Table 2.1; Ivy & Wahl, 2009).

## Vocal Expression

**Vocalics**, sometimes referred to as paralanguage, refers to how people use their voices to communicate and express themselves (Foley & Gentile, 2010; Ivy & Wahl, 2009). Vocalic cues include tone (quality) of voice, volume, articulation, pitch (highness or lowness), rate of speech, and use of silence. The voice reveals our emotions, our thoughts, and the

**Table 2.1  Nonverbal Communication Codes: Consider the Professional Context**

| Nonverbal Code | Consider the Professional Context |
| --- | --- |
| Kinesics (body movement, gestures, and posture) | How do you think gestures and body movement impact professional contexts? |
| Facial/eye behavior | Can you think of some examples of professional face and eye behavior? How can face and eye behavior lead to negative perceptions? |
| Vocalics (paralanguage) | What vocal qualities do you perceive as professional? Unprofessional? |
| Space/territory | How can space and territorial violations impact business and professional contexts? |
| Touch | Can you think of positive ways to use touch in professional contexts? In contrast, can you think of some negative uses of touch? |
| Environment | What are the qualities of a professional environment? |
| Physical appearance | In what ways does physical appearance impact business and professional communication? |

relationships we have with others. A growing body of evidence from multidisciplinary research in acoustics, engineering, linguistics, phonetics, and psychology suggests that an authoritative, expressive voice can make a big difference in one's professional career. Scientific studies show that someone with authority characteristically speaks low, slow, and with vocal intonation (Louet, 2012). Vocalics provide information about our self-confidence and knowledge and influence how we are perceived by others (Hinkle, 2001). Think about the direct impact our tone of voice can have in a professional setting. What does your voice say about you to others?

## Space

The impact of space on communication is called **proxemics**, or how people create and use space and distance, as well as how they behave to protect and defend that space (Foley & Gentile, 2010; Hall, 1959, 1966; Ivy & Wahl, 2009). Violations of territory and our personal space can be detrimental in business and professional settings.

Have you ever been on a crowded elevator and been uncomfortable because it seemed as though people were invading your personal space? When you go to the library, how many of you place your backpacks on the table or chair next to you to claim your space? What would happen if someone sat down in that chair anyway? Violations can be alarming, possibly even threatening. Our relationships with others, power and status, and our cultural backgrounds determine how physically close we get to others and how close we let others get to us (Burgoon & Jones, 1976).

What preferences do you have related to space and distance? Edward T. Hall (1963) identified four zones of space in middle-class U.S. culture. The first is the *intimate zone* (0 to 18 inches). This is usually reserved for our significant others, family members, and closest friends. It is rare that a stranger can enter this space without making us feel violated. These interactions mostly occur in private and signify a high level of connection, trust, and affection. The *personal zone* (18 inches to about 4 feet) is reserved for personal relationships with casual acquaintances and friends. The *social zone* (4 feet to 12 feet) is the distance at which we usu-

This photo demonstrates how people create and use space and distance. What might happen if someone picked up the computer and sat down in the seat next to her?

ally talk to strangers or conduct business. If you went to your professor's office to discuss a grade, for example, you would most likely remain at a distance of 4 to 12 feet. The *public zone* (more than 12 feet) refers to the distance typical of large, formal, public events. In large lecture classrooms, campaign rallies, or public speeches, the distance between speaker and audience is usually more than 12 feet. Understanding these spatial zones is important to your everyday nonverbal communication competency.

## Know Yourself   Nonverbal Communication

*The following report will help you gain a better understanding of your own nonverbal immediacy. Complete each item thoughtfully, and then reflect on the results. How can this knowledge help you be a better communicator?*

### Nonverbal Immediacy Scale-Observer Report

This measure will allow you to assess your own nonverbal immediacy behaviors.

*Directions:* The following statements describe the ways some people behave while talking with or to others. Please indicate in the space at the left of each item the degree to which you believe the statement applies to [fill in the target person's name or description]. Please use the following 5-point scale:

1 = *never*; 2 = *rarely*; 3 = *occasionally*; 4 = *often*; 5 = *very often*.

__ 1. I use my hands and arms to gesture while talking to people.
__ 2. I touch others on the shoulder or arm while talking to them.
__ 3. I use a monotone or dull voice while talking to people.
__ 4. I look over or away from others while talking to them.
__ 5. I move away from others when they touch me while we are talking.
__ 6. I have a relaxed body position when I talk to people.
__ 7. I frown while talking to people.
__ 8. I avoid eye contact while talking to people.
__ 9. I have a tense body position while talking to people.
__ 10. I sit close or stand close to people while talking with them.
__ 11. My voice is monotonous or dull when I talk to people.
__ 12. I use a variety of vocal expressions when I talk to people.
__ 13. I gesture when I talk to people.
__ 14. I am animated when I talk to people.
__ 15. I have a bland facial expression when I talk to people.
__ 16. I move closer to people when I talk to them.
__ 17. 1 look directly at people while talking to them.
__ 18. I am stiff when I talk to people.
__ 19. I have a lot of vocal variety when I talk to people.
__ 20. I avoid gesturing while I am talking to people.
__ 21. 1 lean toward people when I talk to them.
__ 22. I maintain eye contact with people when I talk to them.
__ 23. I try not to sit or stand close to people when I talk with them.
__ 24. I lean away from people when I talk to them.
__ 25. I smile when I talk to people.
__ 26. I avoid touching people when I talk to them.

*(Continued)*

(Continued)

Scoring for Nonverbal Immediacy Scale-Observer Report:
*Step 1.* Start with a score of 78. Add the scores from the following items:
1, 2, 6, 10, 12, 13, 14, 16, 17, 19, 21, 22, and 25.

*Step 2.* Add the scores from the following items:
3, 4, 5, 7, 8, 9, 11, 15, 18, 20, 23, 24, and 26.
Total score = *Step 1* minus *Step 2.*

Source: Richmond, McCroskey, and Johnson (2003).

How did you score? What surprised you about your score? You can also try the measure on others. Simply fill out the measure with another person's behaviors in mind. For instance, you might find it interesting to fill out the survey for your least and most favorite professors to determine whether their nonverbal immediacy might play some role in the degree to which you like them. Do you notice differences in their use of nonverbal immediacy behaviors? Did you learn more in one class? What class did you enjoy more?

## Environment

The constructed or natural surroundings that influence your communicative decisions, attitude, and mood are termed the **environment** (Foley & Gentile, 2010; Ivy & Wahl, 2009). People are influenced by environmental factors such as architecture, design, doors, windows, color, lighting, smell, seating arrangements, temperature, and cleanliness (Harris & Sachau, 2005; Jackson, 2005). Take a moment to think about what preferences would be related to your work environment. How does the environment (e.g., temperature, lighting, color, furniture) impact your communication?

Consider other things in the environment that can serve as nonverbal cues about who you are. These environmental factors you create and control are what serve as nonverbal messages to others who enter the space. As one scholar put it, "People cannot be understood outside of their environmental context" (Peterson, 1992, p. 154). The environments we create for ourselves often speak volumes about those relationships we consider most important (Lohmann, Arriaga, & Goodfriend, 2003).

### Perceptions of Environment

The way we perceive our environment and the environments of others is an important factor in how we respond. Overall, we perceive the environment in six distinct ways (Knapp & Hall, 2006). The first is *formality*, which is an understanding people have of environment that relates to how comfortably they can behave, in light of their expectations. Sometimes it is more about the atmosphere of a certain place than the place itself. The second way we can perceive the environment is *warmth*. This means that the environment gives off a certain sense of warmth, comfort, or a welcoming context based on our past or current experience. Think of a favorite smell from your childhood, for example. Smells in an environment contribute to our perception of warmth.

*Privacy* is another way the environment can be perceived. Do you prefer a crowded and noisy restaurant or a peaceful and quiet one? Do you choose a seat in the back of a movie theater or in the middle next to many other moviegoers? Another perception we have is *familiarity,* which means that we tend to react cautiously when we meet new people or are confronted with an unfamiliar environment. Not knowing where we are and what to expect makes us feel less comfortable. We like knowing what to expect and how to behave in the environment.

Another perception of environment is that of *constraint.* Think about your living situation. Do you like sharing a room or home with another person? Whenever we feel that our personal space is being invaded, we feel constrained. Most of our perceptions of constraint are shaped by the amount of privacy and space available to us. The final perception of environment is *distance.* Our perceptions of distance in an environment pertain to physical arrange-

People are influenced by their environments. What are the nonverbal messages in this professional office environment that could impact communication?

ments. We like to know how far away the closest door is or how many people can fit into an elevator. We create distance by avoiding eye contact or taking a longer route to avoid saying hello to a person we find annoying.

## Physical Appearance

**Physical appearance**—"the way our bodies and overall appearance nonverbally communicate to others and impact our view of ourselves in everyday life" (Ivy & Wahl, 2009, p. 129)—also plays an important role in communication. Making the connection between physical appearance and nonverbal communication is important for two reasons: (1) The way we represent ourselves and our physical appearance reveals a lot about who we are, and (2) the physical appearance of other people influences our perception of them, how we talk to them, how approachable they are, how attractive or unattractive we think they are, and so on.

Clothing is also a part of our physical appearance that is often critical to professional situations. Clothing helps you convey a sense of professionalism. Clothing and other appearance aspects, termed **artifacts** (e.g., jewelry, tattoos, piercings, makeup, cologne, eyeglasses), send nonverbal messages and help others form perceptions of us, both good and bad (Okoro & Washington, 2011; Roach, 1997). The nonverbal message sent by your clothing is a powerful part of professional excellence. Appearance is extremely important in our society. In fact, according to Armour (2005), employers also agree that physical appearance matters. An Intranet software firm in the Northeast requires formal business

The way we represent ourselves and our physical appearance reveal a lot about who we are. The nonverbal message sent by your clothing is a powerful part of professional excellence.

attire on the job. Men must wear ties, cannot have beards, and cannot wear their hair past shoulder length. "Clients like to see a workforce that looks conservative," says the chief operating officer. Although the criteria for what is acceptable in each environment might vary, physical appearance undoubtedly can affect one's perceived professional excellence.

## Body Movement

**Kinesics** is a general term for the study of human movement, gestures, and posture (Birdwhistell, 1970; Foley & Gentile, 2010; Ivy & Wahl, 2009). Kinesics provides valuable information about a person to others. Have you ever heard someone make reference to how a certain person carries himself or herself? Have you ever talked about a person who has a certain presence in the room? Perhaps some of us have said, "He/she walks like a leader." Some people carry themselves in ways that convey pride and confidence, while others have poor posture and seem to lack confidence. Ekman and Friesen (1969b) classified movement and gestures according to how they function in human interaction. The five categories of kinesics are emblems, illustrators, affect displays, regulators, and adaptors.

**Emblems** are specific, widely understood meanings in a given culture that can actually substitute for a word or phrase. An example of this would be placing your pointer finger in front of your lips to indicate to someone to be quiet. **Illustrators** are gestures that complement, enhance, or substitute for the verbal message. If you were describing the length of the biggest fish you ever caught, you might use your hands to illustrate the size. Or when you are giving directions, you might point to show which way to go. **Affect displays** are facial expressions and gestures that display emotion. A smile can be an affect display for happiness, while a scowl can display frustration. **Regulators** are gestures used to control the turn-taking in conversations. For example, we might make a hand motion to encourage someone or raise our own hand to get a turn at speaking. When we are eager to speak, we normally make eye contact, raise our eyebrows, open our mouths, take in a breath, and lean forward slightly. We do the opposite if we do not want to answer. Head nods, vocal expressions (such as *um*), facial expressions, body postures, and eye contact can be seen as connectors that keep the conversation together and make it coherent. When these sorts of nonverbal cues are absent from a conversation, it might trigger a negative reaction, and we could come to believe that our conversational partner is not listening at all. **Adapters** are gestures we use to release tension. Playing with your hands, poking, picking, fidgeting, scratching, and interacting nonverbally with your environment are all adapters that reveal your attempts to regulate situations and to make yourself feel more at ease and able to function effectively. Adapters can alert us that another person is uncomfortable in some way (Ekman & Friesen, 1969b).

## Facial Behavior

Facial expressions (including the study of eye behavior, called **oculesics**) are also critical codes that have been studied by nonverbal communication scholars (Ivy & Wahl, 2009). The face can be considered a gallery for our emotional displays (Gosselin, Gilles, & Dore, 1995). What does another person's face tell you about him or her? What emotion is she expressing? How is he feeling? Are your coworkers surprised to see you? Did your colleagues find your presentation to be entertaining, or were they disappointed? Your face and eye behavior play a huge role in the messages you send in business and professional contexts.

Yet, it is important not only to have a basic understanding of the emotions communicated by the face but also to be aware of how we manage our faces in daily interactions. Social norms and communication expectations in our culture set the rules for what kinds of emotional expressions are appropriate in certain situations. Facial management techniques are categories of behavior studied by Ekman and Friesen (1969a, 1969b, 1975) that determine the appropriate facial response for a given situation. The four most common techniques are neutralization, masking, intensification, and deintensification.

The process of using facial expressions to erase how we really feel is called **neutralization**. People who neutralize their facial expressions are often referred to as having a poker face. **Masking** means hiding an expression connected to a felt emotion and replacing it with an expression more appropriate to the situation. If we use an expression that exaggerates how we feel about something, it is called **intensification**. On the other hand, if we reduce the intensity of our facial expression connected to a certain emotion, it is called **deintensification**.

A significant part of facial expressions involves use of the eyes. About 80% of the information in our everyday surroundings is taken in visually (Morris, 1985). Kleinke (1986) purports that eye contact and gaze functions provide information, regulate interaction, express intimacy, exercise social norms, and facilitate personal, situational, and relational goals. Evasive glances and limited-duration eye contact on the part of a communicator tend to reduce compliance with requests (Gueguen & Jacob, 2002). What can people tell about you by looking into your eyes?

## Your Communication Interaction    When George Met Sally

*Read the passage below, and then answer the questions. As you read, think about ways the KEYS approach could help you improve* **your communication interaction** *if you were in George's or Sally's position.*

Sally began working at a greeting card store in the evening to help pay for her college tuition and books. Her supervisor, George, was very supportive of her goal to do well in all her classes and even allowed her to study when customers were not in the store. For months, Sally shared a lot with George. He was a great listener and always gave her really good advice about how to handle situations in her life, such as car troubles, personal issues, and even tips for studying. Sally felt as though he was the big brother she never had. George found himself growing fond of Sally in a romantic way. He began buying her coffee or dinner and would leave notes at her station just to say thanks for her hard work around the store and how much he appreciated her friendship. Sally had never had a job before and thought she was lucky to have a boss as supportive as George. When Sally found out at the end of the semester that she had made straight As, she rushed to the store to tell George. He was very excited for her. Sally jumped up and down with excitement, and they hugged. George could not help himself and leaned in for a kiss. Sally was surprised and embarrassed. She did not feel the same way about George.

### Questions to Consider

1. How should Sally respond to George?
2. Do you believe that Sally and/or George displayed professional excellence?
3. What nonverbal and verbal cues are important in this exchange?
4. How could the KEYS process help Sally and George in this situation?

## Touch

Touch, also called **haptics** in nonverbal research, "is the most powerful form of nonverbal communication; it's also the most misunderstood and carries the potential for the most problems if ill used" (Ivy & Wahl, 2009, p. 45). Several different systems for categorizing touch have been developed to help us better understand this complex code of nonverbal communication. One of the best means of classifying touch behavior was developed by Heslin (1974). The first, **functional/professional touch**, serves a specific function. These touches normally take place within the context of a professional relationship and are low in intimacy. An example would be the essence of greeting rituals in business situations, the *professional handshake* (Hlemstra, 1999). The handshake is critical to making a good first impression as a professional. Think about what you look for in a handshake. What does a professional handshake feel like?

**Social/polite touch** is connected to cultural norms, such as hugs or pats on the back. Once again, these touches have a relatively low intimacy within a relationship, while **friendship/warmth touch** is the type people use to show their platonic affection toward each other. Hugs and kisses on the cheek might be exchanged between two close friends, for example. **Love/intimacy touch**, on the other hand, is highly personal and intimate.

The handshake is critical to making a good first impression. What are some of the qualities you notice in someone's handshake?

People communicate strong feelings of affection toward each other with these kinds of touches; in this case, hugs may last longer and kisses may be on the lips. The last category involves **sexual arousal**. These touches are extremely intimate.

# Forming Relationships With Verbal and Nonverbal Communication

Developing interpersonal, verbal, and nonverbal communication skills requires you to differentiate between the content and layers of messages. As you communicate with other people, your messages have two layers (Dillard, Solomon, & Palmer, 1999; Watzlawick, Beavin, & Jackson, 1967). The first is the content layer. The **content layer** consists of the "information being explicitly discussed" (Adler & Proctor, 2007, p. 16). The content layer may include descriptive information such as the time of a meeting, a project due date, or the names of the coworkers assigned to a team. You exchange content with others to function and retrieve basic information.

The second layer is relational. The **relational layer** reveals "how you feel about the other person; whether you like or dislike the other person, feel in control or subordinate, feel comfortable or anxious, and so on" (Adler & Proctor, 2007, p. 16). The relational layer may be communicated by your choice of words. For example, an executive may call her employees by their first names, while the employees are required to refer to the executive as Mrs. Villarreal. The difference in formality of names signifies a difference in control. The relational level can also be communicated nonverbally through tone of voice, use of space, and eye contact.

For example, Jason is really nervous about making a deadline, but he can't finish until Rachel completes the financial section of the project. Jason could ask Rachel, "What time will you be done with financials?" to retrieve a specific time reference, such as, "Sometime this evening." These words reflect the content layer. If Jason wants to send the message that he's annoyed with Rachel, he could add a negative tone: "What *time* will you be done with financials?" If Jason is indeed annoyed, then he has effectively communicated both the content and the relational layers of his message. However, if Jason did not intend to express annoyance, then his message is ineffective on the relational level.

There are communicators out there who do not pay attention to the relational layer of their messages. As a result, they don't realize how they're coming across to others. In order to achieve professional excellence, you must think beyond the content layer of your messages and also assess the relational layer. This can be supported by using the KEYS process.

## Verbal and Nonverbal Communication and Their Impact on Professions

In this chapter, we have explored verbal and nonverbal communication—why they are important, their definitions, their principles, and their components. As you consider your professional goals, think about how you will use verbal and nonverbal communication to succeed in your career. We have included the following examples of the importance of verbal and nonverbal communication in a variety of industries. Even if your desired profession is not listed in the sections below, know that developing your professional excellence and communication competence is invaluable no matter what path you may take in life.

Retail companies compete to provide the best products and service to their customers. What does good customer service look and sound like?

### Customer Service and Sales

Recall the importance of proxemics, or the impact of space on communication. Manning and Reece (1989) found that success in productivity and sales was linked to the distance between sales representatives and prospects, salesperson posture, handshake techniques, facial expressions, arm movements, hand movements, and placement of the legs and feet. Those sales representatives who rely primarily on the spoken word to communicate with prospects may be neglecting an important tool for conveying their ideas. In addition, Leigh and Summers (2002) conducted an investigation that examined the effectiveness of nonverbal communication in a sales context. Using videotaped presentations, they found that nonverbal cues (eye gaze, speech hesitations, gestures, clothing, and posture) influenced the experimental buyers' perceptions of the sales representative and their evaluation of the sales presentation.

### Journalism and Television Broadcasting

Those in the public eye must demonstrate effective nonverbal and verbal communication. How many times have you seen a clip of an on-camera flub being played over and over again on YouTube or the local news? In the opinion of some scholars, as well as television commentators, arrogant body language on the part of many journalists in the United States has led to low public respect and esteem for them (Lehrer, 1998).

### Public Service

Individuals who work in environments such as libraries or government offices (e.g., Department of Motor Vehicles, utility companies, etc.) are sometimes criticized for their communication and viewed as distant and unhelpful. There is evidence that individuals who are trained in nonverbal communication can replace negative perceptions of themselves with positive ones (Sampson, 1995).

### Hospitality Management

Customer service is especially important in the hotel and restaurant industries. A number of hotel and restaurant managers have improved their organizations' image among guests by providing client services employees (e.g., hosts, servers, desk clerks, bell hops) with training in verbal and nonverbal communication (Jafari & Way, 1994). In restaurants, eye contact, facial expression, body position, and posture of the staff, including servers and cashiers, affect how customers rate the value of the service (Martin, 1986).

### Medical Professions

Many people can probably share a story about an unpleasant experience at the doctor's office. As physicians compete to attract and retain a strong client base, their services can be interpreted positively by potential patients through correct body language on the part of the physicians and their employees. Patients often choose a physician based on their perceived image of the doctor, as revealed by verbal and nonverbal communications (Hill & Garner, 1991).

### Teaching Professions

There is evidence that the nonverbal communication of teachers influences the evaluation direction (positive or negative) and level of performance they receive from their students (Babad, Avni-Babad, & Rosenthal, 2003). Consider the different teaching and communication styles of your current professors. What do you find are the common communication traits of the professors you enjoy most?

### Legal Professions

A study has indicated that lawyers can project a favorable impression of themselves and their firms for prospective clients through sustained eye contact and other forms of body language, such as an erect but relaxed sitting position and close proximity to the clients (Clarke, 1989).

### Accounting and Finance

In the same vein as lawyers, accountants can benefit through the technique of maintained and appropriate eye contact, good posture, and close proximity to clients (Pickholz & Zimmerman, 2002).

### Management (Private and Public)

Managers in both business and not-for-profit organizations can more effectively convey ideas to their employees through correct use of nonverbal communication (Hancock, 1999; McCaskey, 1979). On the other hand, job evaluations of employees by their supervisors have been found to correlate with smiling, gaze, hand movement, and body orientation (DeGroot & Motowidlo, 1999). In a similar vein, managers can effectively convey impressions of empathy and power through body language (Gabbott & Hogg, 2000).

# KEYS to Excellence in Verbal and Nonverbal Communication

The opener to this chapter discussed how nonverbal communication can affect the quality of interaction (and health outcomes) between medical doctors and patients. Can this same logic be applied to your professional communication? Think about how using the KEYS strategies can positively affect your nonverbal communication with others. The first step, *know yourself*, asks you to inventory the types of nonverbal cues you display to others. This can be difficult, but try to be aware even of the small, unconscious nonverbal cues you create. Sometimes the worst nonverbal cues we display are the ones we are not even aware of making.

The next step, *evaluate the professional context*, requires that you assess what nonverbal signals are considered acceptable in your workplace. Are your meetings informal, or is there a set decorum on how people interact? Notice how both your coworkers and superiors convey nonverbal cues during workplace interactions, and gauge how your nonverbal cues line up with those of others in your company.

The third step, *your communication interaction occurs*, involves taking an immediate reflexive inventory of both your nonverbal communication and your partner's. How do you react to your partner's nonverbal signals? How does he or she react to yours? Think about what sets you at ease when communicating with others, and try to accomplish the same goal when talking with customers, employees, or superiors. The more open people feel when talking with you, the more likely they will disclose information more honestly and comfortably.

The final task, *step back and reflect*, requires you to analyze your communication after the interaction has ended. Did you walk away feeling satisfied with your nonverbal communication? Did your communication partner seem at ease when talking with you? Assess what seemed to be the most effective nonverbal cues and which ones appeared to create a negative perception.

Much like the interaction between doctors and patients, your nonverbal cues can set people at ease and make them feel comfortable talking to you. This can lead to better (and more honest) communication and allow you to practice professional excellence in the workplace.

**K**now Yourself

**E**valuate the Professional Context

**Y**our Communication Interaction Occurs

**S**tep Back and Reflect

## Executive Summary

Now that you have finished reading this chapter, you can do the following.

Define verbal communication:

- Verbal *communication* is both our words and verbal fillers (e.g., *um, like*). Verbal messages are created through language. Effective communication involves accurate interpretations of others' verbal messages as meaning is cocreated (p. 26).

Define nonverbal communication:

- *Nonverbal communication* (also referred to as body language) includes all those ways we communicate without words (p. 29).

Develop your verbal and nonverbal communication skills:

- Developing interpersonal, verbal, and nonverbal communication skills requires you to differentiate between the content and layers of messages. As you communicate with other people, your messages have two layers (p. 41).
- The *content layer* consists of the "information being explicitly discussed" (Adler & Proctor, 2007, p. 16). The content layer may include descriptive information such as the time of a meeting, a project due date, or the names of the coworkers assigned to a team (p. 41).
- The *relational layer* reveals "how you feel about the other person; whether you like or dislike the other person, feel in control or subordinate, feel comfortable or anxious, and so on" (Adler & Proctor, 2007, p. 16). The relational layer may be communicated by your choice of words (p. 41).

Explain the importance of both verbal and nonverbal communication and how they are related:

- Some communicators do not pay attention to the relational layer of their messages. As a result, they don't realize how they're coming across to others. In order to achieve professional excellence, you must think beyond the content layer of your messages and also assess the relational layer (p. 42).

Utilize the KEYS approach to conduct yourself with professional excellence through verbal and nonverbal communication in the workplace:

- The first step, *know yourself*, asks you to inventory the types of nonverbal cues you display to others. This can be difficult, but try to be aware even of the small, unconscious nonverbal cues you create. Sometimes the worst nonverbal cues we display are the ones we are not even aware of making (p. 44).
- The next step, *evaluate the professional context*, requires that you assess what nonverbal signals are considered acceptable in your workplace. Are your meetings informal, or is there a set decorum for how people interact? Notice how both your coworkers and superiors convey nonverbal cues during workplace interactions, and gauge how your nonverbal cues line up with those of others in your company (p. 44).
- The third step, *your communication interaction occurs*, involves taking an immediate reflexive inventory of both your nonverbal communication and your partner's. Think about what sets you at ease when communicating with others, and try to accomplish the same goal when talking with customers, employees, or superiors. The more open people feel when talking with you, the more likely they will disclose information more honestly and comfortably (p. 44).
- The final task, *step back and reflect*, requires you to analyze your communication after the interaction has ended. Did you walk away feeling satisfied with your nonverbal communication? Did your communication partner seem at ease when talking with you? Assess what nonverbal cues seemed the most effective and which ones appeared to create a negative perception (p. 44).

## Discussion Questions

1. What two rules guide communication? Why is appropriateness important when communicating? Share an example of a time when you experienced inappropriate communication. Who was the communicator? Why was it inappropriate?

2. Ethical consideration: In a workplace, when, if ever, is it appropriate to verbally communicate something that is not true? Does this apply to your personal relationships? Ask three people this same question, and note their responses.

3. What are the principles of nonverbal communication? Discuss at least two nonverbal communication codes. Which codes discussed in this chapter are the most important to you as a professional?

4. Name three reasons why nonverbal communication is important. Work through a personal example of a time when you needed to improve your verbal or nonverbal communication. What changes would you have made in the situation?

5. Step back and reflect on a time when you received criticism at work or school. How did you respond verbally? How did you respond nonverbally? How did the environment contribute to your communication?

## Terms to Remember

adapters (p. 39)

affect displays (p. 38)

artifacts (p. 37)

codes (p. 33)

communication rules (p. 27)

constitutive rules (p. 28)

content layer (p. 41)

deintensification (p. 39)

emblems (p. 38)

environment (p. 36)

friendship/warmth touch (p. 40)

functional/professional touch (p. 40)

haptics (p. 40)

illustrators (p. 38)

intensification (p. 39)

kinesics (p. 38)

love/intimacy touch (p. 40)

masking (p. 39)

neutralization (p. 39)

nonverbal communication (p. 29)

oculesics (p. 39)

physical appearance (p. 37)

proxemics (p. 34)

regulative rules (p. 27)

regulators (p. 39)

relational layer (p. 41)

sexual arousal (p. 41)

social/polite touch (p. 40)

verbal communication (p. 26)

vocalics (p. 33)

Visit the Student Study Site at **www.sagepub.com/keys2e** to access the following resources:

- SAGE journal articles
- Video links
- Web resources
- Web quizzes
- eflashcards

## Chapter Outline

**Hearing and Listening**   51

**Barriers to Listening**   53

**Listening Styles and Categories**   59

**Improving Your Listening**   60

**KEYS to Listening Excellence**   62

**Executive Summary**   64

**Discussion Questions**   65

**Terms to Remember**   65

## Chapter Objectives

After studying this chapter you should be able to:

1. Explain the difference between hearing and listening

2. Understand the barriers to listening and how to avoid them

3. Identify and explain strategies for developing and sustaining professional excellence using active listening skills

4. List and define the six-step process of listening (HURIER model)

5. Utilize the KEYS approach to conduct yourself with professional excellence while developing your listening skills in the workplace

# chapter 3

# Listening

**Apple CEO Tim Cook had some large shoes to fill with the death of the legendary Steve Jobs.** Jobs, the former Apple CEO who passed away in October 2011, was widely heralded as one of the greatest inventors and businessmen of his generation. Since taking over, Cook has overseen an increase in revenue and profitability for Apple and has differentiated himself from his predecessor in a number of ways. One major difference is the way Cook uses town hall meetings to seek feedback from his workforce. In an effort to become more employee oriented, Cook allows Apple employees to attend meetings and discuss issues they feel are important to the company. The town hall meetings have already produced two major changes for the Apple corporation. Employees have been given major discounts for Apple products, and the company also introduced a new charitable program that matches employee donations. The overall mood from employees appears to be positive, and Apple's profits continue to increase under new leadership.

A healthy listening environment is essential for any workplace. Whether a health care provider that listens to community/patient concerns, a business that listens to customer feedback, or a university that acknowledges students' needs, listening is critical to workplace success. Having a boss who listens to your input can make you feel valuable and contribute to a better work environment. On the other hand, many of you have probably had a boss who never listened to employees, which can lead to a negative work atmosphere. It is important to note that listening does not apply only to the employee/boss relationship; listening to your coworkers also fosters a good work environment and allows professionals to become more comfortable with one another.

Listening with excellence in the workplace can be much harder than it sounds. It is often easy for us to zone out from other people's input when we are convinced we have the best idea. However, many of the great companies and businesses we know of today owe their success to great listening skills and cooperative teamwork. In this chapter, you will identify several strategies that can help you become a better listener in the workplace.

How important is listening in the communication process? What role does listening play in developing professional excellence? According to Crockett (2011), the average person remembers between 25% and 50% of what he or she hears. That means that when you talk to your boss, your colleagues or customers, your friends and family, they are likely to retain less than half of the conversation. Our poor memories are not to blame for this; rather, most of us simply do not listen well. To compound matters, the diversity and environment of today's workforce makes listening more difficult. In many workplaces, it is not uncommon for work teams to consist of people from several countries or ethnic backgrounds as well as varying levels of technological communication knowledge and practice. Even if everyone speaks English, some might use different dialects and speech patterns. Maximizing performance in such a multicultural and highly technological work environment means learning to listen. We will explore the concept of diversity and communication further in Chapter 5 ("Getting to Know Your Diverse Workplace"). Understanding why listening is important is crucial to help us improve our listening skills overall. The ability to be an effective listener plays a role in one's business and professional communication and is a prerequisite to demonstrating professional excellence. Listening is also vital to the needs of companies of all sizes and dynamics.

According to Stengel, Dixon, and Allen (2003) the most basic principle in the consumer products industry is "listen to the customer." Without an intimate knowledge of ever-changing trends and tastes, you are likely to lose out to competitors who are more tuned in. The notion that success also depends on listening to employees might seem just as basic. Yet this is not as easy as it sounds, and, due to poor listening, a company's leaders—regardless of industry—are often oblivious to what employees are concerned about and why. A good example is the Jayson Blair episode at *the New York Times*. Jayson fabricated and plagiarized multiple articles. By the time senior leaders got around to listening to their employees' concerns about the reporter's misdeeds, damage had been done to the organization's reputation. The problem of managers not hearing what staffers are saying is common in corporate life (Stengel et al., 2003). But the problem is not necessarily whether managers are hearing their staff. The problem lies in the ability to listen. Listening is a fundamental and complex part of the communication process. Let's explore it in more detail.

# Hearing and Listening

In casual conversation, most of us use the words *hearing* and *listening* as if they mean the same thing. However, as a professional striving for communication excellence, it's important for you to have a clear understanding of the difference between these terms. **Hearing** is your physical ability to detect sounds. It is the physiological process or function of receiving sounds. Your hearing is what they test at the doctor's office. Listening, however, is not one's physical ability. Recall the importance of nonverbal communication skills, which help you differentiate between the content and layers of messages. **Listening** requires you to concentrate on the verbal and nonverbal messages being sent and to determine the meaning of those messages. Effective listening is central to fostering interpersonal relationships with coworkers, leaders, and clients. Effective listening can affect one's relationship satisfaction and can be a determining factor in whether someone is an effective communicator.

Maximizing performance in teams means learning to listen.

The effects of one's listening abilities are far-reaching. Sypher, Bostrom, and Seibert (1989) reported that an individual's listening ability has implications for the effectiveness of productivity, teamwork, the overall organization, and perhaps the individual's own success. Listening, in addition to other communication abilities, is a likely predictor of who gets promoted or receives other relevant rewards, such as status and power. Sypher et al. found that better listeners hold higher-level positions and are promoted more often than those with less-developed listening abilities.

Wouldn't life be fantastic if everyone were an excellent listener? Can you imagine an entire career without any misunderstandings? The trouble is, many people make the mistake of thinking excellent hearing equals excellent listening. You have no doubt already experienced communication misunderstandings in the workplace—you know firsthand that excellent hearing does not necessarily equal excellent listening.

Developing excellence as a listener can be difficult, but in order to achieve professional excellence, you must hone your ability to listen effectively. In fact, Haas and Arnold (1995) state that a growing body of research suggests that listening ability, or the perception of effective listening, is inextricably linked to effective individual performance in organizations. Nichols and Stevens (1957) found that good listeners regularly engage in mental activities while listening. A good listener periodically reviews and mentally summarizes the talking points completed thus far. Throughout the talk, the listener "listens between the lines," in search of meaning that is not necessarily put into spoken words. He or she pays attention to nonverbal communication (facial expressions, gestures, tone of voice) to see if it adds meaning to the spoken words. The listener may also weigh the evidence used by the talker to support the points he or she makes. It takes a lot of practice to become a good listener, and listening has become a lot more difficult.

## Step Back and Reflect    Trouble at Home, Trouble With Training

*Read the following passage about Jennifer, and answer the questions that come after.*

Jennifer is a recent college graduate who started a new job as a recruiter for a local nonprofit. Her job consists of placing individuals with employment barriers into jobs. She must build relationships with employers, secure job leads, screen candidates, and report her monthly hires/placements. Her position is commission based, which means she must make placements to earn money. While in training, she found herself preoccupied by several things going on at home. She was fighting with her boyfriend and in a conflict with her roommate. Her boyfriend sent her numerous text messages while her new manager explained the job responsibilities to the class of new hires. Between worrying about her relationship and the pressures of learning a new job, she heard the new manager say that she should do anything in her power to get placements, as this was the most important thing to remember of all the training content.

A few weeks into her position, Jennifer found that she felt really lost about how to do her job well. She was not making any placements. Whenever she approached her coworkers, they did not seem to listen to her. They rarely looked up from their computers or phones, and she had to repeat her questions several times before they answered. When they did respond, they answered only parts of her questions. Jennifer was left confused and frustrated. They all said the same thing, however: Getting placements was the most important thing to focus on no matter how she met her goal. She followed their lead and began claiming credit whenever any of her clients found a job, whether she had assisted them or not. Jennifer was cutting corners to reach her placement outcomes. She had "heard" the message loud and clear. A few months later, Jennifer, her coworkers, and their immediate supervisor were terminated and the nonprofit was under investigation for fraudulent reporting.

### Step Back and Reflect

1. What went wrong?
2. What role did listening play?
3. What are the ethical considerations?
4. How could Jennifer utilize the KEYS approach to improve her communication interaction?

So how can you develop your skills as a listener? The first step is to admit that listening is difficult. Don't fall into the trap of assuming that because you have good hearing, you have good listening skills, too. Take Carey, for example. Carey was born deaf, and while she could not physically hear others speak, she was an excellent listener. She used an interpreter, lip reading, and a highly developed ability to read nonverbal cues to make sense of the messages she received. In fact, her inability to hear may have caused her to develop her exceptional listening abilities. Carey outperformed many of her colleagues who did possess perfect hearing. Although they sat beside Carey in meetings, hearing every word, they fell victim to the barriers to listening excellence. These barriers include failing to limit distractions, failing to focus on the message, and failing to be active listeners.

In any business and professional situation, you'll encounter some or all of these barriers. An important part of professional excellence is being able to develop your listening skills and overcome the barriers.

# Barriers to Listening

## Failing to Limit Distractions

As we covered in Chapter 1, noise is part of every communication interaction. **External noise** includes distractions such as audible talking during a meeting, ruffling of papers, or a cell phone going off in the next cubicle. Whenever possible, you should take steps to control the external noise that might interfere with your ability to listen to others, as well

as their ability to listen to you. For example, when you are talking to someone on the phone, turn away from your computer if you're distracted by messages in your inbox. If you're running a meeting, begin by asking everyone to turn off their cell phones. If the work environment is such that it's difficult for people to break away from distractions, hold a retreat away from your worksite to maximize the team's ability to listen effectively. For example, Jennifer (in Step Back and Reflect on page 52) failed to limit her distractions when she did not turn off her cell phone prior to the new-hire training. Instead, she focused on reading the messages from her boyfriend, increasing her inability to listen to the trainer. We must be conscious of the extent to which environmental, physical, psychological, and experiential factors affect the quality of listening (Highet, 1989, p. 65).

Whenever possible, you should take steps to control the external noise that interferes with your ability to listen to others.

**Internal noise** encompasses any internal condition or state that interferes with the communicator's ability to focus on the message. Even when we are listening in real time—on a cell phone, for example—listening has become more multilayered. During a cell phone conversation, we expect the speaker to be doing something else. Whether we think about it consciously or not, during the conversation we assess what the speaker is saying as well as what she or he is *not* saying because of where she/he is or whom she/he is with. Technology has changed not only the tools we use to listen but also when and where we use them, and even what we think about as we listen (Jalongo, 2008).

Controlling internal noise in others can be difficult, as it may be hard to predict. Still, you can minimize some internal noise in others. For example, holding long meetings without food or bathroom breaks will guarantee internal noise in your team. Minimize the noise by providing food and giving breaks. Say you are a health care provider who has to deliver bad news. News such as "You have cancer" or "You will need surgery" will create

## Your Communication Interaction    Molly, Medical Leave, and Miscommunication

*Read the passage below, and then answer the questions. As you read, think about ways the KEYS approach could help you improve **your communication interaction** if you were in Molly's or Dan's position.*

When Molly learned from her doctor that her recent abdominal pain and nausea could be related to a serious medical condition, she immediately approached her boss, Dan, about taking time off to attend to tests and blood work. Although he was rushing to a meeting, he said he could talk and told her to walk with him to the conference room. She explained that she had a pressing medical issue and would be late for 2 days the following week due to doctor's appointments. Dan said, "Fine," while checking his Blackberry and asked her to provide a doctor's note upon her return. Molly went to her appointments the next week, put a doctor's note in his inbox the same day, and anxiously awaited her test results. During their end-of-week team meeting, Dan started the meeting by stating that the team needed to improve their overall punctuality and attendance. He made eye contact with Molly and listed her name among those who had been late that week.

Molly was shocked and did not know what to say. She had informed him of the time off in advance, had provided documentation, and was not ready to deal with this in addition to everything else on her plate.

### Questions to Consider

1. How should Molly respond to Dan?
2. Do you believe that Molly and/or Dan displayed professional excellence? Why or why not? How could the KEYS process help Molly and Dan in this situation?

---

tremendous internal noise. In situations such as these, allow the listener time to deal with the news before giving additional information or instructions he or she will need to listen to, comprehend, and remember.

As for the internal noise within *you*, you must reflect on what is causing your internal noise and address those factors. If you have an urgent matter to deal with, don't try to hold a conversation with someone. You simply won't be able to listen. Tell the other party you will need to reschedule your conversation for a time when you can give your undivided attention. If you have matters in your personal life that are affecting your ability to listen on the job, you must become aware of those issues and address them. For example, Jason has been experiencing a personal conflict with his wife. They both feel he's been spending too much time at work and not enough time at home. Jason's conflict at home serves as internal noise when his coworker, Rachel, tells him she will not have his part of the project to him on time. As she explains how her workload has doubled over the past few weeks due to some vacant positions in her department and she really wants an extension, all Jason can think about is the fact that his part of the project will now have to be completed over the weekend. For Jason, developing professional excellence includes learning to manage his internal noise so he can listen. If Jason had listened to Rachel, he could have supported her desire for an extension and they could have jointly requested a solution that would benefit them both. Like Jason, Jennifer (from Step Back and Reflect on page 52) was experiencing internal noise as a result of her relationship conflicts at home. Her failure to limit external distractions and to address the factors leading to internal noise prevented her from developing professional excellence.

## Failing to Focus on the Message

In the ever-changing world of social media and emerging technology, we are locked into a mode of continuous partial attention, where we are always scanning our smartphones for the next bit of news or the latest update. Multitasking is the norm, despite some evidence that it prevents us from doing anything to the best of our abilities (Fryer, 2009). In addition to distractions and noise, or maybe because of noise, you may fail to focus on the message being sent. As a result, you are not listening effectively. Beyond noise, some additional factors that may distract your focus on the message include jargon, message overload, receiver apprehension, and bias. Or you may fail to focus on the message because it is difficult to comprehend.

If a speaker uses **jargon** (technical words used by specialized groups) with which you are not familiar, you may think, "What in the world is she talking about? Why should I even pay attention to this stuff?" and then simply tune out. Jargon is a language of familiarity. It can be a useful tool when everyone has a common understanding of the terms at hand. If there is no common understanding, language can separate, insulate, and intimidate. Good communication is the result of the use of common terms that are clearly understood by both parties (Morasch, 2004).

People are unable to listen when they are experiencing internal noise. Reschedule important conversations if you have an urgent matter to deal with.

Message overload can have the same impact as jargon. **Message overload** occurs when a speaker includes too many details in a message, making it difficult for the listener to comprehend. As the listener tries to make sense out of the specific details, he or she loses focus of the primary message. Presenters sometimes make the mistake of including too many graphs and charts during their talks, which leads the audience to message overload. As a listener with professional excellence, you must stay engaged even if the message is difficult to comprehend. Listen for the main points, and request a copy of the notes or PowerPoint slides after the presentation. If the jargon or message overload comes as part of a conversation, not a presentation, engage in active listening.

Have you ever been nervous about listening to a presentation on a foreign subject or being involved in a conversation with a person you want to impress? You might be listening to someone give you specific directions about a complicated task or sitting in a lecture trying to take notes on classroom material. In any of these cases, you might be apprehensive about listening to the speaker. This feeling is called receiver apprehension. **Receiver apprehension** refers to "the fear of misinterpreting, inadequately processing, and/or not being able to adjust psychologically to messages sent by others" (Wheeless, 1975, p. 262). This could mean having a fear of coming across new information or of being judged on

## Ethical Connection

*Please read the passage below, and answer the questions that follow.*

Jennifer and Daniel are both personnel managers at a large company. While both jobs are identical in size and duties, the feedback that Jennifer and Daniel each receive could not be more different. Jennifer's employees feel safe approaching her with new ideas and concerns and are overall satisfied with the feedback they receive. Employees who work for Daniel, on the other hand, often complain that talking to him is like talking to a brick wall. They say that their concerns go unaddressed and that when they forward a new idea for the company, their suggestions are shrugged off without any discussion. At a recent supervisor meeting, the company executives discussed the disparity between Jennifer's and Daniel's employee satisfaction surveys and retention rates. Daniel seemed at a loss as to why his department was underperforming in comparison with Jennifer's.

### Questions to Consider

1. What is the ethical dilemma involved in being a poor listener?
2. Why would employees be happier working in an environment with a manager who effectively listens to their ideas and concerns?
3. Why is it so important that Jennifer provides feedback relating to her employees' communication?
4. Using the KEYS process, how can Daniel become a more effective listener?

A listener with professional excellence stays engaged even if the message is difficult to comprehend.

your ability to remembering the information correctly (Wheeless, Preiss, & Gayle, 1997). Research has demonstrated that a person with high receiver apprehension tends to have more problems with information processing and general listening effectiveness (Chesebro & McCroskey, 2001).

We also need to limit our bias in order to be better listeners. **Bias** is any assumption we make or attitude we have about the person, issue, or topic before we have heard all the facts. If you equate a speaker with subject matter or experiences that have made you feel frustrated or angry in the past, chances are good that you will be biased about that person before he or she gives the speech. That bias may prevent you from listening to what that person has to say, and you may miss some important information. Bias is not limited to individuals; it can also apply to groups. For example, if you feel strongly about a particular topic because of your values, you may refuse to listen to any

## Evaluate the Professional Context    Miguel and the Multitasking Mishap

*Read the following passage about Miguel, and then answer the questions. As you read, focus on evaluating the professional context.*

Miguel had a successful career as an event planner. He originally started off as an assistant at an agency, but through hard work and consistent results, he had developed his own client list and saved enough money to start a company out of his home. He specialized in weddings and took pride in helping couples plan their dream events. As his client base continued to grow due to word-of-mouth referrals, he struggled to keep up with all the client requests but did not have the funds to hire additional employees. Miguel found himself multitasking on most days, and he was often double booked. The summer months were especially hectic.

One of his repeat clients, Tamara, hired him to plan a 50th anniversary party for her parents, as she had been so pleased with how her wedding turned out. It was an especially important event because Tamara's father had been diagnosed with cancer a few months before. A few weeks before the party, Miguel was meeting with a new client when the phone rang. Tamara was on the phone, extremely upset because they needed to move the event up due to a medical procedure scheduled around the original event date. Miguel took the call while working with the new client. While showing the new client fabric samples and place settings, he listened to Tamara, assured her he would take care of it, and they agreed on an available date.

On the day of the event, Tamara, Miguel, her parents, and their guests arrived at the venue to find that another event had already begun. Miguel was mortified when he realized that he had forgotten to reschedule the event with the venue. Although he attempted to apologize and offered alternatives, the damage was done. The family was extremely upset. Tamara began to cry, called Miguel an insulting name, and told him she would be sure to tell all her friends and acquaintances about the experience.

### Questions to Consider

1. What could Miguel have done differently to avoid this situation?
2. Should Tamara have handled the situation differently?
3. How could the KEYS process help Miguel manage his clients' needs and expectations despite his hectic schedule?

other perspective no matter whom it comes from. Effective listening requires us to put our biases aside and regard the other as having a valid point of view worthy of our time and careful attention. To reduce bias, you need to acknowledge that bias might exist and try to remove it from your evaluation of the message.

## Failing to Be an Active Listener

Just as there is a difference between hearing and listening, there are also differences between various types of listening. In your professional career, you will engage in three types of listening: informational, critical, and empathetic. **Informational listening** occurs when you focus on the content of the message to acquire knowledge. Part of learning a new position involves listening to information during new-employee orientation and one-on-one training. **Critical listening** asks you to evaluate the information being sent. For example, Trey has been asked to seek three separate bids from business-development consulting firms. Trey must critically listen and then evaluate the advantages and disadvantages of each proposal. **Empathetic listening** is listening to understand the speaker's point of view without judgment. If a customer comes to you with a complaint and you listen to him to try to understand the problem from his perspective, without countering, criticizing, or judging, you have engaged in empathetic listening. Research tells us that listening with empathy is the basis for a host of important workplace skills and strategies: assessing situations, making rational decisions, generating connections between theory and practice, arriving at deeper understandings of beliefs, adapting to new perspectives, informing instructional decisions, challenging traditions, improving teaching and learning, and validating ideals (Jalongo, 2008).

Where does active listening fit in? Isn't it a type of listening? No, it is not a type of listening; rather, it is a *way* to listen. Every time you engage as a listener, you must consciously decide if you are going to be an active listener or a passive listener. As a **passive listener**, you will simply receive a message and make sense out of that message without feedback or verification. For example, watching the news on television is passive listening, because there is no need to provide feedback since a response is not expected. Poorly run meetings often have everyone but the leader acting as passive listeners. In contrast, as an **active listener,** you are required to make sense out of the message and then verify that your sense making is accurate. In other words, you must verify that you understand the message as the speaker intended. To achieve professional excellence in interpersonal relationships, you must always be an active listener.

An active listener makes sense out of the message and then verifies that the sense making is accurate.

An active listener focuses on asking questions and will often listen to the message and then **paraphrase** it for the sender. Let's say an employee complains to you by saying, "I'm sick of the attitude around here. Some people stroll into work whenever they feel like it, and the customers suffer. The poor customers have to be put on hold forever, and they get really upset." As an active listener, you can summarize that message to check your understanding: "You feel irritated when people are late for work because it means the phones are not covered and we are not providing the best service we are capable of." In some situations, paraphrasing is critically important. At the same time, many professionals view continual paraphrasing as unnatural or mechanical in style. Still, when there's a high likelihood of misunderstanding, a little paraphrasing can make a big difference in the communication interaction.

Another technique is **reflection**. Jalongo (2008) categorizes reflective listening as different from ordinary listening in four important ways. Reflective listening means the listener

(1) listens thoughtfully to the meaning of the speaker's words; (2) considers the content of the message, both stated and implied; (3) thinks about the feelings associated with the message, attending to the speaker's verbal and nonverbal cues; and (4) makes every effort to reflect that message accurately. **Questions** are another tool used by the active listener. By asking questions, you can develop a better understanding of the speaker's message and provide support to the speaker.

Graham, Santos, and Vanderplank (2008) highlight the importance of developing a sense of being "in charge" of the listening process. Being in charge of listening includes both knowing how and knowing when to use which strategies. We have defined listening, discussed why it is important, and revealed the various barriers that may prevent one from listening effectively. Now we will explore in more detail some of the different styles and categories of listening.

# Listening Styles and Categories

Barker and Watson (2000) classified four listening preferences or styles. **People-oriented listeners** are interested in demonstrating concern for others' emotions and interests, finding common ground, and responding. These listeners demonstrate a genuine concern for others' feelings and identify with emotional states of human behavior. This type of listener can become "over-involved with the feelings of others" (Watson & Barker, 1995, p. 3). **Action-oriented listeners** are interested in direct, concise, error-free communication that is used to negotiate and accomplish a goal; these listeners are easily frustrated by disorganized presentations. **Content-oriented listeners** are interested in intellectual challenge and complex information; they want to evaluate information carefully before forming judgments and opinions. At times, it appears as though "they are looking under a microscope and dissecting information" (p. 5). **Time-oriented listeners** prefer brief communication; such listeners seek interaction that is concise and to the point, and they want to know the length of time available before the communication begins. What type of listener are you? Do you recognize the styles of your boss, family, or friends?

In addition to the above-mentioned styles, listening can also be divided into a variety of categories. Listening in interpersonal situations is usually categorized as either conversational or presentational. When the speaking role shifts from one person to another with some degree of frequency, we call it **conversational listening**. In a conversational situation, the person who was actively listening one minute can assume the major speaking role the next, while the previous speaker becomes a listener.

Presentational listening is a type of listening that takes place in situations where clear roles of speaking and listening functions are defined. What are some examples of presentational listening that you have encountered?

Conversational listening is an integral part of meaningful one-on-one social relationships and professional interpersonal exchanges. Conversational listening most often emerges in face-to-face situations but may also take place over the telephone. **Presentational listening** is a type of listening that takes place in situations where a clear role of speaking and listening functions is prescribed. In presentational listening, roles are usually formal and defined as active speaker and responsive listener. The listening environment is based on the following conditions: mode (conversational or presentational), environment (formal or informal), and relationship (social or business; Nelson & Heeney, 1984).

# Improving Your Listening

Now that you have an understanding of the types, styles, and categories of listening, we can share additional ways to improve your listening skills. Becoming a better listener takes time and effort. The **HURIER model** provides a framework for skill-based listening by defining listening as six interrelated components: **H**earing, **U**nderstanding, **R**emembering, **I**nterpreting, **E**valuating, and **R**esponding (Brownell, 1994, 1996).

**Hearing** refers to concentrating on and attending to the message. Our first step toward better listening is making sure we can properly hear the other person. Be sure that you limit any distractions that would prevent you from doing so. **Understanding** is the process of attaching meaning to the verbal communication, or comprehending the literal meaning of the message. We often do this unconsciously. Understanding a message requires that we first hear the message, but it also includes being able to understand the speaker's use of language and the basic context of the information. **Remembering** includes recalling the message so it can be acted on. Listening not only requires us to be present, in the moment, and mindful but also necessitates anticipating future interactions. One way to help yourself remember the message is to create an outline of the main points.

**Interpreting** is the step where we make sense of the verbal and nonverbal codes to assign meaning to the information received or the sensitivity to nonverbal and contextual aspects of the message (Brownell, 1994). Interpreting is an important part of the collaborative process of communication. Ethically interpreting a message means you are not intentionally letting your own bias or beliefs interfere with your interpretation. **Evaluating** is the logical assessment of the value of the message (Brownell, 1994). Learning to evaluate a message without bias, distractions, apprehension, or gender/cultural differences takes time and patience.

After interpreting and evaluating the message, you must decide how to reply or respond. **Responding** is the last step and involves giving some form of *response* to the message, either verbally or nonverbally. Communication would not be collaboration if not for this vital step. Paraphrasing, summarizing, reflecting, and asking questions all demonstrate responsiveness. Using nonverbal cues such as head nods, emotional expressions, or verbal utterances is also a good way to show you are listening. The six-step process, when used in combination with active listening skills and barrier avoidance, will result in development of your professional excellence.

Research in listening has just begun to explore the many aspects of this complex and central communication process. According to Nixon and West (1989), listening is the most basic communication skill and supersedes all learning processes. Historically, listening

## Know Yourself    Listening Anxiety

*The following questionnaire will help you gain a better understanding of your own listening anxiety. Answer each question thoughtfully, and then reflect on the results. How can this knowledge help you be a better communicator?*

The following statements apply to how various people feel about listening to others. Indicate to what degree these statements apply to how you feel, noting whether you:

(5) *strongly agree*, (4) *agree*, (3) *are undecided*, (2) *disagree*, or (1) *strongly disagree*.

1. ___ While listening, I get nervous when a lot of information is given at once.
2. ___ I get impatient and anxious when listening to someone discuss theoretical, intellectual issues.
3. ___ I have avoided listening to abstract ideas because I was afraid I could not make sense of what was said.
4. ___ Many classes are annoying and uncomfortable because the teacher floods you with detailed information in the lectures.
5. ___ I feel agitated or uneasy when someone tells me there is not necessarily a clear, concrete way to deal with an important problem.
6. ___ While listening, I feel tense when I have to analyze details carefully.
7. ___ It is frustrating to listen to people discuss practical problems in philosophical and abstract ways.
8. ___ When I hear abstract material, I am afraid I will be unable to remember it very well.
9. ___ I experience anxiety when listening to complex ideas others tell me.
10. ___ When I listen to complicated information, I often fear that I will misinterpret it.
11. ___ I do not feel relaxed and confident while listening, even when a lot of information is given at once.
12. ___ Listening to complex ideas is not a pleasant, enjoyable experience for me.
13. ___ When listening, I do not feel relaxed and confident that I can remember abstract ideas that are being explained.

Add all scores together: _____
The higher the score, the higher your listening anxiety.

Note: This is a modified version of the Listening Anxiety Test.

Source: Adapted from Wheeless et al. (1997).

has been the most neglected instructional and research area. However, now professional organizations such as the International Listening Association, academic institutions, and other organizations are providing increased training materials, instruction, and institutions devoted to listening research. Through proficient use of listening instruction, people learn listening guidelines and can develop listening skills in ways similar to learning mathematics, physical education, reading, and writing (Nixon & West, 1989).

Gibbs, Hewing, Hulbert, Ramsey, and Smith (1985) assert that listening awareness and instruction can accomplish four major objectives: (1) increasing understanding of the nature of listening and its importance in the total communication process, (2) diagnosing listening abilities and practices, (3) developing skills and techniques to improve listening effectiveness, and (4) creating awareness of the importance of effective listening to personal and professional success. In schools that have instituted listening instruction, students' listening

Technology has affected our ability to listen. Limit distractions by turning off your cell phone before a presentation or professional meeting.

comprehension has as much as doubled in just a few months. Continuous evaluation of one's own listening abilities and participating in listening instruction or learning measures increases retention, promotes critical thinking, and facilitates learning.

Being mindful of your listening effectiveness is valuable in the professional environment. According to Haas and Arnold (1995), listening plays a pivotal role in conceptions of communication competence in coworkers. In other words, your ability or inability to listen will directly affect whether your coworkers perceive you as possessing communication competence. In turn, you will also judge your coworkers' abilities to communicate effectively by how well they demonstrate listening skills. Failure to recognize that listening is just as important as verbal communication is inevitably detrimental. In fact, many Fortune 500 companies, as well as several management training programs used across the United States, identify listening as one of the most important communication skills in the workplace (Haas & Arnold, 1995).

Nelson and Heeney (1984) explain that a truly competent listener goes beyond simply hearing; listening includes comprehending meaning, analyzing relationships, interpreting impressions, and evaluating content. The ancient adage still rings true today—the beginning of wisdom is silence. The second stage is listening (Gibbs et al., 1985). Will you value the knowledge gained in this chapter and improve your listening skills to develop professional excellence? How have your listening skills affected your work, school, or home life?

# KEYS to Listening Excellence

Remember how Apple CEO Tim Cook used excellent listening skills to encourage morale and profit growth in his company? Cook's excellent listening skills have enabled him to fill the rather large shoes of former Apple CEO Steve Jobs. Try to apply Cook's practices to the KEYS strategy. The first step, *know yourself*, allowed Cook to realize he was different from Jobs and to differentiate himself in several important ways. He pushed for a more PR-friendly company and also a more comfortable environment for Apple employees.

The second step, *evaluate the professional context*, involved Cook assessing the professional makeup of the Apple corporation. His predecessor, Jobs, was not only the company head but, in many respects, the advertising face as well. Jobs was not known for his town hall–style meetings with employees and even admitted that other people's input about his product did not significantly influence his business strategies. Cook fulfilled the roles of company head and public face by being open about his communication with employees and starting a charitable foundation within the company. In this way,

Cook successfully differentiated himself from Jobs and kept the company profitable at the same time.

The third step, *your communication interaction occurs*, involved Cook allowing the media to attend his town hall meetings with employees. Both his company and the public were allowed to see Cook's listening skills firsthand. He listened to his employees' concerns and ideas and enacted a generous discount program for Apple employees. His open style of communication can foster more freedom and creativity of expression from his employees.

The final strategy, *step back and reflect*, allows Cook and the public to assess the effects of his open style of communication. By generating goodwill with both the public (the charitable foundation Apple created) and his company (the Apple discount program), Cook allowed Apple to weather the loss of venerated leader Jobs and remain profitable during the transition. Cook listened not only to what his employees wanted but to the public as well. By keeping his two greatest resources happy, Cook finds himself in a great position as the CEO of one of the world's richest companies.

What listening skills do you use when interacting with others? Can Cook's example be used in other companies to generate both profit and goodwill?

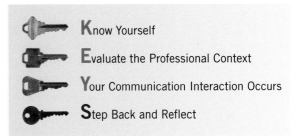

K now Yourself

E valuate the Professional Context

Y our Communication Interaction Occurs

S tep Back and Reflect

## Executive Summary

Now that you have finished reading this chapter, you can do the following.

Explain the difference between hearing and listening:

- *Hearing* is your physical ability to detect sounds. It is the physiological process or function of receiving sounds (p. 51).
- *Listening* requires you to concentrate on the verbal and nonverbal messages being sent and to determine the meaning of those messages. Effective listening is central to fostering interpersonal relationships with coworkers, leaders, and clients (p. 51).

Understand the barriers to listening and how to avoid them:

- *External noise* includes distractions such as audible talking during a meeting, ruffling of papers, or a cell phone going off in the next cubicle. Whenever possible, you should take steps to control the external noise that might interfere with your ability to listen to others, as well as their ability to listen to you (p. 53).
- *Internal noise* encompasses any internal condition or state that interferes with the communicator's ability to focus on the message. Controlling internal noise in others can be difficult, as it may be hard to predict. Still, you can minimize some internal noise in others. For example, holding long meetings without food or bathroom breaks will guarantee internal noise in your team. Minimize the noise by providing food and breaks (p. 53).
- *Message overload* occurs when a speaker includes too many details in a message, making it difficult for the listener to comprehend. As the listener tries to make sense of the specific details, he or she loses focus of the primary message. If the jargon or message overload comes as part of a conversation, not a presentation, engage in active listening.

Identify and explain strategies for developing and sustaining professional excellence using active listening skills:

- An *active listener* focuses on asking questions and will often listen to the message and then paraphrase it for the sender (p. 58).

- Another technique is that of *reflection*. Jalongo (2008) categorizes reflective listening as different from ordinary listening in four important ways. Reflective listening means the listener (1) listens thoughtfully to the meaning of the speaker's words; (2) considers the content of the message, both stated and implied; (3) thinks about the feelings associated with the message, attending to the speaker's verbal and nonverbal cues; and (4) makes every effort to reflect that message accurately (p. 58).
- *Questions* are another tool used by the active listener. By asking questions, you can develop a better understanding of the speaker's message and provide support to the speaker (p. 59).

List and define the six-step process of listening:

- The *HURIER model* refers to a six-step listening process: **H**earing, **U**nderstanding, **R**emembering, **I**nterpreting, **E**valuating, and **R**esponding (Brownell, 1994, 1996). Hearing refers to concentrating on and attending to the message. Our first step toward better listening is making sure we can properly hear the other person (p. 60).
- *Understanding* is the process of attaching meaning to the verbal communication, or comprehending the literal meaning of the message (p. 60).
- *Remembering* includes recalling the message so it can be acted on. Listening not only requires us to be present, in the moment, and mindful but also necessitates anticipating future interactions (p. 60).
- *Interpreting* is the step where we make sense of the verbal and nonverbal codes to assign meaning to the information received or the sensitivity to nonverbal and contextual aspects of the message (Brownell, 1994). Interpreting is an important part of the collaborative process of communication (p. 60).
- *Evaluating* is the logical assessment of the value of the message (Brownell, 1994). Learning to evaluate a message without bias, distractions, apprehension, or gender/cultural differences takes time and patience (p. 60).
- *Responding* is the last step and involves giving some form of response to the

message, either verbally or nonverbally. Communication would not be collaboration if not for this vital step. Paraphrasing, summarizing, reflecting, and asking questions demonstrate responsiveness (p. 60).

Utilize the KEYS approach to conduct yourself with professional excellence while developing your listening skills in the workplace:

- *Know yourself.* Understand the components of being an active listener and critically apply them to your professional interactions. Realize your strengths and weaknesses as a listener and adapt accordingly (p. 61).
- *Evaluate the professional context.* Learn whether your professional environment uses formal or informal communication. Also, pay attention to jargon used at your

work. Use active listening to create understanding of words or phrases you are not familiar with (p. 57).

- *Your communication interaction occurs.* Take what you have learned from the first two steps and try communicating with fellow business professionals. Are you using the workplace jargon correctly and effectively? Be critical about the responses you receive from your peers (p. 54).
- *Step back and reflect.* Ask yourself if both you and your communication partner(s) came away from the interaction with mutual understanding. Think about what was effective and what was not. Repeat the process to gain greater and more effective strategies for being both a good listener and a good communicator (p. 52).

## Discussion Questions

1. What is the difference between hearing and listening, and why does it matter?

2. List three barriers to listening. Which barriers most frequently affect your ability to listen? List the steps you will take to improve your ability to avoid these barriers.

3. What is listening bias, and how has it affected your communication interactions in the past? What can you do to avoid it in future interactions?

4. List and define the four listening styles. Which style do you most relate to? Will this change now that you know how listening impacts your professional excellence?

5. What is the difference between active and passive listening? Conversational and presentational listening?

## Terms to Remember

action-oriented listeners (p. 59)

active listener (p. 58)

bias (p. 56)

content-oriented listeners (p. 59)

conversational listening (p. 59)

critical listening (p. 58)

empathetic listening (p. 58)

evaluating (p. 60)

external noise (p. 53)

hearing (p. 51)

HURIER model (p. 60)

informational listening (p. 57)

internal noise (p. 53)

interpreting (p. 60)

jargon (p. 55)

listening (p. 51)

message overload (p. 55)

paraphrase (p. 58)

passive listener (p. 58)

people-oriented listeners (p. 59)

presentational listening (p. 60)

questions (p. 59)

receiver apprehension (p. 55)     remembering (p. 60)     time-oriented listeners (p. 59)
reflection (p. 58)                responding (p. 60)      understanding (p. 60)


Visit the Student Study Site at **www.sagepub.com/keys2e** to access the following resources:

- SAGE journal articles
- Video links
- Web resources

- Web quizzes
- eflashcards

part I

# Entering the Workplace

Chapter 4: Résumés, Interviews, and Negotiation

Chapter 5: Getting to Know Your Diverse Workplace

## Chapter Outline

The Job-Seeking Process    73

Stage One: Exploring    73

Stage Two: Researching    75

Stage Three: Applying    77

Stage Four: Interviewing    88

Stage Five: Following Up    96

Stage Six: Negotiation    97

KEYS to Excellence in the Job-Seeking
    Process    99

Executive Summary    100

Discussion Questions    101

Terms to Remember    101

## Chapter Objectives

After studying this chapter, you should be able to:

1. Identify the six stages of the job-seeking process

2. Understand the important role of exploring and researching in the job-seeking process

3. Develop a customized résumé and cover letter

4. Interview and negotiate successfully

5. Utilize the KEYS approach to conduct yourself with professional excellence throughout the job-seeking process

# chapter 4

# Résumés, Interviews, and Negotiation

**Jenson Crawford, like many people in the United States today, was having trouble landing a career in a very tight job market.** He decided to try the nontraditional route of job seeking by posting his résumé on the popular professional networking site LinkedIn. Through the site, Crawford found a listing for a management position near his home. He submitted his résumé to the company's website and mentioned that he'd found out about the position through LinkedIn. "The hiring manager was able to immediately get on LinkedIn to see my experience and whom I'm connected to," Crawford reported (Johnston, 2011). With all the attention concerning new social media, it is interesting to see how the idea of online networking has successfully been implemented in a professional setting. LinkedIn shows no signs of slowing down either; the exploding unemployment rate had some impact on LinkedIn's *growth*, as people used it and other tools to look for employment. Membership numbers for LinkedIn in 2007 were 15 million and shot up to more than 40 million by 2009, the years when unemployment began to climb sky-high (Slutsky, 2010).

Jenson's story is becoming increasingly common as unemployment continues to be an issue and the populace becomes increasingly familiar with online networking. Other sites such as monster.com, careerbuilder.com, and Job.com have also increased in popularity in recent years. Besides offering users a chance to search easily for job openings in a specific area and/or field, many sites also offer templates and tips for creating an effective résumé. With current job opportunities being extremely competitive, knowing how to effectively utilize these sites can mean the difference between finding a successful career and being unemployed.

The job search after college can be one of the most difficult tasks facing graduates during their professional careers. It is not uncommon for new graduates to spend years finding a good job in a career that interests them. In this chapter, we will focus on several aspects of the job hunt that are essential to securing a desired career in a timely fashion.

What do you want to be when you grow up? This is a question you have been asked from the time you were old enough to speak. Back then, you probably had no trouble responding. "I want to be an astronaut, a movie star, a princess." These are all common responses from children and, indeed, all interesting occupations. However, as you aged, most of you probably became less certain about what you wanted to be when you grew up.

This uncertainty makes selecting a major in college a daunting task for many students. Once you *have* selected, the uncertainty remains as you face the plethora of career choices available to every major. For example, communication is a highly sought-after skill but not a job title. So in a way, a degree in communication makes you qualified for nothing and everything all at once. The communication major must explore various areas of the discipline to find his or her individual focus. Within each of those areas are countless opportunities that can be both exciting and overwhelming.

Even seemingly defined majors such as nursing, accounting, and teaching require career exploration. You may want to be a nurse, but what kind of nurse? Do you want to work for a doctor's office, a clinic, or a hospital? With what kind of population do you wish to work? Would you prefer to work with children, women, the elderly, diabetics, burn victims, or cancer patients? The choices are many.

Fortunately, there is no need to fear. Considering that the average person holds numerous jobs in his or her lifetime, you'll have your entire career to grow, develop, and find your perfect fit. However, getting started on the right path can help maximize success and minimize frustration. By applying KEYS to the job-seeking process, you can start on the right path.

The sign in this picture is a reminder that sometimes the job-seeking process can make you feel as though you're applying for any job out there. But in reality, the job-seeking process is about finding the position that matches your professional skills and qualifications.

# The Job-Seeking Process

What is the job-seeking process? What does it entail? Seeking a job is a multifaceted process that is part research, part performance, and part rollercoaster ride. The **job-seeking process** involves six stages: exploring, researching, applying, interviewing, following up, and accepting.

We have integrated the KEYS process into our discussion of the stages of job seeking. By doing this, we hope that you will begin to see how the KEYS process can be applied to this communication situation, as well as to others that we cover in later chapters. Our discussion of the job-seeking process will be skills based. In other words, we are going to focus on communication skills (e.g., writing résumés, being interviewed) that will help you excel in the job-seeking process.

As a student of communication, it's important to realize that the discussion of communication skills is, in fact, the application of communication theory. As you read about the various skills, reflect on the theories and concepts we covered in Chapters 1, 2, and 3. For example, you learned that communication is a transactional process, not a pipeline. In this chapter, you will apply that concept by developing audience-centered messages. You also learned in the opening chapter that the communication context impacts messages. Being offered a job changes the context and thereby changes the rules. So the question "What is the salary range and the benefits package?" sends two very different messages depending on when it is asked during the interviewing process. You learned in Chapter 2 that nonverbal communication is a vital component in any message. This chapter shows how the regulative rules for nonverbal communication (e.g., clothing, handshakes, eye contact) matter in the job-seeking process. In Chapter 3, you learned strategies to improve your listening. Excellent listening is a critical first step to successfully answering questions during interviews.

# Stage One: Exploring

The **exploring stage** begins with you, the **job seeker**. During this stage, you will need to explore both yourself and potential careers.

## Self-Exploration

The first step in the KEYS approach is *know yourself,* so begin there with **self-exploration**. Take time to explore your goals and priorities. Here are just a few questions you should consider: What are you best at? What do you enjoy doing the most? What motivates you? What salary range do you need to live the lifestyle you desire? Is a family-friendly career a priority for you? Would you prefer to work in a large or small organization?

Taking time to think about your goals and priorities is an important part of the job-seeking process—it will help you determine what type of career you wish to pursue and what types of organizations you wish to work for.

## Know Yourself    Ron Explores His Career

*The following reading and questions will help you gain a better understanding of things you should consider when exploring your career options. Answer each question thoughtfully and then reflect on your answers. How can this knowledge help you with your career search?*

Ron was an outstanding student who was driven to succeed. As graduation approached, however, he was shocked to realize he had never clearly defined his goals for his future career or for his life. He had never thought about his priorities as they related to the type of position he wanted after graduation. "I guess I just thought I would graduate and someone would knock on my door and say, 'Come work for us. We have the perfect job for you!'" When he came to the realization that such a knock was never coming, he began with the first step in the KEYS approach to professional excellence, *know yourself*. He determined he wanted a position that gave him autonomy, allowed him to lead groups, would pay for graduate school, and would not make him wear a tie. He also discovered that his interviewing skills needed some polishing. Armed with this insight, Ron began searching for a position that would meet his criteria, simultaneously practicing his interviewing skills. After a few months of searching and interviewing, Ron found a position that was the perfect fit. Five years later, he has completed his MA, received a promotion, and not worn a tie since his initial interview. If you find yourself in the same position as Ron, use the following question to guide your career exploration.

### Questions to Help You Explore Your Career

1. What are my greatest strengths?
2. What are my greatest weaknesses?
3. What kind of organization do I want to work for? What kind of organization do I not want to work for?
4. What do I know about this organization?
5. Where do I really want to work?
6. Why do I want to change jobs?
7. What do I expect as far as salary and benefits?
8. Where do I see myself going in the next few years?
9. What makes me stronger than other applicants?

## Career Exploration

**Career exploration** requires you to research opportunities in your major that correspond with your goals and priorities. Being a foreign correspondent may sound like a wonderful career, but if being a highly involved parent is your top priority, foreign correspondent would not be a wonderful career for you. Instead, you could use that same skill set to work for a local public relations firm, which would not require you to spend long periods of time away from your children.

As you narrow down career opportunities, it's important to develop a clear understanding of what each career truly entails. When you find a career that seems interesting, you need to do some investigating. Interview several people in that line of work and find out what the job involves. Ask questions that will help you determine if this career lines up with your goals and priorities. If it seems like a good fit, **shadow** someone in the field for a week or two. Then seek an

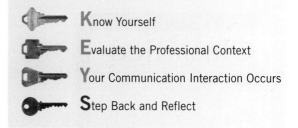

**Know** Yourself

**Evaluate** the Professional Context

**Your** Communication Interaction Occurs

**Step** Back and Reflect

**internship** that will allow you to develop a clearer understanding of this career choice. To many, this may seem like an unnecessary step, but the interviewing phase of the job-seeking process isn't about finding the candidate with the most qualifications; it's about finding the person who is best fit for the job and the company. The more you know about a given occupation, the more effectively you will be able to describe how your skills line up with the position.

# Stage Two: Researching

The **researching stage** of the job-seeking process comprises two components: researching openings and researching potential employers.

## Researching Openings

Once you have an idea of what you are looking for in theory, you must begin to seek positions that exist in reality. For some students, this can be disappointing. Your dream job may require 5 years of experience that you do not have. The honest truth is that few students land their dream job right out of college. So become aware of the steps or experiences you'll need to get to your dream job, and begin working your way up the ladder.

When should you start your job search? This is a process that will take months, so plan accordingly. A good rule of thumb is for graduates to allow between 3 and 6 months to find that first job after graduation.

Where should you look for a job? The answer is simple: everywhere! Begin by using the resources available at your college or university. Most institutions of higher education have **career planning centers**. Your center may go by a slightly different name, such as career services, career placements, career development, or career consulting; regardless of the name, these centers are a vital resource in your job search.

Career services centers will often hold **job fairs** on campus or have information about job fairs in the surrounding community. Find out the dates for these job fairs and come ready to be interviewed. This means you should dress in business attire and have a résumé with you.

Once upon a time, the **classified/help-wanted ads** in the newspaper were the place to go when looking for a job. When job seeking, you should make it a habit to check the newspaper(s) in the city or cities that interest you. However, realize that in the 21st century, many organizations no longer post positions in the newspaper.

Today's job-seeking process may entail a lot of time spent using online employment systems.

The **Internet** has become an excellent tool for locating employment opportunities. There are multiple websites dedicated to matching employees to jobs, including monster.com, snagajob.com, careerbuilder.com, Job. com, jobs.com, Jobs.net, jobsonline.net, USAJOBS.gov, job-search-engine.com, and WorkTree.com. In addition to employment-based websites, many organizations now post job openings on their company websites.

Another useful tool for finding openings is **word of mouth**. Tell everyone you know that you are job searching, making certain to be specific about the kind of job you are looking for. Saying "I am looking for a job in business" is very different from saying "I am looking for a job in hotel management." Who should you tell? Tell family, friends (your friends and your parents' friends), classmates, professors, former employers, people at church, contacts from your internships—tell anyone who will listen.

One family member you should be certain to contact is your Uncle Sam. Yes, Uncle Sam (aka the U.S. government) can help you find a job. If you are looking for jobs with the federal government, you must go through the U.S. Office of Personnel Management, which is easily accessed via http://www.opm.gov/.

If you don't wish to work for the federal government, Uncle Sam can still be of help. According to the U.S. Bureau of Labor Statistics' (2010) *Occupational Outlook Handbook*,

> The **State employment service**, sometimes called the Job Service, operates in coordination with the U.S. Department of Labor's Employment and Training Administration. Local offices, found nationwide, help job seekers to find jobs and help employers to find qualified workers at no cost to either. To find the office nearest you, look in the State government telephone listings under "Job Service" or "Employment." (p. 21)

In addition to state employment agencies, which are run by the government, **private employment agencies**, also known as head hunters, can assist you in your job search. Unlike state agencies, private agencies are for-profit organizations that charge a fee for their services. The amount of the fee and who pays it vary.

An often overlooked place to find openings is **professional associations**. Almost every industry has a professional association that sponsors meetings and conferences. Joining the local, regional, or even national chapter of a professional association will greatly enhance your ability to network with other professionals that may be looking to hire. When joining a professional association, be certain to inquire about outlets for job postings as well as student membership fees/dues.

## Researching Potential Employers

At this point, it should be clear that job searching is time-consuming. Therefore, you do not want to waste your valuable time and energy on positions and organizations that do not fit your desires, goals, and priorities. Think about this stage of the job-seeking process as job researching, not job searching. You are not simply searching for vacant positions. You are researching positions and companies to find the right fit between your skills and desires and their needs and opportunities.

Before applying, take a few moments to research the position and the company. This research will not only help you determine if you truly wish to apply for this position with this organization but will also help you down the line when you customize your résumé and prepare for your interview. Remember, excelling as a communicator means you must be audience centered. You can't be audience centered if you do not know your audience.

Where do you find information on potential employers? You can begin by researching their websites, but remember that the purpose of company websites is to make the organization look appealing, so you do not want to end your research there. If you know anyone who works for the organization in question or has a similar type of position with a different organization, interview him or her for insights. Other sources of information that may be helpful include the Chamber of Commerce, Better Business Bureau reports, the *College Placement Annual*, and CollegeGrad.com. According to Crosby (2000),

> Public libraries and career centers have valuable information about employers, including companies' annual reports to shareholders, reports kept by local chambers of commerce, trade journals, and business indexes, such as *Hoover's Business Index* and *Dun and Bradstreet* (pp. 15–16).

# Stage Three: Applying

Once you have researched someplace you would like to consider for employment, it's time to turn your attention to résumés and cover letters.

## Developing Résumés

A **résumé** provides a picture of who you are as an employee by highlighting your skill set. An excellent résumé illustrates how you fit this position and this organization and highlights the skills you possess relevant to the skills required by the position to which you are applying.

There is no one standard form for a résumé—it's not one size fits all. When selecting the format for your résumé, select a format that will highlight your strengths and downplay your weaknesses. Regardless of which format you select, whenever possible, you should customize your résumé to each

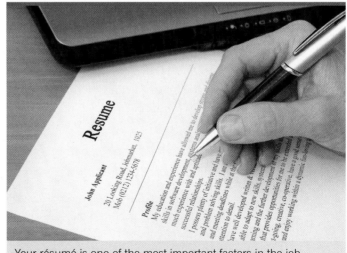

Your résumé is one of the most important factors in the job application process.

## Your Communication Interaction    Audrey's Negative Job Reference

*Read the passage below, and then answer the questions. As you read, think about ways the KEYS approach could help you improve* **your communication interaction** *if you were in Audrey's position.*

Audrey is a recent college graduate who is trying to find a career in her field of study. While working on her résumé, Audrey was concerned because she had left a previous employer on bad terms. She and her boss had a heated confrontation about her schedule, so she never went back. To avoid a negative reference, Audrey decided simply to omit the employer from her résumé although she had worked there for several years. Audrey was thrilled when she was offered a job, but the offer was revoked the day before she was set to begin. She was told that she could not be hired because her application was fraudulent.

### Questions to Consider

1. What ethical boundaries were crossed when Audrey omitted employment history from her résumé?
2. If you were Audrey's new boss, what would you do when you learned about her "incomplete" application?
3. How can a lack of professionalism in one place of employment impact professional excellence in other workplaces?
4. Using the KEYS process, how could Audrey improve her communication when seeking a new position?

position and organization. Although formats vary, every résumé should be no more than one page and must be visually appealing.

Chances are you'll be applying for multiple positions while you're job seeking. Therefore, it's important to develop a **generic résumé** that you can use as a starting point for the **customized résumé** you develop for each position.

When developing your résumé, you will have to determine if you plan to use a chronological, functional, or combination résumé. These résumé types are defined as follows.

### Chronological

This is the most common form and probably the easiest to prepare. The chronological résumé emphasizes employment and/or experience history, listing elements in reverse chronological order (i.e., your most recent experience first). This format is especially useful to new graduates or those with limited work experience.

### Functional (Skill Based)

This functional résumé emphasizes skills and attributes that can be applied to a variety of employment situations; your skills are broken down into categories that quickly communicate to employers what you can do for them. This format is useful for candidates without direct employment-related experience or for those who wish to work in fields unrelated to their academic major.

## Combination

For many candidates, a combination of elements from the chronological and functional résumé formats works best. Regardless of which résumé type you select, your résumé will include some or all of the following sections.

## Contact Information

Begin your generic résumé by listing your **contact information**. You should include your name, address, phone number, and e-mail address. Believe it or not, many prospective job seekers are taken out of the running due to their contact information. You should make certain the address you provide will be valid throughout your job search. The same holds true for phone numbers and e-mail addresses.

When it comes to the telephone, remember that your ring tone and message are going to make an impression on prospective employers. If you want to communicate with professional excellence, use a standard ring tone (no songs) and record a professional message for your voice mail. This same level of professionalism should extend to your e-mail address. An e-mail address such as "partygirl2010" or "mrtequila" is going to land your résumé in the trash. Addresses such as "snugglebear" or "cutiepie" are unprofessional as well. Choose an e-mail address related to your name, and be certain to check it regularly.

It's also important to make sure there is nothing in cyberspace that you would not want your future employer to see. What comes up when you "Google" your name? What information can be found on your MySpace and Facebook accounts? If you think prospective employers don't bother to check these sites, you're wrong. Not only do employers use Google and Yahoo to run background checks on potential employees, they also check Facebook, MySpace, Twitter, and Friendster (Finder, 2006; Slovensky & Ross, 2012).

## Objective and Summary

An **objective** is a one- or two-sentence declarative statement about your career goals. An example of an objective would be: "To obtain a position as a reading specialist with the Altoona Area School District." The benefit of including an objective is debatable. Some argue it can be beneficial and has been a résumé standard for years. Others argue that since the objective is clear (to obtain the position), there is no need wasting space stating the obvious. Many résumés have moved away from the objective to a **summary** of your skills and traits.

## Education

If you're a recent college graduate, your education is, in all likelihood, the most important thing you want future employers to consider, so your **education** section should be prominently displayed. Include the name of any college or university from which you have graduated or are currently attending. As a general rule, a college graduate should not list his or her high school education or high school accomplishments.

List the name of your degree and your major (e.g., bachelor of science in biology). You may also wish to state a minor if you have one. Include the date of graduation (e.g., "Degree conferred December 2011"). If you're in your final semester, you can use something such as "Degree anticipated May 2013."

## Ethical Connection    Maya's Facebook Problem

*Please read the passage below, and answer the questions that follow.*

Maya had excellent experience, credible references, and an outstanding GPA. Nonetheless, she was repeatedly passed over while less-qualified friends were interviewed and then hired. Maya could not understand what was going wrong, so she went to her university's career service center for some help. Her counselor commended her on her résumé and cover letter but told her she must do something about her Facebook account. Maya was shocked. She could not believe her private social-networking account was being viewed by employers.

### Questions to Consider

1. Do you think it's ethical for employers to run background checks using search engines or to evaluate job candidate information posted on social-networking sites such as Facebook? Why? Why not?

2. If you were Maya, would you change your Facebook account?

You may also wish to list some relevant courses. For the purposes of the generic résumé, list all the courses you think may be relevant during your job-seeking process. You can narrow the list during the customizing step.

Students often ask if they should include their grade point average (GPA) on their résumé. The answer is simple—it depends on your GPA. If your GPA is a 3.0 or higher, include it. For some students, the overall GPA is under a 3.0 but the GPA for coursework in their major is much higher. If that's the case, then list your major GPA.

### Experience

A section on experience is a standard part of the résumé. As you advance in your career, you will most likely label this section as **employment experience**, which will take prominence over your education. Yet, for most college graduates, including **relevant experience**, not just employment experience, is more beneficial. Using the general title "Relevant Experience" allows you to incorporate a broader range of information. In this section, you can list your relevant employment history as well as internships, relevant class projects, relevant work with student organizations, or volunteering. For example, you may be applying for a job that requires leadership and grant-writing experience. During college, you worked as a waitress, but you were also the president of two student organizations, and as part of an English course, you wrote a grant for the local food bank, which was funded. All this information can be included in the "Relevant Experience" section because it's all relevant to the position to which you are applying.

### Skills

**Skills** may be incorporated under your experiences or may be a separate category. Some students opt for a résumé format that includes a separate skills section or lists skills rather than integrating them into the "Relevant Experience" section. Which format should you use? The answer is in whichever format does a better job of highlighting you.

### Employment Experience

If you've been lucky enough to work at a job that's relevant to the position you're seeking, prominently display that experience and your job duties. For most college graduates, however, this will not be the case.

Let's look at a few possible scenarios. In the first scenario, your work history is by and large unrelated to the career you are pursuing, but your work on campus through class projects, internships, and student or volunteer organizations is related. To best showcase your skills in this situation, list the class projects, your internship, and your work with the Sociology Club under "Relevant Experience," as previously discussed. Give some details about each experience. Then you can simply list your places of employment, job titles, and employment dates later in the résumé in a section titled "Employment Experience," "Employment History," or "Work History."

If your work history is not directly related to the position you are pursuing, list the place of employment, job title, employment dates, and some skills you acquired at this job. Even if the job is not directly related to your career, it is highly likely that you did gain or hone some skill(s) that will make you a more appealing applicant. For example, if you worked as a waiter, you have developed your customer-service skills, worked both independently and as part of a team, handled difficult situations with professionalism, and demonstrated the ability to multitask.

### Awards and Hobbies

Should you include awards and hobbies on your résumé? As always, the answer is, it depends. Include an **awards and honors** section only if you have multiple listings and they are relevant to the position. Academic awards and honors strengthen you as a candidate, but noting that you were Homecoming Queen will not. If you have only one award or honor but you think it is relevant, make sure to include it somewhere but do not set aside an entire section of the résumé to highlight it. It may be best to discuss it in your cover letter.

As for hobbies, do not put a **hobbies and interests** section in your résumé. If you do have a hobby or interest directly relevant to the position, work it into your résumé as a skill or experience. Otherwise, leave it out.

### References

**References** should not be listed on your résumé. You can make a note about references at the bottom of the page (e.g., "References available on request"), but the purpose of the résumé is to highlight you, so don't waste space listing references. This is not to imply that securing good references is not an important step in the job-seeking process; references are an extremely important part of the process.

Do not ask your references for generic letters of recommendation. You should submit letters of recommendation only to positions that request such letters. If letters of recommendation are required, then and only then should you solicit them from your references.

## Customizing Résumés

The second step in the KEYS model is to *evaluate the professional context,* which includes your audience and the organization. All the research you have gathered during the previous stages of the job-seeking process will enable you to do just that. During the remaining stages of the process, you must take the information you have gathered and apply it to your communication interactions. These interactions include customizing your résumé and cover letter, as well as being interviewed (see Figures 4.2 and 4.3).

### Review Your Audience

The research you have done on the organization will give you some insight into the organization's mission and values. In addition, the job posting will tell you exactly what they are looking for in terms of this position.

How do you customize your résumé? Begin with the generic résumé you have already developed. Systematically go through the generic résumé, identifying the information that is most relevant to this position. During the first round of cuts, delete all the information that is not relevant to this position. If the remaining information does not fit on one page, go back and eliminate the information that is least relevant to the position. When customizing your résumé, the goal is to include information about yourself that addresses every qualification noted in the job posting without exceeding the one-page limit.

Your first audience may be an employee in the Human Resources (HR) Department whose job is to determine if you meet the minimal qualifications for this position. In some cases, the HR Department may use a computer scanning program that counts the number of key words from the job posting found in each résumé. Because of these types of HR screening processes, you must make certain that the language on your résumé matches the language in the job posting exactly. Once you have determined which information will be included in this customized résumé, go back and customize the language. Let's say, for example, that you have applied for a position that requires "proven leadership experience." You believe your 2-year tenure as the president of the Kinesiology Club demonstrates your leadership experience. In your generic résumé, you've listed this experience and you've included "leadership" as one of your skills—this is not enough. The job posting specifically states "proven leadership experience," so you should not imply or dance around the wording used in the posting. To customize your résumé, change the wording in the skills section from "leadership" to "proven leadership experience."

### Creating Visual Appeal

Although résumés can come in a variety of different forms, all résumés should be visually appealing and utilize a parallel structure. In terms of visual appeal, you need to include a balance between text and **white space**. Too much white space indicates a lack of qualifications. On the flip side, too much information jammed on a page does not make you look more qualified. Instead, it makes your résumé difficult to read, which makes you less appealing. Remember, a résumé is a snapshot. You can't include every detail of your life, so make sure to include the information that is most relevant to this position at this organization.

The font you select for the text of the résumé should be 12 point—no less than 11 point if you need more space—for easy reading. When selecting a font, you want to stick with standard fonts such as Arial, Helvetica, and Times New Roman to ensure easy electronic transfer.

As for parallel structure, decide on a heading system, and keep it consistent throughout the résumé. If your first major heading is bold, 14 point, and all capitals, then all major headings should be bold, 14 point, and all capitals.

The use of a parallel structure can also be applied to your word choices. For example, when listing your duties/work experience, use active verbs (see Figure 4.1). In addition, you may utilize a list of bulleted duties/skills. Whichever format you select, remember to use that format throughout that section of the résumé.

It's also critical to edit résumés, applications, and cover letters carefully. Make it a habit to check, double-check, and triple-check. Spelling errors seem to jump off the page at potential employers. If you want to be considered for an interview, there can be no spelling errors. Remember, spelling and grammar check catches only misspelled words, not incorrect words. Also, make certain your grammar is correct. For example, when discussing a former job or experience, use past tense; when discussing a current job or experience, use present tense.

Once your résumé and cover letter are complete, you should laser print them onto $8\frac{1}{2}$" by 11" bond paper, also known as résumé paper. Pink paper with a spritz of perfume may have helped Elle Woods get into Harvard Law School in *Legally Blonde*, but that works only in the movies. Your best bet is to select white or off-white paper—unscented, of course.

## Developing Electronic and Scannable Résumés and Online Applications

Back in the day, résumés and cover letters were either mailed or hand-delivered to organizations. Today, organizations are requesting that résumés be submitted electronically or that the information traditionally found in a résumé be submitted via an **online application**.

When it comes to submitting **electronic** or **scannable résumés**, you must be sensitive to the style and formatting of the document. Electronic résumés should be prepared in common programs, such as Microsoft Word. Scannable résumés should be simplistic; so avoid any decorative fonts or graphics.

### Figure 4.1 Résumé Action Words

| | | | |
|---|---|---|---|
| Achieved | Established | Launched | Produced |
| Administered | Evaluated | Maintained | Programmed |
| Analyzed | Examined | Managed | Proposed |
| Budgeted | Expanded | Mediated | Recommended |
| Built | Expedited | Motivated | Recruited |
| Calculated | Explained | Negotiated | Reduced |
| Composed | Facilitated | Obtained | Reinforced |
| Conducted | Formulated | Operated | Researched |
| Created | Generated | Organized | Reviewed |
| Delivered | Handled | Participated | Scheduled |
| Demonstrated | Implemented | Performed | Supervised |
| Developed | Improved | Planned | Translated |
| Directed | Increased | Presented | Updated |
| Distributed | Initiated | Processed | Utilized |

## Evaluate the Professional Context    Customizing the Résumé

*Read the following passage about James, and then answer the questions. As you read, focus on evaluating the professional context.*

James Cox will soon be graduating from college. He has taken time to know himself and has developed clearly defined career goals. He is currently pursuing positions that will allow him to combine his love of sports, commentating, and computers. He has found a position with XYZ Studios (see the job posting below). After doing some research on XYZ, he is certain he would be a good fit for both the position and the organization. In Figures 4.2 and 4.3, you will find (1) his generic résumé, (2) his cover letter, and (3) his customized résumé.

### Questions to Consider

1. How does the customized résumé differ from the generic résumé?
2. Has James effectively adapted his experience to this professional context?
3. Has he done an effective job in customizing his résumé and cover letter?
4. Do they reflect the information found in the job posting?
5. Are they visually appealing?
6. What advice would you give James?

### Job Posting

#### Network Studio Host

*XYZ Sports in Omaha, Nebraska, seeks candidates for a full-time, on-air radio position. The primary responsibilities include writing and broadcasting in-game scoreboard updates for various NCAA Division-I athletic programs. Candidates must display professionalism with a strong work ethic, be proficient with computers, be web savvy, and be able to work at a fast pace with excellent time-management, communication, and organizational skills. Prior on-air experience is preferred. Candidates must have a flexible schedule, which includes working nights and weekends.*

*Please send cover letter, résumé, and score update demo only (please do not include play-by-play) to Rosalinda Garcia at XYZ Studios.*

For electronic applications, you'll most likely be cutting information from your résumé and pasting it into the application. Although this may allow you to include more information than the standard one-page résumé, the information presented should still be concise and relevant.

## Developing Cover Letters

**Cover letters** accompany your résumé and serve to introduce you as a potential employee, highlight your résumé, and demonstrate your writing skills. According to Buzzanell (1999),

> The goal of the cover letter is to get prospective employers to look at your résumé, the goal of a résumé is to get the prospective employer to ask you on an interview, and the goal of the interview is to get you the job (p. 155).

**Figure 4.2 Generic Résumé**

James T. Cox
1111 Airline Rd.
Apt. 2222
Corpus Christi, TX 78412
jtcox123@yahoo.com
Cell: 361-123-4367

---

EMPLOYMENT

---

May 2011–Present
United Championship Wrestling—Corpus Christi, TX
Ring Announcer/Commentator/Webmaster
   Announce wrestling competitors to and from the arena and the winner after the conclusion of the contest. Conduct play-by-play commentary on wrestling matches for DVD purposes. Perform light webpage design duties, keeping up the Facebook page and websites with current information. Supervisor is Marty Green. Hours are varied, with largest working periods being 6 to 10 hours one Saturday a month. Currently a volunteer position.

July 2011–March 2012
TAMU–CC Island Waves Student Newspaper—Corpus Christi, TX
Sports Editor
   Researched and wrote sports stories, copyedited content, performed light page design duties, all on heavy deadline pressure. Supervisor was Lisa Perez. Office hours were Tuesday and Thursday 11:00 a.m. to 12:00 p.m., with sporadic additional working hours throughout the week for research/writing. Starting/ending wage was $5.85/hr.

January 2010–December 2010
TAMU–CC Recreational Sports—Corpus Christi, TX
Official/Scorekeeper
   Officiated and kept score for basketball, dodgeball, flag football, and volleyball games. Supervisor was Andy Cox. Hours were afternoons and evenings Monday through Friday. Starting wage was $5.30/hr. Ending wage was $5.50/hr.

May 2010–August 2010
Riverbend Retreat Center—Glen Rose, TX
Summer Staffer
   Performed kitchen work, handled office/clerical duties, acted as programs staff (archery, paintball range, paintball course, pool assistant, waterfront assistant), attended snack shop/ice cream shop. Left because it was a temporary job and summer was over. Supervisor's name was Debi Lancaster; however, she is no longer employed with Riverbend, so Alton Belew would be a better contact. Hours were 7:30 a.m. to 9:00 p.m. every day. Starting/ending salary was $600/month.

August 2007–December 2009
Coastal Bend College–Beeville Campus—Beeville, TX
Work Study
   Carried out clerical duties in an educational setting. Reason for leaving was graduation. Hours were afternoons Monday through Friday. Starting/ending wage was $6.00/hr.

*(Continued)*

**Figure 4.2  Generic Résumé (Continued)**

## EDUCATION

Working toward a Bachelor of Arts in communication, with media studies concentration
Anticipated graduation August 2013; current GPA 3.2
Texas A&M University–Corpus Christi, January 2010–Present

Coursework:
Media News Writing and Performance: developed and delivered radio PSAs
Public Relations Techniques: developed a public relations campaign for Islander Athletics
Persuasion
Technical Writing: wrote a grant for the local food bank
Voice and Diction
Organizational Communication
Video Production: produced a 20-minute video PSA
Web and Graphic Design
Journalism
Media and Technology
Public Speaking
Television Criticism
Media Criticism
Legal and Ethical Issues in Communication

Associate of Arts/Associate of Science (dbl. major), music education/accounting
Graduated December 2009; GPA 3.2
Coastal Bend College–Beeville Campus, August 2006–December 2009

## SKILLS/TRAINING

Spanish (bilingual) – proficient – 3 years' experience
Clinical understanding of music – highly proficient – 11+ years' experience
Computer literate – highly proficient – 11+ years' experience
Microsoft software knowledgeable – highly proficient – 7 to 10 years' experience
Curriculum design – proficient – 3 years' experience

## REFERENCES

Juan Perez
Director, Baptist Student Ministry
Coastal Bend College–Beeville
361-888-1212
forjesuschrist@yahoo.com

Jane Smith
Director
Riverbend Retreat Center
888-111-2222
smith@riverbendretreat.org

Nora Cortez
Director/Editor
Cortez Productions
361-333-4444

John Miller
Promoter
United Championship Wrestling
361-555-6666

Begin the cover letter by stating that you're interested in a specific position (state the exact position title). In the next paragraph or two, highlight why you are qualified for this position, making specific reference to the required skills and qualifications noted in the job posting. End the letter by expressing your desire to discuss your qualifications further during an interview. Like the résumé, your cover letter should be concise, no more than one page. Use the same paper and font for both your résumé and cover letter.

---

**Figure 4.3 Customized Cover Letter and Résumé**

To:     Rosalinda Garcia
From:   James T. Cox
Date:   January 17, 2013
RE:     Network Studio Host, XYZ Studios

Dear Ms. Garcia,

I am writing in regard to the position for a Network Studio Host at XYZ Studios in Laredo. Having reviewed the requirements and duties, I believe I am an ideal candidate for this position.

For the past 4 years, I studied communication–media at Texas A&M University–Corpus Christi. My education developed and honed the skills needed to be a successful on-air personality and an asset to your radio station. I will graduate in August 2013 with outstanding oral and written communication skills. In addition, I am highly proficient with computers, having demonstrated my web savvy both in the classroom and on the job.

Clearly, my experience for this position extends beyond the classroom. While pursuing my degree, I have worked as an on-air announcer for United Championship Wrestling, broadcasting play-by-play commentary for DVD recordings. I have provided in-game scoreboard updates for a variety of sports. Furthermore, I am an experienced sports writer for an NCAA Division-I athletic program.

By taking a full course load every semester and working full-time I have proven my strong work ethic and time-management skills. I pride myself on my professionalism, dedication, and flexibility. I thoroughly enjoy working in the fast-paced environment provided by on-air sports broadcasting, and I look forward to discussing my qualifications with you further. Thank you for this opportunity.

Sincerely,
James T. Cox

*(Continued)*

**Figure 4.3 Customized Cover Letter and Résumé (Continued)**

James T. Cox
1111 Airline Rd.
Apt. 2222
Corpus Christi, TX 78412
jtcox123@yahoo.com
Cell: 361-123-4367

**SKILLS/TRAINING**

Experienced writer for NCAA Division-I athletic programs
Experienced sports announcer and scorekeeper
Computer skills – highly proficient – 11+ years' experience
Spanish (bilingual) – proficient – 3 years' experience

**EDUCATION**

**Texas A&M University–Corpus Christi**          Degree anticipated August 2013
Bachelor of Arts in communication–media studies
Coursework:
Media News Writing and Performance          Web and Graphic Design
Technical Writing          Journalism
Voice and Diction          Media and Technology

**RELEVANT WORK EXPERIENCE**

United Championship Wrestling          Corpus Christi, TX
**Ring Announcer/Commentator/Webmaster**          May 2011–Present

Announce wrestling competitors to/from arena and winners at the conclusion of the contest.
Conduct play-by-play commentary on wrestling matches for DVD purposes.
Perform light webpage design duties.
Maintain the Facebook account and supporting websites with current information.

TAMU–CC Island Waves Student Newspaper          Corpus Christi, TX
**Sports Editor**          July 2011–March 2012

Researched and wrote sports stories for NCAA Division-I athletic programs.
Copyedited content.
Performed light page design duties.
Worked effectively under heavy deadline pressure.

TAMU–CC Recreational Sports          Corpus Christi, TX
**Official/Scorekeeper**          January 2010–December 2010
Officiated and kept score for basketball, dodgeball, flag football, and volleyball games.

# Stage Four: Interviewing

When your average college graduate thinks of the job-seeking process, he or she thinks about the fourth stage, interviewing. But for students such as yourself who wish to achieve professional excellence, the work you have done in the previous stages will benefit you immensely during the interviewing stage. As you prepare for the interview, you already have a clear sense of who your audience is and what they are looking for in a candidate. Furthermore, your first communication interactions with the potential employers (your résumé and cover letter) not only highlighted you as a candidate but began to demonstrate how you'll fit into their organization.

Although securing an interview is an exciting milestone in the job-seeking process, you're still several steps away from being hired. To land the position, you must do two simple tasks: prepare and practice.

# Before the Interview

To truly demonstrate professional excellence, you will need to prepare your message, anticipate the questions, script your answers, practice your answers, prepare your appearance, and reduce your nervousness.

## Preparing Your Message

A student once remarked, "Preparing for an interview would be simple if we knew the questions in advance." The bad news is that you do not have a crystal ball that will magically reveal your interview questions, but the good news is that you have something almost as telling. By reviewing your skills, the job posting, and your research, you can determine exactly what information to present during the interview.

Prior to walking into your interview, you should have a clear understanding of the information you plan to present. Begin by looking at the job posting. What qualifications are a must for this position? How do you meet each of these qualifications? For example, if the position states that the candidate must be highly organized, make a list of examples that demonstrate your organizational skills. Review the duties you'll be responsible for in this position. If you'll have to write, make a list of examples that show you are an effective writer. Then gather some samples of your writing to bring along to the interview.

Next, review your résumé and cover letter. Are there areas where you might need to elaborate? What information do you want to restate in the interview? What are some examples or experiences that illustrate the skills highlighted on your résumé? In the end, you should be ready to discuss specific examples, stories, and experiences that are relevant to this position.

Finally, make a list based on important points you learned while doing your research. This list should include things you learned about this company that made it appealing to you and questions you may have about the position or the organization.

## Anticipating Questions

Once you have completed your lists and reviewed your research, it's time to practice answering questions. You can never be 100% certain about what's going to be asked during the interview, but you can make some educated guesses.

Begin by imagining yourself as the interviewer. If you were going to hire someone for this position, what questions would you ask? How could you learn more about the interviewee's qualifications and skills? What would you be looking for in his or her answers? This exercise can help you anticipate possible questions, but it should also help you formulate stronger answers to those questions when the time comes for you to answer them. (Conducting job-seeking interviews, as well as appraisal and disciplinary interviews, is covered in Chapter 8.)

Next, check out some resources that include sample interview questions as well as some helpful tips. Books such as *Best Answers to 201 Most Frequently Asked Interview Questions*, *301 Smart Answers to Tough Interview Questions*, and *The 250 Job Interview Questions You'll Most Likely Be Asked* provide a variety of possible questions.

Be certain to practice both **behavioral questions** and **traditional questions**. Behavioral questions explore how you have handled past situations, as well as asking you to respond to hypothetical situations. For example: "Tell about a time when you had to meet a very short deadline" or "Give me an example of a time you served as a leader." Traditional questions include some of the old standards listed below:

Tell me a little about yourself.

Why did you apply for this position?

What makes you qualified for this position? Why should we hire you?

What are your strengths? What are your weaknesses?

What would your former employer (professor, friend) say about you?

What are three words that describe you?

What are your short-term goals? What are your long-term goals?

Do you have any questions for us?

### Scripting Answers

When it comes time for the interview, remember you are in control of your answers. The interviewer may ask slightly different questions from the ones you've practiced. Yet the information you present during the course of the interview should be the same information you practiced prior to the interview. The purpose of practicing is not to guess the exact questions that will be asked—it's to learn to professionally present important information about your qualifications for this position and your fit in this organization.

If possible, you should prepare by **scripting answers** that follow a three-part formula. First, directly answer the question. Then, back up your answer with a specific example that supports your answer. Finally, connect the answer back to this company and/or this position.

Let's say you are applying for a position managing a retail team for Company A. The interviewer asks, "Have you had much experience working with groups?" Begin by answering the question: "Yes, I have had extensive experience working with groups, both as a group member and as a leader." That would be an average answer.

Some interviewers will inquire further about your experience; others may not. You do not want to miss this opportunity to highlight your experience, so extend your answer to include an example:

Yes, I have had extensive experience working in groups, both as a group member and as a leader. For example, last semester, I worked with a group of graduating seniors on a semester-long marketing project. It was a challenging experience, because the majority of the group had senioritis. At first, they didn't care much about the assignment, but I knew I could change that attitude, so I volunteered to be the leader. Once I was elected, I made certain everyone in the group participated when selecting the topic. This helped get everyone involved from the beginning. Then we divided the project into manageable pieces that allowed everyone to have a balanced workload and a sense of ownership. In the end, we received the highest grade in the class.

This is a good answer, but to turn it into an excellent answer, the job seeker needs to take one more step by relating the answer back to the position and the organization:

> In fact, one of the things exciting to me about working for Company A is the opportunity to lead teams. I realize the challenges on the job will be different from what I faced in the classroom, but that is precisely the kind of challenge I am looking for in a position.

When it comes to answering questions, you want to be strategic. Answering strategically means discussing and emphasizing your skills and experiences that relate to this position. It means applying the KEYS of knowing yourself and evaluating your professional context. It does not mean you can lie, exaggerate, or fudge your answers. Lies, even little white lies, are unethical in any interview situation. If you have to lie to get the job, then this is not the right job for you.

How do you answer questions strategically? Let's say that during your research you learned that Company A has won awards for its customer service. During your interview, you might emphasize your desire to work for a company that has been recognized for excellence and/or highlight your excellent customer service skills—assuming, of course, that both these things are true.

In many interviews, the interviewer will allow some time at the end for you to ask a few questions. Therefore, you should prepare several questions for the employer. Although you would love to ask about salary, benefits, and vacation, this is not the time. That comes after they offer you the job. At this stage in the process, your questions are more about showing your research and interest in the position than about getting additional information. It is an opportunity for you to demonstrate that you have researched this company and will be a valuable asset. So you might ask something like, "When researching Company A, I noticed you have a 6-month training program. Can you tell me a little more about what that program entails?"

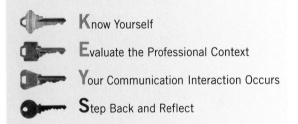

Know Yourself

Evaluate the Professional Context

Your Communication Interaction Occurs

Step Back and Reflect

*Practicing Answers*

Reading questions and thinking through the answers is an effective way to begin practicing, but to be fully prepared, you must take part in **mock interviews**. Enlist the help of family members and friends to run through questions with you. Have different people take different approaches to the interview. Have some mock interviewers smile and give you a lot of feedback. Have others be stern and cold and provide little feedback.

One of the best tools in improving your skills as an interviewee is the video recorder. On most college campuses, the career services center can help you in this process. Receiving professional feedback from the career services staff will be helpful, but watching yourself in action is truly the most powerful tool available for improvement. If your campus does not have a career center or if your career center does not tape mock interviews, find someone with a camcorder and tape it yourself.

Job interview formats can be one-on-one, as seen in this picture, but be prepared for a variety of formats, including those that involve a committee and/or technology.

When practicing, keep in mind that there are a wide variety of interview formats. The good news is, although the settings vary, the basic rules for an effective interview remain the same across situations.

**Telephone interviews** are often used during the early screening phases of the interview process. When doing a phone interview, remember to block the call-waiting feature if you have it. Using a land line is preferred to using a cell phone; however, if you have access to only a cell phone, make sure the battery is charged. Never chew gum, smoke, eat, drink, or use the bathroom during a phone interview, because the noise will be picked up on the other end. When you have finished delivering your answer, wait for the next question. Even if it takes the interviewer(s) a moment or two to ask the next question, do not try to fill that silence. When being interviewed via **videoconference,** try to imagine the camera is a person and respond accordingly. This means making eye contact with the camera and smiling.

**Face-to-face interviews** also come in a variety of formats, which include the standard **one-on-one interview**, a series of one-on-one interviews, **panel interviews,** and interviews with multiple interviewees. The same rules that apply in the standard one-on-one interview apply in each of these settings, but keep a few things in mind for each context. If you have a series of one-on-one interviews, you may feel as though you are repeating yourself. But remember, each interviewer is hearing your information for the first time, so it is not only okay to repeat yourself, it is necessary. If you find yourself answering questions for a panel of interviewers, always acknowledge the person who asks the question but address your answer (and make eye contact) with the entire group when responding. If you find yourself being interviewed with a group of other candidates, always treat your competition with respect and professionalism. The way you treat the other candidates is indeed part of how you will be assessed.

On occasion, your interview may be conducted during a meal. In this context, answering questions, not eating, is your priority. Keeping this in mind, order food that will be easy to eat. This is not the time to order barbequed ribs or crab legs, even if the interviewers order it for themselves. The same goes for alcohol. During the meal, follow all the basic rules of etiquette. If you are not certain of all the rules, review an etiquette book prior to the interview—at the very least, review the different types of silverware. And never talk with your mouth full.

### Preparing Your Appearance

For many students, preparing for the interview begins and ends with purchasing a suit. Although presenting a professional image is an important part of your nonverbal communication in the interview, wearing an Armani suit will not land you the job. Your interviewing attire is in a sense a uniform that identifies you as a professional. Many books and articles have weighed in on the subject of the appropriate interview attire (Dorio & Axelrod, 2000; Molloy, 1988, 1996; Ruetzler, Taylor, Reynolds, Baker, & Killen, 2012). In the end, these books can be summarized in a few basic rules job seekers should follow when putting together their interviewing uniform.

The main piece in an interviewing uniform is the standard business suit. For men, that suit includes a jacket and pants. For women, it includes a jacket and skirt. Many female students question the necessity of wearing a skirt. For better or worse, even in the 21st century, the standard interviewing uniform for women is the suit with a skirt. Some interviewers may not think twice if you elect to wear pants, but some might. The jackets, pants, and skirts should be black, dark gray, or dark blue. The business suit should be coupled with a light-colored shirt or blouse, preferably white. Men should wear a silk tie with a conservative pattern.

Modern technology has opened the door for videoconferences hosted by interview committees, which saves company money on travel. How would you prepare for a phone or videoconference interview?

Interviewers do not expect to see new college graduates in expensive, designer-label suits, nor do they expect to see them in ill-fitting suits. When purchasing your suit, the fit is extremely important. There is nothing professional about sleeves that cover your hands or a too-short skirt. Spend the extra $20 to have your suit professionally altered.

Female job seekers should wear a black or dark blue, closed-toe pump with a small heel, no higher than 2 inches. If you are not comfortable walking in heels, practice far in advance of your first interview. Your pantyhose should be flesh-colored. (Always keep an extra pair of hose on hand in case you get a run. Runs look very unprofessional.) You can wear jewelry during the interview, but you want to keep it simple. The rule of thumb for women is no more than five pieces of jewelry. Those five pieces consist of a watch, a pair of earrings (counts as two pieces), a necklace, and a wedding/engagement ring. The earrings should be small posts, and the necklace should be very simple.

Men should wear basic black dress shoes. Both men and women need to polish their shoes prior to the interview. Men should wear dark, over-the-calf dress socks that correspond with the outfit. (When you sit down, your pant leg will rise and the interviewer will see if you have on your white running socks!) Men should keep a two-piece rule in mind for jewelry: one watch, as long as it appears professional with the suit, and one ring, such as a wedding band or college class ring.

Both men and women should carry a briefcase, portfolio, or some sort of professional bag. Under no circumstances is it acceptable to carry your backpack. For women, it is a wise idea to put your essentials in your briefcase and leave your purse at home. Carrying two bags can make you appear cluttered. Your bag must look professional and correspond with your outfit. Inside your bag, you should include extra copies of your résumé, contact information for your references, samples of your work, and mints or a breath freshener. What you should not have in your bag is your cell phone. Nothing will lose you a job faster than your phone going off during the interview. Don't take any chances; leave it in the car.

When it comes to makeup, gentlemen are advised not to wear any and ladies are advised to wear only light makeup. Dark lipsticks, dark eye shadows, and fake lashes should be avoided. Everyone's nails should be clean and filed. If women wear polish, it should be a light, neutral color. With the exception of one small pair of earrings for women, all other piercings should be removed. In addition, tattoos should be covered. Both men and women should also avoid perfumes and colognes when interviewing. Your interviewer may not like your fragrance or, worse yet, may be allergic to it. If you are a smoker, take extra measures to ensure that you do not smell like smoke. If possible, don't smoke in your suit, wash your hands after smoking, and freshen your breath.

As for your hair, it should be neat and clean. If you have long hair, pull it back. If you wear it short, make sure to schedule a trip to the hairstylist prior to your interview. You don't want to look like a shaggy dog. Gentlemen should avoid facial hair, which includes beards, mustaches, goatees, soul patches, and sideburns. Ladies should avoid big hair, mall hair, pageant hair—whatever you call it, it went out in the 1980s.

Where do the personal touches fit into the interviewing uniform? They don't fit in anywhere. Putting on the interviewing uniform may make you feel like a bit of a conformist, but in the end, it's your interviewing skills and qualifications that will set you apart as an individual, not your clothes or tattoos.

### Reducing Nervousness

For many job seekers, interviewing is an uncomfortable communication interaction for several reasons. First, it is a high-pressure situation in which all eyes are on you. Next, your desire to land the job increases whatever anxiety you might normally feel when communicating with strangers. Finally, many job seekers do not feel comfortable "tooting their own horns." Although you will not be able to eliminate these feelings completely, you can minimize them by practicing. Learning to feel comfortable talking about your skills and accomplishments is a must for successful interviewing. After all, if you don't promote yourself, no one will.

Being at your best mentally and physically reduces nervousness. Preparing and practicing will help you be at your best mentally. But you also need to be at your best physically. This means getting a proper night's sleep before the interview. If you have failed to prepare in advance, staying up all night prior to your interview will only make you look and feel less than your best.

If you have to travel to the interview, it is wise to scout out the location a day or two in advance. Be certain you know the route to the building and the interview location inside the building. Always allow plenty of extra time for unexpected obstacles, such as traffic. If the interview is outside your local region, it's wise to drive or fly there the day before the interview and stay in a hotel or with friends. This will allow you to come to the interview fresh and well rested—as opposed to tired, wrinkled, and sleep deprived, all of which will increase your nervousness.

## Step Back and Reflect    Trying to Fit In

*Read the passage about Malia below, and answer the questions that follow.*

Malia was excited about the possibility of working as a computer programmer with Company Y. Company Y had a reputation for being an organization with high-quality professionals who enjoyed a laidback environment. It was not uncommon for these award-winning employees to come to work in shorts and flip-flops. Given their reputation, Malia took a more relaxed approach to her attire when interviewing with Company Y. She wanted to demonstrate that she could fit in at the organization, so she came to the interview dressed in a business-casual outfit (khakis and a blouse). Although her interview went well, Malia was not offered the position.

### Step Back and Reflect

1. What went wrong?
2. How should you dress for an interview?
3. Should organizational culture influence interview attire? Why or why not?
4. How could Malia use the KEYS approach to improve her communication?

## During the Interview

Arrive to the interview at least 10 minutes early. When waiting for your interview to begin, show patience and professionalism. Remember that you are being interviewed during every interaction with the organization, whether you're interacting with the official interviewer or not. So treat everyone from the parking attendant to the receptionist to the CEO with the same level of professionalism and respect. When you meet the interviewer, look him or her in the eye and shake his or her hand. Your handshake should be firm. This means you do not want an overpowering, bone-crushing shake, nor do you want a wimpy, limp-wristed shake (Ivy & Wahl, 2009; Bass, 2010).

First impressions are extremely important when interviewing. Research has found that it takes as much as double the information in the opposite direction to change an interviewer's initial impression of an interviewee (Huffcutt, 2010; Judge, Higgins, & Cable, 2000). This means if you make a good first impression, you will have to work pretty hard to turn it into a negative impression.

During the course of the interview, try to monitor your nonverbal communication. Sit up straight, maintain eye contact, and avoid speaking too quickly or using vocal fillers. If you are asked a question that you need a moment to think about, take that moment to think. Do not fill the silence with "umms" and "aahs." Bottom line, nonverbal cues do bias interviewer ratings (Bass, 2010; Dipboye, 1992).

Central to being an excellent interviewee is being an excellent listener. Focus on each question asked. If you are unclear about what the interviewer wants, ask for clarification. If the interviewer asks a question with multiple parts, make a mental note of each part and then begin to answer.

If you have prepared and practiced, you will be ready to answer the questions. Include as much of the information you practiced as possible in your answers. Ask the follow-up questions you prepared. Know that your preparation and practice will help you stand out as a candidate.

Remember to remain positive about your qualifications, your experiences, your former employers, your major/field, the job, and the organization. It's important to remain positive even when discussing weaknesses or failures. This can be accomplished by discussing a weakness or failure that will not affect you in this position (Crosby, 2000; Gray, 2011).

### Illegal Questions

Ideally, you will never encounter an interviewer who asks **illegal questions**, but you should prepare in case it happens. What is an illegal question? According to the Civil Rights Act of 1964, Title VII, and subsequent legislation, employers may not consider race, color, religion, sex, national origin, disability, or age when hiring or promoting employees. Therefore, they legally can't ask questions related to these categories.

When an interviewer said to Yelena, "I see you worked for the Jewish Community Center. Are you Jewish?" she was not sure how to respond. There are several ways Yelena could approach this question. First, she could answer it directly and move on: "Yes, I am Jewish." She could directly answer the question with a follow-up: "Yes, I am Jewish. Why do you ask?" She could use humor to deflect the question: "Is this a test to see if I know which questions are illegal?" Or she could refuse to answer: "I do not see how that question is relevant to my qualifications." What is the correct way to handle this situation? Although many students would prefer to use one of the last three approaches, they often are afraid such an answer will hurt their chances of getting the job. Regardless of how you answer the question, make note of what occurs. If you believe your answer negatively impacted your chances of being hired, then you have a discrimination case on your hands. If you are offered the job, you may decide not to take it because this question might be an indicator of a hostile work environment. At the very least, you should report this behavior to someone higher in the organization.

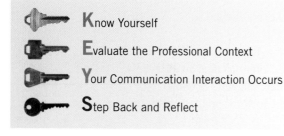

K now Yourself

E valuate the Professional Context

Y our Communication Interaction Occurs

S tep Back and Reflect

### Salary Questions

Although you should never bring up the issue of salary prior to being offered the position, you should be prepared in case the interviewer asks about your salary expectations. To prepare, research the appropriate pay for the position you are seeking. Be sure to examine pay-scale variations related to credentials, experience, and location. If asked, you can give a vague response such as, "I expect a salary that is competitive in this market." If the interviewer requests something more specific, give a range starting with the employer's probable salary and ending with a little above what you are willing to accept.

# Stage Five: Following Up

When the interview ends, be certain to thank your interviewer verbally. Once you return home from the interview, formalize your thank you with a card. A handwritten thank-you card for the interviewer is not only the kind of touch that demonstrates professional excellence but also guarantees that the interviewer will think of you favorably after the interview. If you were interviewed by more than one person, you can either send a thank-you card to everyone who interviewed you or send just one card to your main contact and mention the other parties in the message (Crosby, 2000; Vanevenhoven, Delaney-Klinger, Winkel, & Wagner, 2011). If you have been communicating with the interviewer via e-mail, then you can send the thank-you message through e-mail.

If any additional information was requested during the interview, get that information to your potential employer immediately. This will demonstrate your enthusiasm for the position and your attention to detail.

For many, what comes next is the most emotionally draining part of the job-seeking process—the waiting. It may take days, weeks, even months until you hear back about the position. Remain patient. Under no circumstances do you want to appear like a stalker, calling twice a day to see if a decision has been made.

Use this time to engage in the last of the KEYS, *step back and reflect*. How would you rate your

Thank-you letters, especially handwritten ones, are an excellent way to follow up after an interview.

communication interactions? How did you perform during the interview? What did you do well? What can you improve for next time? What have you learned about the job-seeking process? What have you learned about interviewing? What have you learned about yourself?

# Stage Six: Negotiation

Although it may seem at times that the job-seeking process will never end, it will—and it will end with you accepting an offer. Yet the sixth stage of the job-seeking process involves more than just saying "yes."

Once an offer is made, the ball is in your court. This is the time to ask clarification questions about salary, benefits, work conditions, and the like. This is also the time to negotiate. A **negotiation** is a discussion between two or more parties to reach an agreement that concludes some matter. In this case, the matter being concluded is the terms of your employment. However, the skills and strategies used to engage in employment negotiations are the same skills and strategies needed to successfully negotiation personnel issues, contracts, legal matters, and other workplace issues.

The first rule to good negotiation is to act with professional excellence. The authors of "Negotiation Strategies" (n.d.) stress the need to maintain a polite, collegial, and

You may have to make a difficult decision in the process of negotiating your salary.

collaborative tone. During negotiations, both parties should be looking for the best solution to meet the needs of both sides. Using the unite approach, described in detail in Chapter 7, is an excellence strategy for achieving this objective.

According to Hansen (n.d.), you should let the employer make the first offer, but you should not feel obligated to accept that offer if it is inadequate. How will you know if it is inadequate? You must do your homework and research salary norms, as well as benefits and other perks, for the industry, region, and this organization. In fact, doing your homework and thoroughly researching the situation is critical for all types of negotiation. You can't negotiate a contract if you have no idea what is acceptable and expected in the industry.

According to Johnson (2012), you must also research your value. Your value is based on factors such as education, length of experience, certifications, and management responsibility. Throughout your career, your value will increase, as will your ability to negotiate better contracts for yourself. In other words, the need to negotiate effectively becomes increasingly important as your career progresses.

One common mistake made during negotiations is failing to negotiate for things other than salary. For example, performance expectations, benefits, moving expenses, equipment, and vacation time are all extremely valuable. It may be beneficial to accept a lower salary if the offer includes a company car and great health benefits. Again, keep in mind that your counteroffer must be reasonable and in line with the research you have done.

To make a counteroffer, you can state something such as, "I am very interested in working for your company. Although I would love to be a part of your team, I would like to discuss a few small issues. First, would it be possible to increase the salary offer by $5,000? This would put my starting salary in line with other entry-level salaries for folks with similar education and experience in your organization."

Once you have received the final offer, *step back and reflect*. Take into account all you have learned about this organization and position during your research and the interviewing process. Compare this information with your goals and priorities. If you believe you are a good fit for this position and this organization and that the organization is a good fit for your goals and priorities, accept the offer. If it's not a good fit, then politely and professionally decline the offer. Declining may be difficult if you do not have another job lined up, but saying yes to the wrong job will be more difficult in the long run.

# KEYS to Excellence in the Job-Seeking Process

In the beginning of the chapter, we noticed that Jenson Crawford used some excellent tools (along with KEYS strategies) to land a job in a tight market. When examining the first key, *know yourself*, Jenson determined that he wanted a high-paying career that allowed him to capitalize on his strength as a persuasive communicator. He wanted a career in management. He examined his strengths and weaknesses as a potential candidate. He created a viable résumé that could be easily found by potential employers in an online database. He made sure to note that he was available through LinkedIn and encouraged employers to search there. He then began a formal search for positions.

The next key, *evaluate the professional context*, was time-consuming, but Jenson knew investing time here would give him an edge over other candidates. He searched for positions, researched each company, and then customized his résumé and cover letter for each position. Prior to his interview for the managerial position, he knew precisely how he wanted to present himself and exactly what information he planned to share.

The third key, *your communication interaction occurs*, began when his résumé and cover letter were reviewed. Although he had no clear affiliation with the company, he clearly communicated how his skill set fit into this organization and landed an interview. He prepared for the interview knowing his competition would likely have more experience than he had. He used all this information about his audience and the context to answer the interview questions strategically.

Jenson was also able to effectively utilize the last strategy, *step back and reflect*. His preparation and practice had served him well. If he did not land this position, he would continue to present the same level of professional excellence with other companies until he did land a job. He had presented his strengths and experiences in a positive way, and he had tailored his message to the audience and context. Not surprisingly, later that week he was offered the job and completed the job-seeking process by accepting a position with the company. Do you think more students approach job seeking like Jenson? Do you believe being audience centered while interviewing will really have an impact on your ability to land a job?

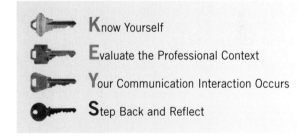

**K**now Yourself

**E**valuate the Professional Context

**Y**our Communication Interaction Occurs

**S**tep Back and Reflect

## Executive Summary

Now that you have finished reading this chapter, you can do the following:

Identify the six stages of the job-seeking process:

- The *exploring stage* begins with you, the job seeker. During this stage, you will need to explore both yourself and potential careers (p. 73).
- The *researching stage* of the job-seeking process comprises two components: researching openings and researching potential employers (p. 75).
- Once you have researched someplace you would like to consider for employment, it's time to turn your attention to résumés and cover letters in the *applying stage* (p. 77).
- The *interviewing stage* involves utilizing your work from the previous stages to project a professional and competent image of yourself to a potential employer (p. 88).
- *Following up* after the interview is the next stage. A handwritten thank-you card to the interviewer is not only the kind of touch that demonstrates professional excellence but also guarantees that the interviewer will think about you favorably after the interview (p. 97).
- Although it may seem at times that the job-seeking process will never end, it will—and it will end with you accepting an offer. Yet the sixth stage of the job-seeking process, *negotiation*, involves more than just saying "yes" (p. 97).

Understand the important role of exploring and researching in the job-seeking process:

- Self-exploration is important; taking time to think about your goals and priorities is an important part of the job-seeking process— it will help you determine what type of career you wish to pursue and what types of organizations you wish to work for (p. 73).
- As you narrow down career opportunities, it's important to develop a clear understanding of what each career truly entails. When you find a career that seems interesting, you need to do some career exploration (p. 75).
- You do not want to waste your valuable time and energy on positions and organizations that do not fit your desires, goals, and priorities. Think about this stage of the job-seeking process as job researching, not job searching. You are not simply searching

for vacant positions; you are researching positions and companies to find the right fit between your skills and desires and their needs and opportunities (p. 77).

Develop a customized résumé and cover letter:

- There is no one standard form for a résumé— it's not one size fits all. When selecting the format for your résumé, choose one that will highlight your strengths and downplay your weaknesses (p. 77).
- Cover letters accompany your résumé and serve to introduce you as a potential employee, highlight your résumé, and demonstrate your writing skills (p. 84).

Conduct all phases of job interviewing successfully:

- To demonstrate professional excellence, you will need to prepare your message, anticipate the questions, script your answers, practice your answers, prepare your appearance, and reduce your nervousness before the interview (p. 89).
- During the interview, remember that you are being evaluated during every interaction with the organization, whether you're interacting with the official interviewer or not. So treat everyone from the parking attendant to the receptionist to the CEO with the same level of professionalism and respect (p. 95).

Utilize the KEYS approach to conduct yourself with professional excellence throughout the job-seeking process:

- *Know yourself* by capitalizing on your strengths and realizing your weaknesses (p. 99).
- *Evaluate the professional context* by searching for positions, researching each company, and then customizing your résumé and cover letter for each position (p. 99).
- *Your communication interaction* begins when your résumé and cover letter are reviewed, making it important to treat each step with care and diligence (p. 99).
- *Step back and reflect.* Your preparation and practice have served you well. If you do not land this position, you will continue to present the same level of professional excellence with other companies until you do land a job (p. 99).

## Discussion Questions

1. Discuss the experiences you've had interviewing. How did the interviews go? Were you nervous? What will you strive to do differently in preparation for future interviews?

2. Take a moment to reflect on your dream job. Have you conducted an electronic search of the organization? What is it about the organization that makes you want to work there?

3. What are the qualities you're looking for in an employer? Related to some of the information in this chapter, how could you retrieve information to see if those qualities exist?

4. Discuss the resources your campus has in place to support the job-seeking process. Do you plan to utilize these resources?

5. Take an inventory of your e-mail address and any virtual networks such as MySpace or Facebook where you have a membership or maintain a profile. Is there any information an employer could retrieve on the web that may be perceived as negative?

## Terms to Remember

awards and honors (p. 81)
behavioral questions (p. 89)
career exploration (p. 74)
career planning
  centers (p. 75)
classified/help-wanted ads
  (p. 75)
contact information (p. 79)
cover letters (p. 84)
customized résumé (p. 78)
education (p. 79)
electronic résumés (p. 83)
employment
  experience (p. 80)
exploring stage (p. 73)
face-to-face interviews (p. 92)
generic résumé (p. 78)

hobbies and interests (p. 81)
illegal questions (p. 96)
Internet (p. 76)
internship (p. 75)
job fairs (p. 75)
job seeker (p. 73)
job-seeking process (p. 73)
mock interviews (p. 91)
negotiation (p. 97)
objective (p. 79)
one-on-one interview (p. 92)
online application (p. 83)
panel interview (p. 92)
private employment agencies
  (p. 76)
professional associations
  (p. 76)

references (p. 81)
relevant experience (p. 80)
researching stage (p. 75)
résumé (p. 77)
scannable résumés (p. 83)
scripting answers (p. 90)
self-exploration (p. 73)
shadowing (p. 75)
skills (p. 80)
State employment service
  (p. 76)
summary (p. 79)
telephone interviews (p. 92)
traditional questions (p. 89)
videoconference (p. 92)
white space (p. 82)
word of mouth (p. 76)

Visit the Student Study Site at **www.sagepub.com/keys2e** to access the following resources:

- SAGE journal articles
- Video links
- Web resources

- Web quizzes
- eflashcards

# Chapter Outline

Learning Your Workplace Culture    104

Assimilating College Students    107

Diversity in Your Workplace: Some Important
    Concepts    112

Examples of Diversity in Professional
    Contexts    114

KEYS to Excellence in Getting to Know the
    Diverse Workplace    120

Executive Summary    122

Discussion Questions    123

Terms to Remember    123

# Chapter Objectives

After studying this chapter, you should be able to:

1. Understand each phase of the assimilation process

2. Assess the culture in your organization

3. Define cultural diversity awareness and worldview

4. Understand the important role of cultural competence, perception checking, and mutual respect as you enter the diverse workplace

5. Utilize the KEYS approach to conduct yourself with professional excellence as you get to know your diverse workplace

# chapter 5

# Getting to Know Your Diverse Workplace

**Hani Khan's former employers found out the hard way that workplace discrimination can have severe negative repercussions.** Khan, who is of Indian and Pakistani descent, was fired from a Hollister store (owned by Abercrombie & Fitch) based on the perception that wearing her traditional Muslim hijab, or head scarf, violated the store's "look policy." The stated policy requires workers to represent the company with a "natural, classic American style" and to "look great." Khan was contacted by a human resources representative, who told her to remove the hijab. When Khan refused on religious grounds, she was told she was being taken off the schedule. Khan's subsequent firing has sparked a storm of controversy and caused a public relations fiasco for Abercrombie & Fitch (Knowles, 2010).

Workplace discrimination is a hot topic in the media and can irreparably damage a company's image. Khan's case is just one example of how a lack of compassion or understanding can have negative consequences for both the employee and the workplace. With workplace diversity becoming increasingly common in the United States (Miller, 2008; Okoro & Washington, 2012), it is vital for workers to understand how to cooperate with individuals different from themselves. It is important to be sensitive to gender, ethnicity, religion, disability, and other differences. Different companies can have widely diverse cultures, and with this trend continuing in the 21st century, new members of the workforce must be cognizant of what is appropriate behavior. For many people, college can be the first exposure to diverse cultures and ways of life, but students should be aware that the workplace can be just as unique and assorted.

Learning your workplace culture is critical to your success. Cultural competence, perception checking, and mutual respect are necessary for any member of the workforce. As a student, it is important to begin assessing the culture of your environment now to help you do so again in the workplace. In this chapter, we will focus on the aspects of workplace diversity and the methods by which you can analyze, engage, and assimilate to your working environment in a healthy manner.

After weeks, or more likely months, of job seeking, the day you have been waiting for will finally arrive. You will begin your life as a professional. You can finally step off the emotional rollercoaster known as job seeking, but don't unbuckle your safety harness quite yet. Beginning a new job, even if it's a promotion or a different position within the same company, brings with it almost as many emotional ups and downs as job seeking. This chapter explores the importance of getting to know your diverse workplace. As you enter any workplace for the first time, it's critical to get to know not only the organizational or workplace culture but also the array of diverse people with whom you'll be working. Advocating for the need to prepare professionals for the diverse workplace, Raymond Pomerleau (1994) argues that "the American workplace is at a crossroads; workforce demographics powerfully suggest that managing diversity to meet the effective utilization of personnel from different backgrounds and cultural perspectives" will take up much managerial attention for years to come (p. 85).

We will begin by examining the assimilation process you will go through as a new employee. We will then explore issues related to diversity in the workplace.

# Learning Your Workplace Culture

Just as every other new employee does, you will learn about your workplace's organizational culture through an assimilation process. The assimilation process is really part of a much larger phenomenon known as **socialization**—the experiences that shape our attitudes, perceptions, emotions, and communication choices (Bremner, 2012; Myers & McPhee, 2006). From the day you were born, your parents, your siblings, your relatives, your friends, your teachers, and even strangers have been working to socialize you into the **culture** or cultures that make up their experiences. So what is a culture? Put simply, culture is the rules of living and functioning in society (Bremner, 2012; Gudykunst, 2004; Samovar, Porter, & McDaniel, 2007). How you talk, behave, dress, and think is heavily influenced by the ways others have socialized you into various cultural groups.

Just as you took part in the assimilation process as a child learning how to function in family and community, you now will undergo an assimilation process on the job, learning how to function in this organization. Every organization has its own organizational culture. Two organizations known for their unique cultures are Southwest Airlines and Starbucks (see Figures 5.1 and 5.2). Review the corporate profiles on each organization. Do the organizational cultures of Southwest Airlines and Starbucks appeal to you as a customer and/ or employee?

To excel in your new position, you must learn the unique culture of the organization that has hired you. **Organizational culture** refers to the way an organization operates,

---

### Figure 5.1 Workplace Culture at Southwest Airlines

*Cul' ture: The development, improvement, and refinement of the originality, individuality, identity, and personality of a given people*

The May 2008 issue of *Spirit* magazine, the official in-flight magazine of Southwest Airlines, featured company president Colleen Barrett addressing airline service culture. The internal operations at Southwest encourage employees to practice people skills, to have fun at work, and to make an emotional breakthrough with customers on the ground and in the air. Take a look at part of what she wrote in the section of the magazine titled "Colleen's Corner":

Southwest Airline's Culture permeates every aspect of our company. It is our essence, our DNA, our past, our present, and our future. It is so important, in fact, that I wish I had more space to discuss it. We often say that other airlines can copy our business plan from top to bottom but Southwest stands apart from the clones because of our People. But I would still wager that if another company somehow managed to hire all of our fantastic Employees, that company might see its best performance but still wouldn't match up to Southwest. Why? The new employer wouldn't possess the Southwest Culture, the secret sauce, if you will, of our organization. That culture motivates and sustains us. For so many of us, being part of Southwest is not just a vocation, but a mission. I don't dictate the Culture; neither do our other officers. Rather, it stems from the collective personality of our Employees. . . . Those definitions are laid out in what we call "Living the Southwest Way." That creed consists of three values:

*A Warrior Spirit that recognizes courage, hard work, and a desire to be the best, a Servant's Heart that follows the Golden Rule and treats others with respect; and a Fun-LUVing Attitude that includes FUN, of course, but also passion and celebration.*

As you can see, Southwest Airlines emphasizes a positive workplace culture. What challenges, if any, can a culture of fun bring to business and professional communication? Would a fun-loving attitude work in other industries? Why or why not?

Source: Barrett (2008, p. 12).

---

the attitudes the employees have, and the overall tone and approach to any given business. Taking time to learn the organizational culture is essential to your success as a communicator and a necessary part of the KEYS approach. Learning an organization's culture provides you with information necessary to evaluate the audience and context. Furthermore, you can't effectively step back and reflect on your communication without taking into account the organizational culture in which it occurred.

Learning a new culture is stressful. In fact, for many new employees, the excitement felt prior to starting a new position quickly plummets as they undergo the **assimilation process**—the adjustment period and "settling in" that's common for anyone starting a new job. During this time, you will learn the organization's culture. If you successfully assimilate into the organizational culture, your job satisfaction should increase and you can begin to excel. If you don't effectively assimilate into the organizational culture, chances are you will remain at a low level of job satisfaction and will once again begin job seeking. To help you better negotiate this assimilation process, as well as help you establish yourself as someone with professional excellence, let's walk through the assimilation process and discuss the keywords noted above in more detail.

## Figure 5.2 Starbucks Coffee Mission Statement

**Mission Statement**

Establish Starbucks as the premier purveyor of the finest coffee in the world while maintaining our uncompromising principles as we grow.

The following six guiding principles will help us measure the appropriateness of our decisions:

- Provide a great work environment and treat each other with respect and dignity
- Embrace diversity as an essential component in the way we do business
- Apply the highest standards of excellence to the purchasing, roasting, and fresh delivery of coffee
- Develop enthusiastically satisfied customers all the time
- Contribute positively to our communities and our environment
- Recognize that profitability is essential to our future success

**Environmental Mission Statement**

Starbucks is committed to a role of environmental leadership in all facets of our business.

We fulfill this mission by a commitment to

- understanding of environmental issues and sharing information with our partners,
- developing innovative and flexible solutions to bring about change,
- striving to buy, sell, and use environmentally friendly products,
- recognizing that fiscal responsibility is essential to our environmental future,
- instilling environmental responsibility as a corporate value,
- measuring and monitoring our progress for each project,
- encouraging all partners to share in our mission.

Does the mission of Starbucks resonate with you? As you can see, Starbucks has a separate Environmental Mission Statement. What are some other issues a company such as Starbucks could add to its mission?

Organizations begin to assimilate you into their culture before you are even hired. Websites are developed to attract not only customers but future employees. The recruitment process, from the way the job posting is written to the signing of the contract, contributes to your socialization into an organization. Most likely, this will be a positive experience; otherwise, you would not have taken the job. But remember, both you and your future employer are putting your best foot forward, which may result in unrealistic expectations for both parties.

Once hired, you step out of the fantasy world and into the reality of your new organizational culture. Every organization, large or small, has its own culture. According to Edgar Schein (1992),

An organizational culture is a pattern of shared basic assumptions that have been invented, discovered, and/or developed by a group as it learns to cope with problems of external adaptation and internal integration in ways that have worked well and are considered valid, and, therefore, can be taught to new members of the group as the correct way to perceive, think, and feel in relation to a problem. (p. 247)

As a new member of an organizational culture, you will be formally and informally taught the acceptable ways to think and behave. According to Jablin (1987), "The newcomer learns the requirements of his or her role and what the organization and its members consider to be 'normal' patterns of behavior and thought" (p. 695). In many ways, it's like entering a foreign land.

As you get to know the diverse workplace, you should begin asking yourself reflective questions, including the following: What is the mission statement? Did you have an employee orientation? What was discussed in orientation? Where are the offices located (for workers, supervisors)? What do the offices look like (e.g., small, large, cubicles)? Are the furniture and computers old or new? What kinds of items are displayed (e.g., cartoons, degrees, awards, family photos)? How do people dress? What metaphors do employees use to discuss the organization (e.g., family, team)? What stories do employees tell about the organization, about leadership, about each other?

What would a boardroom such as this say to you about organizational culture?

What jargon is specific to this company and/or this department? What rituals are present (e.g., office birthday parties, having lunch together)? What behaviors are rewarded? How are employees rewarded?

## Assimilating College Students

To illustrate the assimilation process more concretely, let's examine an assimilation process you've experienced—entering a college or university as a new student. How do you learn information about the college or university you are currently attending? Most likely, you learned formally through things such as first-year orientation and welcome packets that included brochures and student handbooks. In addition, you learned informally by watching other students and observing how they did things.

How did you gain information about the organizational culture? According to Jablin (1987), there are seven tactics a newcomer can use to learn about an organization. They include **overt questioning**, **indirect questioning**, **third-party questioning**, **testing limits**, **disguising conversation**, and **surveillance**. Although overt questioning is obviously the most direct way to gain information, there may be reasons to use the other tactics. For example, if the person you would like to question directly is not there, you may need to ask a third party. Or, depending on the question, you may feel that you can get a more accurate answer through observation or thorough surveillance, rather than asking directly only to receive the politically correct response, not the truth.

## Your Communication Interaction    A Shift in Organizational Culture

*Read the passage below, and then answer the questions. As you read, think about ways the KEYS approach could help you improve* **your communication interaction** *if you were in Ashlee's position.*

When Ashlee entered college, she thought to herself, "Succeeding in college will be no different than succeeding in high school." During her first semester, she took a course with Professor Grassman. Although she was told the exams would include information from both lectures and assigned readings, she tested her limits by studying only her class notes. Not surprisingly, her score on the first exam was low.

Ashlee then began using some of the other tactics for learning the culture. For example, she tried surveillance by monitoring the behavior of students who did well on exams. She also used disguising conversation and indirect questioning to gauge her test results. Instead of asking her classmates if they had done the reading, she would make disguised conversational comments such as, "I don't know what Professor Grassman was thinking giving such a hard exam," or would ask indirect questions such as, "Do you think Dr. Grassman assigns too much reading?" Then Ashlee would wait to see how her classmates responded. She also utilized third-party questioning and asked her roommate, who took the course the previous semester, for some study tips.

Ashlee did learn some useful information using these tactics, and her scores did improve some.

### Questions to Consider

1. Which tactic do you think is most successful for gaining information?
2. Which tactic do you use most often? Why?
3. If Ashlee had visited Professor Grassman during office hours and used overt questioning, do you think her scores would have improved even more? Why or why not?

You will also gain information about your organization's culture by evaluating artifacts, rituals, language, and narratives/stories. Let's look at some examples of each.

**Artifacts** are temporary embellishments (e.g., jewelry, sunglasses, perfume) or objects characteristic of a particular culture or institution (e.g., furniture, buildings, technology, artwork, logos) that provide information about personalities, attitudes, group affiliation, and organizational membership (Ivy & Wahl, 2009; Varlander, 2012). According to Goodall (1991), artifacts found in parking lots can provide valuable insight into an organization's culture. The alma maters (Penn State and Nebraska) of the coauthors of this text have highly competitive football programs. The importance of football to these organizations' cultures is manifested in many ways, including in bumper stickers. At either university, it's rare to see a vehicle that does not have some sort of university, football-fan bumper sticker. Attending sporting events, particularly football games, and being a proud fan is a big part of the organizational culture at both campuses.

While writing this book, both coauthors were employed by Texas A&M University–Corpus Christi. At A&M–CC, sports teams have been on campus for only a few years and there is no football program. To date, sports have had little impact on the organizational

# Know Yourself   The Organizational Assimilation Index

*The following index will help you gain a better understanding of your skills at organizational assimilation. Answer each question thoughtfully and then reflect on the results. How can this knowledge help you be a better communicator?*

This questionnaire contains statements about your assimilation into your workplace. Indicate the extent to which you agree with each statement according to the following scale.

If you *strongly agree* with the statement, write 5 in the blank.
If you *agree* with the statement, write 4 in the blank.
If you *neither agree nor disagree* with the statement, write 3 in the blank.
If you *disagree* with the statement, write 2 in the blank.
If you *strongly disagree* with the statement, write 1 in the blank.

_____ 1. I feel like I know my supervisor pretty well.

_____ 2. My supervisor sometimes discusses problems with me.

_____ 3. My supervisor and I talk together often.

_____ 4. I consider my coworkers friends.

_____ 5. I feel comfortable talking to my coworkers.

_____ 6. I feel like I know my coworkers pretty well.

_____ 7. I understand the standards of my organization.

_____ 8. I think I have a good idea about how this organization operates.

_____ 9. I know the values of my organization.

_____ 10. I do not mind being asked to perform my work according to the organization's standards.

_____ 11. My supervisor recognizes when I do a good job.

_____ 12. My supervisor listens to my ideas.

_____ 13. I think my supervisor values my opinions.

_____ 14. I think my supervisor recognizes my value to the organization.

_____ 15. I talk to my coworkers about how much I like it here.

_____ 16. I volunteer for duties that benefit the organization.

_____ 17. I talk about how much I enjoy my work.

_____ 18. I often show others how to perform our work.

_____ 19. I think I'm an expert at what I do.

_____ 20. I have figured out efficient ways to do my work.

_____ 21. I can do others' jobs, if I am needed.

_____ 22. I have changed some aspects of my position.

_____ 23. I do this job a bit differently than my predecessor did.

_____ 24. I have helped to change the duties of my position.

*(Continued)*

(Continued)

## Scoring:

1. Add your scores for items 1, 2, and 3. This is your familiarity with supervisors score.
2. Add your scores for items 4, 5, and 6. This is your familiarity with coworkers score.
3. Add your scores for items 7, 8, 9, and 10. This is your acculturation score.
4. Add your scores for items 11, 12, 13, and 14. This is your recognition score.
5. Add your scores for items 15, 16, and 17. This is your involvement score.
6. Add your scores for items 18, 19, 20, and 21. This is your job competency score.
7. Add your scores for items 22, 23, and 24. This is your role negotiation score.
8. Add your scores for all 24 items. This is your overall organizational assimilation score.

How did you score? What surprised you about your score? Does your score ring true with your personality or feelings about having to adjust to a new job?

Source: Galliard, Myers, and Seibold (2010).

How would you describe the organizational culture at your college or university?

culture. However, the university is located on an island, and that has been highly influential on the culture. At the Island University, there are few university bumper stickers in the student parking lots, but the majority of student vehicles display beach permit stickers. Relaxing and socializing at the beach is an important part of this organization's culture. What do the artifacts on your campus tell you about the organizational culture?

As a new student, you learned **cultural rituals**—practices, behaviors, celebrations, and traditions common to people, organizations, and institutions. Rituals include activities such as professors passing out syllabi on the first day of class and rush for Greek organizations. Graduation is the most important ritual at a college or university and one you most certainly aspire to take part in someday. What are some other rituals on your campus? What do they tell you about the organizational culture?

As a new student, you also had to learn the jargon of higher education. For example, students seeking admittance into college learn acronyms such as SAT and ACT. Those graduating learn new acronyms such as GRE, MCAT, and LSAT. Every organization and profession has its own language or **jargon** that you must learn in order to communicate effectively in your chosen field. Part of your education will be learning that jargon so you can communicate with other professionals once you graduate. Can you think of any examples of miscommunication that

# Evaluate the Professional Context    Jonathan's First Day

*Read the following passage about Jonathan, and then answer the questions. As you read, focus on evaluating the professional context.*

Jonathan arrived to work early on the first day, dressed in his best suit. He was greeted by his direct supervisor, Dan, and given a quick lay of the land. The supervisors were housed on the second floor in offices with doors. Jonathan noticed that the supervisors' doors, which were shut and remained shut most of the day, displayed only a nameplate and title. The midlevel employees, such as Jonathan, had cubicles on the first floor. The administrative staff shared one large open desk area. All the employee spaces on the first floor were decorated with family photos and cartoons. The cartoons poked fun at the dysfunction of corporate America and bureaucracies. The administrative staff had similar cartoons, as well as a large sign that read, "I have one nerve left, and you are on it."

Jonathan was introduced to a coworker, Ann, who was responsible for training him. Once the supervisor walked away, Ann told Jonathan that the department was understaffed and she had a lot of work piled up on her own desk, so she hoped he learned quickly. She ran him through his duties using a lot of acronyms and jargon he did not understand. By lunch, his head was swimming.

About that time, the rest of Jonathan's coworkers assembled at his cubicle. They were all dressed casually and seemed friendly. They invited him to a local pizza buffet for lunch. During lunch, they told him stories about "their team." He was pleased to hear some of his coworkers' comments, such as, "We are a really tight-knit group" and "Welcome to our team." However, some of the comments about the supervisors caused him some concern. Supervisors were continually referred to as "them" and "those people," never part of "we." Many of the stories included advice on how to manage the administrative staff.

For example, Lisa told a story about the last new hire, who quit after 3 weeks. "She was rude to the administrative staff. She demanded things, and they did not like it. So all of her stuff was 'accidentally' processed inaccurately. She got so frustrated that she quit."

When Jonathan returned from lunch, almost 45 minutes late, he was told to work on some of the things Ann had taught him. As he began, he discovered he had no computer access. When he asked the administrative assistants for help, they started laughing. "You don't have a computer account or password yet." Jonathan just smiled and said thank you. Jonathan left work that day worried that he had made the wrong decision by accepting this job.

## Questions to Consider

1. Put yourself in Jonathan's place for a moment. What have you learned so far about the organizational culture?

2. How should Jonathan use information about the context and organizational culture to guide his communication interactions at work on the second day?

3. How can the KEYS approach help Jonathan communicate effectively in this situation?

occurred as you were learning the jargon? What is some of the jargon you have learned as part of your major? What jargon is used in your current workplace?

Communication scholar Walter Fisher (1984) argues that humans are all storytelling creatures. Through our **narratives** or stories, we come to understand the organizational culture and one another. Paying attention to an organization's stories is important to understanding the culture (Briody, Pester, & Trotter, 2012; Mitroff & Kilmann, 1975). Many of you probably used stories to determine which courses to take and from which professors. All of you have heard delightful tales and horror stories about various faculty members on your campus. In fact, today's high-tech world has taken organizational story-telling to a whole new level with programs such as Pick-a-Prof and RateMyProfessor .com, allowing students to hear stories from students they have never met (Edwards, Edwards, Qing, & Wahl, 2007; Zhu, 2012). Listening to what students use as criteria to deem a professor good or bad will tell you a lot about your campus's culture. What are the criteria on your campus? What stories helped you assimilate into the culture on your campus? How will what you learned assimilating into the organizational culture in college help you in "the real world"?

# Diversity in Your Workplace: Some Important Concepts

Part of the assimilation process is getting to know the people that make up your organization. A common mistake among so-called professionals is neglecting to take an inventory of others in the working environment. In today's world, getting to know your diverse workplace is important for the following reasons: (1) In order for you to succeed in any professional environment, you must be aware of and sensitive to differences between yourself and others, and (2) your ability to communicate effectively when encountering difference (e.g., ethnicity, race, language barriers, religion, spirituality, marital status, sexual orientation) is an essential component of professional excellence. Our point is this: The people you'll be working with may present you with differences you've never encountered before, and your communication choices will make or break the experience. Let's begin by exploring a few important concepts related to effective communication and workplace diversity.

## Cultural Diversity Awareness and Worldview

As a professional beginning a new job, it's critical to strive for **cultural diversity awareness**—being aware of diversity that's present in any working or social environment (Fine, 1996; Muir, 1996; Trenerry & Paradies, 2012). You may be thinking, "How do I prepare for the diverse workplace? What do I need to do to achieve cultural diversity awareness?" These questions are not easy to answer, because we all have varied worldviews.

According to Samovar et al. (2007), the term **worldview** is culture's orientation to supernatural, human, and natural entities in the cosmological universe and other philosophical issues influencing how its members see the world. How can we understand what makes up our worldviews? Redfield (1953) devised a system that includes some of the following elements: self, other, gender differences, "us versus them," religious differences, various ways people manage time (e.g., fast-paced, relaxed), and spirituality.

## Ethical Connection    Caleb's Blunder

*Please read the passage below, and answer the questions that follow.*

Growing up and in college, Caleb was not exposed to Hispanic, Chicano, or Latino people. In fact, he had no idea what these terms meant. He had always been comfortable using the term *Mexican* with his Caucasian friends and family in West Virginia. There was no negative intention in their use of the term, and Caleb never dreamed that another person would be offended by the word. During one of his first days on the job, Caleb spent several hours with a trainer named Rosa from the Human Resources Department. As Caleb and Rosa were in conversation, Caleb said the following: "I've noticed that there are lots of Mexicans who work around here." He continued, "But you don't really look like a Mexican, Rosa. You have a very fair complexion." Not surprisingly, Rosa was offended. In response to Caleb's comment, Rosa took the time to explain that some people who identify as Hispanic may be offended if labeled "Mexican." She went on to explain that in her case, her mother was of Irish descent and her father's family came from El Salvador, so she was not Mexican. She also added that Hispanics are a diverse group and do not all have one look. Caleb did not set out to offend anyone, but by failing to understand and evaluate his professional context, he offended Rosa just the same.

### Questions to Consider

1. Do you consider Caleb's communication unethical? Why or why not?
2. How could Caleb have handled the situation with cultural competence?
3. What are the ethical issues that could/should be considered in regard to not respecting workplace diversity?
4. Using the KEYS process, how can Caleb develop more effective cultural competence?

The preceding foundations of worldview give you a sense of how complicated it is to understand the variety of viewpoints in our world. Indeed, it's a challenge to prepare for and predict the diverse people you'll encounter at work. What are some ways to approach the diverse workplace to avoid misunderstanding? What's the connection between getting to know the diverse workplace and professional excellence?

## Cultural Competence

As the economy has gone global and customers/clients have diversified, many organizations have increased their efforts to diversify their workforces. There are many advantages to diversity among employees, such as multiple perceptions in decision making and increased understanding of the customer base. With professional excellence as your goal, you must engage in the diverse terrain of your workplace environment. One way to engage and get to know the diverse workplace is by striving to improve your cultural competence. The term **cultural competence** refers to the level of knowledge a person has about others who differ in some way in comparison with himself or herself.

Diverse teams of professionals have many advantages over teams that lack diversity. Can you name some of those advantages?

A culturally competent professional not only has the knowledge of difference but is always striving to learn more. People who are viewed as having cultural competence are usually masters of a practice called **perception checking**—asking others if their perceptions or sense of understanding is correct or incorrect. Let's remember that even if our intention is one of respect for other people, the way we communicate messages regarding difference can make or break us as professionals and tarnish our journey toward excellence.

## Mutual Respect

When getting to know the diverse workplace, it's important to foster relationships. We can develop positive personal and professional relationships with people who are different in terms of race, ethnicity, religion, gender, and sexual orientation by coming to understand those differences. When individuals and groups communicate with the goal of **mutual respect**—also known as mutual understanding—cultural tensions, misunderstandings, and conflict can be avoided (Christian, Porter, & Moffit, 2006; Kals & Jiranek, 2012). Mutual respect is about people seeking understanding through the vehicle of open dialogue; attempting to understand others with an open mind leads them to respond with mutual respect and understanding. When cultural competence and mutual respect are absent, **discrimination**—the act of excluding or denying people of products, rights, and services based on their race, ethnicity, religion, gender, age, sexual orientation, or disability—can occur. As a result, organizations are implementing workforce training programs to increase cultural sensitivity, tolerance, and appreciation of diversity in the workplace (Burkard, Boticki, & Madson, 2002; Okoro & Washington, 2012). Professional excellence can't happen in a diverse workplace without cultural competence, perception checking, and mutual respect.

# Examples of Diversity in Professional Contexts

In the previous sections, we've established the importance of getting to know the diverse workplace. In this section, we survey a number of examples of diversity that you may encounter in professional contexts. Gender, ethnicity and race, language differences, religion, and people with disabilities are just a few examples of the diversity you'll encounter in the workplace.

## Gender

You will no doubt encounter gender-related diversity in your workplace. You may not think of men and women as being part of different cultures, but communication scholar Deborah Tannen (1990) argues that men and women are indeed part of very different cultures. Further, according to communication and gender scholar Julia Wood (2008), women have a different way of knowing and communicating than do their male counterparts. As a result, you should get in the habit of approaching gender diversity in the same fashion you would approach any other form of diversity—with cultural competence.

Let's look at some examples. Women are more likely to use communication to establish relationships, resulting in something known as rapport talk (Ford & Stickle, 2012; Tannen, 1990). If asked, "How was your weekend?" a woman is likely to give a detailed description of the events that occurred. Furthermore, women often add tag questions to their statements to invite conversation and help develop rapport. So a woman might say, "That is an excellent opportunity for the department, isn't it?" By adding the tag question, she has invited a response from the other party. Conversely, men are more likely to communicate in a style know as report talk (Stamou, Maroniti, & Dinas, 2012; Tannen, 1990). If asked, "How was your weekend?" a man might reply, "Great. We took the kids to a Giants game." He reports what occurred without much detail. Men are also more likely to talk in statements and commands, excluding tag questions: "That is an excellent opportunity for the department."

Understanding the cultural differences in the ways men and women communicate can help you avoid miscommunication and false stereotypes. For example, a woman who uses tag questions is not unsure of herself; she is simply developing rapport and inviting conversation. Similarly, a man may still consider rapport and relationships important even if he communicates using report talk.

## Ethnicity and Race

Differences in race or ethnicity often come to mind when we think of diversity in the workplace. Although the terms *race* and *ethnicity* are often linked to each other, when it comes to communication competence, you will be focusing on differences based on ethnicity, not race. **Race** is the categorization of people based on physical characteristics such as skin color, dimensions of the human face, and hair. The old typology placed people into one of three races. Today, those typologies are no longer deemed useful and have been replaced with ethnic identifications or classifications. **Ethnicity** refers to a social group that may be joined together by factors such as shared history, shared identity, shared geography, or shared culture. If you rely on nonverbal cues to detect someone's ethnic background, you do so without taking into account that what you see visually may not always be accurate. In other words, a person's physical qualities may lead you to perceive them as being a part of one particular ethnic group, when in fact they identify with a difference ethnic group. Thus, as you get to know the diverse workplace related to ethnicity, it's important to remember that what you see visually through nonverbal dimensions of physical appearance does not always shape accurate perceptions of another person's ethnicity.

To understand the impact of ethnicity on communication, you must understand **stereotypes**. While this term tends to have a negative connotation, stereotypes merely describe the way humans categorize or understand. This may cause one to perceive others as belonging to a particular ethnic or social group. These perceptions can be positive, neutral, or negative. When developing professional excellence as it relates to cultural competence, it is important to begin by *knowing yourself*. What are your experiences with this ethnicity? What stereotypes (positive or negative) do you hold? What questions or concerns do you have about communicating with someone from this ethnicity? The next step is to *evaluate the professional context*. You can do this by researching a culture to increase your understanding of difference. You can also ask questions of the person with whom you are communicating in the professional context. Open and respectful communication is a must when getting to know people in the workplace of diverse ethnic backgrounds.

When James traveled to India on business, he researched ethnic differences. He learned that the custom in India is to get to know the other party prior to doing business. In New York City, he had always made it a point to do business first and, once an agreement was reached, then go for dinner or a drink. Understanding this difference increased his cultural competence. When Suzette traveled from France to Iowa for a business meeting, she greeted her coworker, Sam, with a hug and a kiss on each cheek. She noticed that Sam seemed a bit uncomfortable. Instead of ignoring her perception, she asked, "What is the customary greeting in the United States?" Sam explained the simple handshake, and Suzette increased her cultural competence with perception checking.

## Language Differences

According to intercultural communication scholars McDaniel, Samovar, and Porter (2009), the impact of **globalization** is "a seemingly unstoppable process that brings each of us into greater contact with the rest of the world and gives our daily lives an increasingly international orientation" (p. 6). Have you thought at all about globalization and how it will impact your career? Keeping your own professional goals in mind, how do diversity and globalization impact the industry or profession in which you're interested?

One way globalization will impact your communication is through differences in accents, dialects, and languages. The word **accent** refers to a person's pronunciation of various words in a language. An accent can give us a clue as to where a person is from. For example, "She speaks with a French accent." **Dialect** differences include variations in the pronunciation of words, as well as in vocabulary and syntax. You may encounter a coworker or customer who does not speak the same language as you. Nevertheless, you will still need to communicate with each other. Clearly, accent, dialect, and lack of a shared language impact communication effectiveness in professional settings both with coworkers and customers. Language differences will compound other cultural differences that surely exist.

When you experience **language barriers,** be prepared to ask and answer many questions to ensure a clear understanding. Try to avoid the common mistakes of losing patience and giving up or speaking to the person as if they can't hear you. Speaking louder or, even worse, yelling at another person when a language barrier is present can often lead to frustration and further misunderstanding.

Many industries regularly deal with language barriers. Service industries such as health care facilities, airports, and hotels have implemented **translation services**—interpretation systems available to assist with language barriers and other communication-related concerns. If your organization offers translation services, be certain to use them.

In addition to language differences, language preferences can also create language barriers. For example, all employees in one department can speak English, but three of them prefer to speak Japanese. When they are speaking to one another, they use Japanese. The rest of the department is unable to understand what is being said and often feels left out. If the manager tells the Japanese-speaking employees to stop using their language, is she discriminating against them or violating their rights? Bergman, Watrous-Rodriguez, and Chalkley (2008) considered the use of foreign language in a professional setting—specifically, the way individuals perceive those who speak a foreign language in the workplace. While a group of coworkers speaking a foreign language together may signal camaraderie, it may also cause them to be labeled as outsiders by those who do not speak the language. While the choice to speak a foreign language is based on personal and professional factors, the results of this study indicate that language use has important implications for the way individuals are treated in the workplace.

As a leader or manager, what would you do to manage a conflict resulting from a language barrier? Consider the following example:

How have you handled language barriers in your own life?

Terry was a new a shift leader at a manufacturing plant. Half the unit he was in charge of spoke English as a second language, preferred to speak Spanish, and identified as Hispanic. The other half of the unit all spoke English as their first language and identified as White or Black. Terry was warned by some of the other shift leaders that he really needed to pay attention to the cultural tensions before they got completely out of hand. The guy he replaced, Cecil, had never taken the time to do anything about the tensions and conflict taking place in the unit. Miguel, one of Terry's best employees, stopped by to report that there had been several verbal and physical confrontations that needed to be addressed. Miguel explained that the Whites and the Blacks had a problem with the Hispanics speaking Spanish at work. Miguel was one of the employees who liked to speak Spanish. He expressed that the Whites and the Blacks felt as though they were being talked about in a negative way. Terry decided to take action. He wrote up a policy for his unit to

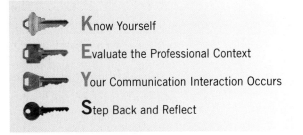

Know Yourself

Evaluate the Professional Context

Your Communication Interaction Occurs

Step Back and Reflect

## Step Back and Reflect    Abby Decorates for the Company Holiday Party

*Read the passage below about Abby, and answer the questions that follow.*

Abby was in charge of decorating for the annual company holiday party. She had been working in financial planning for 5 years, but this was the first time she'd been able to help with the decorations. The prior year, Abby had helped decorate for the annual Christmas play at her church. Since she had paid for the Christmas play decorations with her own money, she felt comfortable reusing them at her work party. This would allow her to save money on decorations and purchase more door prizes. One of her favorite decorations was a nativity scene. It fit perfectly on the head table; Abby just knew that the scene would be a big hit with everyone! She also had a beautiful tree to display in the entryway. As Abby started to decorate for the party, the lead partner called her to the side and asked her to rethink the decorations. One of his concerns was that the decorations were culturally insensitive to some of the people at the office. Abby was asked to remove the nativity scene from the head table, and the tree had to come down. Abby was devastated.

### Step Back and Reflect

1. What went wrong?

2. What had Abby failed to consider about the professional context in a diverse workplace?

3. How could Abby utilize the KEYS approach to improve her communication interaction?

speak "English Only Please" and gave it to Miguel. Terry never communicated with his unit in person about the situation. The conflicts continued to get worse. After several more complaints, Terry decided to put up a sign in the break room asking everyone in his unit to speak "English Only Please." Soon after, Terry started to see production problems as tensions increased. Terry couldn't figure out what he was doing wrong. After all, he had communicated the new policy in writing twice. Why wouldn't the guys in his unit simply follow his new rule? How could the KEYS approach help Terry with this problem?

## Religion and Spirituality

Religion and spirituality are other areas of diversity among coworkers (Deshpande, 2012; Driscoll & Wiebe, 2007). How can religion or spirituality come into play with people you're working with or serving professionally? Let's turn back to Jonathan's experience getting to know the diverse terrain at his new job. One guy on the team whom Jonathan really related to was Alex. Jonathan had observed that several members of the team would get together for happy hour on Fridays, and he thought it would be fun if he and Alex joined the group. Jonathan invited Alex out for happy hour several times, but Alex always declined. After the third rejection, Alex took the time to explain to Jonathan that he and his family were members of the LDS Church (also known as the Church of Jesus Christ of Latter-Day Saints). Alex further explained that he did not drink alcohol. What can we learn from Jonathan's experience? Clearly, people from various religious perspectives make up your diverse work environment (Bhunia & Das, 2012; Lewis & Geroy, 2000). Can you think of other ways religion and spirituality impact professional contexts? Take a look at Step Back and Reflect on page 118, which features Abby's experience with the company holiday party.

## People With Disabilities

Your diverse workplace may also include people with disabilities. We recognize that some of you are limited in your experience with people with disabilities, while other readers live with a disability or have friends, loved ones, or significant others with a disability. Regardless, we can all develop cultural competence in this area and support fair treatment and respectful communication.

People with disabilities work in a variety of business and professional contexts.

Your communication with people with disabilities is important in your personal and professional life. We usually know that a person is living with a disability based on his or her physical appearance, but remember that some forms of disability are invisible (Braithwaite & Thompson, 2000; Houtenville & Kalargyrou, 2011). The physical appearance of a person with a disability can lead you to communicate or act differently (Braithwaite, 1990, 1996; Braithwaite & Braithwaite, 2009; Braithwaite & Thompson, 2000; Ivy & Wahl, 2009; Konrad, Moore, Doherty, Ng, & Breward, 2012). In an interview situation, how would you react to a potential employee who arrives in a wheelchair or with a seeing-eye dog? Can you think of other situations or experiences to increase knowledge and awareness of this topic related to business and professional contexts? People with disabilities have a major presence in professional settings today, and it's critical that you as a professional strive for respectful communication with people with disabilities and promote a supportive and considerate attitude in the professional environment where you work (and that you may in some cases be responsible for maintaining). There is also a certain legal factor at play here due to state and federal laws promoting equal and fair treatment of people with disabilities in professional contexts, but we encourage you to go beyond legality and minimal compliance by educating yourself and striving to communicate with and respect people with disabilities in any personal or professional setting.

Dealing with differences can seem like an overwhelming task when, in reality, it is a simple process. You can come to understand your coworkers and customers, even if they have views and practices different from your own, if you practice cultural competence, perception checking, and mutual respect.

# KEYS to Excellence in Getting to Know the Diverse Workplace

Remember Hani Khan, who lost her job because her traditional cultural clothing didn't comply with Abercrombie & Fitch's "look policy"? In studying the KEYS approach to professional excellence in the diverse workplace, we can see that Abercrombie & Fitch made some questionable decisions regarding Hani's employment. In relation to the first key, *know yourself*, Abercrombie & Fitch should have practiced cultural competence, and part of that entails improving communication with people from different cultural backgrounds and worldviews. The company's rigid adherence to an inflexible "look policy" led to poor communication choices. The company might be better served by asking how its policies affect people from different backgrounds. The goal should be to check perception more and focus on open and honest conversations with people about areas with which the company is not familiar. In all, the company simply needed to get to know its employees better in relation to cultural diversity.

The next key, *evaluate your professional context,* is essential for Abercrombie & Fitch because the company should strive to become more audience centered and aware of the potential for cultural differences in both professional and personal contexts. Company managers should become more mindful of differences in their surroundings and use the skill of perception checking to avoid making assumptions about other people.

The third key, *your communication interaction occurs,* can make Abercrombie & Fitch a more successful communicator. Company officials should start to think before making statements or assumptive comments to coworkers with diverse cultural backgrounds. As the communication interaction occurs, managers should work more at planning their messages and asking for clarification to avoid misunderstanding.

Once supervisors for Abercrombie & Fitch finish implementing good communication practices with their employees, it becomes necessary to *step back and reflect*. The company should become more open to reflecting on communication with others. Managers should ask themselves some of the following questions as they step back and think about the communication that has occurred: Was I respectful to him/her in our conversation? Did I ask questions that revealed a genuine interest and human decency toward others different from me? Was I a good listener? Was I open to the other person's point of view? If something seems off or the manager/employee is uncomfortable, it is important to be careful to revisit the conversation or check in with the other person to make sure the situation was handled well. The fourth phase can help people be more thoughtful about both verbal and nonverbal communication.

Have you ever seen mistakes similar to those made by Abercrombie & Fitch? Do you think it is or will be difficult to communicate in a diverse workforce? Do you have any concerns? How can the KEYS approach help you succeed at understanding the organizational culture and communicating with coworkers and customers from other cultures?

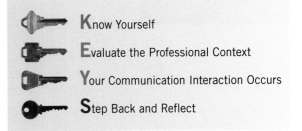

**K**now Yourself

**E**valuate the Professional Context

**Y**our Communication Interaction Occurs

**S**tep Back and Reflect

## Executive Summary

Now that you have finished reading this chapter, you can do the following:

Understand each phase of the assimilation process:

- The *assimilation process* is the adjustment period and "settling in" that's common for anyone starting a new job (p. 105).
- Organizations begin to assimilate you into their culture before you are even hired. The recruitment process, from the way the job posting is written to the signing of the contract, contributes to your socialization into an organization (p. 106).
- Once hired, you step out of the fantasy world and into the reality of your new organizational culture. Every organization, large or small, has its own culture (p. 106).
- As a new member of an organizational culture, you will be formally and informally taught the acceptable ways to think and behave (p. 107).

Assess the culture in your organization:

- From the day you were born, your parents, siblings, relatives, friends, teachers, and even strangers have been working to socialize you into the *culture*(s) that make up their experiences (p. 104).
- Learning an organization's culture provides you with information necessary to evaluate the audience and context. Furthermore, you can't effectively *step back and reflect* on your communication without taking into account the organizational culture in which it occurred (p. 105).

Define cultural diversity awareness and worldview:

- *Cultural diversity awareness* involves being aware of diversity that's present in any work or social environment (p. 112).
- *Worldview* is culture's orientation to supernatural, human, and natural entities in the cosmological universe and other philosophical issues influencing how its members see the world (p. 112).

Understand the important role of cultural competence, perception checking, and mutual respect as you enter the diverse workplace:

- *Cultural competence* refers to the level of knowledge a person has about others who differ in some way in comparison with himself or herself. A culturally competent professional not only has the knowledge of difference but is always striving to learn more (p. 113).
- *Perception checking* involves asking others if one's perceptions or sense of understanding is correct or incorrect. Remember that even if our intention is to show respect for other people, the way we communicate messages regarding difference can make or break us as professionals and tarnish our journey toward excellence (p. 114).
- *Mutual respect* is about people seeking understanding through the vehicle of open dialogue; attempting to understand others with an open mind leads them to respond with mutual respect and understanding (p. 114).

Utilize the KEYS approach to conduct yourself with professional excellence as you get to know your diverse workplace:

- *Know yourself*—You should want to achieve professional excellence, and part of that entails improving your communication with people from different cultural backgrounds and worldviews (p. 120).
- *Evaluate your professional context*—It is essential for you to become more audience centered and aware of the potential for cultural differences in both professional and personal contexts (p. 120).
- *Your communication interaction* can make you a more successful communicator. Start to think before making statements or assumptive comments to coworkers with diverse cultural backgrounds (p. 120).
- *Step back and reflect*—Try to become more open to reflecting on your communication with others (p. 120).

## Discussion Questions

1. Discuss the attitude or mind-set you have about work and finding a job. What are the primary factors (e.g., family, prior work history) that have influenced your attitude? Do you think these factors will positively or negatively influence you as you assimilate into your new organization?

2. How would you describe the organizational culture at your college or university? How were you assimilated into the culture?

3. What artifacts, rituals, jargon, and stories have you observed in your workplace?

4. Can cultural diversity be fostered in the workplace through employee education and training? What experiences have you had, if any, concerning diversity training or education?

5. Related to organizational culture, what are your impressions of companies such as Starbucks Coffee and Southwest Airlines? What, if anything, stands out to you about their organizational culture that makes them different in comparison with others? What other companies stand out to you as having a unique culture?

## Terms to Remember

accent (p. 116)
artifacts (p. 108)
assimilation process (p. 105)
cultural competence (p. 113)
cultural diversity awareness (p. 112)
cultural rituals (p. 110)
culture (p. 104)
dialect (p. 116)
discrimination (p. 114)

disguising conversation (p. 107)
ethnicity (p. 115)
globalization (p. 116)
indirect questioning (p. 107)
jargon (p. 110)
language barriers (p. 116)
mutual respect (p. 114)
narratives (p. 112)
organizational culture (p. 105)
overt questioning (p. 107)

perception checking (p. 114)
race (p. 115)
socialization (p. 104)
stereotypes (p. 116)
surveillance (p. 107)
testing limits (p. 107)
third-party questioning (p. 107)
translation services (p. 117)
worldview (p. 112)

Visit the Student Study Site at **www.sagepub.com/keys2e** to access the following resources:

- SAGE journal articles
- Video links
- Web resources

- Web quizzes
- eflashcards

part III

# Developing in the Workplace

Chapter 6: Interpersonal Communication at Work

Chapter 7: Strengthening Teams and Conducting Meetings

## Chapter Outline

Exploring Relationship Types at Work   129

The Line Between Professional and Personal   135

Professional Etiquette   139

KEYS to Excellence in Interpersonal Communication   142

Executive Summary   144

Discussion Questions   145

Terms to Remember   145

## Chapter Objectives

After studying this chapter, you should be able to:

1. Define interpersonal communication

2. Identify and explain strategies for professional excellence in supervisor–subordinate and coworker relationships

3. Improve customer relationships at work

4. Understand the difference between professional and personal communication

5. Utilize the KEYS approach to conduct yourself with professional excellence in interpersonal communication in the workplace

# chapter 6

# Interpersonal Communication at Work

**James Lynn was a factory inspection manager for Wal-Mart Stores in 2002 when he developed feelings for a female coworker.** While he was in Guatemala City touring a facility with his female colleague, they developed a romantic relationship outside of the workplace. Lynn was surprised when he returned to the United States to find out that he was being terminated for violating Wal-Mart's strict "no fraternization" policy. There had never been any romantic interaction between Lynn and his partner at work, and they had kept the physical aspect of their relationship hidden in the privacy of their hotel room. However, other employees had reported suspicion about Lynn's relationship, which led to Wal-Mart officials dispatching a private investigator to spy on Lynn and his companion during their trip. After 4 days of surveillance, the investigator reported back to officials that Lynn was having a romantic relationship with another employee, which led to his termination ("The Office Romance," 2010).

In a professional environment, it is important to build strong relationships with your coworkers through interpersonal communication. However, James Lynn's relationship with another employee put an end to his leadership career at Wal-Mart. It is important to understand your workplace environment to know if office romances are tolerated or not. While traditionally held as acceptable in most job settings, the growing threat of sexual harassment or hostile work environment lawsuits has many companies banning the practice altogether. While realizing the professional consequences of having an office relationship, it is important also to be aware of how your coworkers may react to office romance. Some coworkers can feel uncomfortable or threatened by working closely with a romantic couple, or can become jealous if they are interested in one of the people themselves.

Romantic relationships are certainly not the only aspect of interpersonal office communication. You will also have to deal with coworker relationships, superior–subordinate relationships, and customer–client relationships, to name a few. This chapter will outline the important functions and methods for building healthy interpersonal relationships in an office environment. While maintaining a professional appearance, you should be able to interact with coworkers in a friendly and disarming manner.

Interpersonal communication at work occurs between supervisors, subordinates, coworkers, and customers. Beyond policies about appropriate relationships in the workplace, employees have problems communicating with clients as well as coworkers. This chapter will review the essentials to connecting with other people professionally on an interpersonal level. Much, if not all, of the information we will cover on interpersonal communication can help people achieve professional excellence. Interpersonal communication, also referred to as people skills or soft skills, is an area you will need to develop and foster throughout your career if you wish to achieve professional excellence (Conrad & Newberry, 2011; McKnight, 1995; O'Connor, 1993).

As we established in Chapter 5, once you begin a new position, getting to know the organizational culture and diverse workforce is essential. Part of that process will no doubt include the formation of relationships in the workplace. These relationships are developed through interpersonal communication. **Interpersonal communication**, the cocreation of meaning as people interact, is a powerful skill that will help you *develop* in the workplace. Interpersonal communication is dyadic, meaning it occurs in **dyads** (two people). Through these dyads, you'll make connections with others and come to establish a network of professional relationships. As you strive for professional excellence, your interpersonal communication with coworkers, leaders, and clients is critical.

You might be thinking, "I'm a people person. Friendships and interacting with others come naturally to me, so why do I need to study this stuff?" If you've had a positive experience with interpersonal communication in other jobs or as you've made progress in college, it's natural to think that you do not need to work on your people skills. However, interpersonal communication is a process that we need to understand *at* work and *as* work. That is, even if you've had positive experiences in the past, part of striving for professional excellence is to hone your skills and be as effective as possible in your connections with other people in any given professional environment. We describe interpersonal communication as work because it's something you must always be aware of and always seek to improve. There's always a need to connect and relate with others, whether they're our coworkers, leaders, or clients. Further, interpersonal communication skills are not just about developing relationships or getting along with others. You will also encounter difficult people and conflict (a topic covered in Chapter 10); the way you respond in these not-so-comfortable situations or with not-so-nice people will be informed by our focus on interpersonal communication in this chapter.

Interpersonal communication is important for the following reasons: (1) Your ability to relate with other people is central to achieving professional excellence; (2) interpersonal communication helps you form professional connections with other coworkers, leaders, and clients; and (3) your interpersonal relationships at work provide a supportive social system that will increase your job satisfaction (Karl & Peluchette, 2006; Simon, Judge, & Halvorsen-Ganepola, 2010). Remember the huge impact effective communication played when you were *entering the workplace?* Well, effective people skills and interpersonal communication will play an equally important role in your

Interpersonal communication is important in the employee interview but continues as you build professional relationships with your colleagues.

success as you *develop in the workplace*. Let's begin this chapter with a look at the important role of interpersonal communication at work.

# Exploring Relationship Types at Work

Interpersonal communication at work can be classified into three dyadic interactions or relationships: superior–subordinate relationships, coworker relationships, and customer–client relationships.

## Superior–Subordinate Relationships

In the language of the workplace, the **superior** (supervisor/employer) is typically the higher-status person and the **subordinate** (employee) the lower-status person.

### Communicating Information

The interpersonal communication between supervisors and subordinates is not limited to the **relational layer**, nor does it exclusively focus on conveying status. After all, some content does have to be communicated if any work is ever to get done. Unfortunately, the status differences between supervisors and subordinates do contribute to the creation of less-than-ideal communication conditions.

One such condition is known as **semantic information distance**—a term that describes how employees and supervisors do not share the same view of some fundamental areas such as organizational issues or basic job duties (Jablin, 1979). Furthermore, employees and supervisors do not have the same view of employees' participation in decision making (Harrison, 1985; Zhou, Hirst, & Shipton, 2011). For example, Tom believes his employees are highly involved in decision making. Tom's employees, on the other hand,

# Your Communication Interaction   Suzette's Customer Service Experience

*Read the passage below, and then answer the questions. As you read, think about ways the KEYS approach could help you improve **your communication interaction** if you were in Phil's position.*

When Suzette arrived at the store, she had a clear plan mapped out. She was going to return her shoes for the full value without a receipt. She had purchased the shoes 2 months ago, and she had worn them several times to work and once to a wedding. They were okay for work, but after a night of dancing, she decided the heels were too high, so she wanted to return them.

The store policy, which was prominently displayed behind the cash register, stated, "Shoes can be returned only if they have not been worn. You have 30 days to return a purchase, and all returns must include the receipt." Although she was in violation of every part of the policy, Suzette was not worried. She was certain if she threw a big enough fit, she would get her way. After all, the customer is always right.

When Austin, the sales representative, waited on Suzette, he was friendly, asking, "How may I help you?" Suzette immediately began to demand her money back. Although her tone was rude and aggressive, Austin remained calm. He listened to her. He expressed empathy. His manner remained polite and professional even as Suzette raised her voice and began to cause a scene.

Phil, the manager, heard the noise and came to see what was wrong. Phil decided to end the situation as quickly as possible, so he gave Suzette her money back. Suzette walked out smiling, but Austin was now furious.

## Questions to Consider

1. Why was Austin upset by Phil's response to Suzette?
2. Should Austin have handled the situation differently?
3. Should Phil have handled the situation differently?
4. How can the KEYS process help Phil manage customer confrontations?

believe they have little input in decision making because even when Tom asks for their opinions and insights, they are rarely implemented. The good news is, even though supervisors and employees may suffer from semantic information distance, chances are good that neither party realizes it—and in most cases, the organization continues to function effectively (Eisenberg, Monge, & Farace, 1984).

In addition to the communication problems resulting from semantic information distance, communication between supervisors and subordinates often is affected by a communication phenomenon known as upward distortion (Foste & Botero, 2012; Fulk & Mani, 1986). **Upward distortion** occurs when the messages sent up the chain of command, from subordinates to supervisors, are altered (see Table 6.1).

According to Fulk and Mani (1986), messages are altered in one of four ways: gatekeeping, summarization, withholding, or general distortion. **Gatekeeping** occurs when some,

**Table 6.1 Self-Monitoring Questions**

- Can you remember a time when you altered a message?

- In what way did you alter it?

- Why did you alter it?

- Could your supervisor have done something differently to cause you not to alter the message?

- What could he or she have done?

but not all, of the information is passed on to the supervisor. **Summarization** occurs when the employee summarizes the messages in such a way that emphasis is placed on certain aspects of the message. **Withholding** occurs when information is not passed on to the supervisor. And **general distortion**, a close cousin to out-and-out lying, occurs when the message is changed to serve the subordinate's purposes. As a supervisor, you must take steps to limit message alteration by doing some, if not all, of the following: (1) Limit the number of people a message must travel through before it gets to you, (2) go to the source of the message for clarification, (3) keep communication channels open with subordinates and customers, and (4) never "shoot the messenger."

### Communicating With Your Supervisor

In Chapter 10, we will spend some time discussing how you should communicate with subordinates when you become a leader/supervisor; so in this chapter, we are going to focus our discussion on strategies you can use as a subordinate for effectively communicating with your supervisor(s).

No doubt, you are familiar with terms such as *teacher's pet* and *brown-noser*. These terms are often reserved for individuals who ingratiate themselves with or "suck up" to the person in authority, and the terms have a negative connotation. Still, **ingratiation**, which occurs when an employee acts warm and friendly toward the supervisor, can be an effective strategy for communicating with the boss. However, if the ingratiation is insincere, not your style, or if your boss doesn't like the attention, your resulting communication will come across as less than professional. For those seeking professional excellence, advocacy is the strategy of choice when communicating with supervisors. **Advocacy** utilizes a simple persuasive technique. Specifically, you evaluate your boss's needs and preferences and then

Wouldn't it be great if you had some sort of cue to let you know about a distorted message? Be aware of ethical problems such as lying in the workplace—set boundaries and try to stay away from toxic people.

develop messages, arguments, and proposals that line up with those needs and preferences (Foste & Botero, 2012; Riley & Eisenberg, 1992). Advocacy falls in line with the KEYS process, as it requires you to know yourself and evaluate the professional context.

There is no single effective strategy that works every time when communicating with supervisors. To communicate effectively with your supervisor, you must evaluate him or her in the same way you evaluate everyone else. As you strive for professional excellence as superiors or subordinates, remember the power of communication; appropriate verbal and nonverbal behaviors often make or break your chances of being viewed positively on the job. Please note that in terms of interpersonal communication in the workplace, it is important to consider the way a supervisor communicates with a subordinate. We will discuss this in more detail in Chapter 8.

## Coworker Relationships

While communication with your boss is important, effective interpersonal communication with your coworkers is equally important. Across industries, employees need to work together to complete common tasks. In fact, the "co-" in *coworker* is a prefix meaning "together or jointly." Common tasks are what bring you together and form that working relationship—some professionals form personal relationships initiated from the time spent completing workplace tasks and assignments.

Coworker relationships may also be based on needs or, more accurately, the fulfillment of needs. These needs may be task related. For example, if your computer is not working properly, you may need the expertise of the computer specialist, resulting in an interpersonal communication interaction between the two of you. Coworkers can also fulfill the need for support on the job. Having coworkers that can help you complete tasks, provide professional advice, and laugh with you is a real plus to your professional development and stress level on the job.

Physical and spatial closeness also has an impact on which coworkers you will develop relationships with. Coworkers "who work in adjacent desks, cubicles, or offices are more likely to develop closer relationships than people who work for the same company, but on different floors or opposite ends of a building" (Ivy & Wahl, 2009, pp. 369–370). Professionals today stay connected with technology, such as e-mail or instant-message exchanges, text messaging, social-networking sites, and virtual work teams (Diaz, Chiaburu, Zimmerman, & Boswell, 2012; Riggio, 2005).

Another common factor that serves as the basis for coworker relationships is shared communication networks. A **communication network** is defined as "a group of individuals who regularly share a line of communication" (Eisenberg, Goodall, & Trethewey, 2007, p. 256). In some cases,

Remember that your workplace environment has a major impact on interpersonal communication.

these lines of communication are predetermined by the organization. For example, the **organizational chart** at Company U indicates that Ethan, Virginia, and Diana report to their supervisor, Don. If they have information that needs to be shared with the district manager, Richard, they must first report it to Don, who will then pass the information on to Richard. This type of communication network is known as a **formal communication network** because it is formally prescribed by the organization. But, as we all know, this is not the way all communication flows in the workplace. The majority of communication occurs in what is known as the **white space**, the part of the organizational chart that has not been prescribed.

The communication networks that develop in this white space are collectively known as the **informal communication network**, also commonly referred to as the **grapevine**. As someone with professional excellence, you should avoid the grapevine, right? Wrong. According to a study by Hellweg (1987), the information found on the grapevine is more efficient and more accurate than the information shared through formal communication channels. Communicating via the informal communication network allows employees to speak directly and not chance the message being altered as it moves its way through several people in the formal communication network. Just remember, when using the informal communication network, continue to communicate with professional excellence. For example, be certain that you are not disrespecting anyone by going "over his or her head" without permission. So if you need to discuss an issue with a coworker in a different department, be certain to get your superior's okay first. Furthermore, make certain that the information you give and receive is professional in nature. The grapevine is often associated with gossiping. You will encounter difficult people in the workplace, which we will discuss in detail in Chapter 8, but gossiping about them and/or their behavior with other coworkers only makes you a difficult employee as well. If you have an issue with a coworker, you must discuss it with that person face to face or with the appropriate supervisor. Don't turn it into a hot piece of grapevine gossip or office drama. And remember, listening to gossip is just as bad as spreading it.

In the 21st century, the channels for communicating with coworkers seem to expand daily. Should you send the message via a phone conversation, a voice message, a text, an e-mail, a memo, or a meeting? Although each channel has strengths and weaknesses, when it comes to developing interpersonal relationships, good old-fashioned face-to-face communication is still the best way (Rhoads, 2010; Waldeck, Seibold, & Flanagin, 2005).

Unfortunately, gossip and rumors can serve as roadblocks to business and professional excellence. How would you manage gossip in your own professional life?

People or entities that your organization serves or provides products to are known as customers. For our purposes, we are going to refer to them as **external customers,** because they are external to the company. An **internal customer,** then, is an employee—an internal part of the organization—who needs services or products from other parts of the organization to complete his or her work. If you take a holistic view of any organization and see serving the external customer as the ultimate mission, then the vast majority of employees are directly or indirectly one another's internal customers.

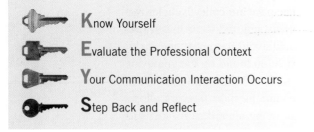

**K**now Yourself

**E**valuate the Professional Context

**Y**our Communication Interaction Occurs

**S**tep Back and Reflect

Do you think of your coworkers as internal customers? Do you give your coworkers the same respect and professional courtesy that you give your external customers? How do you treat your external customers? In the following section, we will discuss how to achieve professional excellence with the customers. All this information is applicable to your communication with your coworkers, as they should be treated as your internal customers. Achieving professional excellence with your coworkers is most easily accomplished by following the KEYS process and thinking of your coworkers as internal customers.

## Customer–Client Relationships

Maintaining positive customer relations centers on effective communication and is essential in today's business world. **Customer relations**, or customer service, "is the interaction between employees or representatives of an organization or business and the people the organization sells to or serves" (Ivy & Wahl, 2009, p. 370). All organizations have customers or clients, and anyone claiming to have professional excellence must excel at communicating with these individuals. Sprint, for example, won the 2002 Call Center of the Year award from *Call Center Magazine.* What did it do to excel? It trained employees in services and products, and it established a fun work environment that made its customer service agents feel, and ultimately sound, upbeat and friendly when talking to customers.

Excellent customer service is ingrained in the organizational culture of successful organizations; therefore, you should seek out organizations that value and foster customer service when you are job searching. Such organizations see customer service as the central focus and avoid defining the customer as a nuisance (Albrecht, 1992; Teece, 2010).

Communication can be extremely challenging when dealing with angry customers or coworkers.

According to Tom Peters (1987), organizational cultures that foster excellent customer service provide quality as defined by the customer, respond quickly, and are obsessed with listening.

# The Line Between Professional and Personal

Given the vast amount of time you will spend in the workplace, chances are some of your interpersonal relationships at work will include intimacy. **Intimacy** is characterized by feelings of closeness and trust that you share with other people. What comes to mind when you hear the word *intimacy*? Most people typically think of physical intimacy, but it's important to understand that there are other types of intimacy as well. Intimacy is not just about romantic or sexual activity. In situations where you share physical closeness with others (e.g., coworkers, clients, close friends), you have intimacy. As communication scholars Andersen, Guerrero, and Jones (2006) explain, intimacy is defined as "an experience consisting of felt emotions and perceptions of understanding, or as a relationship that is characterized by affection and trust" (p. 260). And as you develop a feeling of trust and affection toward coworkers, even toward clients and bosses, you will find yourself maintaining interpersonal relationships with coworkers *at* as well as *away* from work.

However, in order to develop professional excellence in the workplace, you must have a clear understanding of the line between personal and professional relationships, as well as what constitutes professional versus personal communication.

## Romance in the Workplace

In some ways, developing personal relationships, affection, and trust with coworkers, clients, and supervisors is not only a positive experience for you but good for your employer as well. After all, having a sense of social belonging is a core motivational factor on the job (Kirkhaug, 2010; Maslow, 1965). But what happens when feelings between cohesive colleagues turn into something more? Be forewarned that many organizations have norms and in some cases written policies that discourage or forbid romantic relationships in the workplace.

Why do such policies exist? One reason workplace romance is discouraged or forbidden is because it's a distraction. Flirting, courting, and breaking up can all distract from the work that needs to be done. In fact, the plots of many television shows center on the distraction and drama created by romance in the workplace. What would *Grey's Anatomy* be without romance?

Another reason romance is discouraged in the workplace is favoritism. The fear is that romantic relationships and sexual favors, as opposed to hard work and merit, can be used to advance one's career. A study by Dillard and Segrin (1987) found that of women who had been involved romantically with someone at work, 86% reported motives that were not job related, while 14% did report job-related motives. Clearly, the vast majority of those surveyed entered relationships for other reasons, but 14% with the wrong motive is more than enough to create problems in the workplace.

## Sexual Harassment

What is sexual harassment? The Equal Employment Opportunity Commission (1980) defines sexual harassment as follows:

> Unwelcomed sexual advances, requests for sexual favors, and other verbal or physical conduct of a sexual nature constitutes sexual harassment when (1) submission to such conduct is made either explicitly or implicitly a term or condition of an individual's employment, (2) submission to or rejection of such conduct by an individual is used as the basis for employment decisions affecting such individuals, or (3) such conduct has the purpose or effect of substantially interfering with an individual's work performance or creating an intimidating, hostile, or offensive working environment (pp. 74676–74677).

Understanding sexual harassment is tied to communication excellence because sexual harassment is a result of communicative behaviors and sense making (Bingham, 1991; Dougherty, 2001; Scarduzio & Geist-Martin, 2010; Taylor & Conrad, 1992). As clearly stated by the Equal Employment Opportunity Commission, sexual harassment is not only quid pro quo (i.e., something for something) but also the creation of a hostile work environment. Saying to an employee, "Have sex with me or you are fired," is clearly sexual harassment. But eyeing an employee up and down, referring to someone's spouse as hot, displaying beefcake calendars, or making someone uncomfortable by pursuing them romantically are also forms of sexual harassment.

As you strive for professional excellence, continually monitor your own communication for comments or behaviors that might be inappropriate. If you're doing anything that might be questionable, stop it immediately. Furthermore, if a colleague demonstrates a behavior, makes comments, or creates an environment that could be construed as sexual harassment, don't ignore it. If you sit by and allow someone else to be sexually harassed, you are contributing to the problem even if you are not the perpetrator.

What should you do if you are sexually harassed? Tamaki (1991) provides the following steps for dealing with a harasser. If you feel comfortable doing so, confront the harasser. You may not feel comfortable confronting the harasser directly, or you may confront the harasser but still the behavior continues. In either case, you should report the behavior to a supervisor and/or your human resources department. In addition, you should keep a written record of the behaviors and comments that you feel constitute harassment. It may also help to have a support system. Talking to supportive individuals, whether they are from your personal or professional life, is recommended.

Creating a hostile work environment is a form of sexual harassment.

## Step Back and Reflect    Jessica and Vinnie

*Read the following passage about Jessica, and answer the questions that follow.*

Jessica had recently been promoted into a new position with Company K when she was instructed to work with Vinnie on a project. When their meeting ran late, Vinnie suggested that they continue talking over some food. He commented that his wife and kids were out of town so he did not have to hurry home that evening. Jessica saw nothing unprofessional about the invitation. She was starving, and they were in the middle of an excellent brainstorming session, so she agreed. At dinner, Jessica began to feel uncomfortable. Twice, Vinnie brushed his hand against hers. It did not seem professional, but she excused it as an accident. Then he began making personal comments such as, "I just can't believe a gorgeous woman like you is single. You are too attractive to be spending your evenings alone." Jessica responded by mentioning the photos of his wife and kids displayed in his office. "I am sure one day I will be lucky enough to have a beautiful family like yours. Now about the project timeline . . . ." When the meal ended, Jessica declined the offer for a nightcap and headed for the parking lot. Vinnie followed her to her car, at which point he physically stood in front of her car door, blocking her access to the vehicle. He then stated, "Well, if you will not have a nightcap with me, at least give me a hug." Jessica replied, "I'm not much of a hugger," and she extended her hand. Vinnie grabbed her hand with both of his and began to caress it. Luckily, at that moment her cell phone rang; she pulled her hand free and answered it. She stayed on the phone, saying, "I have to take this." Vinnie backed up a bit, and Jessica threw her car door open, jumped in her car, and sped off.

Jessica did not know what to think. Was she overreacting? Could she have misunderstood? The next day, she approached a female supervisor, Michelle, described what had happened, and asked for her thoughts on the situation. Michelle listened to the events of the evening and then replied, "If someone as good-looking as Vinnie hit on me, I would be thrilled. Anyways, if you were not interested in him you should not have gone to dinner with him. I think you should be flattered, not whining." Jessica did not mention the situation again, but she did start searching for a new job that afternoon.

### Step Back and Reflect

1. What went wrong?
2. Was Vinnie's behavior appropriate? Was it professional? Was it sexual harassment?
3. Was Michelle's reaction appropriate? Was it professional?
4. What advice would you give Jessica?
5. How could Jessica or Michelle have utilized the KEYS approach to improve her communication interaction?

## Communication Privacy Management at Work

Because most employees do develop friendships with people they meet in the workplace, non-work-related conversations are fairly commonplace. What topics are deemed acceptable or professional? What constitutes friendly office chitchat? What topics are too personal for the workplace or invade coworkers' privacy? According to Sandra Petronio

(2000, 2002, 2007), who developed **Communication Privacy Management** theory, privacy is regulated by rules. We each develop our own set of rules that helps us determine what information we share, or **self-disclose,** and what information we keep private. For instance, many people in leadership positions believe that sharing private information with their employees is inappropriate and can confuse the relationship between leader and employee.

To understand the relationship between privacy management, interpersonal communication, and professional excellence, let's look at an example you are likely to encounter in the workplace. You're on a job interview and your future boss asks you about your marital/relational status. Does this question display professional excellence? In fact, as noted in Chapter 2, this question is illegal.

Now, let's say you have the job and you are getting to know your coworker. The two of you are making small talk. Since you are both already employed by the company, it's perfectly fine to ask a coworker about his or her marital/relational status, right? Although you may be asking this question to show interest in your new coworker, he may have been raised believing that this sort of questioning is intrusive and "none of your business." Some people feel that details about their love lives are not to be shared with many people, especially with someone at work.

Because family and loved ones are a fairly common discussion topic, it may seem natural when getting to know someone to ask if the person is married, dating, or single. Are you comfortable with people at work knowing about your marital/relational status? If you're married, in a traditional heterosexual relationship, and have children, you likely don't have much trouble at all talking about your family and spouse: "Yeah, my wife and I are settling into the community. Julie loves her new job at the art museum. The kids are both playing soccer for Hamlin Middle School. We really like it here." The person on the receiving end of this message, if he or she also has a family, would likely reciprocate with his or her spouse's name and number of kids. Topics such as family and kids are safe, professional topics of conversation, right?

What information about yourself do you view as private and would not want to be revealed in the workplace?

Let's flip the situation around a bit. Emma is a single professional. When her coworkers ask about her marital status, she feels as if her privacy is being violated, but she answers, "I'm single," and tries to change the topic. Her less-than-professional coworker then goes on to ask questions such as the following: "Are you dating anyone? So, you don't have a boyfriend yet? Would you like for me to set you up on a blind date with my friend Darren?" While some professionals are open about their marital/relational status and enjoy sharing information about their family life at work, it's important to realize that not everyone feels the same way about the disclosure of marital/relational information.

| Table 6.2 Sexual Orientation in Professional Contexts: Some Important Terms | |
|---|---|
| Heterosexuality | Physical and romantic attraction to people of the opposite sex |
| Homosexuality | Physical and romantic attraction to people of the same sex |
| Bisexuality | Physical and romantic attraction to people of both sexes |
| Asexuality | Having little, if any, interest in sex |

In Emma's case, she wishes to maintain privacy around her relational status and her sexual orientation in the workplace. **Sexual orientation** refers to the sex of a person with whom we wish to engage in sexual activity (Cavico, Muffler, & Mujtaba, 2012; Fleming, 2007). Lesbian, gay, bisexual, and transgender (LGBT) people will no doubt make up part of the diverse population in any professional setting (Bell, Özbilgin, Beauregard, & Sürgevil, 2011; Fleming, 2007; McDermott, 2006). For the LGBT readers of this text, we also want to recognize the choice you'll have to make regarding being open or private about your sexual orientation at work. Being "out" at work is easier for some LGBT people than for others. Regardless of your own sexuality, it's critical to recognize that LGBT communication and culture is present in both professional and social contexts (Eadie, 2009; see Table 6.2).

Single, married, gay, or straight, it's unprofessional to ask about the relationship statuses of others at work. As you're adjusting to new coworkers or taking a new role as a leader, be sensitive to the varied degree of acceptance when it comes to talking about marital/relational status in the workplace. You'll find that there are varying levels of acceptance regarding discussion of marital/relational status, from personal preferences to organizational policy.

Keep in mind that marital/relational status is just one example of a topic that might be deemed private. Other topics, such as religion, political affiliation, and even hobbies, may be private issues for your coworkers, clients, and/or supervisors. To maintain professional excellence as it relates to privacy management is to avoid asking questions that may be deemed private, unless the other party initiates the topic. Do not feel pressured to reveal information about yourself that you deem private. And if you do develop a personal relationship with another professional, keep your personal conversations private. As we discussed in the last section, sharing personal information about others through the company grapevine is completely and totally unprofessional.

# Professional Etiquette

It doesn't take a rocket scientist to understand that you can't have professional excellence if you don't display professional etiquette. **Professional etiquette** is practicing the

## Evaluate the Professional Context　Katie and Joey's Misunderstanding

*Read the following passage about Katie and Joey, and then answer the questions. As you read, focus on* **evaluating the professional context.**

When Katie learned a good-looking guy had been hired in the marketing department, she quickly found an excuse to head that way and check him out. Joey *was* cute and did not have on a wedding ring, so Katie wasted no time making her move. Joey had heard through the grapevine that Katie often planned company events and happy hours; so when she extended an invitation to him, he accepted. Joey had relocated for this job, and he had not yet made any friends in the community. He was excited about the opportunity to hang out with coworkers. It seemed as though things were going well at work, and now he was even establishing what seemed to be a new social network.

Friday afternoon arrived, and Katie met Joey at the local club. After grabbing a table, Katie said the following to Joey: "Wow, I have not been on a date with a nice-looking guy like you in several months."

Joey was shocked and didn't know what to say. He was just looking for another coworker to hang out with. He had just come through a painful divorce, and he did not want to discuss it.

### Questions to Consider

1. How should Joey respond to Katie?
2. Do you believe Katie and/or Joey displayed professional excellence? Why or why not?
3. How could the KEYS process help Katie and Joey in this situation?

behaviors of social etiquette or good manners in a professional setting. You have been taught good manners. You know not to talk with your mouth full and to cover your nose when you sneeze. So do we really need to talk about professional etiquette? You bet we do, because the workforce is increasingly full of people who lack professional etiquette; therefore, your ability to display it will not only help you achieve professional excellence but will set you apart from the pack.

Let's begin with the basics: politeness. Greet people when you see them. Do not interrupt others when they are speaking or when they are having a conversation with another party. Make requests in a manner that is polite as opposed to demanding. Respect your supervisors', coworkers', and customers' time. Say "please" and "thank you." Turn off your cell phone in a meeting. Be punctual. Don't eavesdrop on conversations. And, as noted earlier, don't spread gossip.

You may be thinking, "Don't patronize me. I know all this." Of course you do, but do you practice it? We have been in meetings and witnessed all the following (more than

## Know Yourself    Understanding Professional Etiquette

*The following quiz will help you understand your own professional etiquette. Answer each question thoughtfully, and then reflect on the results. How can this knowledge help you be a better communicator?*

A great place to begin practicing your professional etiquette is in the classroom. Take the following quiz and see how many times you have displayed less-than-professional etiquette during your college career. Place a check beside every violation you have committed.

_____ 1. Came to class without completing the homework.

_____ 2. Came to class without completing the required readings.

_____ 3. Made the following statement or one like it: "I missed class last week. Did we do anything important?".

_____ 4. Asked your professor: "Will this be on the test?".

_____ 5. Forgot to turn off your cell phone during class.

_____ 6. Left class to answer your cell phone.

_____ 7. Answered your cell phone during class.

_____ 8. Sent a text or instant message during class.

_____ 9. Surfed the net during class.

_____ 10. Sent an e-mail with punctuation and/or spelling errors.

_____ 11. Called your professor by the wrong title—for example, "Mrs." instead of "Dr.".

_____ 12. Requested a reference letter via e-mail.

_____ 13. Requested a reference letter less than 2 weeks before it was due.

_____ 14. Gossiped about a professor or classmate.

How did you do? For true professional excellence, you should not have a single check. Take some time to explore why each of the above behaviors is considered an example of poor professional etiquette. If you did earn some checks above, what can you do to eliminate those behaviors in the future? Are there other behaviors that you believe should be listed above? What are those behaviors, and why do you consider them violations of professional etiquette?

once, we might add): so-called professionals showing up late, wasting everyone else's time, and then asking, "What did I miss?"; high-level employees not only getting cell calls but answering them during meetings; a complete lack of manners displayed by employees on all levels; customers being ignored; employees being reprimanded in front of others; gossip and office drama getting so out of hand that work literally stops. Despite the fact that many people in professional positions display poor manners, it is still not professional and certainly is unacceptable behavior for someone striving for professional excellence.

# KEYS to Excellence in Interpersonal Communication

Remember James Lynn, who developed intimate feelings for another coworker even though it was a violation of company policy? Was James able to keep his job and develop toward professional excellence? James lost his job because he did not follow company rules and did not keep his relationship with a coworker professional. Think about how you should strive for excellence during interpersonal communication. When studying the KEYS approach to professional excellence as you develop in the workplace, try to make some changes and improve your people skills and interpersonal communication.

When examining the first key, *know yourself*, decide if you want to achieve professional excellence, and know that part of that entails improving your interpersonal communication with both your coworkers and clients. Realize that getting to know yourself better involves adjusting your communication style in professional settings. Remember that using your cell phone and texting in front of your coworkers and the customers can be rude or insensitive. Examine your strengths and weaknesses as they relate to interpersonal communication. Set a goal to improve your impression management and be more mindful of your communication decisions at work. For example, avoid making comments in front of coworkers about things going on in your personal life. In addition, review your company's performance standards and try to improve both verbal communication and body language in service encounters. Smiling and tone of voice can be improved—these are both factors that can positively impact the way other people view you.

The next key, *evaluate the professional context*, is essential because you want to become more audience centered and aware of how you come across to coworkers and clients. Become more mindful of the topics you bring up at work, and give more attention to how loudly you talk about particular topics when customers are present. The evaluation of your audience and workplace context can lead to improved interpersonal communication with your coworkers and clients.

The third key, *your communication interaction occurs*, can make you more genuine during interpersonal encounters with coworkers and clients. Start to practice good eye contact as well as active listening strategies, and realize that these skills are valuable to your development as a professional. As you walk away from interpersonal conversations and service encounters, think about what you communicated both verbally and nonverbally. As your communication interaction occurs, work more at making appropriate decisions regarding your people skills and interpersonal communication.

As you strive to improve your people skills, engage in the fourth key, *step back and reflect*. Become more open to reflecting on your interpersonal communication with others. Ask yourself some of the following questions as you step back and think about the message you sent: Was I communicating a positive attitude to the customer? Was I engaged in active listening rather than passive? Did I sound sarcastic when I responded to the customer's complaint? Did I talk about personal issues that other people may have viewed as offensive or unprofessional? Revisit the conversation or check in with the other person, whether coworker or customer, to make sure you handled it well.

Do you need to improve your interpersonal communication in the workplace? What have you learned in this chapter that could help you improve?

**K**now Yourself

**E**valuate the Professional Context

**Y**our Communication Interaction Occurs

**S**tep Back and Reflect

## Executive Summary

Now that you have finished reading this chapter, you can do the following:

Define interpersonal communication:

- *Interpersonal communication*, the cocreation of meaning as people interact, is a powerful skill that will help you develop in the workplace. Interpersonal communication is dyadic, meaning it occurs in *dyads* (two people) (p. 128).

Identify and explain strategies for professional excellence in supervisor–subordinate, coworker, and customer relationships at work:

- To communicate effectively with your supervisor, you must evaluate him or her in the same way you evaluate everyone else (p. 132).
- Appropriate verbal and nonverbal behaviors often make or break your chances of being viewed positively on the job (p. 132).
- If you have an issue with a coworker, you must discuss it with that person face to face or with the appropriate supervisor (p. 133).
- Organizational cultures that foster excellent customer service provide quality as defined by the customer, respond quickly, and are obsessed with listening (p. 135).

Understand the difference between professional and personal communication:

- As you develop a feeling of trust and affection toward coworkers, even clients and bosses, you will find yourself maintaining interpersonal relationships with coworkers *at* as well as *away* from work (p. 135).
- To maintain professional excellence as it relates to privacy management is to avoid asking questions that may be deemed private, unless the other party initiates the topic (p. 139).

Utilize the KEYS approach to conduct yourself with professional excellence in interpersonal communication in the workplace:

- *Know yourself.* Know how you want to achieve professional excellence, and know that part of that entails improving your interpersonal communication with both coworkers and clients (p. 142).
- *Evaluate the professional context.* This is essential for you because you will become more audience centered and aware of how you come across to coworkers and clients (p. 142).
- *Your communication interaction occurs* when you are critical during your interactions with others. This makes you more genuine during interpersonal encounters with coworkers and clients (p. 142).
- *Step back and reflect.* Become more open to reflecting on your interpersonal communication with others (p. 142).

1. What are your strengths when it comes to interpersonal communication? What areas do you plan to develop?

2. Make a list of several positive customer service experiences you've had. Did interpersonal communication impact your service experience? If so, what makes the difference in these experiences compared with others?

3. As a manager or leader, what steps would you take, if any, to educate your employees about interpersonal communication?

4. Do you believe companies should have policies that forbid dating among employees? Why or why not? Should companies have policies forbidding supervisors and subordinates to have nonromantic relationships outside work? Why or why not? Should companies have policies that forbid coworkers to develop nonromantic relationships outside work? Why or why not?

5. Make a list of private topics that you believe should not be discussed in professional settings, and then think of a time when your privacy was violated by someone. Was it an invasion of your private space or of your private information? How did the invasion make you feel, and how did you react?

**Terms to** Remember

advocacy (p. 131)

communication network (p. 132)

Communication Privacy Management (p. 138)

customer relations (p. 134)

dyads (p. 128)

external customers (p. 134)

formal communication network (p. 133)

gatekeeping (p. 130)

general distortion (p. 131)

grapevine (p. 133)

informal communication network (p. 133)

ingratiation (p. 131)

internal customer (p. 134)

interpersonal communication (p. 128)

intimacy (p. 135)

organizational chart (p. 133)

professional etiquette (p. 139)

relational layer (p. 129)

self-disclose (p. 138)

semantic information distance (p. 129)

sexual orientation (p. 139)

subordinate (p. 129)

summarization (p. 130)

superior (p. 129)

upward distortion (p. 130)

white space (p. 133)

withholding (p. 131)

Visit the Student Study Site at **www.sagepub.com/keys2e** to access the following resources:

- SAGE journal articles
- Video links
- Web resources

- Web quizzes
- eflashcards

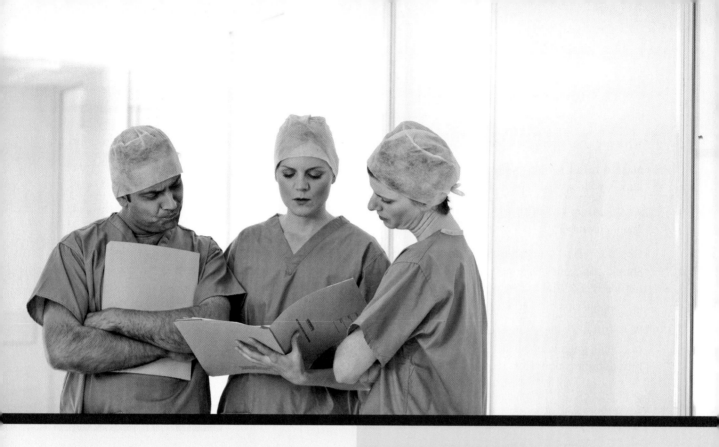

## Chapter Outline

**How Do Groups Differ From Teams?**   148
**Conducting Meetings**   149
**Team Roles**   156
**Team Norms**   156
**Problem Solving**   158
**Cultivating Innovative Thinking**   166
**Conflict in Team Meetings**   169
**KEYS to Excellence in Team
   Communication**   174
**Executive Summary**   176
**Discussion Questions**   177
**Terms to Remember**   177

## Chapter Objectives

After studying this chapter, you should be able to:

1. Distinguish between a group and a team

2. Recognize the impact of the environment, the topic(s), and the participants on communication within meetings

3. Analyze the roles and norms displayed by a group or team

4. Apply the concepts for effective problem solving and innovative thinking to a team context

5. Understand the need for conflict and the strategies for productive conflict

6. Apply the KEYS process to professional excellence as you develop your groups into teams

chapter 7

# Strengthening Teams and Conducting Meetings

**For 2 years Ani Chopourian was a member of the cardiovascular surgical team at Mercy General.** During her time there, she made numerous reports of inappropriate conduct, bullying, and retaliation at the Sacramento hospital. She recalled several instances of poor conduct, including a doctor routinely greeting her with "I'm horny!" and a slap on her bottom, and one frightening instance where a surgeon, in a fit of rage, broke the ribs of an anesthetized heart patient. Other doctors would make fun of her Armenian heritage by teasing her about joining Al-Qaeda. Chopourian was fired shortly after she posted her final complaint about the surgical team at her hospital. In her ensuing legal battle, Chopourian was awarded $168 million in damages for her harassment lawsuit, the single largest judgment in U.S. history for an individual victim of workplace harassment (Williams, 2012). Because Chopourian was so ostracized by her team members, both she and the hospital she worked for faced serious injury and consequences.

Team communication is a crucial aspect for creating workplace excellence. In the example above, it is easy to see how a toxic team environment can have serious penalties. The consequences do not necessarily have to deal with lawsuits, however. Poor team communication generally leads to a decrease in the quality, quantity, and satisfaction of workplace interaction. A healthy team environment should aid business professionals in problem solving, innovative thinking, and effective conflict management. Also, it is important to remember that practically every job environment is going to require some type of team interaction. New professionals entering the workforce should be adequately prepared to thrive in a group setting.

Many college students make the mistake of picking a career under the assumption that it will not require them to interact with other people on a regular basis. In the communication age, however, you will almost certainly be expected to work well with others in a team environment. This chapter will identify the needs and functions of communication in a team setting and will show what benefits can be gained by working well in a group with your coworkers.

Have you had unpleasant group experiences? Are there times you'd prefer just to do the project yourself because it would be easier? Well, if you don't like working in groups, we have some bad news for you—working with others is part of every job, regardless of the field. If you want to excel in your field of interest, you need to learn how to work with others. The good news is that by using the KEYS process, you can turn your groups into innovative, functional teams. In this chapter, you'll be introduced to a variety of communication strategies that will help you lead this transformation.

Team communication is important for the following reasons: (1) Your ability to relate with other people in teams is central to achieving professional excellence, (2) team communication helps you form professional connections with coworkers and accomplish professional projects, and (3) your ability to work effectively in teams is a critical skill that will play an important role in your success as you *develop in the workplace*. Let's begin with a look at the important role of team communication at work.

## How Do Groups Differ From Teams?

Is there a difference between groups and teams? While executives and managers often use these terms interchangeably, their definitions do differ (Katzenbach & Smith, 1993; Kinlaw, 1991; West, 2012). For those seeking professional excellence, understanding this difference is essential. The small-group theorist Marvin Shaw (1981) states that a group is "two or more persons who are interacting with one another in such a manner that each person influences and is influenced by each other person" (p. 8). Central to this definition are the concepts of relationship, interaction, and influence.

If you go to see a blockbuster movie on opening night, you'll be part of an audience that you might refer to as a "group" of people. While you may call the audience a group, it would not fit our definition of a group since the moviegoers have no relationship, interaction, or influence on one another. For our purposes, a **group** is defined as three or more individuals who are working toward a common goal or share a common purpose. As a result of their common goal or purpose, they have relationships, interaction, and influence with one another.

Similar to groups, teams also have common goals and purposes. Further, like group members, team members have relationships, interaction, and influence with one another. The difference between groups and teams resides in the nature of those relationships and interactions (Levi, 2011; Myers & Anderson, 2008). A **team** is defined as a group in which members share leadership responsibility for creating a team identity, achieving mutually defined goals, and fostering innovative thinking (Lumsden & Lumsden, 1997; Moe, Dingsøyr, & Dybå, 2010). This definition highlights four key differences between groups and teams. First, unlike group members, team members share leadership responsibilities. There may be one team member who has a leadership title such as manager, vice president, or coach, but all team members demonstrate leadership when it comes to defining goals, making decisions, and implementing ideas. Second, team members share an identity. They refer to their team as "us" and "we," as opposed to "the group" or "them." Third, group members work toward common goals, while team members not only work toward common goals but also help define what those goals will be. Finally, teams strive for innovation. According to Katzenbach and Smith (1993), "A working group relies primarily on the individual contributions of its members for group performance, whereas a team strives for a magnified impact that is incremental to what its members could achieve in their individual roles" (p. 88).

Team communication exists in a variety of industries.

# Conducting Meetings

According to an old adage, groups outperform individuals, and teams outperform groups. If you wish to achieve professional excellence in the workplace, you must learn to transform your groups into teams. Effective communication is essential for this transformation.

Meetings are the central form of team communication (Boerner, Schäffner, & Gebert, 2012; Myers & Anderson, 2008). During meetings, leadership can be shared, goals and purposes can be defined, a team identity can be developed, and innovation can be fostered. The ability to effectively participate in and lead meetings is an important component of professional excellence and a key to transforming groups into teams. On the flipside, poorly run meetings are a major roadblock stopping many groups from ever becoming teams and many group members from achieving professional excellence.

In order for meetings to run effectively, there are a few basics that must always be considered. These basics include the meeting environment, the meeting topics, and the meeting participants.

Meetings can be stressful, especially when you have too many projects to keep up with. In our consulting practices, we have met numerous professionals frustrated with their time spent in meetings just thinking about the stacks of information waiting for them at the office.

# Know Yourself   Understanding Group Behavior

*The following quiz will help you gain a better understanding of your own behavior in groups. Answer each question thoughtfully, and then reflect on the results. How can this knowledge help you be a better communicator?*

Most students have many opportunities to develop their communication skills during class projects that require group work. The first step in developing your group into a team is to know yourself. Think about the last group project you completed for school. Take the following quiz and see how many times you have displayed behaviors that did not reflect a team attitude or professional excellence while working with that group. Place a check beside every violation you have committed.

_____ 1. Came to meeting without completing your assigned task

_____ 2. Made the following statement: "No one told me what I had to do" or "I was not sure what to do, so I didn't want to do it wrong"

_____ 3. Missed a meeting without giving your group members advance warning

_____ 4. Missed a group meeting and did not proactively find out what you needed to do for the next meeting

_____ 5. Participated in a meeting without an agenda

_____ 6. Gossiped about a fellow group member

_____ 7. Pushed your ideas forward without allowing others to express their ideas

_____ 8. Did not share a concern because you did not want to start a conflict or cause the meeting to last longer

_____ 9. Discussed a problem with the professor before discussing it with your group member(s)

_____ 10. Wasted others' time by coming to a meeting late and/or discussing issues that were not relevant to the project

_____ 11. Accepted the first okay solution, as opposed to working toward an innovative idea

How did you do? For true professional excellence, you should not have a single check. Throughout this chapter, we will discuss why each of these areas is important for excellence in team communication. If you did earn some checks above, what can you do to eliminate those behaviors in the future? Are there other behaviors that you believe should be listed above? What are those behaviors, and why do you consider them violations of excellence as a team member?

## Meeting Environment

Creating the proper meeting environment is a vital but often overlooked component of effective communication. What is a **meeting environment**? It includes both the time and place a meeting is held. The meeting environment is as much a part of the communication that occurs as the words that are said. Unfortunately, despite the importance of the meeting environment, most people spend little time thinking about it when they plan their meetings.

Currently, there are hundreds of shows and entire television networks dedicated to designing the perfect room or creating the perfect space. Why? The physical environment, from the color on the walls to the furniture to the lighting, has a major impact on us (Ivy & Wahl, 2009; Kupritz & Hillsman, 2011). Look around the room you are in right now. Why did you select this room for studying? How does this room make you feel? How does the room positively impact your studying? How does it negatively impact your studying? Now think about various places where you have attended meetings. How did those environments impact communication? Hopefully, you are beginning to see the importance of meeting environment (see Table 7.1).

If you wish to create an effective meeting environment, what factors should be considered? First, you must consider the time. Time of day, time of week, and time of year can all influence communication. For example, holding a meeting at 8:00 on a Monday morning, 4:30 on a Friday afternoon, or right after lunch may not be the best choice if you want your team members to be fully engaged and alert. Trying to implement a large-scale change is probably a bad idea during the busy holiday season in November and December, but it may be the perfect thing to do in January to kick off the new year. When selecting meeting times, be aware of differences in team members' schedules. If team members work different shifts with different days off, meeting times should be varied. For example, if half the team works from 7:00 a.m. to 3:00 p.m. and the other half from 3:00 p.m. to 11:00 p.m., holding every meeting at 9:00 a.m. would repeatedly inconvenience the same half of the team. When team members work varied schedules, there is no ideal time to meet. Yet alternating the meetings between shifts shows that all team members are valued and respected, which positively impacts communication interactions.

Location is also an important component in creating a positive meeting environment. In fact, you should consider the convenience, aesthetics, and comfort of the location. As far as convenience, Maelia learned the impact it can have on communication in a meeting. When Maelia began her job as the district supervisor, she held all the district meetings at 8:00 on Monday mornings in her office. Her intention was to start each week fresh by clearly communicating goals and priorities. Unfortunately, this was not

---

**Table 7.1  The Meeting Environment: Questions to Consider**

- Is the time convenient to those who will be attending?
- Has enough time been allotted to discuss all the topics?
- Are there too many topics?
- How long is the meeting? Will we need breaks?
- How long is the meeting? Will we need beverages and/or food?
- Are there audio–visual needs? Is the location equipped to meet the audio–visual needs?
- Does the furniture support conversations? Can everyone see one another easily?
- Is the furniture comfortable? Is there enough elbow room?
- Is the location convenient to those who will be attending?
- Does the location send any unintended messages? Is the location considered anyone's turf?
- Is the location aesthetically pleasing?
- Is this the best time and location available?

A meeting or seminar room, as shown in this photo, may seem like an ideal place to hold a meeting, but be aware of environmental factors such as lighting, temperature, and overall comfort.

the message Maelia sent; both the time and the location were inconvenient for the rest of the group. Most of the managers found themselves commuting to and from Maelia's office during rush-hour traffic. Furthermore, the managers felt they were needed in their stores first thing on Monday mornings, not at a meeting across town. The location and time of the district meetings indirectly sent the message that Maelia considered herself the most important person in the group and that she didn't care about her managers' schedules or duties. This message didn't support the notion of shared goals and shared leadership necessary for transforming groups into teams. In fact, it created a negative environment that hindered communication during the meetings. Fortunately, Maelia realized her mistake. When she moved the district meetings to Mondays at 2:00 p.m., she allowed her managers to have the time they needed in their stores on Monday mornings. She also varied the location from week to week, holding meetings at different stores throughout her district. By considering the time and location, she was able to improve the meeting environment and begin transforming her group into a team.

What is your impression of the meeting setup displayed in this photo?

When selecting a meeting location, you should also consider aesthetics and comfort. Many leaders get in the habit of holding all their meetings in the same room. For example, there is only one conference room in our building, so a lot of meetings are held there. The problem is that the conference room has an extremely long and narrow table. When sitting at the table, team members can't see one another, making it very difficult to hold discussions or brainstorming sessions. Further, the room is very dull and uninspired, with no windows and poor lighting. Fortunately, there is another room two floors down that has movable tables, excellent lighting, and a great view outside the window. Using this room does require proactive scheduling, a short elevator ride, and some furniture rearranging, but the aesthetics create an atmosphere that is more conducive to effective communication.

The length of the meeting should factor into your assessment of comfort. Pay close

## Step Back and Reflect     A Day at the Museum

I (Kelly Quintanilla, one of your coauthors) have taught many successful workshops to business professionals over the years, workshops in beautiful locations with enthusiastic participants. I also taught one workshop that appeared to be doomed to fail before it even began. The topic of this 6-hour workshop was conflict management. The group was a department whose members were currently engaged in a battle with one another. Literally, half the department was not speaking to the other half. Some of the best department members had put in for transfers. Productivity and customer service were suffering.

Knowing all this in advance, I had carefully selected a large room with comfortable chairs, round tables, and good lighting. I had planned for several breaks with food and drinks in an attempt to foster informal communication. The meeting environment was ideal. Unfortunately, an emergency water outage caused the workshop to be moved to a room in one of the local museums. The meeting was scheduled to begin at 8:00 a.m., but many people arrived late due to the last-minute change in location. Those who arrived on time became increasingly agitated as they waited. Part of their agitation stemmed from the fact that there was no coffee, no food, nothing. Despite several calls, the food order never made it to the new location. The only place to get a drink or snack was a small, extremely overpriced gift shop that did not open until 10:00 a.m. To make matters worse, the room had about 40 mounted animal heads hanging from the walls. The animal heads, most of which were in a growling pose, were very dusty, causing anyone with allergies to begin sneezing and sniffling. The final problem was the furniture. The chairs were the small, metal, folding kind. The tables were also small, and there were not enough of them; so the participants were crammed together. I could not imagine a worse meeting environment for any group, let alone a group already engaged in conflict. I needed to do something quickly.

### Step Back and Reflect

1. What went wrong?
2. What would you do if you were in my position?
3. Could you overcome the meeting environment?
4. Could the situation be used to your advantage somehow?
5. Should the workshop be called off and rescheduled?
6. How could I utilize the KEYS approach to improve this communication interaction?

attention to the furniture. Make certain that the chairs are comfortable and that team members have enough elbow room. If you cram your team members into a small space with uncomfortable furniture for any length of time, it will be difficult for them to remain productive.

Keep in mind that comfort extends beyond furniture. For longer meetings, you should consider taking short breaks, allowing people to stretch, visit the restrooms, and refresh their perspective. If your budget allows for it, consider providing food and beverages in meetings.

In the end, you may not always have the ability to change the time or location of your meetings. Regardless, considering both time and location for every meeting is part of professional excellence.

## Meeting Topics (Agenda)

One essential component to any well-run meeting is an agenda. An **agenda** is a guide or an overview of the topics that will be covered during the meeting. An agenda can be simple or complex. Either way, an agenda is a useful channel for informing team members about meeting topics and, if used properly, can serve as a communication tool for facilitating meetings (see Table 7.2).

Agendas should be distributed several days in advance of the meeting. This will allow team members to comment on the agenda items and give the leader time to revise the agenda if necessary. It will also allow team members time to think about issues in advance of the meeting. If you'd like the group to brainstorm ideas or share information, the agenda is a valuable preparation tool for team members.

Noting the allotted time for each topic also helps the leader determine which topics and how many can be covered in any given meeting. Leaders with professional excellence prioritize agenda items. Items should be prioritized based on importance and urgency. Items that require extensive discussion time should be handled as a separate meeting or series of meetings dedicated solely to that topic area. If a leader is truly seeking the input of team members, then he or she should not try to force too many items into one meeting.

### Table 7.2 Agenda Format

**Heading:** Should include date, time, and location. May include a list of participants.

I. **Welcome/opening**
   The leader should always orient the team and focus the meeting during the opening.

II. **Approve minutes from the previous meeting**
   Minutes are a written record of the meeting.

III. **Specific points to be discussed**
   The majority of the agenda will be a list of the specific items that will be covered during the meeting. Beside each item, state who will lead the discussion and/or report on this item. It is also wise to include the estimated time it should take to cover each item.

IV. **Old business**
   Allow time for the team to discuss items from previous meetings that may still be unresolved.

V. **New business**
   Allow time for the team to discuss any new items that may have come up after the agenda was finalized or during the meeting itself.

VI. **Arrangement of the next meeting**
   Summarize any assignments that must be completed by the next meeting. Also make certain to discuss the time and location of the next meeting.

VII. **Closing**
   Always provide some sort of closing statement.

## Ethical Connection    Overtalking vs. Undertalking

*Please read the passage below, and answer the questions that follow.*

Team leaders can also use an agenda as a tool for facilitating communication during meetings. Let's say one member of your team, Parker, tends to dominate conversations, occasionally leading the discussion on irrelevant tangents. Parker is an **overtalker**. Another member of your team, Alyssa, tends to sit silently during meetings, failing to participate or give input. Alyssa is an **undertalker**. The few times Alyssa has tried to communicate during meetings, she is constantly cut off by Parker, who often moves the conversation in a different tangent. During several of your one-on-one sessions with Alyssa, you have noticed that she is very insightful and has many great ideas to help out the company. While Parker is motivated and eager to participate in meetings, you notice he has a hard time focusing on one topic at a time. In order to keep your meetings moving effectively and professionally, you must find a way to curtail Parker's speeches while not cutting him off entirely. Also, you need to encourage Alyssa to interact more and to have the confidence to state her ideas to the entire staff.

### Questions to Consider

1. What are the ethical issues with allowing one person to dominate or one person not to participate in a team or staff meeting?
2. How could you limit Parker's speaking without making him feel as though he is being cut off?
3. What methods or communication could you use to encourage Alyssa to be more active in team meetings?
4. Using the KEYS approach, how could both Alyssa and Parker strengthen their team communication skills?

## Meeting Participants

When it comes to planning meetings, you should ask yourself two important questions. First, who should be at this meeting? Determining the participants in a meeting should not be based on office politics. Leaders with professional excellence avoid the trap of inviting a representative of each department to be politically correct. Invite people who can contribute to the purpose of the meeting. Take time to assess the meeting's purpose, and then determine who can best serve that purpose. Second, can all key members attend this meeting at this time? If key team members can't be present, the meeting should be rescheduled. For example, you should not hold a meeting about budgetary issues if the CFO (chief financial officer) can't attend. You'll waste the time of everyone who does attend, and the team will still need to meet again with the CFO.

Failing to consider meeting environment, meeting topics, and meeting participants hinders the chances for a successful meeting, but covering the basics does not, in and of itself, guarantee success. For meetings that will transform groups into teams, all members must share leadership, develop positive problem-solving strategies, participate in productive conflict, and strive for innovation. Let's take a moment to explore each of these important elements.

# Team Roles

As you learned earlier in this chapter, teams require members to share leadership. How do team members share leadership? What is the role of the designated leader if all members are sharing his or her duties?

There are many designated leadership titles (e.g., director, manager, supervisor, vice president, president, queen). Regardless of your title, if you're the designated leader, think of yourself as a **coach**. A coach has a very distinct role in meetings. Remember, a coach does not play the game. The coach must remain on the sidelines. The coach doesn't have to be an expert on everything, have all the answers, or do all the talking. However, the coach does need to call the meetings, set the agenda, and then facilitate the discussion. A coach facilitates the discussion by supporting positive team roles and norms while eliminating self-centered roles and unproductive norms.

Within every team, members can play a host of possible roles. Some of these roles are functional roles that help the team achieve goals or maintain positive relationships among members (see Table 7.3). These roles are known as **task roles** and **relationship roles**, respectively. Unfortunately, there are also many dysfunctional roles that can interfere with the positive functioning of the team. These roles are known as **self-centered roles**. In order for a group to become a team, all team members must actively engage in the functional roles while working to limit the dysfunctional roles.

As a coach utilizing the KEYS approach, you should *know* the skills and strengths you bring to the team and *evaluate* the skills and strengths of your team members. After *your communication interaction occurs,* coaches must *step back and reflect* to determine if all the functional roles are being covered. If not, redesign the agenda or add team members who will cover the gaps. For example, if no one is giving his or her opinion, the coach might add an agenda item that calls for everyone to provide input on a topic. If the group lacks a harmonizer, the coach may add a new member to the team who is skilled at handling conflict. You should never hesitate to talk about the way the team is interacting. It's a sign of professional excellence to address weaknesses head-on. So if you're the coach, make certain your team is aware of the various tasks and relationship roles. Make it a habit to discuss the team's strengths and weaknesses. Make it a habit to step back and reflect on the communication as individuals and as a team. And when the team notes dysfunctional roles, be prepared to address those behaviors directly. (We discuss dealing with difficult people in more detail in Chapter 10.)

**K**now Yourself

**E**valuate the Professional Context

**Y**our Communication Interaction Occurs

**S**tep Back and Reflect

# Team Norms

When you attend class, you probably sit in the same desk every time. Why? You don't own the desk; it's not yours. Still, if someone else sat in the desk, it would bother you, right? You might even ask that person to move. There's no written rule, no seating chart stating that this is your desk—it's simply a norm.

## Table 7.3 Team Roles

**Task roles**: Roles that help the team carry out tasks and get the work done

| | |
|---|---|
| Initiator | Proposes solutions; suggests ideas; introduces new approaches to problem solving |
| Information giver | Offers facts or generalizations; relates one's own experience to the problems to illustrate points |
| Information seeker | Asks for clarification of suggestions; requests additional information or facts |
| Opinion giver | States an opinion or belief concerning a problem and suggests solutions to that problem |
| Opinion seeker | Looks for an expression of feelings from group members; seeks clarification of values, suggestions, or ideas |
| Coordinator | Shows relationships among various ideas or suggestions; tries to pull ideas and suggestions together |
| Procedural developer | Takes notes; records ideas; distributes materials; guides group through the agenda |
| Summarizer/evaluator | Restates ideas and describes relationships; details agreements and differences |

**Relationship roles**: Roles that strengthen or maintain team relationships

| | |
|---|---|
| Supporter | Expresses togetherness; encourages others; gives praise; suggests solidarity |
| Harmonizer | Mediates and reconciles differences; suggests areas of agreement between disagreeing members; suggests positive ways to explore difference |
| Gatekeeper | Asks opinions of members who are not participating; prevents dominance by others; facilitates overall interaction |

**Self-centered roles**: Roles that interfere with the team's ability to complete tasks

| | |
|---|---|
| Blocker | Gives negative responses to most ideas; is negative about any positive solutions; raises continuous objections |
| Dominator | Controls through interruptions; superiority of tone and length of conversation control |
| Attacker | Aggressive to achieve personal status; expresses disapproval; critical of status of others |
| Clown | Disrupts with jokes and other diverting behavior; brings up tangents; refuses to take ideas seriously |

Source: Adapted from Benne and Sheats (1948).

Smartphones, cell phones, and other electronic devices can serve as major distractions during meetings. What is your view of the use of technology in the classroom or other professional settings?

What's a norm? A **norm** is an unwritten rule of behavior. While norms are unwritten, they are as powerful (if not more) as the written rules. Think about the organizations for which you have worked. Do they have an employee handbook or a policy book? Ever taken the time to read a handbook? Many employees fail to take the time to learn the written rules. Instead, they follow the unwritten rules or norms they see other people enacting in the workplace.

Our point is this—if you want to function with professional excellence, you should read your employee handbook! You should know the written rules and expectations. (We also recommend you spend some time familiarizing yourself with your student handbooks.) Knowing both the written and unwritten rules is important for communicating with professional excellence. At times, these written and unwritten rules will complement each other and lend themselves to norms that are productive for your team. At other times, the written and unwritten rules can contradict each other, resulting in negative consequences for both you and the team.

Let's look at Lina for an example. In Lina's office, the written rule related to cell phones was very clear: "No use of personal cell phones during company time." Yet the norm was for employees to take personal calls all day long. Further, employees would leave meetings to answer their cell phones and/or send text messages during the middle of group discussions. This was clearly a negative norm.

All groups have both positive and negative norms. The important thing is to step back and reflect on the norms and assess how various norms are affecting your group. Your objective is to turn your group into a team by eliminating the negative norms and building on the positive norms.

But how do you eliminate negative norms? You have to address them. You can't ignore them and just expect them to fix themselves. To achieve professional excellence, you must be willing to say, "Here is something that is going wrong; let's find a way to correct the problem as a team." It's equally important to recognize the positive norms. When a norm is contributing to the success of the team, it should be acknowledged and actively supported by the team.

# Problem Solving

In the opening section of this chapter, we introduced you to the definition of a team. If you recall, a team is defined as a group in which members share leadership responsibility,

## Your Communication Interaction    The Cussing Jar

*Read the following passage about Tyrone and Company B, and answer the questions that follow.*

Company B is a large retail department store. Every Monday morning, the managerial team of Company B assembles to go over the goals and challenges for the upcoming week. The managers are a diverse group representing multiple sales departments, human resources, advertising, accounting, maintenance, and shipping/warehouse. Overall, these managers have proven to be excellent problem solvers and possess a good rapport with one another. But there are some problems. Although all the managers are effective in their various departments, the norms across departments vary. For example, the shipping and warehouse managers work in the back storeroom, dealing with truckers as opposed to customers. Amongst this group, swearing is a common, acceptable practice. It is a norm. However, this communication style is deemed offensive by some of the managers from other departments.

Tyrone Jackson, the general manager, leads the Monday morning meetings, and he has noticed this negative norm. To solve this problem, he addresses the norm directly. The following Monday, he states, "In our past few meetings, I have noticed that we have gotten into a bad habit of swearing during our Monday morning meetings. Given the nature of these meetings, they need to have a more professional tone, so we need to watch our language. However, I realize this is a norm and it may be hard to break. Any ideas on how we can make this change?" The group began to toss out ideas, and in the end, they agreed to use a cussing jar. Each word was assigned a dollar amount—$5 for this cuss word, $1 for that cuss word, and so on. Whenever anyone cussed, he or she had to put money in the jar, and the money would then be used to pay for lunch.

The first day, everyone was careful and $22 ended up in the cussing jar. The next week, some of the managers fell back into the negative norm and $87 ended up in the cussing jar. The entire group, even the managers who had to put the most money in the jar, had fun trying to break this bad habit. They had collectively come up with the idea of the jar, and they all supported its use. From that week forward, the amount in the jar steadily decreased, and the team was able to change this negative norm collectively.

### Questions to Consider

1. What role did Tyrone Jackson play in facilitating this change?
2. Do you agree with his approach?
3. What problems could result from this approach?
4. Have you ever been part of a group that was trying to change a negative norm?
5. Was your group successful? Why or why not?
6. How was the KEYS approach utilized in this situation?

create a team identity, engage in problem solving, foster innovative thinking, and achieve mutually defined goals.

To achieve mutually defined goals, teams engage in problem solving. *Problem solving* and *decision making* are not interchangeable terms. Decision making is actually a step in the problem-solving process. According to Dennis Gouran (1982/1990), a leading scholar in group communication, **decision making** is "the act of choosing among a set of alternatives under conditions that necessitate choice" (p. 3). **Problem solving** involves not only making a choice but also coming up with quality alternatives from which to select and then working to implement the choice your team selects.

How can you ensure that your team generates innovative alternatives and/or successfully implements its choice? Begin by understanding all the steps in the problem-solving process. At some point in your academic career, you probably learned John Dewey's **Reflective Thinking Process** or some other problem-solving model based on his process. According to Dewey (1910), five steps make up problem solving. These steps include

1. describing and analyzing the problem,

2. generating possible solutions,

3. evaluating all solutions,

4. deciding on the solution, and

5. planning how to implement the solution.

Within each step, you have the opportunity to excel or struggle. Let's examine each of the steps to see how effective communication can help team members achieve professional excellence.

## Describing and Analyzing the Problem

It seems only logical that the first step in problem solving is to describe and analyze the problem. After all, how can you solve a problem if you do not know what the problem is? Alas, this vital step is often shortchanged or skipped altogether. The reason for this mistake is simple. There is an assumption that "we already know what the problem is." The leader has defined the problem in his or her own mind, so he or she may feel that the group's time would be better spent discussing solutions. Group members are comfortable with skipping this step because they, too, have defined the problem in their minds. Unfortunately, the group leader and various group members, in all likelihood, do not share the same definition. Based on their individual experiences and perceptions, they probably have a different take on the nature of the problem or unsatisfactory state. By failing to understand the problem from all sides, a group limits its chances of generating a solution that will truly correct all facets of the problem.

Teams take time to discuss the problem. Team members share their own insights and experiences. In addition, they actively seek and share feedback from other employees and relevant parties who are not part of the team. When determining meeting participants, careful consideration is given to the makeup of the team in an attempt to include diverse perceptions of a problem. When analyzing a problem, group members must look at the current conditions realistically to determine the nature, extent, and probable cause(s) of the problem (Choy & Oo, 2012; Gouran & Hirokawa, 1996; Kauffeld & Lehmann-Willenbrock, 2011). Further, failure to recognize potential threats or clearly understand the situation can result in poor decisions.

## Generating Possible Solutions

Once a problem is clearly understood, team members can begin generating possible solutions. Avoid tossing around a few ideas; find one that is satisfactory, and then move on to the next step. Do not stop with an okay solution. Teams seek innovative solutions that address all facets of a problem.

For better or for worse, your formal education has trained you to look for the "right answer" (Von Oech, 1983). One consequence of taking thousands of multiple-choice exams in your lifetime is that you have become skilled at marking the right answer and then moving to the next question. This skill is useful when demonstrating your knowledge of a given subject area, but it's not very useful when trying to think critically and develop innovative solutions. There's an old proverb that states, "There are seven right answers to every question." Teams subscribe to the wisdom of this proverb.

Fortunately, there are many tools that can aid your team in generating possible solutions. Those tools include brainstorming, nominal group technique, idea writing, role playing, and sensing. See Table 7.4 for a detailed description of each tool. (We will continue our discussion of innovative problem solving later in this chapter.)

### Table 7.4 Tools for Innovation

| | |
|---|---|
| Brainstorming | A technique for generating many ideas quickly. The goal is quantity, not quality; so all ideas should be expressed and written down. No ideas should be criticized or praised. Members are not permitted to speak for longer than 10 seconds at a time— no long explanations. Ideas will be evaluated and elaborated on at a later point in the problem-solving process. |
| Nominal group technique | A type of brainstorming designed to incorporate all team members. Rather than having team members yell out their ideas, nominal group technique has members brainstorm independently, writing down their ideas on a piece of paper. After a set amount of time has passed, members stop writing and read what they have written. All the ideas are then recorded on a chalkboard or somewhere the entire group can view them. |
| Idea writing | This technique combines brainstorming and the nominal group technique. Under this technique, team members begin brainstorming and write their first idea down on the top of a piece of paper. Each member then passes his or her paper to the right, reads the idea on the paper, and then adds another idea. This process continues until the paper is full. All the ideas are then read aloud and displayed for the group to see. |
| Role playing | A technique used to increase team members' understanding of various points of view. A team member will put himself or herself in the place of someone else. It may be another group member or someone not present at the meeting, such as the customer. The team member will then try to answer questions about the problem from the point of view of the person he or she is playing. |

## Evaluating All Solutions

Once possible solutions have been generated, the team must begin the process of evaluating the merit of each solution based on criteria. **Criteria** refers to the standards used to make a decision. For example, if your company was developing a new advertising campaign, the criteria might include that it must reflect the company's current image, be easy to remember, have a positive feel, reach the target audience, be in place within 6 months, and not cost more than $10,000 to implement. Your criteria should always include budgetary considerations and deadlines. Your team may come up with a highly innovative solution, but if you can't afford to implement it or if it can't be implemented by a preset deadline, then that solution is not the right choice.

How do you evaluate solutions? Teams develop a systematic process for evaluation. Just as there are tools to help generate possible solutions, there are also tools to help teams evaluate solutions. These tools include keep/scratch, T-chart, decision matrix, and value rating. See Table 7.5 for a detailed description of each.

If the leader is actively facilitating discussion and if the team members are actively engaged, a thorough evaluation of solutions will be a natural function of the team. All teams should routinely test and question the quality of information used as the basis for both the problem analysis and the possible solutions. In addition, teams should routinely question their assumptions and biases.

### Table 7.5  Tools for Evaluation

| | |
|---|---|
| Keep/scratch | A technique for limiting the number of alternatives the team will discuss in detail. Display all the alternatives so all team members can see them. Have the leader read each alternative. If a member of the team wishes an alternative to be considered further, he or she will yell "keep." If no one yells "keep," the leader will cross out or scratch the alternative. No one should ever yell "scratch." |
| Value rating | A technique for reducing the number of alternatives the team will discuss in detail. Team members are given a set number of points (or stickers). Each member distributes his or her points to the alternatives he or she would most like to discuss. If each team member has 10 points, he or she may give 5 points to Alternative A, 3 points to Alternative C, and 2 points to Alternative F. The alternatives that receive few or no points will be cut before the discussion begins. |
| T-chart | A visual representation of the pros and cons of each alternative. Team members draw a T, large enough for everyone to view easily. One side of the T is labeled "Pros," and the other side is labeled "Cons." The team then brainstorms the pros and cons of the alternative in question, recording their comments on the chart. The pros and cons are rated in accordance with the criteria. |
| Decision matrix | A decision matrix is similar to a T-chart. It is a visual representation of the merits of various plans. It allows team members to compare various alternatives easily. The merits are rated in accordance with the criteria. |

### Table 7.6 Questions to Guide the Evaluation

- Do we have enough information?
- Do we understand the information we have?
- Are we missing any information? Are any areas not covered by the information we have?
- Are our sources reliable, credible, and appropriate?
- Are the criteria appropriate given our objectives and constraints?
- Did we generate a variety of innovative alternatives?
- Did we limit our alternatives?
- Did we apply the criteria to each alternative fairly and appropriately?
- Did the team agree on the mode of decision making?

Source: Gouran (1982/1990).

If this type of critical evaluation is not occurring naturally, one or more team members should be assigned to the role of **devil's advocate**. The devil's advocate has the task of making sure dissenting points of view are discussed. The questions provided in Table 7.6 can help guide the team through this evaluation process.

## Deciding on the Solution

Once the merit of all the solutions has been thoroughly evaluated and discussed, it's time to make a decision. This decision will become the goal or desired state that the team will then work toward. There are four approaches to decision making available to the team. These approaches include decision by the leader, voting, compromise, and consensus.

Team communication is the foundation of negotiation and problem solving seen across industries.

### Decision by Leader

When the **decision by the leader** approach is used, members are not truly functioning as a team. The role of the members is to recommend or advise the leader. The leader then makes the ultimate decision. As a result, the goal is not mutually defined. In some instances, this approach may be the best way to make a decision. For example, if an emergency room team needs to make a quick decision about an unfamiliar medical situation, the physician in charge may ask the advice of colleagues and/or medical staff. Yet, due to the need for a quick decision, the physician will ultimately determine the course of action. Although this approach has benefits in pressure situations, it's not the preferred approach for building teams.

### Majority Rule

The concept of **voting** is another way to reach a decision. With this approach, team members cast a vote for the solution they find most meritorious. The solution that receives the most votes is implemented. There are some obvious advantages to voting. First, all team members have equal input in the decision. Next, it is an easy process that often requires little more than raised hands or slips of paper for casting votes. Finally, it requires little time in comparison with the compromise or consensus approaches. However, voting as a decision-making approach also comes with some disadvantages. Because it is quick and easy, voting is often used to speed up the decision-making process and avoid any lengthy discussions or conflict. Conflict, as we will discuss later in this chapter, is a valuable, needed resource in innovative problem solving and team building. Limiting this process can result in quick decisions that lack innovation and cause division. Voting is a win–lose approach to decision making. Unfortunately, not everyone makes a good loser—or a good winner, for that matter—so voting can divide the group and stop it from becoming a team.

### Compromise

Team members approaching decision making with a "let's compromise" attitude is a positive thing, right? After all, compromise is a win–win approach, isn't it? Actually, **compromise** is a lose–lose approach to decision making. Although it is a commonly held belief that compromise is a good thing, compromise can limit innovation. With compromise, all parties are willing to give something up in order to gain something they want; so the goal becomes narrowing options, not developing innovative ideas. Jake and Marilyn used the compromise approach on their last date. Jake wanted to eat ribs and see an action movie. Marilyn wanted sushi and a romantic comedy. So they compromised and spent their evening eating ribs, which made Marilyn miserable, and watching a movie that Jake hated. Both parties were unhappy for half the evening; it was a lose–lose situation. If they had searched for some additional options, they would have discovered that pizza and bowling would have made them both happy for the entire evening.

### Consensus

The final approach to decision making is consensus. **Consensus** occurs when a solution or agreement that all team members can support is reached. This does not mean that the final solution is one that all team members prefer; rather, it means that the solution has the support of all team members. In an ideal world, team members might be able to come up with an idea that everyone loves and thinks is the best way to go, but most times that doesn't occur. Thus, finding a solution that everyone supports has many positive benefits. This support results in a stronger commitment to implementing the solution and strengthens the relationship between team members. Further, working through the consensus process lends itself to innovative decision making.

So why aren't all decisions made using consensus? Because consensus is time-consuming. Many leaders and/or groups do not see the value in spending time working through the consensus process. Although consensus is more time-consuming as a decision-making approach, decisions reached using consensus can often be implemented quickly because they have the support of all members. As a result, consensus may be less time-consuming than voting or compromise, especially when the process is looked at from beginning to end. It certainly is the most likely to result in mutually defined goals.

## Evaluate the Professional Context    Winter Carnival in Snowy Mountain

*Read the passage below, and then answer the questions. As you read, think about ways the KEYS approach could help you improve* **your communication interaction** *if you were in Sasha's position.*

The Snowy Mountain Tourist Department was tasked with developing some new promotional events to attract skiers during the upcoming season. Over the years, this resort community had been steadily losing business to other ski destinations. Sasha Adams, the department manager, was willing to admit that her ideas were just not competitive, so she turned the task over to her department.

Sasha was thrilled to learn that her department generated three creative ideas. The problem was that supporters of each idea felt very strongly that their idea was the best, and they could not narrow it down to one event. Sasha honored her commitment to allow the group to make the decision, so she had department members vote. Three votes went to a winter comedy festival, three votes went to a winter sports event, and four votes went to a winter carnival.

Sasha had high hopes that the winter carnival would increase tourism, but it decreased department morale instead. The four members who had voted for the carnival were very involved, but more than four people were needed to run the event. In the end, it was not a success. The other six members felt that their events would have achieved much better results. Were they right?

### Questions to Consider

1. What went wrong?
2. Was majority rule the best way to make this decision? Why or why not?
3. How would you have handled the decision-making process?
4. Could the KEYS approach have helped Sasha? If so, in what way?

## Planning How to Implement the Solution

Once the solution is reached, it must be implemented. Walking away from the table with a great solution is not a success if that solution never comes to fruition. Teams make certain their solutions are implemented by developing a thorough, detailed plan. When implementing a solution, all facets of the implementation must be accounted for in both a timeline and a budget. In addition, a **lead**—the person who's accountable for a given task—must be designated. Designating leads is an excellent opportunity to share leadership. The team member with the leadership title should not be the lead in all facets of the implementation plan. Rather, leads should be selected based on their areas of expertise and their passion for various parts of the plan. In order to ensure a thorough plan, your team should address all the questions found in Table 7.7.

> **Table 7.7  Implementing Your Plan**
>
> - State the objective clearly and concisely.
> - List the major steps that must be completed in order to accomplish the objective.
> - Prioritize the steps. What are the most critical elements? Which are less critical? What can you do now? What will you need additional resources for?
> - Under each major step, list all the tasks (substeps) that must be completed in order to accomplish the step in question.
> - Place all the steps and tasks on a timeline. Focus on the sequence in which steps and tasks must be completed. Adjust the timeline accordingly.
> - Estimate the cost of each step and begin to develop a budget. Revisit the budget often.
> - Assign a lead for each step. Multiple leads may be needed for some steps—different leads for different tasks.
> - Anticipate obstacles. What obstacles stand in the way of success? How will your team deal with these obstacles?

# Cultivating Innovative Thinking

While groups conduct problem-solving meetings with little thought of innovative solutions, teams structure their meetings and facilitate the problem-solving process in such a way that innovation is stimulated. After all, teams, by their very definition, must foster innovative thinking.

One way to foster innovation in team problem solving is to incorporate Von Oech's (1986) explorer, artist, judge, and warrior into the process. Incorporating Von Oech's cast of characters doesn't require team members to dress up in costumes and run around acting like explorers or warriors. Rather, the skills and tools displayed by explorers, artists, judges, and warriors are meant to highlight or reinforce the skills and tools essential to creative problem solving. Let's examine each character to better understand its role in cultivating innovative thinking.

## Explorer

When analyzing a problem and preparing to generate solutions, team members should act as explorers. **Explorers** seek out new information in uncharted lands. As explorers, team members follow their curiosity, create a map, leave their own turf, and look for a lot of ideas and information (Von Oech, 1986). A team in the explorer mode might ask, "What's the problem?" or "Why aren't we the leader in sales?" or "How can we do it better?" Then, team members are given the task and the time to seek new information that addresses the question(s). This task turns into a map of sorts, as it provides team members with a general guideline to follow when searching. The interesting thing is, once this map is in your mind, you will begin to see relevant information everywhere. If you have your doubts, think about the last time you purchased a car—did you suddenly start seeing similar cars (color and type) everywhere you went? Were they there before? Of course they were, but they were not on your map, so they blended into the background scenery. As long as you have your map, leaving your turf can become a rewarding adventure. For example, the famous football coach Knute Rockne discovered his "four horsemen defense" while watching a chorus-line dance, and Picasso's art was the inspiration for World War I military camouflage (Von Oech, 1986). Looking both inside and outside your field and your type of business/ industry for information and insight is what will make your team innovative. In fact, one distinct advantage of team members with diverse backgrounds is that they bring different perspectives into the team. Put simply, send the team out to explore and make certain they come back with lots of information that can be molded into innovative solutions during the artist phase.

## Artist

As the team begins to generate solutions, members move from the role of explorer to the role of artist. The **artist** puts ideas together in new ways. When you hear the word *artist*, what images come to mind? Do you see a painter, a sculptor, or someone who's handy with a hot-glue gun? That's certainly one way to look at an artist, but in reality an artist includes those images and so many more. Someone who puts ideas together in a new way is an artist. You may not be able to paint or sing, but if you can develop a chart or a schedule, you, too, are an artist. Earlier in this chapter, we discussed some tools useful to the artist (see Table 7.4). Three additional tools your team can utilize to enhance the artist are asking "what if" questions, connecting concepts, and incubating (Von Oech, 1986).

Two small words—"what if"—are essential to finding innovative solutions. For example, a team of hospital administrators were determined to improve patient satisfaction scores. During the explorer phase, they examined successful hospitals and medical arenas for information. In addition, they left their turf and explored other places where people stay overnight, such as hotels. In the artist phase, they asked themselves "what if" questions, such as, "What if we were a five-star hotel?" By connecting hotels and hospitals, they gained a new perspective on the problem. They began to offer free valet parking at the emergency room, and they added a staff position—patient and family liaison—that functioned much like a concierge in a hotel. Not surprisingly, patient satisfaction scores went up.

Just as explorers need time to explore, artists need time to incubate. When do you have your most inspired ideas? Is it during a meeting within moments after a problem has been thrown on the table? Or does your inspiration come to you in the shower or after a good night's sleep? Maybe your creative ideas come when you're on the treadmill, sweating away your stress or singing along with your iPod? Truth be told, we have yet to meet a single person who can achieve creative inspiration on command. We certainly can't. If you want innovative solutions, your team needs time to explore resources and discover information. Then they need time to allow that information to germinate in their minds and grow into something that is more than just okay or so-so.

## Judge

Once a team has developed lots of innovative ideas, it moves into the **judge** mode as team members evaluate the possible solutions and then select one solution for implementation. Judges begin with the question, "Are we meeting our objective?" Then, they systematically examine the positives and negatives of each solution and render the decision (Von Oech, 1986).

## Warrior

Innovative problem solving does not end with the judge mode. Warriors are needed to make certain that the plan is successfully implemented. The role of the **warrior** is to develop and carry out the plan. We have already discussed how to develop a thorough plan and the importance of leads who will act as warriors overseeing and/or carrying out various parts of the plan. Yet warriors must do more than that. Ask yourself, "Why did Von Oech select a warrior to represent the skills needed in this phase of innovative problem solving?" First, all plans will hit obstacles and roadblocks. As a result, team members must be strong and ready to overcome inevitable difficulties. Furthermore, innovative ideas are more likely to be criticized and attacked because they are different. When your team moves forward with a plan that is outside the box, others may want to stuff it back in the box. Therefore, team members must act like warriors, carrying out the plan with persistence (see Table 7.8).

---

**Table 7.8  Quotations for Warriors**

"Always bear in mind that your own resolution to success is more important than any other one thing." —*Abraham Lincoln*

"We are all failures—at least the best of us are." —*James M. Barrie*

"I didn't fail 3,000 times; I documented 3,000 ways not to make a light bulb." —*Thomas Edison*

"Try not. Do or do not. There is no try." —*Yoda*

"Failure is not falling down but refusing to get back up." —*Chinese proverb*

"Only those who dare to fail greatly can ever achieve greatly." —*Robert F. Kennedy*

---

## Supporting Each Role

As you reviewed the skills and qualities of each role, you may have noticed that you are stronger in some roles than in others (this is normal). Some of us are natural artists, while others are outstanding warriors. The benefit of working in a team is that you don't have to be strong in every area to ensure innovative solutions. To ensure innovation, teams must have at least one member who is strong in each area and share leadership to maximize those strengths. In addition, meetings should be structured to support each phase of the innovative problem-solving process. For example, begin exploring the problem at your first meeting. Then send every member of the team out to explore the problem further and collect information that might aid in finding solutions. Dedicate at least one meeting, more if time allows, to the artist. Allow team members time to brainstorm, ask "what if" questions, and so on. Develop criteria and a clear process for assessing solutions during the judge phase. And finally, as a warrior, develop a clear plan and work as a team to overcome roadblocks, obstacles, and setbacks. Being innovative is not easy, but it's a central component to functioning as a team and achieving professional excellence. In the 21st century, innovation is no longer an option; it's a necessity.

# Conflict in Team Meetings

When was the last time you thought to yourself, "I have a meeting today. I hope it's full of conflict"? Chances are you've never had those thoughts. In fact, you may have thought the exact opposite on occasion: "I hope my meeting today has no conflict." Believe it or not, lack of conflict isn't a good thing. Lack of conflict is a strong sign that your group has some serious problems, will not develop innovative ideas, and will never reach "team" status. The whole purpose for having meetings is to get different people together to share a variety of ideas and develop innovative solutions to problems. If this is to occur, then conflict must occur, too.

The problem for most of us is that the word **conflict** has a negative connotation. So let's use a different word. If you replace the word *conflict* with something such as *discussion* or *sharing of ideas*, then the phrase sounds more appealing: "I hope my meeting today is full of discussion and sharing of ideas." To better understand the need for conflict in meetings and strategies for facilitating productive conflict, let's explore each area in more detail.

## Need for Conflict

As groups develop into teams, some naïve leaders think that a positive byproduct of this transformation will be a lack of conflict—nothing could be further from the truth. If you're part of a group that is not experiencing conflict, chances are you're part of either a groupthink or a meetingthink situation.

### Groupthink

**Groupthink** is the tendency of highly cohesive groups to suspend critical thinking and make faulty decisions (Janis, 1982, 1989; Shirey, 2012). You may recall from history class that in 1961, President John F. Kennedy supported a group of Cuban exiles who returned to Cuba in an attempt to overthrow the communist government headed by Fidel Castro. Instead of claiming a quick and easy victory as Kennedy and

Some people are difficult to work with and play the role of Mr. Shouty—especially when they have emotional outbursts and bully other people in meetings.

his advisors had planned, the mission failed. The scholar Irving Janis studied the incident, known as the Bay of Pigs, and concluded that the defeat was a result of groupthink.

***Causes of Groupthink.*** For groupthink to occur, several conditions must exist. First, the group must be highly cohesive. Not all highly cohesive groups suffer from group-think; however, if highly cohesive groups are combined with other elements, the chances of groupthink increase. For example, if the group functions in isolation, is very homo-geneous, lacks norms for critically analyzing information and/or is dealing with high-stress threats, groupthink is more likely to occur. In addition, these groups are often headed by a charismatic, directive leader. Because of the strong desire to maintain the cohesiveness with leader and group, group members begin to self-censor. No one in the group wants to be the voice of dissent, so members remain silent even though they have doubts or concerns. If a group member does voice disagreement, "mind guards" jump in and silence the dissent until the dissenting member begins self-censoring. (Just as bodyguards protect the group from physical harm, mind guards protect the group from conflict and dissen-tion.) Since these groups often function in isolation, they do not receive feedback from the outside. In the end, it appears as if everyone agrees, assumptions go unchallenged, and faulty decisions are made.

***Avoiding Groupthink.*** The way to avoid groupthink is to introduce conflict systemati-cally. Norms should be developed for seeking additional information, testing assumptions, and incorporating the role of devil's advocate. Having the larger group divide into sub-groups when brainstorming and/or having the leader withhold his or her thoughts are additional strategies used to reduce groupthink.

### Meetingthink

As consultants, we both have seen the byproduct of groupthink occur in many different organizations—not groupthink itself but the byproduct of groupthink, which is the suspen-sion of critical thinking that results in faulty decisions. The groups we have observed are not highly cohesive, don't have charismatic leaders, and don't function in isolation. Yet their members still make faulty decisions due to a lack of critical thinking. We refer to this phenomenon as meetingthink. **Meetingthink** has the same outcome as groupthink, but it doesn't require the same inputs. It's the suspension of critical thinking due to more com-mon variables, such as false empowerment, overload, or poorly run meetings.

***False Empowerment.*** **False empowerment** occurs when a leader acts as if he or she plans to involve the group in the decision-making process when, in reality, the leader is going to make the decision regardless of the input received from the group. At first, group members believe they are empowered to make a decision, but in the end this proves to be false. Over time, group members learn that their opinions, ideas, and thoughts are not valued, so they remain silent during meetings. As a result, critical thinking is suspended.

***Overload.*** **Overload** occurs when group members have so much on their plates that they cannot truly concentrate on and engage in the meeting at hand. While the meeting is occurring, group members are thinking about the 10 other items they have to do that day at work, as well as the list of things they must take care of when they leave work. Being over-loaded may also cause members to come to meetings without preparing. Because mem-bers fail to read the report in advance of the meeting, they may be unable to take part in the discussion. Overloaded group members also withhold valuable input because they fear it will somehow lead to more work. They are afraid the boss will say, "Great idea, Susan. I'd like you to head up a committee examining that issue and report back in 2 weeks."

***Poorly Run Meetings.*** Poorly run meetings are a third contributor to the meetingthink problem. The next time you are at a meeting, look around the room. How many people appear to be engaged and listening? How many people are glazed over, sleeping with their eyes open, doodling, or looking out the window? If the majority of the group is not engaged, chances are the meeting is being poorly run. Poorly run meetings can be the result of some or all of the factors we discussed earlier. The meeting may be disorganized due to a lack of an agenda. It may be too long and/or include too many topics. The meeting may include the wrong participants. Overtalkers may be dominating the meeting. The leader may be doing all the talking and failing to do any facilitating. Regardless of the reason, poorly run meetings result in group members disengaging, which results in poor decision making.

***Avoiding Meetingthink.*** What can you do about it? How can you avoid this in your own groups? First, make it a practice to follow the suggestions discussed earlier in this chapter. Consider the meeting environment. Always evaluate the meeting topics and use an agenda. When determining the meeting, ask the following questions: Is this topic relevant to the participants? (If you are not positive, ask them.) Am I being respectful of my team's time? If you have a meeting scheduled but some of the key participants can't make it, cancel the meeting. Similarly, if you have a standing meeting scheduled but there are no agenda items, cancel it. Your team members will be more engaged in the meetings they do

This photo suggests one of the worst possible versions of a poorly run meeting.

attend if you respect their time. Finally, if you have the leadership title, facilitate the discussion. Make certain all the functional roles are present. If they're not, bring it to the attention of the team.

What if you're not the leader of the meeting in question? What can you do to avoid meetingthink? On a personal level, challenge yourself to be fully prepared and engaged in every meeting you attend. Avoid becoming overloaded by actively managing the number of meetings you attend. If you are invited to participate in a meeting, ask the leader why you were selected to participate. What role does he or she want you to play? If you will play a valuable role, attend the meeting. If you were invited out of courtesy, decline to attend. Similarly, ask if you are the person who needs to attend or if a representative from your team is needed. If a representative is needed, look within your team for support. There may be equally qualified members of your team who could go in your place. What may have been a burden to you might well be an exciting opportunity to another member of your team.

Whether group members are suffering from groupthink or meetingthink, the results are the same—critical thinking is suspended, and faulty decisions occur. By design, groups and teams should have conflict. The trick is to make sure the conflict is positive and productive.

## Productive Conflict

By now, you may be convinced that conflict is a necessary part of teams, but you still may not be excited about the idea of engaging in conflict, especially if you've experienced negative, counterproductive conflict in the past. Achieving professional excellence in teams involves the utilization of positive, productive conflict as a valuable resource.

### Stages of Team Development

Conflict is actually present in three of the five stages that make up team development (Posthuma, 2012; Tuckman & Jensen, 1977). The five **stages of team development** include forming, storming, norming, performing, and adjourning. During the *forming stage*, group members tend to be polite and impersonal as they test the waters. Conflict appears in the second stage, known as storming. During the *storming stage*, members engage in infighting and often clash with the leader. In the *norming stage*, the group develops procedures for organizing, giving feedback, and confronting issues. In the *performing stage*, the members carry out the duties of the group. In the final stage, *adjourning*, the group completes its work, resolves issues, and comes to a close. It's important to realize that this is not a linear process. Group members don't march neatly from stage to stage. It's normal for groups to revisit stages and circle through the process repeatedly. The point here is that groups encounter conflict in the storming, norming, and performing stages of development. If a group is going to become a team, it will encounter conflict in the storming stage, develop productive ways to handle conflict in the norming stage, and utilize the kind of innovative thinking in the performing stage that can come only through productive discussion or conflict.

### Handling Conflict

In order to achieve professional excellence, you must determine the best way to handle conflict so it's both positive and productive. Every time you are faced with a conflict, you must select one of three modes of conflict resolution: flight, fight, or unite. Let's take a look at each.

**Flight** occurs when you choose not to engage or deal with a conflict. There are times when this is the appropriate strategy. Some issues are not worth the time or the energy. However, if there is a problem that must be solved or a behavior that must be changed, flight is not the appropriate response and avoidance only makes the problem worse.

**Fight** is another alternative for handling conflict. Using the fight approach will require you to engage in some type of confrontation. This approach is also known as a win–lose approach to problem solving. Both parties face off as opponents, and one party will come out the winner, while the other party will come out the loser. Clearly, this approach can have some negative consequences. In fact, the losing party often holds a grudge, which can damage relationships in the long run. However, there are times when an issue is important enough to warrant the fight approach. If handled properly, even conflicts that are solved using the fight approach can be positive.

# The Unite Approach

The third mode for conflict resolution is the **unite** approach, which requires team members to move away from stating positions to exploring interests (Fisher, Ury, & Patton, 1991; Hackman, 2012). The unite approach defines team members as joint problem solvers rather than adversaries. Instead of approaching the conflict as team member against team member, it becomes the team united against the problem. A **position** is a demand that includes each person's solution to the problem. Under the unite approach, team members look beneath the surface of each position to see all the interests. **Interests** are the needs and concerns underlying each position.

An example of two competing positions might be, "The wait staff should only wait tables and not do side jobs such as filling ketchup bottles or rolling silverware in napkins" and "The wait staff must wait on tables and do side jobs." There are only two positions, but under each position are many interests. For example, under the wait staff position are interests (needs and concerns) such as, *I want to be a good employee. I like working here. I want to do a good job. I want to be a team player. I do need to have the ketchup filled and silverware rolled. I do not have time to do side jobs and properly serve my customers. I want to earn the most tips possible. Not all the wait staff take turns with the side jobs. Hostesses and busboys do not do side jobs. I am paid only $2.00 an hour, while hostesses and busboys are paid $6.00 per hour.* Under the manager position are some similar needs and concerns: *My wait staff are excellent servers. I want to retain this wait staff. I want my wait staff to get the most tips possible. I want the customers to have an excellent dining experience. The side jobs must be done. Traditionally, wait staff do the side jobs. I want the entire staff to function as a team.*

When the team looks beyond the positions and focuses on the interests, they are able to identify interests they share and establish common ground for joint problem solving. Instead of arguing positions, the team can look for solutions that support the interests or common ground they share.

## Raise the Issue

In order for this approach to work, it's critical for the opening communication to reflect the unite attitude. According to Fisher et al. (1991), you should begin by preparing to raise the issue. The preparation includes many of the elements we have already discussed, such as considering the meeting environment, meeting participants, and meeting topic. Because this process can take some time, be certain to schedule the meeting at a time when participants are not rushed (Chen, Zhao, Liu, & Wu, 2012).

Begin the meeting by stating the issue concisely and in a neutral tone. Focus on behaviors and facts, not opinions. For example, you would not want to begin by saying, "Clearly, the wait staff think they're too good to take care of the side jobs, and it's causing us to lose business. Do I have to fire someone in order to get this problem resolved, or do you have a better idea?" Rather, begin with something such as, "Recently, there has been a shortage of rolled silverware and filled condiments during peak serving times." The latter statement is concise with a neutral tone.

When stating the problem, be as brief as possible. As illustrated in the example above, you should keep it to a sentence or two. Leaders have a tendency to state the problem and the solution without allowing others to talk—this will shut down the entire communication process.

*Invite Cooperation*

Once the problem is stated, invite cooperation (Fisher et al., 1991; Kress & Schar, 2012). For example, you might say, "How can we solve this problem together?" By listening, you and the other team members will gain a better understanding of everyone's perceptions of the issue.

If your team is not familiar with this approach, you may need to guide team members through the process. Prior to addressing any issues, talk to the team about the benefits of using the unite approach. Have the team imagine themselves on one side of the table, united against whatever issue or problem arises. Emphasize that the unite approach requires effective listening and participation from all team members. To develop listening and participating as a norm, incorporate the **round robin technique**. After you've raised the issue and invited cooperation, go around the circle and allow everyone to share his or her perceptions of the issue. The round robin technique requires members to listen and not interrupt while other team members are speaking. Team members may ask one another clarification questions to improve understanding, but they can't argue for or against positions. As the team discusses their perceptions of the issue, the underlying interests will become clearer. Only then can the team begin generating options and selecting the best solution(s).

# KEYS to Excellence in Team Communication

Think about Ani Chopourian from the beginning of the chapter. She found herself in a toxic environment with coworkers who did not practice excellence in their team communication. As a result, the hospital that employed her faced serious fines and a drastic blow to its public image. When thinking about how you interact with others in a team setting, be aware of the KEYS process to improve your communication. During the first step, *know yourself*, do a self-inventory of how you have interacted with others in the past and how your team members reacted to your communication. Did they react positively or negatively to the way you communicated with them? Understanding different workplace cultures is critical to avoid offending the people you work with.

The second step, *evaluate the professional context*, requires you to identify what is considered professional communication and what is not. What types of jokes are tolerated in your working environment? Is cursing frowned upon or ignored? What behavior is considered acceptable when venting your frustrations to your coworkers? Try to make sure that your team communication fits the culture of your workplace.

The third step, *your communication interaction occurs*, requires you to be critical of your communication while talking with your team members. Be sensitive to others' nonverbal cues, and try to notice when somebody feels threatened or offended by your communication. Take what you have learned from evaluating your professional context to craft a message that can be well received by your coworkers.

The final strategy, *step back and reflect,* involves taking a reflexive inventory of your communication with other team members. Both verbally and nonverbally, how did your coworkers react to what you said? Was your body language offensive or threatening, or did you choose a more amiable approach in your communication? Constantly be aware of how others react to your communication, and make the proper changes to your approach when necessary.

Think of a group/team to which you belong. How does that group/team make decisions and handle conflict? Are your decisions innovative? Are your conflicts productive? Based on what you have learned, could you improve the group/team communication?

**K**now Yourself

**E**valuate the Professional Context

**Y**our Communication Interaction Occurs

**S**tep Back and Reflect

## Executive Summary

Now that you have finished reading this chapter, you can do the following:

Distinguish between a group and a team:

- A *group* is defined as three or more individuals who are working toward a common goal or share a common purpose (p. 148).
- A *team* is defined as a group in which members share leadership responsibility for creating a team identity, achieving mutually defined goals, and fostering innovative thinking (p. 148).

Recognize the impact of the environment, the topic(s), and the participants on communication within meetings:

- Location is an important component in creating a positive *meeting environment*. In fact, you should consider the convenience, aesthetics, and comfort of the location (p. 151).
- You should also consider aesthetics and comfort when selecting a meeting location (p. 152).
- An *agenda* is a useful channel for informing team members about meeting topics and, if used properly, can serve as a communication tool for facilitating meetings (p. 154).
- Leaders with professional excellence avoid the trap of inviting a representative of each department just to be politically correct. Invite people who can contribute to the purpose of the meeting. Take time to assess the meeting's purpose, and then determine who can best serve that purpose (p. 155).

Analyze the roles and norms displayed by a group or team:

- Within every team, members can play a host of possible roles. Some of these roles are functional roles that help the team achieve goals or maintain positive relationships among members. These roles are known as *task roles* and *relationship roles* (p. 156).
- A *norm* is an unwritten rule of behavior. All groups have both positive and negative norms. The important thing is to step back and reflect on the norms and assess how various norms are affecting your group (p. 158).

Apply the concepts for effective problem solving and innovative thinking to a team context:

- *Problem solving* involves not only making a choice but also coming up with quality alternatives from which to select and then working to implement the choice your team selects (p. 160).
- Remember John Dewey's *Reflective Thinking Process*. According to Dewey (1910), five steps make up problem solving. These steps include describing and analyzing the problem, generating possible solutions, evaluating all solutions, deciding on the solution, and planning how to implement the solution (p. 160).
- One way to foster innovation in team problem solving is to incorporate Von Oech's (1986) explorer, artist, judge, and warrior into the process (p. 160).

Understand the need for conflict and the strategies for productive conflict:

- Lack of conflict is a strong sign that your group has some serious problems, will not develop innovative ideas, and will never reach "team" status. The whole purpose for having meetings is to get different people together to share a variety of ideas and develop innovative solutions to problems. If this is to occur, then conflict must also occur (p. 169).
- To achieve professional excellence, you must determine the best way to handle conflict so it's both positive and productive. Every time you are faced with a conflict, you must select one of three modes of conflict resolution: *flight, fight,* or *unite* (p. 172).
- To develop listening and participating as a norm, incorporate the *round robin technique*. After you've raised the issue and invited cooperation, go around the circle and allow everyone to share his or her perceptions of the issue (p. 174).

Apply the KEYS process to professional excellence as you develop your groups into teams:

- *Know yourself.* Be aware of the strength and weaknesses you bring to the group or team (p. 174).
- *Evaluate the professional context.* Know your workplace culture and the personalities of other people in your group or team. This will enable you to foster a positive group interaction (p. 174).
- *Your communication interaction occurs.* Develop an agenda and send it to the group a week before the meeting, giving everyone time to acquaint themselves with it (p. 174).
- *Step back and reflect.* Listen to the input from your peers to better understand what is important to the group and company as a whole (p. 174).

**Discussion** Questions

1. Think about the last project you worked on with others. Would you define that as a group or a team experience? Why would you use that label?

2. Step back and reflect on some meetings in which you have participated. How did the environment, topics, and participants contribute to the communication at those meetings?

3. During meetings, do you share in the leadership? What roles do you play? When you have a designated leadership title, do you act as a coach? What norms do you use to help facilitate effective communication and shared leadership?

4. When it comes to innovative problem solving, in which role (explorer, artist, judge, or warrior) do you excel and which role must you work to develop?

5. How do you handle conflict? Have you ever tried a unite approach? Why or why not?

**Terms to** Remember

| | | |
|---|---|---|
| agenda (p. 154) | flight (p. 172) | Reflective Thinking Process (p. 160) |
| artist (p. 167) | group (p. 148) | relationship roles (p. 156) |
| coach (p. 156) | groupthink (p. 169) | round robin technique (p. 174) |
| compromise (p. 164) | interests (p. 173) | self-centered roles (p. 156) |
| conflict (p. 169) | judge (p. 167) | stages of team development (p. 172) |
| consensus (p. 164) | lead (p. 165) | task roles (p. 156) |
| criteria (p. 162) | meeting environment (p. 150) | team (p. 148) |
| decision by the leader (p. 163) | meetingthink (p. 170) | undertalker (p. 155) |
| decision making (p. 159) | norm (p. 158) | unite (p. 173) |
| devil's advocate (p. 163) | overload (p. 170) | voting (p. 164) |
| explorer (p. 166) | overtalker (p. 155) | warrior (p. 168) |
| false empowerment (p. 170) | position (p. 173) | |
| fight (p. 172) | problem solving (p. 160) | |

Visit the Student Study Site at **www.sagepub.com/keys2e** to access the following resources:

- SAGE journal articles
- Video links
- Web resources
- Web quizzes
- eflashcards

## part V

# Excelling in the Workplace

**Chapter 8:** Technology in the Workplace

**Chapter 9:** Business and Professional Writing

**Chapter 10:** Leadership and Conflict Management

## Chapter Outline

Communication and Technology: Tools for
  Professionals   182
Drawbacks of Technology   190
Professional Etiquette With
  Technology   197
KEYS to Excellence With Communication
  and Technology   198
Executive Summary   200
Discussion Questions   201
Terms to Remember   201

## Chapter Objectives

After studying this chapter, you should be able to:

1. Understand the impact technology has on business and professional communication

2. Explain how emotion is expressed with technology

3. Understand how the drawbacks of technology can prevent you from excelling as a professional

4. Utilize the KEYS approach to achieve professional excellence regarding communication and technology

# chapter 8

# Technology in the Workplace

**Peter Miscovich, a managing director for the consulting firm Corporate Solutions, understands the growing trend of using technological solutions to increase workplace productivity and excellence.** "Emerging technologies are enabling new levels of workplace optimization and utilization as well as boosting productivity to levels never seen before in global organizations" (Musgrove, 2011). While conducting a survey of corporate business practices, Miscovich reported that nearly 90% of companies plan on incorporating new communication technologies in their workforce to increase productivity and interaction among employees (Musgrove, 2011). New technologies include smartphones, PDAs, tablets, and videoconferencing software. The idea is to give employees the means to generate immediate feedback and new information while also allowing for an increase in workplace mobility. The "office" can be wherever an employee is at a given time, so people are not constricted to a specific geographic space to be productive for the company.

The increase in workplace technology, while convenient, presents new challenges to workplace communication. There are issues of employee surveillance, time management, electronic aggression, and professional etiquette associated with computer-mediated communication. Personal social-networking sites have introduced many people to Internet communication in the information age but have placed little emphasis on professional excellence in online business communication. Many companies have explicit rules concerning the use of social media and electronic devices in the workplace, and a poor understanding of your expectations can lead to poor performance or even job termination.

This photo illustrates the use of conference phone technology opening more participation in common professional tasks such as interviewing, planning, and negotiation.

Knowing how to interact with colleagues professionally in an online environment will enable you to become an effective member of your business community. In this chapter, you will learn the essentials for effective professional communication while also becoming aware of the potential drawbacks associated with new technology.

Communicating excellence through technology is a necessary skill in the current workforce. Learning to communicate effectively while utilizing technology is important for the following reasons: (1) The way you communicate when using technology influences the impressions other people have of you, which is central to achieving professional excellence; (2) communication and technology help you establish contact and maintain professional networks and relationships with coworkers, leaders, and clients; and (3) communication and technology lead to a number of obstacles that can hinder professional excellence. Recall the important role professional excellence played when you were *entering and developing in the workplace*. Put simply, the KEYS process will help bridge professional excellence with communication and technology and help you *excel in the workplace*.

## Communication and Technology: Tools for Professionals

When you communicate by using any form of technology, you are taking part in **computer-mediated communication (CMC)** (Diaz, Chiaburu, Zimmerman, & Boswell, 2011; Li, Jackson, & Trees, 2008; Walther, Loh, & Granka, 2005). Your methods of communicating with clients, colleagues, and managers with technology must be thought out carefully.

Communication and technology have helped people conduct business virtually instead of communicating face-to-face (Couch & Liamputtong, 2008; Langan, 2012). No doubt, many of you are or will be members of a **virtual work team**—tasks and professional projects traditionally accomplished face-to-face that are computer mediated to save on time and travel (Schiller & Mandviwalla, 2007; Staples & Webster, 2007; Watson-Manheim, Chudoba, & Crowston, 2012). When team members are located all around the country or the world, technology is an excellent tool to enhance communication. But if you use technology to avoid face-to-face communication with people in your office, technology can become a barrier to effective communication.

### Table 8.1 Selecting the Channel: Pros and Cons

| Channel | Pros | Cons |
|---|---|---|
| Desktop/ network e-mail | • Robust software provides a full range of features and functions <br> • Provides lots of storage for your e-mail messages <br> • Provides offline access to your e-mail; don't have to be connected to e-mail provider to compose new messages or read replies | • Limited mobility: must use desktop/laptop computer or be signed in to network to access software |
| Web e-mail | • Freedom of movement: don't have to be logged on to own computer to send and receive e-mail | • Limited features and functions compared with desktop e-mail software <br> • No offline access to e-mail <br> • Access to attachments is limited to the computer or network you are using at the time |
| Instant messaging | • Instant give-and-take associated with phone chat; unlike standard e-mail, which involves composing and sending messages and then waiting for replies, instant messaging takes place in real time | • Incompatibility issues between competing instant-messaging software providers <br> • Lack of basic e-mail features and functions available on most desktop or web e-mail programs |
| Personal digital assistants (PDAs) | • Portability: Slip it into your pocket or briefcase, and off you go <br> • Offline access to e-mail received and messages being composed <br> • Ability to sync PDA to desktop computer so e-mail can be transferred between hardware devices <br> • Touch-screen technology <br> • Full keyboard function (QWERTY) | • Inconsistent coverage: If you are out of cell phone range, you are probably out of range to transmit and receive wireless e-mail messages <br> • Although manufacturers are beginning to offer keypads that enhance ease of use, many PDAs have small keypads, while others have no keypad at all. To write messages, you write or tap letters on the screen with a stylus or your thumb. |
| Two-way text pagers | • Portable <br> • Small and lightweight | • Inconsistent coverage: Unlike one-way pagers (which never have great coverage), the coverage for two-way pagers is about the same as for cell phones. <br> • Small keypads: Most people learn to type with their thumbs. <br> • Limited message size |
| Standard cell phones | • Portability and convenience: One device handles phone calls and text messages | • Coverage can be spotty <br> • Small keypads <br> • Limited message size |

Sources: Flynn (2009) and Flynn and Flynn (2003, pp. 95–99).

Images such as this are what some employers are looking for as a red flag in hiring particular applicants. Do you have any pictures posted on the web that could potentially lead to a negative impression?

If you decide to use technology, how do you determine which communication channel works best for the situation? Is e-mail the best way to get a message out? Is a text the best way to make an urgent request? Is your cell phone the best device to use when participating in a phone conference or interview? Table 8.1 features the pros and cons of many common devices designed to help us stay connected and manage information as professionals. Review the table and think about your technology preferences.

## Maintaining Professional Excellence Online

Social networking can be a wonderful tool for sharing information and maintaining professional connections. However, one area to be especially mindful of is the kinds of information about you others can retrieve from the Internet.

Important to your study of business and professional communication is learning to assess and improve your effectiveness when utilizing technology in your communication (Hewett & Robidoux, 2010; Shipley & Schwalbe, 2008). Since much of our communication occurs through technology, we must make sure we present ours as professionals both online and in person (Ivy & Wahl, 2009; Jovin, 2007; Locher, 2010; Walther et al., 2005; Wright, 2004).

The way people present themselves online does matter in professional life. Remember, even "private" electronic communication can easily become public (Table 8.2). What do your Facebook page, text messages, and e-mail name say about you? What impression will others have of you based on what you post to online social-networking sites such as Facebook and Myspace (see Table 8.3)? Is your image online different from the image you present in person? If they are different, how are they different? What does each say about you as a professional? Understanding the impact of technology on your communication is critical to achieving professional excellence.

## Electronic Communication

Have you thought about how communication has changed as a result of technology such as e-mail, instant messaging, social networking, and texting? With each change in technology, there are changes to our communication as professionals (Barley, Meyerson, & Grodal, 2011; Hermes, 2008; Ivy & Wahl, 2009; Yee, Bailenson, Urbanek, Chang, & Merget, 2008). And, as noted earlier, some of the changes that result from technology positively

## Table 8.2 Who's Watching? Who Wants to Know? Will They Really Look at My Facebook?

Business communication experts Sherry Roberts and Terry Roach (2009) have specific suggestions regarding how information you post about yourself online can impact your professional life. Social networking once meant going to a social function such as a cocktail party, conference, or business luncheon. Today, much social networking is achieved through websites such as Myspace, Facebook, or LinkedIn. Many individuals use these sites to meet new friends, make connections, and upload personal information. On social-networking websites (SNWs) that focus more on business connections, such as LinkedIn, individuals upload job qualifications and application information. These SNWs are now being used as reference checks by human resources personnel. For this reason, SNW users, particularly university students and other soon-to-be job applicants, should ask themselves the following questions:

- Am I loading information that I want the world to see?
- Does this picture really show me in the best light?
- What impression would another person have of me if he or she went through my site?

Although SNWs are a great way to connect with friends, family, and friends-to-be, they can present problems when potential employers begin to search through them for information concerning job applicants. Many potential employees would be mortified to learn that employers could read the personal information posted on Myspace, Facebook, LinkedIn, or other SNWs. Searches on SNWs allow employers to look into what the applicant does "after hours," socially or privately.

Source: Roberts and Roach (2009).

## Table 8.3 Thinking Critically: Facebook and Online Social-Networking Sites

What are some ways for you to be proactive when your experience at work fuses with what you have posted online? Genova (2009) argues that employers have legitimate business interests in monitoring workplace Internet use: to minimize legal exposure, to increase productivity, and to avoid proprietary information loss. Since employees arguably have no expectation of privacy in their work on employers' computers, there are few grounds for complaint if they are disciplined for straying from corporate policy on such use. In this heavily scrutinized work environment, it is no small wonder that employees crave a place to unwind and play "electronically" after hours. In unprecedented numbers, America's workers are visiting online social-networking sites and posting tidbits that their employers might not consider job appropriate. Here, many postulate that they do have an expectation of and, indeed, a right to privacy, especially in arenas that are used to express personal freedoms and exercise individualism and have no bearing on the workplace. Whether employers agree with this stance or not, an increasing majority are using employees' presence on these sites to support discipline, termination, or simply not hiring an individual. But is this fair if those actions are based on off-the-clock Internet use?

Source: Genova (2009).

Blogs now have a presence in a variety of business and professional settings. In fact, some executives are now using blogs as a way to share information about topics such as organizational change or as a way to launch new initiatives.

influence our communication, while others have a negative influence.

As we move into the sections that follow, there are a number of things to keep in mind about technology, especially when writing and sending e-mail professionally. Before composing and sending an e-mail, consider the information provided in Table 8.4. Keep in mind that these rules also apply to text messages, blogs, and other electronic messages.

Using an e-mail system, as well as many other forms of technology, allows a sender to avoid some of the unpleasant parts of face-to-face confrontation. For example, if you had to fire an employee, you would not have to see anyone cry if you delivered the bad news via e-mail, nor would you have to worry about the physical side of an angry

### Table 8.4 Being Aware of E-mail

- E-mail is never secure.
- E-mail can lead to misunderstanding.
- Inappropriate e-mail can lead to workplace lawsuits.
- Your e-mail may be monitored by the company.
- Spending too much time on e-mail can hinder your productivity and focus.
- E-mail abuse can lead to employee termination.
- Sending inappropriate e-mails can harm your reputation as a professional.

Source: Flynn (2009).

outburst over the telephone (Li et al., 2008; Locher, 2010). Getting fired over e-mail is just one example of a change resulting from increased accessibility to and affordability of technology. How we communicate with one another in professional settings continues to evolve. While some people welcome the constant evolution and emergence of new communication technology, others find it difficult to adjust to these changes and feel pressured to keep up. Clearly, advantages and disadvantages emerge when it comes to the use of technology in managing our professional relationships. You've likely heard great stories about making professional connections online, then face-to-face, and then negotiating a big contract. On the other hand, you've probably also heard stories about

# Know Yourself    CMC Competence

*The following scale will help you gain a better understanding of your own CMC competence. Answer each question thoughtfully, and then reflect on the results. How can this knowledge help you be a better communicator?*

*Directions*: The following statements, modified from Spitzberg's (2006) CMC Competence Scale, describe the ways some people use and feel about new CMC. Please indicate in the space at the left of each item the degree to which you believe the statement applies to you. Please use the following 5-point scale:

1 = Not at all true of me

2 = Mostly not true of me

3 = Neither true nor untrue of me; undecided

4 = Mostly true of me

5 = Very true of me

_3_ 1. I enjoy communicating using computer media.

_4_ 2. I always seem to know how to say things the way I mean them using CMC.

_1_ 3. I don't feel very competent in learning and using communication media technology.

_2_ 4. Communicating through a computer makes me anxious.

_5_ 5. I know I can learn to use new CMC technologies when they come out.

_4_ 6. I manage the give and take of CMC interactions skillfully.

_4_ 7. I can show compassion and empathy through the way I write e-mails.

_4_ 8. I take time to make sure my e-mails to others are uniquely adapted to the particular receiver I'm sending it to.

_3_ 9. I try to use a lot of humor in my CMC messages.

_2_ 10. I use a lot of the expressive symbols [e.g., ☺ for "smile"] in my CMC messages.

_3_ 11. I have no trouble expressing my opinions forcefully on CMC.

_3_ 12. I avoid saying things through e-mail that might offend someone.

_4_ 13. My interactions are effective in accomplishing what I set out to accomplish.

_4_ 14. My comments are consistently accurate and clear.

_4_ 15. I am generally pleased with my interactions.

_4_ 16. I come across in conversation as someone people would like to get to know.

_3_ 17. My CMC interactions are more productive than my face-to-face interactions.

_3_ 18. CMC technologies are tremendous time-savers for my work.

_4_ 19. I rely heavily on my CMCs for getting me through each day.

_3_ 20. I can rarely go a week without any CMC interactions.

Source: Spitzberg (2006).

How did you score? What surprised you about your score? You can also try the assessment on others. Simply fill out the measure with another person's behaviors in mind. For instance, you might find it interesting to fill out the survey for one of your friends to determine whether his or her use of CMC might play some role in the degree to which you interact with him or her online. Do you notice differences in that person's use of CMC and face-to-face interactions? Be aware of how you assess communication between CMC and face-to-face interactions among your friends, family, coworkers, and acquaintances.

## Your Communication Interaction    Aaron's Communication Problem

*Read the passage below, and then answer the questions. As you read, think about ways the KEYS approach could help you improve* **your communication interaction** *if you were in Aaron's position.*

Aaron is a project manager for a large pharmaceutical company. Aaron's employees often have a hard time keeping up with him in meetings, which results in many follow-up e-mails with him after the meetings are concluded. While Aaron is pleasant enough in person, he has little patience for writing e-mails and often becomes belligerent with his employees during their e-mail interactions. Aaron writes in all capital letters, attacks his employees for not paying attention during the meetings, and, more often than not, never answers the original questions his employees asked him. As a result, many of his employees are still confused and are reluctant to try e-mail communication again. Recently, Aaron was demoted from his position after his department made a critical mistake in the production of a pain reliever that hit the market, resulting in a massive recall. Aaron was criticized by both his employees and his bosses for not communicating effectively and professionally with his staff.

### Questions to Consider

1. Is being confrontational in e-mails with employees an effective way to communicate?
2. Does it demonstrate professional ethics?
3. What are some other examples of negative effects that can result from poor CMC?
4. Using the KEYS process, how can Aaron use technology more effectively to communicate with his staff?

employees shopping online or viewing porn on the company computer when they should be working. As communication scholars Diana K. Ivy and Shawn T. Wahl (2009) argue: "Technological innovation regarding communication isn't going away; it's only going to increase as newer, faster, more convenient, and more affordable gizmos will continue to be developed for our [professional] use" (p. 321).

People working in businesses and professional organizations increasingly rely on their e-mail systems to communicate with colleagues and accomplish their work (Ivy & Wahl, 2009; Kibby, 2005; Lawson & Leck, 2006; Shipley & Schwalbe, 2008; Thompson, 2008; Young, Kelsey, & Lancaster, 2011). Considering how prevalent e-mail usage is in business and professional communication, let's examine how this form of technology impacts professional image.

As we suggested in Chapter 4, you should review and perhaps change your e-mail address when applying for jobs. Think about the impression a job recruiter would have when receiving an e-mail message from <pimpinout@university.edu> versus <gabe.martinez @university.edu> (Ivy & Wahl, 2009). Which address implies more professionalism? Which address communicates a better first impression? You need to think about the perception of you that others may form based on your e-mail (Byron & Baldridge, 2007; Ivy & Wahl, 2009; Welch, 2012).

### Table 8.5 Checklist for Appropriate E-mail Content

✓ Spell-checked to clean mechanical and grammatical errors

✓ Free of jokes

✓ Doesn't contain harassing, negative, or aggressive language

✓ Illustrates professional excellence

✓ Free of racist, sexist, or discriminatory language

✓ Free of sexual language, violence, and pornographic images

Source: Flynn (2009).

But communicating effectively through e-mail involves much more than just having a professional e-mail address (see Table 8.5). Again, the checklist in Table 8.5 also applies to other forms of electronic communication, such as text messages and blogs. Unfortunately, many people fail to put the same level of professionalism into their e-mail messages. This can lead to the start of conflicts or the escalation of existing conflicts. According to Wollman (2008), electronic conflicts are very common. Can you think of a time when you sent an e-mail message that was less than professional? How could you have changed the message to present yourself with professional excellence?

Professional excellence requires you to know yourself as a communicator. Using the KEYS approach, you must know what kind of e-mail style you have, both in sending and receiving, to see what impression you communicate through your e-mailing behavior. You also need to expand that self-analysis to all forms of CMC. For example, do you have a habit of using smiley faces and "lol" with friends? Have you carried those habits into your professional texts? Do you carefully proofread your memos but send text messages and e-mails full of typos and errors? Do you forward things you think are funny or inspirational to colleagues or other professional contacts? Now ask yourself, "Would I pass that same information

This photo gives you a sense of how negative a response to unprofessional electronic communication can be.

on in hard copy? Would I repeat that joke in person?" As you analyze yourself online, remember that you want to portray the same image and the same level of communication professionalism electronically that you would portray in person or in written, hard-copy correspondence, because the need for professionalism is the same. This is a different channel, but the same rules apply. Similarly, remember that you must evaluate the audience or the receiver of the message. For example, some people love to text,

## Ethical Connection     Mr. Billig's Nasty E-mail

*Please read the passage below, and answer the questions that follow.*

A new associate sends a request to her team leader for information on a work project that she did not understand during the team meeting. Examine the e-mail exchange that follows.

(NEW HIRE, SHAWANA)

Dear Mr. Billig,

This is Shawana. I'm the new hire on your special projects team. Can you explain the harmful effects of our product on pregnant women? I am having a difficult time understanding the effects. Thanks for your time.

Sincerely,

Shawana

(MANAGER, MR. JERRY BILLIG)

SHAWANA, I KNOW WHO YOU ARE. DID YOU NOT GET TRAINED IN THIS AREA DURING ORIENTATION? WE HAVE DEADLINES AND LITTLE TIME TO PLAY CATCH UP. MAYBE IF YOU WOULD TAKE THE TIME TO GET TO KNOW YOUR OTHER TEAM MEMBERS, YOU WOULD NOT HAVE TO COME TO ME. WE SURE NEED TO CHANGE OUR ORIENTATION FOR NEW HIRES.

MR. BILLIG

NEW PROJECTS MANAGER

E-MAIL: BILLIG@LACTIDES.COM

### Questions to Consider

1. How can the e-mail exchange between Shawana and Mr. Billig be evaluated from an ethical perspective?

2. What would your impression of Mr. Billig be, based on this e-mail message?

3. Was Shawana's e-mail appropriate and professional?

4. How do you think this e-mail exchange will impact Shawana and Mr. Billig's future communications?

5. Have you ever sent e-mails or text messages like this? Did you consider this type of communication unethical and/or unprofessional? Why or why not?

and others love virtual meetings, but some people and some topics require good-old face-to-face communication. If you apply the KEYS approach and carefully select the communication channel you use, you will be one step closer to communication excellence with technology.

# Drawbacks of Technology

We recognize that communication and technology will help you be more productive, network, and *excel* as a professional. However, part of professional excellence is also

## Evaluate the Professional Context    Emily and Ryan's E-mail Affection

*Read the following passage about Emily and Ryan, and then answer the questions. As you read, focus on evaluating the professional context.*

Emily and Ryan had been working together on a virtual team for close to a year. They also hung out after work a few times a month and had become friends. Emily and Ryan used e-mail constantly to get their work done. After the first few weeks working on the project, Emily stopped using Ryan's name during e-mail openings. For example, Emily would open her e-mails to Ryan with "Hey, Sexy." She would end her e-mails to Ryan with "Love, Em." He really didn't have a problem with Emily's playfulness via e-mail, and he began replying in a similar way. They were just having some fun. However, they both ended up getting in trouble with their project manager. Emily and Ryan both received a warning for abusing the company e-mail system for "relational purposes" and for being "unprofessional."

### Questions to Consider

1. What can you learn from Emily and Ryan's experience?
2. What kinds of greetings and closings do you use regularly in e-mails you send? Does your style depend on the recipient of the e-mail?
3. How can the KEYS process be used to help Ryan and Emily?

being able to recognize the drawbacks of technology and avoid violating professional etiquette (explained further in Chapter 4). Those of you who excel into leadership positions should be aware of the drawbacks of technology, as the need for more workplace policies is emerging to help manage risks associated with technology (e.g., security breaches, privacy violations, decreased production, employee conflict, viewing of pornography, miscommunication; Diffle & Landau, 2007; Kelleher & Hall, 2005; Roberts & Wasieleski, 2012).

## Employee Surveillance

How privacy is managed in the workplace is certainly part of the organizational culture that you need to get to know (Cozzetto & Pedeliski, 1996; Langan, 2012; Rule, 2007). Be aware of the private information you communicate to other people (e.g., relationship problems, health, money troubles), as well as the private information or activities you might manage at work (e.g., personal e-mail, virtual communities, online banking; Cho & Hung, 2011; Solove, 2008). In

As suggested in this photo, computer crashes, e-mail aggression, and other technology breakdowns can be extremely frustrating.

Computer viruses and security breaches can tarnish professional activities and productivity.

fact, companies and organizations are using **workplace surveillance systems** in an effort to monitor and track employee behavior in terms of the information they access or communicate while at work.

The goal of workplace surveillance is to alleviate productivity concerns and discourage employees from looking up personal banking information or viewing pornography at work (Sheriff & Ravishankar, 2012; Watkins-Allen, Coopman, Hart, & Walker, 2007). In addition to blocking employee access to particular sites or tracking web-surfing behaviors, companies are now asking employees to waive their privacy rights when it comes to using work-related e-mail (see Table 8.6). That is,

| Table 8.6 Ways of Addressing E-mail Security Issues | |
|---|---|
| *Issue* | *Possible Solution* |
| Technology | Install firewall, antivirus, and antispam software as a minimum requirement. |
| | Consider encryption software by weighing the chances of e-mail interception against costs of interception. |
| Policies | As a minimum requirement, provide a written policy covering |
| | • viruses—for instance, what to do in cases of receiving suspicious mail from unknown sources; |
| | • misuse of the system—for example, the organization's view on what constitutes personal/ work e-mail and appropriate/inappropriate material; |
| | • e-mail etiquette—such as the extent to which e-mail correspondence should replicate the format of written correspondence and how to handle organizational opinion in e-mails; |
| | • employee privacy rights—for example, statements on whether or not employees should expect that their e-mail correspondence will be subject to scrutiny if necessary; |
| | • policies on monitoring and scanning—including, for example, the extent to which e-mail will be subject to monitoring and scanning; and |
| | • storage and archiving of e-mail—for example, statements on the permanency of e-mail and organizational archiving procedures. |
| User education | Issue employees copies of the written policy. |
| | Train employees so they know why e-mail may be insecure—for example, e-mail correspondence as legally binding. |
| | Train employees in secure e-mail handling practices—including, for example, password protection and discrimination in selecting recipients. |

Source: Table adapted from Kelleher and Hall (2005).

personal or private affairs are not to be included in any company e-mail. Remember, the intensity of workplace surveillance depends on the industry, but holding a conversation on your cell phone as you walk down the hallway or sit in a meeting is unprofessional regardless of the topic of the conversation. Let's explore in more detail the concerns or problems that emerge with communication and technology in business and professional situations.

## Time Management

**Chronemics** is the study of time as communication and/or as a communication function. Drawing from research on the nonverbal dimensions of time in CMC, Ivy and Wahl (2009) explain that, "while electronic messages occur in **asynchronous time**—messages are posted at one time, then read at another time— CMC also offers more interactive features, such as communication in **synchronous time**" (p. 332). As a result, e-mail systems and other forms of communication

Managing all the information sent electronically can be especially distracting when you're trying to meet a deadline.

technology make employees more efficient while simultaneously increasing their workload (Ballard, 2008; Biggiero, Sammarra, & Dandi, 2012; Bruneau, 2012; Ivy & Wahl, 2009). Do you think technology helps or harms your own time management? How, if at all, do you use technology to help manage your time? What expectations do you have related to response time for text messages, e-mail, instant messages, etc.?

| Table 8.7  Information Overload: Ways to Manage E-mail Clutter |
| --- |

- Don't feel as though you have to respond to every e-mail.
- Develop a strategy for managing information overload.
- Ignore and delete what you can. Read and respond to messages that are important. Utilize the subject line to read quickly for junk mail and spam.
- Time management is critical. Block out some time to delete inbox clutter.
- Develop on organizational system with files and archives.
- Use your professional e-mail address for work-related communication only. Set up a personal account to check during off time.

Source: Flynn (2006b).

In virtual meetings and with the use of messaging features such as Instant Messenger or text-message composition on PDAs (e.g., iPhones, Blackberries, smartphones), professionals can communicate with little delay between messages (Ivy & Wahl, 2009; Wang et al., 2012). Indeed, technology helps professionals be more productive and stay connected with clients; respond quickly; and accomplish tasks despite geographic distance, travel time, and the like. But what are the drawbacks when we consider how much of the time we are wired? A good friend of ours gets so stressed out with e-mail responses and phone calls at work during the week that he advocates for times of being **unplugged**—a term referring to the avoidance of checking e-mail, sending text messages, watching television, or answering the phone (see Table 8.7). No doubt, some of you might think of watching television, talking to your friends on the phone, sending text messages, or listening to your iPod as ways to recharge—the use of technology may very well make your downtime possible. We must also consider the demands of many of your jobs, which would never allow several days without communication.

## Information Overload

Spending a lot of time on tasks that seem to take away from your productivity instead of helping you accomplish your work can make you feel off balance and stressed, leading to burnout (covered at length in Chapter 14). You might be experiencing **information overload**—when information, requests for feedback, taking on new projects, responding to questions, answering the phone, and completing required online classes for work, on top of taking care of loved ones, children, pets, and other family matters, leaves us feeling as though things are spinning out of control (Chen, Pedersen, & Murphy, 2012; Savolainen, 2007).

Contributing to information overload are several unprofessional distractions or threats to privacy. Here are a few examples:

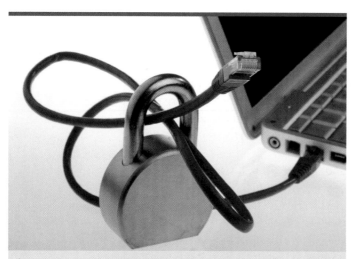

Are policies that establish a sense of respect and courtesy related to technology use a good idea? Why? Why not?

1. **E-mail forwards** consist of virus alerts, chain letters, stories disguised as warnings, petitions or calls for help, jokes, pictures, and the like (Kibby, 2005; Vorakulpipat, Visoottiviseth, & Siwamogsatham, 2012).

2. **Spam** is the use of a user's e-mail address for a purpose to which the user didn't agree. It is junk e-mail sent by "spammers" who obtain e-mail addresses by buying company customer lists or using programs to produce e-mail addresses randomly.

3. **Phishing** is sending authentic-looking but fraudulent e-mails designed to steal sensitive personal information.

## Step Back and Reflect    Barb's E-mail Response

*Read the following passage about Barb, and answer the questions that follow.*

Barb was having a bad day. One of her coworkers, Alex, whom she had been dating for several years, broke up with her using a text message! Needless to say, Barb was angry—she couldn't believe that Alex was impersonal and cold enough to break up with her in that way. They both worked in an accounting office at a large oil refinery. Alex and Barb socialized with a group of coworkers on Friday nights—a social network clearly existed outside of work. In order to get back at Alex, Barb wanted to make a statement. She decided *not* to use a text message to respond to Alex and didn't want to confront him face-to-face at work. Instead, she used the workplace e-mail list (the same list used to organize the Friday night gatherings for everyone in the accounting office). Barb sent a "Reply All" e-mail in response to one of Alex's old e-mail messages and told the entire story about the text-message breakup. The next day, Barb received a formal reprimand from her boss and almost lost her job. As you can see, this is an example of someone using e-mail to attack another person.

### Step Back and Reflect

1. What went wrong?
2. Was Barb out of bounds sending this message to coworkers, since this group socialized outside of work?
3. Have you ever used text messages or e-mails to break up with someone or to display your anger about a breakup?
4. How could Barb utilize the KEYS approach to improve her communication interaction?

As you can see, information overload is more than just deleting e-mails; there are threats to your privacy and to the overall security of your computer (Flynn, 2009). While information overload is certainly a drawback to technology and serves as more of a maintenance function for professionals globally (Flynn, 2006b; Marulanda-Carter & Jackson, 2012), we want to return to the implications the drawbacks of communication and technology have for professional excellence. We turn to Barb and Alex—two professionals who happen to work at the same company and maintain an intimate relationship. As you'll see, technology can be used to attack other people when romance in the workplace goes south.

While Alex and Barb's breakup may sound rare, it should encourage you to think about how communicating with technology requires the same level of consideration as face-to-face communication. Sometimes you may get mad at another coworker inside and outside of work, but that doesn't mean the confrontation needs to be distributed to everyone in the company. Do you know someone who has the bad habit of using the "Reply All" function in e-mail? How would you respond, if at all, if you were in Alex's situation? How could the KEYS process help Alex and Barb with this problem?

**Table 8.8 Tips for Avoiding Electronic Aggression**

- Would you say the same thing to someone in person?

- Would this message be seen as unprofessional by anyone?

- Is your read of the electronic aggression correct? Give people the benefit of the doubt and request a face-to-face conversation.

- Avoid the temptation to use the "Reply All" option.

- Avoid using obscene or threatening language.

- Control your emotions. Revisit the issue when you've had time to calm down.

Source: Flynn (2009).

## Electronic Aggression

Electronic communication allows people like Barb in any workplace situation to sit behind their computer screens or other digital devices and fire off responses in many forms (see Table 8.8). Professionals in a variety of industries take topics in need of discussion, or controversial topics, and place them in electronic formats, often termed **e-mail dialogues**—exchanges of messages about a particular topic using e-mail, professional blog space, and other electronic tools to encourage participation that will ideally lead to new ideas, strategic planning, and sound decision making.

E-mail dialogues can be fruitful, and we don't want to advocate avoidance of this type of exchange; however, e-mail dialogues have a drawback that many of you have already experienced. The dark side of these electronic exchanges is **electronic aggression**—a form of aggressive communication filled with emotionality that is used by people who are interacting on professional topics. Topics that begin with a professional spirit can get unprofessional when people don't agree with the direction of the discussion or if particular language is used to disagree about a program or idea others support. One way to fuel the aggression is to send an **e-mail flame**—"a hostile message that is blunt, rude, insensitive, or obscene" (Flynn & Flynn, 2003, p. 54; Nitin et al., 2012).

Electronic aggression and e-mail flames, similar to the one we discussed in Step Back and Reflect 8.1, can occur when someone posts a highly charged message to a **corporate blog**, a web log used to improve internal communication at work or for external marketing and public relations (Flynn, 2006a; Jang & Stefanone, 2011); a **listserv**, a computer service that facilitates discussions by connecting people who share common interests; or an **electronic bulletin board**, an online service that anyone, not just a subscriber, can access to read postings (Doyle, 1998; Hult & Huckin, 1999; Ivy & Wahl, 2009).

# Professional Etiquette With Technology

The previous sections of this chapter explored the advantages and disadvantages of communication and technology in professional contexts. Remember to think about professional etiquette when communicating with technology (see Table 8.9). Again, a great place to begin practicing your professional etiquette with technology is in the classroom. Students and teachers alike are using technology in the classroom. Laptop computers, PDAs, cell phones, blogs, and pagers are the beginning of a long list of electronic devices that help us manage our everyday lives (Arlat, Kalbarczyk, & Nanya, 2012; Flynn, 2009;). What concerns, if any, do you have regarding technology use during class? Have you ever been

Text messaging, tweeting, checking e-mail on smartphones, and ringing cell phones reflect the noise and distractions brought on by new communication technology.

### Table 8.9 Professional Etiquette With Technology

| | |
|---|---|
| Voice mail—your personal greeting | Record your own greeting. |
| | Indicate if you will be out of the office. |
| | Refer the caller to another person for help. |
| | Check messages daily. |
| Voice mail—leaving messages | Speak clearly and slowly. |
| | Leave your name and number. |
| | Keep messages short and to the point. |
| | Leave the date and time you called. |
| Ring tones | Use silent or vibrate when a ring tone might be disruptive. |
| | Many ring tones are unprofessional—use the standard tones offered by your provider. |
| Text messaging | Don't replace all communication with texts. |
| | Use texts that leave little room for misunderstanding. |
| | Don't deliver bad or good news in a text. |
| | Don't use text messages to have a conversation. |
| | Don't send texts during meetings. |
| | Don't type in all caps. |
| Cell phone usage | Don't answer your cell during a meeting. |
| | Don't take personal calls at work. |

Source: Flynn (2009).

distracted by other students' use of technology? Similarly, think about how the use of technology (e.g., talking, texting, tweeting, gaming, online social networking) can disrupt the workplace experience. What do you think?

Where's the professional etiquette when employees are texting their friends instead of taking care of work-related tasks? Has professional etiquette changed with the growth of technology? What do you think?

# KEYS to Excellence With Communication and Technology

Remember Peter Miscovich, who asserted that electronic technologies can increase productivity and excellence in the workplace? The tools he is talking about, while allowing for more productivity, also require people to be more reflective about how they use technology to communicate. If you want to excel and get promoted to a higher position in leadership, you need to improve your communication—especially when communicating with technology. When studying the KEYS approach to professional excellence as you try to *excel* in the workplace, make some adjustments and improve your e-mail style. When examining the first key, *know yourself*, know that achieving professional excellence entails improving your communication. Thus, both your electronic and face-to-face communication have to improve if you want to advance professionally. Examine your strengths and weaknesses related to all aspects of your communication (verbal, nonverbal, and electronic). Set a goal to be more respectful of the employees who work on your team when communicating one-on-one, during meetings, or through e-mail. In all, you need to get to know yourself better in all aspects of your communication, with the use of technology being just one of them.

The next key, *evaluate the professional context*, is essential for you to become more aware of your professional context as well as how you come across to other people when sending information via e-mail. Become more mindful of how your communication could be hurtful, even if you are just trying to make a point.

The third key, *your communication interaction occurs*, can make you a more professional communicator. Start to think before making certain statements to members of your team, and be much more mindful of your tone and word choice in e-mails. If you send out information electronically, be careful to think about how your e-mail can be received. Follow up with people in person after sending information electronically. Follow up or ask questions such as, "Did you get my e-mail?" and "I hope my description of the new product was clear. Let me know if you need my assistance with anything that might come up." As your communication interaction occurs, work more at planning your message and not simply relying on sending messages electronically. Realize the value of follow-up, respect, and courtesy in all aspects of your communication.

When you meet a new hire or send out information to your team, engage in the fourth key, *step back and reflect*. Become a more reflective communicator. Ask yourself some of the following questions as you step back and think about the communication that has occurred, especially electronically: "Was my e-mail response appropriate?" "Did my questions in the e-mail sound sarcastic?" "Did my team think it was rude when I answered my cell phone during the meeting?" "Should I use all caps in my text message?" "Was sending a response to everyone inappropriate?" "Did Shawana view my e-mail as negative and critical?" "What will my staff think if I don't respond at all?" The fourth phase can make you more thoughtful about all aspects of communication, not just when you use technology.

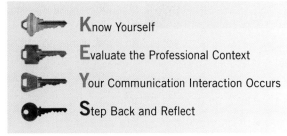

Know Yourself

Evaluate the Professional Context

Your Communication Interaction Occurs

Step Back and Reflect

## Executive Summary

Now that you have finished reading this chapter, you can do the following:

Understand the impact technology has on business and professional communication:

- Communication and technology are important for the following reasons: (1) The way you communicate when using technology influences the impressions other people have of you, which is central to achieving professional excellence; (2) communication and technology help you establish contact and maintain professional networks and relationships with coworkers, leaders, and clients; and (3) communication and technology lead to a number of obstacles that can hinder professional excellence (p. 182).

Explain how emotion is expressed with technology:

- As you analyze yourself online, remember that you want to portray the same image and the same level of communication professionalism electronically that you would portray in person or in written, hard-copy correspondence, because the need for professionalism is the same (p. 189).
- Emotions can be difficult to portray online; what you consider funny or sarcastic, someone else might find rude or inappropriate.

Understand how the drawbacks of technology can prevent you from excelling as a professional:

- Companies and organizations are using *workplace surveillance systems* in an effort to monitor and track employee behavior in terms of the information they access or communicate while at work (p. 192).
- While electronic messages occur in *asynchronous time*—messages are posted at one time, then read at another time—CMC also offers more interactive features, such as communication in synchronous time. As

a result, e-mail systems and other forms of communication technology make employees more efficient while simultaneously increasing their workload (p. 193).

- *Information overload* occurs when information, requests for feedback, taking on new projects, responding to questions, answering the phone, and completing required online classes for work, on top of taking care of loved ones, children, pets, and other family matters, leaves us feeling as though things are spinning out of control (p. 194).
- The dark side of electronic exchanges is *electronic aggression*—a form of aggressive communication filled with emotionality that is used by people interacting about professional topics (p. 196).

Utilize the KEYS approach to achieve professional excellence regarding communication and technology:

- *Know yourself.* Determine if you want to achieve professional excellence, and know that part of that entails improving your communication (p. 198).
- *Evaluate the professional context.* This is essential because you become more aware of your professional context, as well as how you come across to other people when sending information via e-mail (p. 198).
- *Your communication interaction occurs.* This will help you become a more professional communicator. Start to think before making certain statements to members of your team, and be much more mindful of your tone and word choice in e-mails (p. 198).
- *Step back and reflect.* Become a more reflective communicator. This fourth phase will make you more thoughtful about all aspects of your communication, not just when you use technology (p. 198).

## Discussion Questions

1. Discuss an example of a time when you misunderstood another person in a text message, e-mail, or instant message. How did you respond to the misunderstanding? Did you and the other person clear things up in person, or was it done electronically?

2. Do you have a Facebook, Myspace, or related account? Is there anything posted on the page that you think could potentially harm your credibility as a professional?

3. How do you express emotion when communicating with various forms of technology covered in this chapter?

4. Can the drawbacks and risks associated with communication and technology be alleviated with employee education and training? What experiences have you had, if any, concerning training or education related to security, privacy, and professional etiquette?

5. Have you ever experienced information overload? If so, what are some strategies you implement to help you with time management, filtering spam and e-mail forwards, excessive text messages, and other distractions?

## Terms to Remember

asynchronous time (p. 193)

chronemics (p. 193)

computer-mediated
   communication (CMC)
   (p. 182)

corporate blog (p. 196)

electronic aggression (p. 196)

electronic bulletin board
   (p. 196)

e-mail dialogues (p. 196)

e-mail flame (p. 196)

e-mail forwards (p. 194)

information overload (p. 194)

listserv (p. 196)

phishing (p. 194)

spam (p. 194)

synchronous time (p. 193)

unplugged (p. 194)

virtual work team (p. 182)

workplace surveillance
   systems (p. 192)

Visit the Student Study Site at **www.sagepub.com/keys2e** to access the following resources:

- SAGE journal articles
- Video links
- Web resources

- Web quizzes
- eflashcards

## Chapter Outline

The Importance of Written
   Communication   204
Types of Written Communication   207
KEYS to Excellence in Written
   Communication   229
Executive Summary   230
Discussion Questions   231
Terms to Remember   231

## Chapter Objectives

After studying this chapter, you should be able to:

1. Understand the impact of written communication on professional excellence

2. Understand the different indirect messages sent with written communication

3. Identify different types of written communication

4. Utilize the KEYS approach to achieve professional excellence regarding written communication

## chapter 9

# Business and Professional Writing

**George Raab found out the hard way that there can be no expectation of privacy for workplace e-mail accounts.** Raab, a former chief financial officer for the New York City Education Department, was caught using his city e-mail account to line up a future job at a private firm and to manage his real estate holdings, all while still employed by the city (Chapman & Monahan, 2011). The city Conflict of Interest Board fined Raab $6,500 for misuse of city resources. The ensuing investigation found other issues of corruption as well. Investigators also concluded that Raab had paid a former colleague from a private firm upwards of $375,000 to perform new-age hypnosis to boost morale in the Education Department. The findings sparked a major controversy in the city and caused major problems for the Education Department, as accusations of corruption were leveled at the entire office. Even though Raab had left his position and paid the fine, the department was still left to deal with a public relations disaster.

While most people today have private e-mail accounts, many jobs in the professional workplace require that employees have another e-mail account with the company to conduct business. Also, many companies require that employees sign an agreement acknowledging that employee e-mails are the property of the company and can be investigated at any time. This can become dangerous when employees misuse workplace e-mail for personal reasons, or for anything not related to business. Even electronic messages to other coworkers that are critical of a boss or the company in general can be damaging and possibly lead to job termination. That stories such as Raab's are still common in the news indicates that many people need to understand how to communicate with writing in a professional manner.

Writing with professional excellence is another important aspect of succeeding in the workplace. Many jobs will require that you communicate through writing as part of your day-to-day responsibilities. It is important to note that e-mail is not the only medium you are expected to be familiar with; business letters, memos, employee reviews, and proposals or reports also carry the need to write effectively. In this chapter, you will learn more about the types of written communication expected from you, as well as how to be an effective writer at work.

I n this chapter, we explore the importance of *written communication* as it connects to professional excellence. All the chapters in this book have focused on human communication. We have spent a great deal of time emphasizing the importance of culture in the workplace, interpersonal relationships, team communication, leadership, and communication and technology. These topics are essential to your study of business and professional communication. Further, human relationships are essential as you enter, excel in, and survive in your career. Yet our study of business and professional communication is not complete without attention to written communication. In Chapter 4, we reviewed a number of written communication essentials, such as cover letters and résumés, in the process of *getting the job*. Now we will turn our attention to some basic principles for excellence in all types of written communication. In addition, we will cover some specific types of written communication that you are likely to encounter on the job. What types of written communication skills do you think you may use *on the job?* What can you do on the job regarding your written communication that will ensure professional excellence?

# The Importance of Written Communication

What would you do if you were hired for a new position that required you to communicate in a variety of styles and formats? Written communication can challenge professionals entering a variety of positions, regardless of industry. We point this out because many readers of this text may have some of the same concerns as Yolanda (discussed later in this chapter). How do I select the correct format to get the message out? Is it appropriate for me to send this document via e-mail? What tone should I strive for in this message? How much detail about the new company initiative should I include in the press release? How should the memo be organized? Indeed, these questions about written communication that are emerging as you take this course may continue to present a challenge as you transition into your career or excel as a professional.

Written communication is important for the following reasons: (1) Official documents, memos, e-mail, and other forms of written communication reveal something about you as a professional; (2) important policies, requests, and organizational procedures are conveyed through written communication; (3) proposals, employee terminations, media relations, and the like are achieved with written communication; and (4) written communication must be present in order to achieve professional excellence. To address these important topics, let's take a look at ways to strive for written communication excellence.

## Striving for Written Communication Excellence

So how do you develop excellence in written communication? In this section, we review some strategies that will help your development: message structure, message clarity, and message presentation.

Written communication and organizational skills are critical in managing large amounts of information in today's business and professional world.

### Message Structure

The good news is, the principles you learned for developing an excellent presentation are the same principles you need for developing excellent written communication. Excellent written communication begins with a clear general purpose, a clear specific purpose or thesis, and clear organization. Begin by asking yourself, "What is the purpose of this written communication? Am I presenting new information? Am I clarifying? Am I requesting? Am I persuading?" Once you have identified your general purpose, ask yourself, "What is the key message I want my audience to take away from this e-mail, report, or memo?" By answering this question, you will have identified your specific purpose or thesis statement. From there, you can begin organizing your message. We strongly recommend that you develop an outline before you begin writing. This outline will help you determine the organizational structure of your message. Remember this: Poor organization will lead to ineffective communication. Simply put, if the reader cannot follow your message, the reader cannot understand your message.

### Message Clarity

Developing clear organization is the first step to message clarity. However, clear organization alone does not guarantee that your message will be clear. To maximize message clarity, you must evaluate your audience and avoid generalities.

As with all forms of communication, excellence in written communication requires you to evaluate your audience. Ask yourself, "Who will read this written document?" In many cases, you will have both a primary audience—the person or persons the message is addressed to—and a secondary audience—other readers who may need or use this information. Keep all readers in mind as you draft your message. Consider details such as the reader's place in the organization (supervisor, employee, customer), his or her level of understanding (both educational level and experience in your industry), and the amount of interest and involvement with the topic at hand. This evaluation will help you determine if jargon can be used and if background information is needed.

## Know Yourself   Writing Startup Sheet

*The following startup sheet will help you gain a better understanding of your own writing. Answer each question thought-fully, and then reflect on the results. How can this knowledge help you be a better communicator?*

### Audience

1. Who is my primary reader/audience? Who else will be reading this?

   _____

2. Did I provide the necessary information?

   _____

3. How does the information relate to the reader/audience?

   _____

4. How does my reader/audience feel about this information/subject?

   _____

### Purpose

5. The purpose of this written communication is to _____ so that my audience will _____.

### Delivery

6. What's the best channel for this message? Hard copy? E-mail? Phone? In person?
7. When should I send this message?

Would you find the writing startup sheet useful in a professional setting? What types of written communication are you the most concerned about?

Source: Adapted from Lindsell-Roberts (2004, p. 24).

Message clarity is also achieved by using specific language as opposed to general language (Bly, 1999; Travers, 2012). **General language** is usually characterized as vague statements that can easily be misunderstood, whereas **specific language** makes precise references. For example, Dr. Jones could write the general statement that she has excellent patient satisfaction scores, or she could make the specific, clearer claim that 97% of her patients reported the highest level of satisfaction. During a reprimand, the manager could write, "You need to return from lunch in a timely fashion." But his message would be much clearer if he specifically wrote, "You must return from lunch by 1:00 p.m."

### Message Presentation

In addition to considering message structure and message clarity, you must consider message presentation. Unlike spoken communication, there is a lasting visual element to your written communication. Message presentation refers to that visual component. Carelessly written communication will send the message that you are a careless employee or leader. With spelling and grammar check, as well as good old-fashioned proofreading, **typos** (mistakes in typing), **misspellings** (mistakes in spelling), and **grammar** errors (sentence fragments, inappropriate use of punctuation, etc.) can be corrected. Just as a typo on your résumé can lose you a job, a typo on a report can cause you to lose credibility. Misspellings, typos, and sending something to the wrong department are all roadblocks to professional excellence. As the KEYS approach has taught you, know yourself. For some of you, knowing yourself will mean realizing that you are not very good at editing your own work. Many of us who are good at editing others' work struggle to edit our own work. If that is the case, get a colleague to proofread your document before sending it out.

To achieve professional excellence, your documents and e-mails should be typed in black ink and should be legible. In addition, your typeface must be dark enough to read. Documents with poor ink quality look unprofessional and are ineffective.

In addition to the preceding tips for written communication, we recommend using a **writing startup sheet**—a list of questions that encourage the writer to think about audience, purpose, key issues, and delivery.

# Types of Written Communication

What types of written communication will you encounter as a professional? While the various types of business letters, memos, e-mails, and the like depend on the industry you work in, it's important for you to be prepared and begin to form a toolbox from which to work as a professional. In the sections that follow, we cover the following types of written communication: business letters, employee review letters, recommendation letters, thank-you letters, memos, proposals and reports, planning documents, press releases, and e-mail.

## Business Letters

The **business letter** is

used to communicate formal matters in business, jurisprudence, or otherwise. You will use this form of correspondence when you want to write a cover letter to accompany your résumé, write a letter announcing business news to colleagues outside your company, or notify vendors of a change in your ordering procedures. (Bly, 1999, p. 21)

As you strive for professional excellence, remember that business letters, when not composed appropriately, can be ineffective and lead to miscommunication.

Have you ever received a letter that did not keep your attention? What reaction do you have when your name is misspelled in a document? Review the following examples to help you get started. To begin, we've included a basic business letter template, followed by an actual example that includes a price quote for services (see Sample 9.1).

**Sample 9.1 Business Letter With Price Quote**

XYZ Corporation
650 Wayward Avenue
Houston, TX 73850
**(Letterhead)**

September 23, 2012 **(Date)**
ABC Global Services **(Address of the recipient)**
PO Box 32555
Tyrone, PA 16801
Dear Mr. Stobbs, **(Opening/greeting)**

XYZ proposes to furnish all necessary labor, supervision, materials, tools, and equipment for the installation of the electrical work for the above referenced project, as detailed herein, in accordance with our interpretations of the intent of the design for the Lump Sum price of **Fourteen Thousand Six Hundred Forty Nine Dollars and No Cents. . . . $14,649.00.**

*Breakdown:*

1. Labor:       $1,068.00
2. Material:    $13,581.00

*Scope of work:*

1. Furnish and install:
    a. Battery Monitoring System
    b. (1) Duplex Receptacle in computer room
    c. (1) Cat 5E cable from UPS to computer room

*Clarifications:*

1. All work to be based on straight time first shift.
2. Due to rising cost of materials and/or labor, we reserve the right to adjust this proposal if not accepted within thirty (30) days of the above date.

Respectfully yours, **(Closing)**

*Cheryl Banks*

Cheryl Banks
Project Manager

In addition to providing price quotes for services with business letters, you will also communicate with other departments and businesses. Below is a **downsizing letter** (Sample 9.2) used to inform other businesses about skilled employees available for employment due to company downsizing (e.g., layoffs, fired employees).

## Employee Reviews

Written communication is central to providing feedback to employees regarding job performance. **Employee reviews** serve as a form of written communication used in business

**Sample 9.2 Business Letter for Employee Downsizing**

ABC Global Services
PO Box 32555
Tyrone, PA 16801

April 25, 2012
Dear Fellow Employer:

As you may know, Company ABC has announced a plan that will enhance workforce operations and safety. Part of the plan has entailed restructuring the Company ABC workforce. This transition will better the business in a competitive global market. As a result, about 400 dedicated and skilled employees will be separated and ready for employment with your company as early as January. This workforce has been successful in producing the best results in Company ABC history in areas such as productivity, quality, safety, and customer service.

These employees have extensive experience in a variety of areas and have been trained in Customer Service Excellence, Team Work Efficiency, Statistical Process Control (SPC), and Employee Motivation Programs. This is a world-class workforce. They are highly motivated, safety conscious, and have broad experience in a wide variety of disciplines.

To assist our employees in their transition to new careers, we have established a Career Resource Center at the Phoenix Community Center, which will be operational from 9:00 a.m. to 6:00 p.m., Monday through Friday, for several months. If you have employment opportunities available, *I encourage you to contact our Career Resource Center by calling 814-444-1234.* If we are not available, please leave a voice message or send an e-mail to TurnoverTeam@CRC.com. We will be happy to assist you by sending résumés, posting job opportunities, and/or setting up interviews.

You can be assured that inquiries will be handled promptly and confidentially. Thank you for your consideration. We look forward to assisting you in achieving your employment goals.

Sincerely,

*Paul Stobbs*

Paul Stobbs
Human Resources Director

and professional settings to provide feedback to employees about how they are performing on the job. These reviews are typically filed with personnel documents. Written communication related to employee reviews must be accurate and reflect actual employee performance. Remember, this type of document should be utilized carefully to document positive performance and areas for the employee to improve. If an employee is a candidate for mandatory leave, an improvement plan, or termination, these review documents must be used to document a pattern of employee performance. Further, employee review documents serve as a method of informing employees how to improve on the job.

## Recommendation Letters

In addition to employee reviews, another type of letter that is commonplace across industries and academic disciplines is the **recommendation letter**—a form of written communication used to provide a documented reference for students and professionals.

# Your Communication Interaction    Employee Review Letter

*Read the passage below, and then answer the questions. As you read, think about ways the KEYS approach could help you improve **your communication interaction** (in this case, written communication in the form of an annual evaluation) if you were in Samantha's position.*

[COMPANY STATIONERY]
ANNUAL FACULTY REVIEW        March 1, 2012

Dr. Colt Holcomb, Assistant Professor of Communication

To:    Personnel Annual Review File
From:    Samantha Newday, Chair
         Richard Blue, Assistant Chair
         Department of Communication

This review is for the 2012 calendar year. As per the College personnel policy, any additions or corrections to this review may be added to the file by Dr. Holcomb.

*ACADEMIC PREPARATION

Dr. Holcomb earned his PhD from the University of Jackson in May 2005. His areas of specialization include communication and new media.

*EXPERIENCE

Dr. Holcomb has been employed as an assistant professor of Communication since August of 2006.

*TEACHING

Dr. Holcomb taught during the Fall, Spring, and Summer semesters of 2012. Specifically, he taught COMM 5399: Race, Gender, and Class in Media; COMM 3380: Media and Technology (two sections); COMM 3340: Public Relations Techniques; COMM 3311: Nonverbal Communication; and COMM 1315: Public Speaking (five sections). He also taught two sections of COMM 3330: Techniques of Persuasion, which were stacked for graduate credit with COMM 5311. In addition, he supervised one graduate- and one undergraduate-directed individual study. Three of these courses were new preparations for Dr. Holcomb.

As indicated by his overall instructor scores, all of Dr. Holcomb's item scores were below the College goal of 4.0. His overall instructor means ranged from 3.74 to 3.87. Dr. Holcomb is dedicated to teaching but has been receiving

A letter of recommendation is needed when a college/university or employer requests one, and it's something that many, if not all, of the readers of this text will need throughout their careers. Your professors are asked to write many recommendation letters for current and past students. Your careful preparation will help your professor write the best letter below-average scores. Dr. Holcomb focuses on student learning as he designs his courses. His inclusion of service learning in several of his courses increases his workload but enhances the student learning experience. His oral and written student evaluations demonstrate that the students enjoy this approach despite challenging assignments. He attributes the below-average instructor scores to course rigor.

*INSTITUTIONAL, COMMUNITY, AND/OR PROFESSIONAL SERVICE

In terms of professional service, Dr. Holcomb served on the editorial boards for *Communication Teacher*, *Georgia Speech Communication Journal*, and *Basic Communication Course Annual*.

*SCHOLARLY/CREATIVE ACTIVITIES

Dr. Holcomb had a productive year in terms of scholarly activity. In the area of refereed journal articles, he had three pieces in various stages of publication. His piece "Visual Communication Research" was published in *Visual Communication* during 2012. He had a second article in press in *Communication Monographs*. Finally, he was working on a revise and resubmit for an article in *Human Communication Research*.

Dr. Holcomb also remained active by presenting three papers and two panel presentations at the National Communication Association's Annual Conference in Chicago.

Dr. Holcomb exceeded his scholarship goals for 2012. For 2013, he plans to revise and resubmit his article for *Management Communication Quarterly*.

*SUMMARY

Dr. Holcomb's performance is average. His teaching evaluations are below the College goal. His service to the profession is acceptable. Dr. Holcomb's scholarship is exemplary. He is scheduled to participate in a teaching development circle to try to improve his teaching evaluation scores.

## Questions to Consider

1. Do you think this is an effective evaluation? Why or why not?
2. Is the feedback on this evaluation specific?
3. Does Samantha Newday give Dr. Holcomb clear information on future expectations or ways to improve?
4. How could the KEYS approach improve this communication interaction?

possible. You as a student must take responsibility and initiative in the letter-writing process. Although professors will vary in their preferences, Tables 9.1 and 9.2 offer some tips. See Sample 9.3 for an example of a recommendation written by a professor for a student applying for a professional position.

# Ethical Connection    Andrea's Trouble With Plagiarism

*Please read the passage below, and answer the questions that follow.*

Andrea is a graduate assistant in her final semester at the university. She has never been an excellent writer, and her job required her to make significant contributions to an academic paper being published by the university. When Andrea found her contributions to be entirely too short, she took large sections from another article, which was already published, to meet the page requirements. While she did not simply copy and paste entire sections into her paper, she made only trivial changes to the wording and did not give proper credit to the original article's author. Andrea was incredibly surprised when she was informed the university was letting her go. When she talked with the head of her department, Dr. Jones, he said that he was familiar with the paper she got her information from and considered it plagiarism since there were no citations. Dr. Jones also informed Andrea that it would be hard for her to find employment at another university with a plagiarism charge on her record.

## Questions to Consider

1. What ethical boundaries did Andrea cross by taking research from another paper?
2. Why would a charge of plagiarism hurt Andrea's chances of finding another job at a university?
3. How could Andrea have avoided this outcome through the decisions she made about her writing?
4. Using the KEYS process, explain what steps Andrea could have taken to become a more effective writer.

## Thank-You Letters

In our consulting practice, we encourage professionals at all levels across industries to set a goal for using **thank-you letters**—written communication used to express appreciation to coworkers and clients. With the intensity of e-mail, text messages, and all the information professionals manage, it's easy to forget a simple thank you. Thank-you letters can be sent via e-mail (which is great for delivery speed), but think about how impressive it is to actually receive a handwritten note. We encourage you to keep professional thank-you cards in your work area to write letters or notes of appreciation. In addition to thank-you letters helping you achieve professional excellence on the job, they can also be used as **networking notes**—a form of thank-you letter used to remind employers of your interview and to emphasize that you're the right person for the job. In fact, employers often say that a sincere thank-you letter can give a job candidate the edge over another competing candidate. Review the example below (Sample 9.4), and set a goal to use thank-you letters both on the job and to network for new jobs or promotions.

## Memos

Other types of written communication used in professional settings are **memos.** The word *memo* is short for *memorandum* and is typically a short note or update distributed in business. Memos should be reserved for communicating information that's critically important. The memo format we recommend is provided in Sample 9.5.

## Table 9.1 Ten Reasons Letters Fail

1. *Poor message.* The message is poorly written.
2. *Insensitive salutation.* The salutation is too impersonal. For example, avoid "Hey" or just jumping right into the message.
3. *Too much on one page.* People often try to fit too much on one page.
4. *Lack of signature.* Many people forget to sign their names on letters or to include their names in e-mail messages.
5. *Spelling errors.* Spelling errors harm your credibility.
6. *Grammatical errors.* Grammatical mistakes harm your credibility.
7. *Self-absorbed sender.* The letter is focused on the sender, leading the reader to lose interest. Try to focus on "we" instead of "me."
8. *Poor font choice.* The reader should not be exposed to numerous font styles and colors.
9. *Tone.* The tone is not conversational.
10. *Long paragraphs.* The paragraphs are too long, leading the reader to lose focus.

Source: Lindsell-Roberts (2004, p. 4).

## Table 9.2 Tips for Obtaining a Recommendation Letter With Professional Excellence

### A. *Asking the professor to write a letter of recommendation*

**1) Ask the professor in person.**

The important words above are

- "*ask*"—No professor owes you a letter. You are requesting help from that person; make your statement in the form of a request. Be willing to take "no" for an answer.

- "*in person*"—Do not put the request under an office door or leave it in a mailbox or grab the professor in the hallway or after class. Ask the professor to write a letter when he or she will have time to discuss this with you, preferably during posted office hours.

**2) Ask if the professor would be able to write you a *favorable* letter of recommendation.**

- If the professor cannot honestly write a favorable letter, you will want to find another person who will.

**3) Ask if the professor would be able to write you a *specific* letter of recommendation.**

- If the professor does not know you well enough to be specific in his or her comments, the letter will not do you much good anyway. Ask someone else.

### B. *Your responsibility: What you should do for the professor*

**1) Allow ample time for the professor to write the letter.**

- At least *2 weeks* should be allowed.

*(Continued)*

(Continued)

**2)  Provide the professor with *all* the relevant forms and instructions.**

- Put all materials in a large labeled envelope (including your name and phone number) so the materials will not get lost.
- If the organization provides a form for the letter, give the form to the professor.
- If the organization provides general instructions for preparing letters, make a copy of the instructions for the professor. Highlight the instructions.
- Make sure the professor has the *correct address, person/organization to whom the letter is addressed* (make sure all this is spelled correctly), and the *deadline* for submitting the letter. Some will want this information electronically. Check with your recommender.

**3)  Type in all information you are responsible for providing.**

- *Type* your name and other information on *all* forms where needed (do not hand write—it looks tacky and unprofessional).

**4)  Provide the professor with your résumé and statement of your goals.**

- *In writing,* remind the professor of your major(s) and minor(s), which classes you took from the professor, term when you took the classes, and grades received in those classes.
- Provide the professor with any information about your participation in the class, projects completed, etc. Help the professor recall your class performance in as much detail as possible.
- Remind the professor about teaching assistantships, internships, research projects, grants.
- Provide the professor with information on some of your college activities, especially leadership positions held and awards won.
- Provide the professor with a statement of your career goals and/or reasons for choosing the university/ job for which you are applying.

**5)  Provide the professor with an addressed envelope for each recommendation.**

- *Type* the correct address on each envelope (ask for university envelopes if they are needed; some professors will not need envelope types—just ask).

**6)  Make sure the professor has sent the letter of recommendation.**

- *Politely check* with the professor *a few days before the deadline* to make sure the letter has been completed and sent. Don't be shy about this—we do forget! It is your job to make sure the letter has been sent.

**7)  Follow up the recommendation with a thank-you letter to the professor.**

- Letters of recommendation take time, thought, and effort. Let the recommender know you appreciate the effort made on your behalf.

**C.  *Do students get copies of the letters of recommendation?***

**1)  Each professor will have a policy on giving students copies of the recommendations.**

- You may ask the professor what the policy is if you desire a copy.

**2)  Some professors will be willing to discuss their recommendations with you after they are written.**

- If you wish, you may ask the professor if he or she would be willing to discuss the recommendations with you.

Source: Table adapted and reproduced with permission of © Dawn O. Braithwaite, updated 2002, Communication Studies, Department University of Nebraska-Lincoln. Earlier version published in *Association for School, College and University Staffing Annual,* Addison, IL, 1989.

## Sample 9.3 Recommendation Letter

Matt Hicks, General Manager
Clear Channel of Dallas
501 Tupper Lane, Dallas, TX 78915

Dear Mr. Hicks,

I am writing to recommend to you Brad White as a member of your professional staff. I have known Brad as a student in numerous courses at Coastal Wave College. I also have knowledge of his work ethic and dedication to internships in our department as well as in part-time professional work. I would like to note that I choose not to inflate letters of recommendation but rather reflect my honest evaluation of the applicant. With that, I honestly believe Brad would make a good addition to your team.

Brad's work as an undergraduate student has been solid and I believe reflects the type of progress one should make when applying for professional positions. In fact, I have seen Brad's work from a video-production project and public relations campaign, as well as in community relations. His work is simply outstanding, which is proven by his status as an honors graduate. There are only a few students in each class that hold this status. Beyond his proven abilities in the classroom, Brad is the type of person who will go the extra mile in any professional position. He has proven this with both his academic and professional experiences. If you have additional questions, please feel free to call me at 587-222-1234.

Sincerely,

*Molly Duncan*

Molly Duncan, PhD
Assistant Professor of Communication
Coastal Wave College
Phone: 907-123-4567

As you can see, the four major elements of the basic memo are "date," "to," "from," and "re" (regarding what topic). Remember to be careful with memos in terms of frequency and topic. Frequent memos will come to be expected, leaving important information ignored. Employees may also respond negatively to the topics addressed and the tone of a memo. To illustrate our point regarding topic and tone in business memos, review the case study of Yolanda's use of memos (in Step Back and Reflect on page 217) to see what can go wrong with memos if used inappropriately.

Memos can also be used to communicate **process directives**—descriptions of new policies/procedures and changes to those that are already in place. Process directives are distributed to the employees or departments the

Saying thank you is something that is often neglected in our fast-paced society. Those who give attention to expressing appreciation in the form of electronic and handwritten notes tend to have a professional edge over others.

# Evaluate the Professional Context

## Bonnie Needs a Recommendation Letter

*Read the following passage about Bonnie, and then answer the questions. As you read, focus on* **evaluating the professional context**.

Bonnie found out about a new scholarship, and she needed to fill out the application as soon as possible. The only problem was that she found out about it at the last minute, and a recommendation letter from a professor on campus was required. She had taken Dr. Chang for several courses, so she felt it was okay to ask for a recommendation letter. Bonnie had so many things going on and didn't have time to make an appointment or call, so she dropped by during Dr. Chang's office hours. The following interaction took place regarding the letter:

**Bonnie:** Hi, Dr. Chang! I'm really in a bind. I need you to write me a recommendation letter today. I figured that since your office hours were from 1:00 to 3:00 p.m., you would have time to get it done before your next class. I'm really in hurry, and I figured I could count on you.

**Dr. Chang:** Bonnie, I actually have an appointment with another student about a project, and she's about to come in any minute.

**Bonnie:** Oh, that's okay. I'll just wait outside until you're done with the other student. If you can get it done by 2:45 p.m. that will work for me.

**Dr. Chang:** Unfortunately, I will not be able to get to the letter today. I really need more of a notice. I am more than happy to help but would need some specific information about the scholarship and where to send the letter.

Bonnie was not happy about Dr. Chang's response. What was she supposed to do? While we all have busy schedules and encounter sudden deadlines that are out of our control, requesting a recommendation letter has to be done with professional excellence at the core. Clearly, Bonnie was not successful in her approach to getting a letter from Dr. Chang.

## Questions to Consider

1. Did Bonnie act appropriately given the professional context?

2. Was Dr. Chang's behavior professional? Why or why not?

3. What can you learn from Bonnie's experience?

4. How could the KEYS process help Bonnie improve her communication skills?

---

### Sample 9.4 Thank-You Letter: On the Job

Dear Yolanda,

Thank you for all your hard work on the communication audit. Things have been really challenging during this past quarter, and I just wanted to take a moment to express my appreciation for your work ethic and commitment to Company ABC.

Warmest regards,
Virginia

Source: Lindsell-Roberts (2004).

---

**Sample 9.5  Basic Memo**

> **Date:** _____
> **TO:** _____
> **FROM:** _____
> **RE:** _____

Source: Bly (1999).

---

# Step Back and Reflect    The Attitude Memo

*Read the following passage, and answer the questions that follow.*

*Shannon:*   Did you see that memo from Yolanda?

*Joel:*   No, what's going on?

*Shannon:*   She sent another memo about team attitude. The team is getting really annoyed.

*Joel:*   Has anyone responded?

*Shannon:*   No, but I heard that several employees have been complaining.

Based on this brief conversation between Shannon and Joel, it seems that Yolanda has done some damage using written communication. Yolanda is the assistant director of communication at Company ABC. Attitude and having fun are really important to Yolanda, so she decided to communicate her standards of performance with the following memo.

**Date**: October 20, 2012
**TO**: Communication Team
**FROM**: Yolanda Smith
**RE**: Team Attitude

I expect my team to showcase a positive attitude when working on projects. If you all have any questions about attitude, see me in my office.

Yolanda sent out memos like this once a week. Her goal was to have a highly cohesive team, and she wanted to be respected. However, things were not going very well. Her team seemed to get more and more negative and unmotivated as each week passed.

## Step Back and Reflect

1. What went wrong with Yolanda's memo?

2. How would you respond if you received a memo like this at your job? How could Yolanda's memo be improved?

3. How could she benefit from the KEYS process related to her written communication?

directive impacts and are filed as official documents of organizational policy. Yolanda has the task of writing a process directive for Company ABC. Her process directive is to be placed inside a memo and distributed as an internal communication announcement to let everyone know about a new company newsletter. The executive team wants to make sure that everyone in the organization is informed about the newsletter. The goal is for employees to feel a sense of community in the workplace by being informed about Company ABC activities. In addition to the employees knowing about the newsletter, Yolanda includes specific information in the process directive regarding to whom information for the newsletter should be sent, as well as deadlines for submitting information (see Sample 9.6).

---

### Sample 9.6  Process Directive Memo

[COMPANY LOGO]
PROCESS DIRECTIVE 126

**Date:**    November 16, 2012
**TO:**    All Company ABC Employees
**FROM:**    Yolanda Smith
**RE:**    Company ABC Quarterly Newsletter, Process Directive 126

*Objective:* To communicate important information from the Executive Team to the employees of Company ABC, as well as to the community. The primary goals of the Company ABC Quarterly Newsletter are to

- provide a newsletter to distribute information, both internally and externally, about plant operations and employee news in a QUARTERLY format;

- recognize employee social activities, retirements, and accomplishments;

- communicate information from the Lead Team, Gain Sharing, Safety, Employee Social activities, etc.;

- share the Company ABC Values with employee families and community leaders;

- establish a positive impression of the business in the community and enhance the workplace culture.

*Frequency:* The Company ABC Newsletter has been designed and approved to be distributed electronically, mailed to the employees' homes, and mailed to community leaders in a QUARTERLY format.

*Process:* The Lead Team and Business Unit Managers will contribute information to Virginia Wolf to prepare for distribution quarterly.

*Newsletter Contact:* Virginia Wolf will collect information for each section of the newsletter. Members of the Executive Team should

- send information to Virginia Wolf to prepare for distribution each quarter;

- pay attention to activities, such as social clubs and activities, to be included;

- support internal and external distribution of the newsletter;

- respond to calls for information to be included in the newsletter.

*Directive:* Company ABC provides access to the Newsletter in both electronic and printed formats. Members of the Executive Team and all Company ABC employees should support the distribution of the newsletter to institutionalize effective communication, enhance workplace culture, and build positive impressions of the business in the community.

Clearly, Yolanda's memo included specific information about the goals and processes of the Company ABC Newsletter. With so many changes and new initiatives flying around in an organization, effective written communication is a must. What if Company ABC started a newsletter without informing the frontline employees and those in management about what to expect?

## Proposals and Reports

In addition to memos, **proposals** are also utilized in many business and professional settings to propose products and services to potential clients. The sample provided below is a short proposal that describes the major components of a **workforce communication assessment**—an inventory or evaluation of the communication practices of an organization (also known as a communication audit). The proposal in Sample 9.7 describes what the client can expect from the communication assessment. Notice how the proposal includes an objective and description of each component of the assessment (e.g., survey, focus groups, recommendations, project completion, project hours).

Now that you have a basic understanding of how a short business proposal looks, let's review **reports**—written communication used to summarize research or assessment

---

**Sample 9.7  Proposal for Services**

**WORKFORCE COMMUNICATION ASSESSMENT**
**COMPANY ABC**
Prepared By
[INSERT NAME]

**WORKFORCE COMMUNICATION ASSESSMENT**
**PART I: SURVEY**
*OBJECTIVE:* Evaluate communication preferences of Company ABC workforce
*DESCRIPTION:*

1. Survey Planning with Company ABC Leadership Team

2. Workforce Communication Survey will be designed

3. Company ABC survey will

   ✓ focus on communication effectiveness (best way to get the message out),

   ✓ identify what is ineffective (communication channels that don't work),

   ✓ include areas in which the Leadership Team is interested,

   ✓ evaluate important factors related to employees' on-the-job experience (satisfaction, morale, managerial support, communication expectations),

   ✓ be reviewed and approved by Leadership Team.

4. Workforce will be surveyed

5. Information from survey will be prepared and presented to Leadership Team

*(Continued)*

(Continued)

### PART II: FOCUS GROUPS

*OBJECTIVE:* Collect specific preferences about how to communicate effective messages at Company ABC
*DESCRIPTION:*

1. Focus Group Planning with Company ABC Leadership Team
2. Workforce Focus Groups will be designed
3. Company ABC Focus Groups will

   ✓ collect specific information about employee communication needs,

   ✓ identify specific ways to communicate effective messages at Company ABC,

   ✓ include questions in which the Leadership Team is interested,

   ✓ explore specific factors related to employees' on-the-job experience (satisfaction, morale, managerial support, communication expectations).

4. Focus Groups will be conducted
5. Information from Focus Groups will be prepared and presented to Leadership Team

### PART III: RECOMMENDATION

Based on the information collected from the surveys and focus groups, recommendations will be made to the Company ABC Leadership Team. Information will be provided about how Company ABC can communicate effectively during reorganization and as it moves forward.

**PROJECT COMPLETION:** Early January 2013
**PROJECT HOURS:** Not to exceed contract

findings to inform managers about important issues related to business (e.g., customer service, employee satisfaction, employee morale). Remember that reports are used to summarize both **quantitative data** (characterized by numbers, percentages, statistics, and surveys) and **qualitative data** (characterized by actual words, phrases, responses to open-ended questions, and interviews). The report provided in Sample 9.8 is an example of what could be presented at the completion of a workforce communication assessment. As you see, this sample focuses on reporting focus-group data.

This focus-group report with recommendations, as well as other forms of research about businesses and organizations, can lead to changes in business strategies. Once an executive leadership team has had time to review recommendations made by a particular department or outside consulting firm, it's not uncommon to begin planning for the future of the organization. The next section explores the role of planning documents as forms of written communication.

## Planning Documents

Once the organization knows its strengths and weaknesses, business leaders often engage in **strategic planning**—the development of a plan that emphasizes goals, initiatives, strategies, and targets utilized to help employees strive for a shared vision and commitment to the core values in an organization. What do planning documents look like? Virginia has asked Yolanda to put together an **internal communication plan** (a plan that focuses on communication taking place inside the daily operations of any given business) and an **external communication plan** (a plan that focuses on communicating information about the organization or business to citizens or employee families outside any given business). **Planning documents** are forms of written communication usually presented with maps and other visual designs to lay out a broader vision of where the company is going and what specific strategies will be utilized in the near future. Since Yolanda was struggling with her written communication on the job, she asked Virginia to help her come up with some basic planning documents for both the internal and external communication plan at Company ABC. The two samples provided (Samples 9.9 and 9.10) are good starting points to help employees understand components in both the internal and external communication plans at Company ABC.

## Press Releases

When an organization or business wants to make an announcement to the community, it uses **press releases**—forms of written communication used to send messages and make announcements to a variety of media organizations, including newspapers, radio, television news, and Internet

Written communication entails paying special attention to confidential records and information privacy.

---

### Sample 9.8 Focus Group Report and Recommendations

(REMINDER: Reports like the one in this sample usually include an appropriate title page, table of contents, and bibliography.)

**Private and Confidential**
Prepared for Company ABC by Strategic Communication Concepts, March 2012
**Company ABC: Focus Group Report and Recommendations**
*Yolanda Smith,*
*Director of Communications*

### DATA COLLECTION INFORMATION

- Number of Focus Groups: 10
- Number of Focus Group Participants: 99
- Length of Focus Group Interviews: 62–87 minutes

*(Continued)*

(Continued)

## OVERVIEW

The report that follows includes major themes and specific responses to the current communication, morale, safety, and benefits at Company ABC. Hourly, salaried, and executive leadership employees participated in focus group forums in which they discussed major topics connected to communication at Company ABC (communication about change, workforce preferences on how to communicate/get the message out, morale, safety, and benefits). In order to articulate a clear sense of the focus group responses, the report is organized as follows: (1) *overall reaction and tone*, (2) *communication*, (3) *safety*, and (4) *benefits/rewards and recognition*. In addition, the report includes recommendations regarding communication methods and strategies to support the future of Company ABC.

Thematic Analysis of Data

*Overall Reaction and Tone*

The overall reaction and tone in the focus group discussions were extremely negative. Focus group participants all expressed dissatisfaction, low morale, and uncertainty about their jobs at Company ABC. The participants specified that they feel "in the dark" and that all they hear are rumors about people getting fired, big layoffs, and contract negotiations. Lack of communication, job uncertainty, and poor working conditions were central themes in all 10 groups. The participants noted that this is the worst they have ever seen Company ABC in terms of morale. Themes of job uncertainty, low morale, and poor communication were consistent across all groups. The themes are summarized with the following comments:

- "We are completely in the dark about what is going on around here."
- [Insert other responses or comments.]

*Communication*

All 10 focus groups provided insight into specifics and/or priorities for improving communication. In doing so, they addressed what is not currently working and what they would like to see in terms of improvement.
*Communication About Change.* All 10 groups were clearly confused about the direction of Company ABC, as well as organizational changes.

- "They tell us that change is coming, but we don't know what that is. They intentionally keep us in the dark."
- [Insert other comments.]

*Methods of Communication.* All 10 groups noted methods of communication available but not used, such as e-mail, technical tools, electronic message boards, bulletin boards, and memos. This theme was summarized with the following comments:

- "People do not use e-mail. There are over 1,100 employees here; only about 450 use e-mail."
- [Insert other comments.]

Overall, there was an agreement in all 10 groups that there are communication methods (mechanisms) available at the plant that work but are simply not being used. Information is not current.

*Safety*

All 10 focus groups expressed major concerns about safety procedures and poor working conditions.
*Safety Procedures and Workplace Conditions.* In all 10 groups, discussions about safety focused on poor workplace conditions at Company ABC as demonstrated by the following comments:

- "This place gives lip service to safety. They do not care about safety. The only thing they are interested in is production."
- [Insert other comments.]

### Benefits/Rewards and Recognition

Throughout the discussions, all 10 focus groups expressed major dissatisfaction with benefits and a lack of reward/recognition at Company ABC. All 10 groups discussed a need for increased wages and more reward/recognition. Of the 10 groups, 8 specifically discussed the need for more clarity when it comes to gain-sharing goals.

*Benefits and Pay.* All the focus groups made comments about their dissatisfaction with the benefits and pay at Company ABC.

- "We used to make a good living around here. Our health insurance has gone up, our copays are higher, and the company has done nothing to offset our costs."
- [Insert other comments.]

*Gain Sharing.* All 10 focus groups expressed major dissatisfaction with gain sharing.

- "They lie to us about gain sharing."
- [Insert other comments.]

*Rewards and Recognition.* Of the 10 focus groups, 9 expressed major concerns with the current reward and recognition of Company ABC employees. Interestingly, one focus group argued about reward and recognition. Several participants believed that a paycheck should be enough incentive. The individuals who disagreed with the majority contended that reward and recognition are never good enough for people and that someone will always complain. However, the majority of focus group participants emphasized that reward and recognition need to be improved.

- "The newsletter used to let us know who retired and who was new to the plant. They don't inform us about accomplishments or what's going on. We are never recognized and are not appreciated."
- [Insert other comments.]

## Recommendations

### 1. Bulletin Board Locations

*All locked bulletin boards need to be cleaned up. All old announcements need to be removed. There needs to be a date and posting system in place. All messages approved for distribution should be monitored. After a designated period of time, messages/postings should be removed.

*Insert other recommendations.

### 2. Terminate Wide Distribution of Company ABC Daily Report

### 3. Replace Company ABC Daily With Company ABC Monthly Newsletter

*Company ABC must revive a monthly newsletter that is both distributed at work and mailed home so the employees and families are exposed to the message. The newsletter should be made available at designated locations at the plant.

*[Insert other recommendations.]

(Continued)

(Continued)

### 4. *Revive Use of Electronic Message Boards*

*Company ABC must revive use of Electronic Message Boards.
*[Insert other recommendations.]

### 5. *Emphasize Traditional Face-to-Face Communication*

*There must be designated communication and team time.
*[Insert other recommendations.]

### 6. *Train Leaders as Information Facilitators*

*Team leads, managers, or those designated as leaders at Company ABC must be trained in effective oral communication and meeting facilitation.
*[Insert other recommendations.]

### 7. *Town Hall Meetings Hosted by Executive Team*

*After the Journey to Excellence plan moves forward, host town hall meetings about Company ABC.
*[Insert other recommendations.]

### 8. *Craft a Message and Disseminate to Community*

*Advertise positive message about Company ABC to external audience.
*[Insert other recommendations.]

### 9. *Utilize Professional Communication and Marketing Consultants*

*Administration should continue to seek outside professional communication/transition experts (e.g., Strategic Communication Concepts, The Turnover Team) for technical assistance and advice.
*[Insert other recommendations.]

### 10. *Develop Employee Orientation Program*

*As Company ABC makes the transition, develop employee orientation program that can be first used with all current employees who are onboard with the transition. The orientation should be required for everyone who is going to stay and, of course, all new employees.
*[Insert other recommendations.]

### 11. *Employee Development Series*

*As Company ABC makes the transition, develop employee education series on topics that support the Company ABC Values.
*[Insert other recommendations.]

## Appendix A
## Focus Group Participants

|  | Salaried | Hourly | Executive |
|---|---|---|---|
| **Total** | 41 | 58 | 3 |

**Total = 99 participants**
**Executive Leadership representatives = 3 participants**

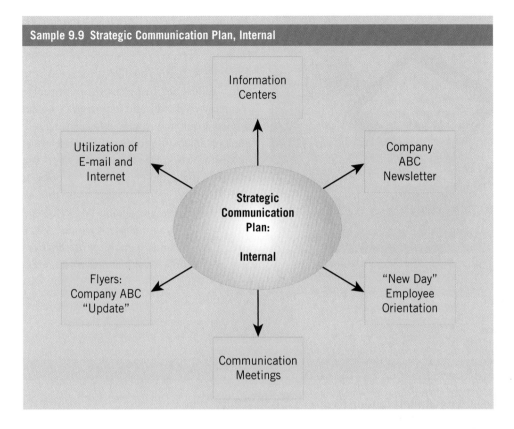

Sample 9.9  Strategic Communication Plan, Internal

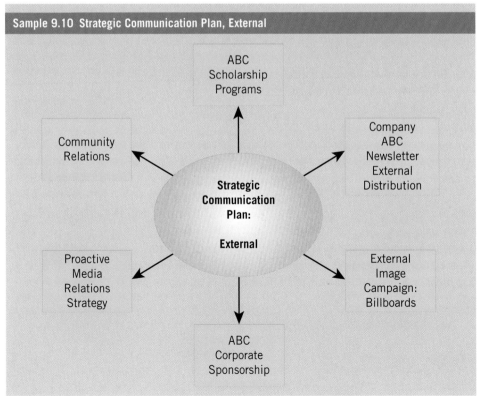

Sample 9.10  Strategic Communication Plan, External

Graphs, charts, and maps are integral to writing with communication excellence.

reporters. Company ABC is experiencing change on a number of levels. While the company is laying off a number of frontline employees, highly qualified managers and team leaders are being hired to encourage company efficiency and improved customer service. Company ABC is also investing millions of dollars in a remodeling project that makes the workplace cleaner and safer. The task is to make the changes taking place at Company ABC sound positive even though many employees are getting laid off. Read the sample press release (Sample 9.11), and grade Yolanda's effort. What changes or edits, if any, could improve the press release? What words did you identify that are vague?

**Sample 9.11  Sample Press Release**

## Company ABC Announces Modernization Plan

Company ABC said today that it is commencing a plan of optimization and modernization. The plan will feature an extensive overhaul and optimization of the company's workforce to improve productivity and coordinated capital investments to modernize key processes and safety in the plant. Both will be accomplished while keeping the plant at full production.

The workforce structure at Company ABC has been essentially unchanged since it was built in the early 1970s. The company underwent its last major expansion in the late 1980s and since has received major upgrades only to certain areas. As a result, the company will address all areas of operations to foster high-quality production in a safe working environment and excellence in customer service.

In an effort to improve productivity in a globally competitive market, an assessment of the plant started in 2008. An assessment team was formed to examine and evaluate every task performed in the company. The evaluation revealed a tremendous amount of underutilized potential in our employees. The Management of Company ABC developed an optimization plan to improve operation safety, productivity, and customer service. The optimization plan will entail reductions, reassignment, and realignments at all levels. A transition plan that offers employees educational and business opportunities has been put into place.

Part of the optimization plan includes an influx of new investment capital to modernize equipment that will improve processing efficiency, energy efficiency, product quality, safety, and customer service.

Our ultimate goal is to secure the long-term potential of this business and to become a serious competitor in the global market.

Contact Information:
Yolanda Smith
Media and Community Relations Coordinator
ABC Company
215-999-0000

**Sample 9.12  Proactive Media Writing**

## Company ABC in Compliance With Mercury Vapor Regulations

In recognition of a recent study released on the link between mercury exposure and cancer, Company ABC emphasizes its commitment to operations and community safety with assurance of state and federal environmental compliance. Company ABC understands the importance of medical and environmental research that helps educate company operations that are safe for its workforce and community. While the recent study raises some important discussion points for future research, the study does not substantiate any links between environmental pollutants and autism. Further, the amounts of mercury vapors released from the plant are minimal according to state and federal environmental regulations.

Realizing that some concern has been raised by one study, here is some information about the role of mercury in our operations at Company ABC. Mercury is a naturally occurring metallic element found throughout the crust of the earth in concentrations averaging about 0.5 ppm (1/2 of 1 part per million, equivalent to about 1/2 a teacup in a railroad tank car). Normally, it is found compounded with sulfur as the mineral cinnabar. In the pure or metallic form, it is a silver liquid at ordinary temperatures and for centuries was called "quicksilver." It has long been used in making pharmaceuticals, in the mining industry, and to treat fur and hides. The most common exposure most people have to mercury is in dental fillings, called amalgams, which are about 50% mercury.

Bauxite, like most soils, contains trace amounts of mercury in amounts ranging up to about 1/2 part per million. Each year, Company ABC processes about 3.8 million tons (about 7.7 billion pounds) of bauxite. Most of the mercury contained in the bauxite, typically 1,200 to 1,400 pounds per year, leaves the plant combined with the plant's main solid waste stream, bauxite residue, in the same solid mineral form in which it arrived. The residue is stored in large surface impoundments. The plant has permits that actually allow it to emit up to about 60 pounds per year into the air, but favorable plant chemistry stabilizes nearly all the material as a solid. Typically only 4 to 7 pounds per year are released into the atmosphere either as metallic mercury vapor or as an oxide.

Company ABC continues to modernize the plant to improve processing efficiency, energy efficiency, product quality, safety, and respect for the environment.

Our ultimate goal is to secure the long-term potential of this business and to become a serious competitor in the global market.

For more information, please contact:
Yolanda Smith
Media and Community Relations Coordinator
ABC Company
215-999-0000

## Proactive Media Writing

Obviously, press releases cover topics beyond workforce layoffs, bankruptcies, and corporate scandals. There are a number of positive things that organizations announce in press releases (e.g., scholarship programs, donations, community events). Industries that impact the environment and community safety (e.g., petrochemical facilities, oil refineries) are often held to standards set by the federal government. If you work for an organization that has the potential to harm people or the environment, it's critical to be ready to respond to news that can put your company in a negative light.

In addition to Yolanda writing the press release about the Company ABC Modernization and Optimization Plan, she also needed to focus on **proactive media writing**—a form of written

Working from home can be valuable during difficult times, but think about the advantages and disadvantages of checking e-mail from your home computer—technology tends to blend our personal and professional lives in many ways.

communication similar to a press release that emphasizes an organization's commitment to safety and compliance. There are certainly other components to a proactive media strategy. For example, oil refineries may choose to post billboards with images of their employees helping kids in the community. Put simply, if citizens in the community maintain a positive image of an organization, they will not immediately think of the potential harms brought on by the industry. Therefore, using written communication as a proactive media strategy helps the organization prepare for negative news that tarnishes the organization's reputation at the local, state, national, and perhaps even global levels. Read the sample proactive media release (Sample 9.12), and grade Yolanda's effort. Do you think she does a good job at damage control? Remember, written communication can make or break the image and overall success of a company, regardless of industry.

## E-mail

People working in businesses and professional organizations increasingly rely on their e-mail systems to communicate with colleagues and accomplish their work (Khan & Khan, 2012; Kibby, 2005; Shipley & Schwalbe, 2008; Thompson, 2008). Given how prevalent e-mail usage is and will continue to be in business and professional communication, we can't emphasize enough how important it is to strive for written communication and professional excellence when using e-mail.

Indeed, written communication is just as important when composing e-mail messages as it is with the other forms reviewed in this chapter. In the next chapter, you will learn about other e-mail concerns such as privacy, surveillance, electronic aggression, and the like as you strive for written communication and professional excellence. Table 9.3 provides a list of tips for writing e-mail with professional excellence.

### Table 9.3 Tips for Writing E-mail With Professional Excellence

✓ Avoid using ALL CAPS.
✓ Avoid the use of graphics, colored backgrounds, and drawings.
✓ Avoid the use of emoticons and acronyms.
✓ Respond to e-mail in a timely fashion.
✓ Don't be informal.
✓ Send only work-related e-mails (not personal e-mails) on the company computer.
✓ Don't use e-mail to replace important face-to-face conversations and phone calls.
✓ Always proofread your e-mail messages and use spell-check.
✓ Don't send e-mail that you wrote while you were upset, mad, or intoxicated.
✓ Send only e-mails that you are comfortable with everyone seeing (e-mails are not private).

Source: Bly (1999, pp. 27–29).

# KEYS to Excellence in Written Communication

Remember George Raab, who did not exercise professional excellence while employed for the City of New York? It is critical that you know how to use professional excellence in writing, not only through electronic communication but in traditional writing as well.

When examining the first key, *know yourself*, determine if you want to achieve professional excellence, and know that part of that entails improving your written communication. Examine your strengths and weaknesses related to all aspects of your written communication. Set a goal to improve your written communication skills, and realize that you need members of your team to edit your writing.

The next key, *evaluate the professional context*, is essential for you to become more audience centered and aware of how you are coming across to other people in your writing. Become more mindful of how your written communication sounds demanding and/or negative.

The third key, *your communication interaction occurs*, makes you a more professional communicator in that you can make better choices when using written communication. Start to think before sending out memos and e-mails, and be much more mindful that your passion to perform and motivate can impact your written communication. When there is a need for a company announcement via written communication, be careful to think about the best way to get the message out. If there is a need for written communication, engage in careful planning and editing of the written message. As the message is sent, also communicate with members of your staff face-to-face to make sure they understood.

When you use written communication, engage in the fourth key, *step back and reflect*. Become more reflective of written communication, and realize how it could be misunderstood and send the wrong signal. Ask yourself some of the following questions as you step back and think about your written communication: Was my memo response appropriate? Did my questions in the letter sound negative? Did my team think it was rude when I passed out the process directives printed in red? Should I use all caps in my e-mail message? Is sending a memo about attitude and productivity to everyone inappropriate? The fourth phase also makes you more thoughtful about all aspects of your written communication, not just when you send out a memo or write a letter. Your evaluation and reflection can result in positive changes that other people can notice.

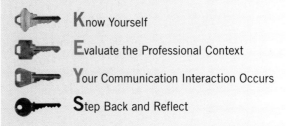

Be aware of how your written communication may come across depending on the topic. Sometimes waiting, picking up the phone, or meeting face-to-face might be more effective than written communication.

**K**now Yourself

**E**valuate the Professional Context

**Y**our Communication Interaction Occurs

**S**tep Back and Reflect

## Executive Summary

Now that you have finished reading this chapter, you can do the following:

Understand the impact of written communication on professional excellence:

- Official documents, memos, e-mail, and other forms of written communication reveal something about you as a professional (p. 204).
- Important policies, requests, and organizational procedures are conveyed through written communication (p. 204).
- Proposals, employee terminations, media relations, and the like are achieved with written communication (p. 204).
- Written communication must be present to achieve professional excellence (p. 205).

Understand the different indirect messages sent with written communication:

- With spelling and grammar check, as well as good old-fashioned proofreading, *typos* (mistakes in typing), *misspellings* (mistakes in spelling), and *grammar* errors (sentence fragments, inappropriate use of punctuation, etc.) can be corrected. Just as a typo on your résumé can lose you a job, a typo on a report can cause you to lose credibility. Misspellings, typos, and sending something to the wrong department are all roadblocks to professional excellence (p. 207).

Identify different types of written communication:

- The *business letter* is used to communicate formal matters in business, jurisprudence, or otherwise. You will use this form of correspondence when you want to write a cover letter to accompany your résumé, write a letter announcing business news to colleagues outside your company, or notify vendors of a change in your ordering procedures (p. 207).
- *Employee reviews* serve as a form of written communication used in business and professional settings to provide feedback to employees about how they are performing on the job (p. 208).

- The *recommendation letter* is a form of written communication used to provide a documented reference for students and professionals (p. 209).
- *Thank-you letters* are written communication used to express appreciation to coworkers and clients (p. 212).
- *Proposals* are also utilized in many business and professional settings to propose products and services to potential clients (p. 219).
- *Reports* are written communication used to summarize research or assessment findings to inform managers about important issues related to business (p. 220).
- *Press releases* are forms of written communication used to send messages and make announcements to a variety of media organizations, including newspapers, radio, television news, and Internet reporters (p. 221).

Utilize the KEYS approach to achieve professional excellence regarding written communication:

- *Know yourself.* Determine that you want to achieve professional excellence, and know that part of that entails improving your written communication. Examine your strengths and weaknesses related to all aspects of your written communication (p. 229).
- *Evaluate the professional context.* This is essential for you to become more audience centered and aware of how you are coming across to other people in your writing. Become more mindful of how your written communication is sounding demanding and negative (p. 229).
- *Your communication interaction occurs.* Make yourself a more professional communicator in that you make better choices when using written communication (p. 229).
- *Step back and reflect.* Become more reflective of written communication and how it could be misunderstood and send the wrong signal (p. 229).

## Discussion Questions

1. Discuss an example of a time when you were offended by written communication. How did you respond? Did you use written communication for your response, or did you respond in person?

2. Are there other forms of written communication not covered in this chapter that you have concerns about? As a professional, what steps would you take if you were asked to use written communication with which you were not familiar? Would you delegate the task to someone else? Would you be honest that you were not comfortable with the project?

3. What steps do you or will you take on the job that will help you strive for professional excellence with written communication? What strategies do you have, if any, that work for you?

4. Take a moment to reflect on your experiences with written communication. Have you ever been caught in an e-mail or letter exchange that crossed the line from professional to uncivil? What can organizations do to prevent uncivil written communication?

5. Some scholars are concerned about the negative impact of text messaging and other forms of technology on written communication. Do you share this concern? Do you think technology encourages you to be less professional in your written communication? Why or why not?

## Terms to Remember

business letter (p. 207)

downsizing letter (p. 208)

employee reviews (p. 208)

external communication plan (p. 221)

general language (p. 206)

grammar (p. 207)

internal communication plan (p. 221)

memo (p. 212)

misspellings (p. 207)

networking notes (p. 212)

planning documents (p. 221)

press releases (p. 221)

proactive media writing (p. 227)

process directives (p. 215)

proposals (p. 219)

qualitative data (p. 220)

quantitative data (p. 220)

recommendation letter (p. 209)

reports (p. 219)

specific language (p. 206)

strategic planning (p. 220)

thank-you letters (p. 212)

typos (p. 207)

workforce communication assessment (p. 219)

writing startup sheet (p. 207)

Visit the Student Study Site at **www.sagepub.com/keys2e** to access the following resources:

- SAGE journal articles
- Video links
- Web resources

- Web quizzes
- eflashcards

# Chapter Outline

What Is Leadership?   234

Utilizing Power   236

Improving Communication With Leadership
   Theories   239

Hiring the Right Team   243

Following Up and Following Through   246

Communicating About Your Team   246

Dealing With Difficult People   248

Giving Feedback   251

Managing Your Public Image   259

KEYS to Excellence in Leadership   260

Executive Summary   262

Discussion Questions   263

Terms to Remember   263

# Chapter Objectives

After studying this chapter, you should be able to:

1. Gain a clear understanding of what constitutes leadership and power

2. Understand the relationship between leadership theory and communication

3. Develop communication strategies for hiring quality employees and leading effective teams

4. Provide feedback as a means to motivate team members and develop difficult people

5. Use the KEYS process to develop professional excellence as a leader

# chapter 10

# Leadership and Conflict Management

**Fourteen workers at a law firm in Florida found themselves jobless after they decided to wear orange-colored shirts to work on the same day.** Employers at the Elizabeth R. Wellborn law firm called the 14 employees into a conference room and said that management took the coordination of their shirts to mean they were staging some sort of protest. Although several employees denied the claim, they were all jobless at the end of the day. Some of the group contended they had established a custom of wearing orange shirts on payday Fridays, to promote a feeling of togetherness when they would go out as a group for drinks. Mailroom worker Yadel Fong told reporters that the perception of a protest was wrong and that employees were conducting business as usual (Farnham, 2012). The management at the law firm did not feel inclined to argue though, and since Florida is an "at will" employment state, the employees can be fired for any reason the employer deems necessary. The workers were understandably frustrated, and the law firm now finds itself facing heavy criticism from the public.

The preceding example shows a severe lack of communication between employees and management. While some workers felt that wearing the same-color shirt promoted togetherness and cooperation, management took the move as a sign of protest or unrest. Because there was no effort to explore what the exact reason was for all the workers to wear orange shirts, the law firm lost many employees for no good reason. It is vital for leaders in the workplace to practice good communication skills and keep a pulse of the attitudes of their employees. A poor understanding of your employees' working environment can lead to decreased productivity, poor job satisfaction, and the loss of quality workers.

Leading with professional excellence is crucial to all bosses in the workplace. Knowing exactly what leadership entails and how to use the power given to you will aid in developing a happy and productive work environment. In this chapter, you will learn about different leadership theories and how to create an effective team from the very beginning. The key to tying all this together is communicating effectively with your employees.

# What Is Leadership?

To develop professional excellence as a leader, you must have a firm grasp of what constitutes leadership. To understand what leadership is, we must first understand what leadership is not. Although leaders may possess some desirable personality traits, be charismatic, be born into a family of leaders, or have a job title such as manager or executive, true leadership is not defined by any of these things. Let's explore each of them more closely for a better understanding of why they don't equal leadership.

We emphasize that leadership is something that takes work—leadership excellence demands constant attention and self-evaluation.

Leadership is not a trait. A **trait** is a distinguishing characteristic or quality that's part of individual character; traits are often seen as inborn or genetically based. For example, some people have the personality trait of being extroverted or outgoing, while others are introverted, less outgoing, or shy. In the 1920s and 1930s, scholars focused on determining the traits that make up a leader, exploring which traits all great leaders share, as well as traits that differentiate *leaders* from *followers*. Scholars studying the leadership traits concluded that there are indeed traits that distinguish a leader from a follower (Barbuto & Gifford, 2012; Mann, 1959; Stogdill, 1948). The traits thought to make up a great leader were many (see Table 10.1). But if you begin to compare various leadership traits to the leaders, you will quickly see that great leaders are not all alike, and the traits they possess can vary greatly. In addition, both leaders and followers have many of these leadership traits. Furthermore, these leadership traits have been criticized for biasing traits that male leaders display while ignoring traits predominantly possessed by female leaders (Powell, 2012; Rosener, 1997).

Extending from the leadership-as-traits approach is the notion that charisma or birthright equals leadership. Definitions for **charisma** include characteristics such as magnetic charm, allure, and the supernatural or magical ability to appeal to followers. "Charisma

| Table 10.1 Leadership Traits | |
|---|---|
| Physical traits | Young to middle-aged, energetic, tall, and handsome |
| Social background traits | Educated at the "right" schools and socially prominent or upwardly mobile |
| Social traits | Charismatic, charming, tactful, popular, cooperative, and diplomatic |
| Personality traits | Self-confident, adaptable, assertive, and emotionally stable |
| Task-related traits | Driven to excel, accepting of responsibility, having initiative, and being results-oriented |

Source: Allen (2002).

is, literally, a gift of grace or of God" (Wright, 1996, p. 194). History is full of charismatic leaders who possessed confident, assertive styles that drew loyalty and support from followers. There is no doubt that charisma is a wonderful characteristic for a leader to possess. Yet charisma alone doesn't make a great leader, nor is the lack of charisma a mark of poor leadership. There are many great leaders who will never be labeled as charismatic. Conversely, there are many people who possess charisma but never ascend to leadership excellence.

Leadership has also often been seen as a **birthright**. The thinking here is that if there are certain inborn traits that make a great leader, then those traits will be passed on from parent to child. Monarchies are based on the notion of birthright. In some cultures, subjects believed that their kings, queens, czars, or chiefs were superior to the rest of the population. In extreme cases, they were elevated to god-like status. Similarly, many business empires are passed on from one generation of a family to the next with the belief that each new generation will bring with it the drive and skills of the business founder. Alas, this concept of leadership is also flawed. Within every monarchy, there are examples of leadership excellence and failed leadership all in the same family tree. In the Roman empire, Claudius and Nero illustrate this point. Claudius, due to a disability, was viewed as a poor choice for emperor—but in the end, he proved to be an effective leader. Under his rule, many public works were built and Rome expanded its territories into Britain. However, his grandnephew and successor, Nero, holds an infamous place in history for being a horrible leader. He is remembered for his extravagant lifestyle and cruelty and for "fiddling while Rome burned." The same holds true in the business world. Conrad Hilton may have built one of the most prestigious hotel chains in the world, but his granddaughter Paris clearly has a different take on leadership than her grandpa did.

In the United States, the break from the English monarchy and the establishment of an elected government reinforced a link between leadership and **job title**. The person who's hired or voted into the leadership role gets the title. Those with the leadership job title lead, and the rest follow. In fact, during the Industrial Revolution, the idea that "management thinks and workers work" was developed, two-way communication was stifled, and managers literally told employees, "We don't pay you to think." Again, a little reflection on your own experiences should help you spot the weakness with the notion that job title equals leadership. Do you know people with leadership titles who are poor leaders? Do you know people without leadership titles who are excellent leaders? Leadership skills and leadership titles are not mutually exclusive. Remember, leadership is something that team members share regardless of title.

If leadership is not a trait, a matter of charisma, a birthright, or a job title, what is it? **Leadership** is "a dynamic relationship based on mutual influence and common purpose between leaders and collaborators in which both are moved to higher levels of motivation and moral development as they affect real, intended change" (Freiberg & Freiberg, 1996, p. 298). As you study this definition, the role of communication should be clear to you. According to this definition, *change* is dependent on a dynamic relationship, mutual influence, and a common purpose. As you've already learned, you can't have a *dynamic relationship* without effective communication. In addition, *mutual influence* and *common purpose* both rely on two-way communication. Furthermore, having leaders and *collaborators,* as opposed to leaders and followers, again implies the need for effective communication. By examining this and other definitions of leadership, the role of communication becomes clear—it's intrinsically woven into every facet of leadership excellence. Everyone has leadership potential, and by utilizing the KEYS process for communication excellence, you can unlock your leadership potential.

This chapter focuses on specific communication skills that you'll need to achieve leadership excellence. The areas that can make or break you as a leader include utilizing power, improving communication with leadership theory, hiring the right team, following up and following through, communicating about your team, giving feedback, dealing with difficult people, and managing your public image.

# Utilizing Power

Let's review for a moment our discussion of superior–subordinate relationships from Chapter 6. **Status** is a person's rank or position in an organization. Typically, the **superior** (supervisor/employer) is the higher-status person and the **subordinate** (employee) is the lower-status person. Typically, people who hold a higher status have more years of experience, training, knowledge, and rank than do those with lower statuses (this may not always be the case). For example, a doctor has the leadership title and status over the nursing staff. This title and status hold true even if the doctor is right out of medical school and the nursing staff is full of veteran nurses with years of experience and hands-on training.

Job title is about status, but as we discussed in the last section, job title does not equal leadership. True leadership is about power. Both professional and personal relationships have a power dimension. So to better understand the role of power in your relationships and the resulting communication, let's look at the five types of power as defined by John French and Bertram Raven (1968): legitimate power, coercive power, reward power, expert power, referent power, and connection power.

**Legitimate power** is based on a position of authority. The manager has legitimate power over the department budget and employee schedules. While a position/job title may give someone legitimate power, it doesn't mean that person exercises that power.

**Coercive power** refers to the ability to control another person's behavior with negative reinforcement, while **reward power** describes control over another person's behavior with positive reinforcement. Clearly, a person with legitimate power has both coercive and reward power over subordinates. For example, a manager could reward an employee with a good schedule and a raise or punish the employee with an undesirable schedule and no raise. But people with legitimate power are not the only ones who have coercive and reward power. Anyone who can offer positive or negative reinforcements has power. So the staff member who can process your paperwork quickly versus slowly and the administrative assistant who can choose to squeeze you in or make you wait for a meeting with the boss both have coercive and reward power.

**Expert power** is based on one's superior expertise in a specific field. In our fast-paced, increasingly specialized world, it is no wonder experts are given power. You may recall the *Saturday Night Live* skit on expert power. The skit begins with a song: "Nick Burns, your company's computer guy. He's gonna fix your computer, and then he's gonna make fun of you." Why would Nick Burns make fun of his coworkers? He finds their lack of knowledge about computers irritating. The coworkers put up with the abuse because they need him. Without Nick's knowledge, they can't do their jobs. He has expertise that gives him power over them.

You give **referent power** to someone because you want that person to like you. You may feel a connection to that person, or you may wish to be like that person—either way, it gives him or her power over you. High school peer pressure is a form of referent power. Kitt has been a member of the accounting firm for years. She's organized, highly knowledgeable, and excellent with customers. Kitt has a positive attitude about life and has found a healthy balance between work life and home life. While she has never taken a leadership title, many of the young accountants look to her as a role model. They follow her lead and seek her advice because they have granted her referent power.

**Connection power** is based on the old expression, "It's not what you know but who you know." Having a connection to people in positions of power or having a strong support system definitely acts as a source of power. If the CEO's son works in the mailroom, he will likely be treated differently than the other members of the mailroom staff.

Examining types of power reveals a critical difference between managers and leaders. *Manager* is a title, which brings with it legitimate power. **Managerial functions** include important duties such as being in charge of and responsible for various goals and functions in an organization. It also involves supervising subordinates. Leaders may be managers, and they may have legitimate power, but neither is a requirement for leadership. **Leadership functions** include influencing and guiding followers as opposed to subordinates, as well as being innovative and creating a vision for future direction. Leaders often have multiple types of power, with referent power likely in the mix.

Leaders face both positive and negative confrontations. Leadership excellence is about turning those negatives into positives.

## Step Back and Reflect    Rosa's Review

*Read the following passage about Rosa, and answer the questions that follow.*

A regional manager could not make sense out of the dramatically different ratings that were given to Rosa, the administrative assistant for the western office. Some members of the team had given her extremely high ratings, while others had given her extremely low ratings. The written comments ranged from "She is glue that holds us together" to "She plays favorites, deliberately delays projects, and should be fired." How could they be talking about the same person?

During her annual review, Rosa explained the office dynamic as follows:

I have worked here for 15 years, and I know how everything is run. I know the procedures like the back of my hand. The problem is, some people don't care about the procedures. They don't listen to me when I tell them they are doing it wrong, and then they want me to fix their messes. That's not my job. Another problem is timelines. I am busy, and I will get to things when I get to them. But poor planning on their part does not equal a crisis on my part. Plus, when I have bailed them out or dropped everything to help them, they are never grateful. They have no respect for me or my job.

Now I will bend over backwards for the people who follow the rules and respect my time. And you know what, those people are always grateful. They give me thank-you cards, take me to lunch, and remember my birthday. They see me as part of the team, not "the secretary."

### Step Back and Reflect

1. What went wrong?
2. What types of power are coming into play in this office?
3. Does Rosa have power in her position?
4. Is Rosa's behavior professional?
5. How could the regional manager improve the communication using the KEYS process?

Now that you understand the different types of power as well as the difference between status and power, it is important to apply this knowledge to the KEYS process. *Know yourself.* Begin by asking yourself, "What kind of power do I possess? How does my power affect my communication interactions? How do I react when communicating with coworkers or supervisors who possess each of the types of power noted above?" When *evaluating the professional context,* ask yourself, "What kind of power do various members of my workplace exhibit? How effective are the legitimate leaders and people with status? What are their strengths? How could they improve?" Make it a habit when *your communication interactions occurs* to *step back and reflect.* Ask yourself, "How does power affect communication in my workplace?"

Ineffective leaders rely solely on their legitimate power to motivate others and fail to take into account the power of other members in the workplace. As you achieve professional excellence, you will reflect on the role power plays in all your communication interactions.

# Improving Communication With Leadership Theories

Just as understanding theories on power can improve your communication as a leader, so too can studying leadership theories. Over the past century, scholars have studied leadership-developing theories and models designed to help us understand what effective leadership is and train us to be better leaders. Implementing the knowledge and insight contained in various leadership theories is a must if you ever plan to excel as a leader.

Imagine yourself at a fork in the road. Each path before you represents a different choice you could make as a leader. If you select the wrong path, you may never find your way. If you select the right path, you will still have a journey ahead of you, but your chances for success will improve dramatically. Each leadership theory discussed in the following section will help you select the right path for communicating as a leader given your team, your task, your situation, and your vision. Let's begin by reviewing various leadership theories developed through the years.

## Behavioral Theories

As we noted above, the traits approach to leadership was among the first formal attempts to study leadership. But when it became clear to scholars that leadership was more than merely a list of traits, they began to turn their attention to the behaviors of leaders.

In elementary school, you were probably taught three leadership styles: authoritative, laissez-faire, and democratic. Under the **authoritative** style, the leader makes all the decisions with little input from the team. With the **laissez-faire** style, the team makes the decisions with little input from the leader. (*Laissez-faire* is a French expression meaning "allow to do.") In the **democratic** style, the leader follows the will of the people, or at least the majority of the people, with decisions often being made through voting. While these terms create a classification for leaders based on behaviors, they were designed as broad categories for explaining systems of government, not as a formal study of leadership behavior.

Fortunately, behavioral theorists such as Douglas McGregor did develop categories for leaders that were based on research into leader/manager behavior. McGregor (1960) observed two very different leadership styles that he labeled **Theory X** and **Theory Y**. The differences between Theory X managers and Theory Y managers are derived from their opposing views of employees. Theory X managers believe that

- the average employee dislikes work;
- because most employees dislike work, they must be controlled, directed, and threatened so they will perform their job duties; and
- employees prefer to be told what to do, avoid responsibility, have little ambition, and value job security above all.

On the other hand, Theory Y managers believe that

- the need and desire to work is as natural as the need and desire to play or rest;
- controlling, directing, and/or threatening are not the only means for getting employees to perform their job duties;
- the average employee is motivated by achieving goals;

- the average employee not only accepts responsibility but many times seeks it; and
- the average employee's full intellectual and creative potential is not utilized in most organizations.

What can you learn from studying McGregor's work that will make you a better leader? Managerial attitudes about employees have a direct effect on communication style. It should come as no surprise that Theory X managers have a very different communication style from that of Theory Y managers. Theory X managers support a top-down communication. The vast majority of information flows down the organizational chart from managers to employees in the form of commands. Since employees are seen as disliking work, rewards and punishments are used to keep them motivated. The idea that managers think and workers work stems from Theory X's roots in classical management theories.

Leadership is about bringing people together.

Those subscribing to a Theory Y style of management support two-way communication. The Theory Y manager acts more as a facilitator or a coach working to empower employees. He or she seeks employee feedback and insight. Employees are encouraged to take part in decision making.

So which communication style is more effective: (a) the top-down style of Theory X or (b) the two-way communication of Theory Y (see Table 10.2)? It actually depends on the situation. There are times when the authoritative communication styles associated with Theory X are a must for effective leadership. Think about an emergency situation: A building is on fire; a platoon is under attack; a patient has been wheeled into the ER with life-threatening injuries. Having the senior-most person take charge and begin barking orders as the rest of the team perform their duties with speed, without question, is not only appropriate but necessary in these examples. This realization led researchers to the next wave of leadership theories, known as the situational leadership approach.

**Table 10.2 Self-Monitoring: What Is Your Attitude About Work?**

- Do you subscribe to the Theory X or Theory Y style of management? Why?
- Do you believe people inherently dislike work, or do you believe work is as natural as play?
- Have you ever worked for a Theory X manager? Was this style effective or ineffective?
- Have you ever worked for a Theory Y manager? Was this style effective or ineffective?

## Situational Leadership Theories

According to Sadler (1997), one of the major limitations of the traits approach was its failure to take into account the importance of the situation. This same limitation holds true for the work of McGregor. However, researchers such as Blake and Mouton, Fiedler, and Hersey and Blanchard studied the impact of situation on assessing leadership effectiveness.

The **Managerial Grid**, developed by Robert Blake and Jane Mouton (1964, 1978), includes five managerial styles: impoverished, country club, authoritative, middle-of-the road, and team. Unlike researchers before them, Blake and Mouton's model incorporates two dimensions: concern for people and concern for task (see Figure 10.1). The impoverished manager has a low concern for both people and task. The country club manager has a high concern for people and a low concern for task. The authoritative manager has a high concern for task and a low concern for people. The middle-of-the-road manager has a moderate level of concern for both people and task, while the team manager has a high concern for both people and task.

What can you learn from studying Blake and Mouton's Managerial Grid? When selecting an effective leadership style, you have to consider multiple factors. Be careful not to make the mistake of glancing at the grid and thinking that team manager is the best way to lead. There may be times when the task at hand is small or less than urgent, so an effective leader might use the country club style to increase the cohesion of the group. At another time, the task might be urgent, opening the door for an authoritative style—it depends on the situation.

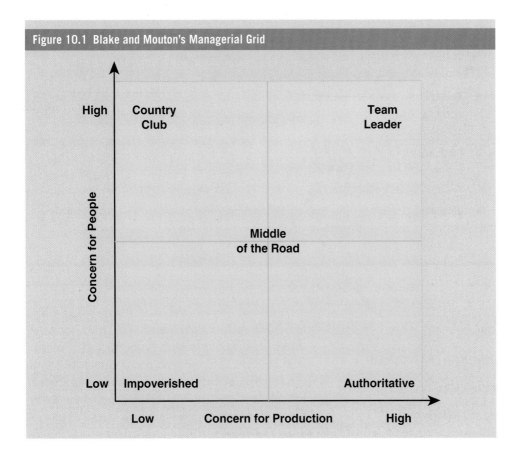

Figure 10.1 Blake and Mouton's Managerial Grid

This idea was reiterated and expanded on by other researchers, such as Fiedler. According to Fiedler's **Contingency Theory,** there's no best way for managers to lead. Excellent leaders assess the situation and then select the leadership style and accompanying communication style that best fits the situation. When assessing the situation, Fiedler reports the need to look at three factors: the leader–follower relationship, the task structure, and the position power (Fiedler, 1997; Fiedler & Garcia, 1987; Wisse & Rus, 2012). Let's say that Christy and Michael are both trying to determine how best to lead their respective teams. Christy has a positive relationship with her team, and they share a history of mutual respect. The structure of the task is clearly defined, and she has strong position power because the executive team has given her the funds and the order to get the job done. Michael has just started his position, so there is little history or trust between him and the team. The task at hand is somewhat ambiguous. Furthermore, this initiative is Michael's idea. It has not been mandated by the executive team, so he has little position power. How should Christy communicate with her team? Should Michael use the same style as Christy since she has the kind of relationship with her team that he wants with his team?

Before you give any advice to Christy or Michael, you should first review Hersey and Blanchard's (1977) **Situational Leadership Theory** (see Table 10.3). According to this theory, leaders should take into account task behavior, relationship behavior, and level of maturity/readiness of the followers to select the most effective communication style.

---

**Table 10.3 Hersey and Blanchard's Situational Leadership Styles**

- **Telling** (high task/low relationship behavior/low level of readiness): Leader provides detailed instructions; a useful style with new employees, when things must be completed quickly, or when employees lack motivation.

- **Selling** (high task/high relationship behavior/moderate level of readiness): Leader works to persuade the team to support the task; involves two-way communication, but the leader is still in the position of authority.

- **Participating** (high relationship/low task behavior/moderate to high levels of readiness): Leader facilitates the discussion, and the decision making is shared between leaders and followers, the main role of the leader being to facilitate.

- **Delegating** (low relationship/low task behavior/high level of readiness): Leader assigns the task or identifies the problem, but the team is empowered to develop and carry out the plan of action.

---

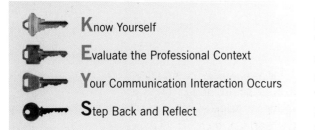

**K**now Yourself

**E**valuate the Professional Context

**Y**our Communication Interaction Occurs

**S**tep Back and Reflect

Based on Hersey and Blanchard's work, which leadership style should Christy use with her team? Which style would work best for Michael given his task, his relationship, and his team's readiness? As you can see, the research of situational leadership scholars will allow you to better *evaluate the professional context* as you work your way through the KEYS process to professional excellence as a leader.

## Transformational Leadership

One final area that must be addressed is that of transformational leadership. **Transformational leaders** are defined as leaders who articulate a goal or vision to an organization and then inspire followers to make that vision a reality, requiring them to transcend their own personal interests for the good of the organization (Bolman & Deal, 1997; Wright, Moynihan, & Pandey, 2012). Transformational leaders are often known for being charismatic. In addition, their leadership style can be characterized as empowering, which helps develop innovative thinking and initiative among followers. Be warned—the effectiveness of transformational leaders is difficult to measure (Den Hartog & Belschak, 2012; Wright, 1996).

What you learn from this research into transformational leadership is that truly outstanding leaders in the 21st century have a vision of where their teams and/or organizations are heading and communicate that vision to their teams. They also empower their teams, allowing them to become a part of that vision.

# Hiring the Right Team

Leadership should be something that you share with the other members of your team. You will be acting as a coach, so you should be engaged in the recruitment process. It's highly unlikely that you'll be placed in a leadership position that allows you to select your entire team or department; it just doesn't work like that. You will most likely accept a leadership position and begin working as the titled leader with a preexisting group. Developing this group into a team may be challenging. Our point is this: You must begin by developing the players you have been given. Over time, some of those players will leave or your organization will grow, and you'll have the opportunity to hire new team members. Leaders with professional excellence know that hiring is a process that begins long before the first candidate arrives for an interview and lasts long after orientation and training. Let's review each step in this process from a leader's perspective.

Leadership excellence focuses on hiring the right people.

## Developing the New Employee Profile

When hiring opportunities occur, it's incredibly important that you, as the leader, participate in every stage of the hiring process. It's also important to get the rest of the team involved. So begin by framing the problem as a challenge facing the team—there's a vacant position that must be filled. If someone has left an existing position, there's a tendency among status quo groups simply to place an advertisement for that identical position. In contrast, innovative teams use the vacancy as an opportunity to evaluate team duties and needs as they currently exist, not as they were written years ago. As companies grow and change, so do the duties of their employees. In addition, according to McGregor's Theory Y, each new team member brings with him or her a host of skills not being utilized.

As the leader with professional excellence, you should facilitate a discussion about the opportunities this new position creates and what the team really needs. This may be the time when some current team members shift their duties, allowing them to put some of their underutilized skills to work. It also might be the time to add new skills to the team.

As the team evaluates which skills will be needed, make certain that people skills and attitude are part of the conversation. As a professional, you should not only pay attention to your own people skills and attitude—you should also pay attention to the people skills and attitudes of those hired into your team. If you make a hiring decision based solely on technical training, you'll be making a terrible leadership error. Successful organizations focus on how people skills and attitude contribute to a positive organizational culture with enhanced employee and customer satisfaction (Gilbert, Carr-Ruffino, Ivancevich, & Konopaske, 2012; Krapels, 2000). When hiring new employees, you must be certain the employees have all the following: the competencies needed for the position, an openness and excitement about training and developing new skills, a positive attitude, career goals that will fit into your organizational culture, and, most important, professional excellence.

## During the Interview

Once the position has been advertised, the interview questions must be drafted. You may or may not be responsible for drafting the questions, but as the leader, you should always review the questions, giving your input and ultimately your approval. When drafting and/or reviewing questions, keep your purpose in mind. What are we looking for in a candidate? Then ask, how do these questions inform us about those skills or qualifications? Let's say you need an employee who can work under the pressure of a short deadline. You could ask, "Do you work well with deadlines?" Any smart interviewee will answer, "Yes, I do." So a better question might be, "Tell me about your experience working under deadlines." As the interviewee provides examples, you can probe each situation to determine how successfully he or she really functioned. This would also be a good question to ask professional references to verify the information the interviewee gave you.

During the interviewing process, professionals set the tone. As the leader, you may not be the one conducting the initial interviews. Yet you should meet with all potential team member(s) *before* they are hired and engage in open dialogue with others who will be participating in the interviewing process about the importance of hiring people with professional excellence.

When conducting an interview, it's important to remember that everyone gets nervous—you should take the first few minutes to help put the interviewee at ease. Make some small talk and allow the interviewee to get comfortable with you and the setting. This will create an environment in which you can see beyond the nerves to the true potential of this prospective team member.

## Evaluate the Professional Context    I Hire Only Nice People

*Read the following passage about Paul, and then answer the questions. As you read, focus on evaluating the professional context.*

Paul was the branch manager of a car rental chain. Although the chain had thousands of branches all over the globe, Paul's branch stood out. Their customer satisfaction scores were exceptionally high. Their turnover was very low. They had promoted a record number of entry-level employees into managerial positions throughout the corporation. When problems arose, such as low sales or budget cuts, the team members worked together to address issues, as opposed to bickering and backbiting. To what did Paul attribute the success of his team? He attributed it to the "nice" factor.

When Paul interviewed potential employees, he made sure they met all the qualifications listed in the job posting, and then he asked the deal-breaking question: "How would you describe your personality? What kind of person are you?" If they gave an answer that included the word "nice" or a self-description that translated into "nice," they were still in the running. He would also check references, always asking, "Would you describe so-and-so as a nice person? Why would you describe him or her this way?" He would then ask various members of the staff who had interacted with this potential employee to describe their interactions. Of course, he was looking for interactions that would indicate a "nice" quality. Once he hired a new employee, he would provide him or her with an orientation and training process that included frequent reminders that "we hire only nice people around here."

### Questions to Consider

1. What do you think of Paul's hiring strategy?
2. What qualities will you look for when you hire new employees?
3. How will you know if a candidate has these qualities?
4. Should "nice" be a goal when developing a professional context?

As you learned in Chapter 4, interviewees are also assessing the organization to determine if they even want this position. As the leader, you must be sure you and your team treat all interviewees with professional excellence.

## After the Interview

A leader with professional excellence makes certain that new team members feel like part of the team from Day 1. You should make it a point to greet all new employees on the day they arrive. In addition, you must make certain they will be properly oriented and trained. Training and orientation may or may not be part of your job duties. Regardless, you must make sure new employees are given the tools they need to succeed. As we discussed in Chapter 3, those tools include an understanding of the organizational culture and their job duties. Assign training duties—don't just think training will magically occur—and follow up to make sure the new employee is getting what he or she needs to succeed.

# Following Up and Following Through

Excellent leaders know the meeting does not end when they say "adjourned." As we discussed in Chapter 7, teams must allow for innovation and shared leadership. To achieve these goals, team members should leave most meetings with homework—send them out to explore information. Allow them time to incubate so they can brainstorm more effectively. Give them tasks to complete as the team accomplishes its goals. Remember, excellent leaders don't do all the work alone. Excellent leaders involve the team so they, too, can share in the leadership, which will make your job more manageable.

To achieve this, you must follow up after each meeting. A poor leader makes one of two mistakes. First, some poor leaders assign homework but then fail to ask about the results at the next meeting. If this occurs once or twice, team members will stop participating and will not bother to do the things you have assigned. The second mistake is "taking care" of team members who don't perform their duties. If tasks are assigned but the team members fail to perform those assigned tasks, they must be held accountable. Poor leaders see that an assignment has not been done and just do it themselves. This teaches team members that they are not accountable or responsible, and the leader will end up doing most, if not all, of the work.

As the leader, you must create a "follow up and follow through" norm within your team. To begin enacting this norm, send out an e-mail thanking the team members for their participation in a recent meeting, state the homework to which each team member has agreed, and remind them of the next meeting time. By doing this, you have reaffirmed in their minds what they have to do for the next meeting. Let's say this team meets once a month. Two weeks before the next meeting, send out a reminder to each team member saying, "You are on the agenda for our next meeting." Then, ask if there are any additional items they would like included on the agenda or if they need any supplemental materials. One week prior to the meeting, send out the agenda, and be sure to list the name of each team member who will be reporting during the meeting. Also note areas in which the entire group should be prepared, and be ready to discuss. During the meeting, call on each person even if he or she isn't prepared. Make the individual responsible for saying, "I did not do my assigned task." Do not remove that person from the agenda. Make him or her accountable. This will set up a norm in which you follow up so team members follow through. As a result, your meeting will be more productive and everyone can share in the leadership.

# Communicating About Your Team

As we discussed in Chapter 6, no matter how many times you say, "This is confidential," "What happens in this room stays in this room," or "This is just between us," information still leaks out. Somehow, some way, gossip almost always finds its way to the informal communication network (aka the grapevine). So you can rest assured that the way you communicate about your team will get back to your team. And your message, positive or negative, will have a major impact on the way you and your team interact. Furthermore,

## Your Communication Interaction    The Buck Stops Here

*Read the passage below, and then answer the questions. As you read, think about ways the KEYS approach could help you improve* **your communication interaction** *if you were in a leadership position.*

On the desk of President Harry S. Truman was a sign that read, "The Buck Stops Here." According to Mathews (1951), the expression "the buck stops here" is a play on the words of the common expression "pass the buck." When people passed the buck, it meant they passed the problem or the responsibility to someone else. So "the buck stops here" was President Truman's way of telling the American people he would take responsibility.

### Questions to Consider

1. Do you believe the buck should stop with the leader?
2. As a leader, will the buck stop with you?
3. How does this attitude reflect the kind of professional excellence supported by the KEYS process?

the way you communicate about your team will have a major impact on the way others view you as a leader. When it comes to communicating about your team, follow two simple rules: When there are problems, the buck stops with you; when there are successes, you never take the credit. Let's explore each rule in more detail.

If your team makes a mistake, if your department has a shortcoming, if something goes wrong in your department, or if there is an error, the buck stops with you. You're the leader of that team; therefore, in a public forum, you assume responsibility for whatever the problem may be. Excellent leaders don't make excuses. They take responsibility when their teams do not perform at the expected level. In doing so, you'll earn the respect of your coworkers, supervisors, customers, and team. Your professionalism and integrity will be remembered. Watch an episode or two of *The Apprentice* if you want to see how unprofessional a leader appears when he or she starts blaming team members and pointing fingers because the team failed to meet expectations. Leaders with professional excellence acknowledge the problem, apologize if necessary, and correct the problem. Privately, some team members' behavior may need to be addressed, but publicly, the professional leader stands up and takes responsibility.

On the flip side, when your team has met expectations, exceeded expectations, or had an outstanding performance, you don't take the credit. In fact, you should publicly give credit to your team. You may be thinking, "Wait a minute. I have to take responsibility for the mistakes, but I don't get credit for the successes. That seems unfair." Fair or unfair, it's a characteristic that all leaders with professional excellence must demonstrate. Don't worry, others know that you led the team, and they understand that great teams are a product of great leaders. If it's a team effort, the whole team should share in the praise, and you should be the first one cheering for them. Even if they are not there to hear your praise, it will get back to them. The results will lead to strong morale and loyalty from your team members.

# Dealing With Difficult People

As consultants and corporate trainers, we often ask employees, "What is it like working in your department or organization?" The vast majority of them reply, "We are like a family." The idea that employees and supervisors function as a family and/or a team is heavily promoted in corporate America. Since we already have explored the team metaphor, let's use the family metaphor to examine an extremely important duty of every leader who aspires to professional excellence: namely, dealing with difficult people.

## Meet Your Organizational Family

The family metaphor can have both positive and negative ramifications. To many supervisors, the thought of employees running around saying, "We are all one big, happy family here at Company X," is wonderful. Let's remember that families can be dysfunctional, too. In fact, even the most functional families have problems from time to time. So let's begin our discussion by meeting some of the difficult people you might encounter in your organizational family.

Brother Steven is a **bully** (Bernstein, 2001). As is the case with most schoolyard bullies, Steven has a bad temper. He uses aggression and anger to get his way. Other family members allow him to have what he wants to avoid a blowup. Steven's behavior also gets him out of a lot of responsibilities, because no one wants to work with him or hold him accountable.

It takes a leader with integrity to hold difficult people accountable for their actions.

Sister Angela is a **sniper**. During meetings or discussions, she pops in with nasty comments meant to wound her targets. She's full of sarcastic remarks and masks inappropriate comments with humor. Some of Angela's comments include, "Who came up with that lame idea?"; "That's a great suggestion coming from a blonde"; and "That never worked before, but I am *sure* it will work now."

Aunt Madison is a **drama queen**. She loves to create drama in the workplace by starting arguments, gossiping, holding grudges, and the like. She will blow small things out of proportion for attention. Her communication includes angry outbursts, tearful breakdowns, and the silent treatment.

Uncle Jason is a **slacker.** He finds any excuse not to work. His excuses include, "I don't know how," "No one trained me," "That's not my job," and "You didn't tell me to do that."

Cousin Kathy is a different type of slacker known as a **vampire**. She is more appealing than your run-of-the-mill slacker. When Kathy is around, there always seems to be laughter and fun, but in the end, others always do her work. Like a vampire, she draws you in and then drains you dry (Bernstein, 2001).

Cousin Paul is the office **grump**. A dark cloud follows him wherever he goes. He often rolls his eyes, breathes hard, and presents a bad attitude. He makes comments such as, "I can't believe we have to do this," "This is stupid," and "Why do I always have to do all the work?"

Grandpa is the **roadblock to change**. He doesn't like change. In fact, he often refuses to carry out changes in his duties. Grandpa can be heard saying, "Back in my day" or "Things used to be different (or better) around here."

Grandma can be a **distracter**. While she may mean well, she often leads the team on tangents. Her examples, comments, and questions are longwinded and stray from the purpose of the meeting.

Nephew Robert is a **patient,** turning his coworkers and sometimes even bosses into his counselors. He brings personal problems to

Workplace bullying is a serious problem that shouldn't be ignored by anyone in leadership.

work and discusses them on company time. His personal life often impacts his attendance and performance on the job.

Finally, there are the nieces. Niece Elaine is the **team player**. Niece Marie is the **star**. Both nieces are hardworking and dependable. For Elaine, the goal is to complete her tasks, get along with her coworkers, and serve her customers. As for Marie, she shares Elaine's goals, but in addition, she wants to take on extra duties, learn more, and advance in her career. Unfortunately, in many organizations, both nieces are rewarded for a job well done with extra work and little praise.

It's quite likely that your workplace will have a different mix. For example, none of these labels is gender specific. You can have female grumps and bullies as well as male drama queens and stars. You may not have all these family members in your workplace, and you may have some others we didn't mention. Even worse, you may have one person who embodies several (or all) of these dysfunctional roles.

So take a moment to reflect on your workplace. One important step in achieving professional excellence, even with difficult people, is *knowing yourself.* As our 86-year-old neighbor often says, "A skunk never smells its own tail." In other words, everyone around the skunk knows he stinks, but the skunk doesn't have a clue. You don't want to be that skunk, so take a long, hard look at yourself and determine which family member best represents you. You may come to realize that while most of the time you are a star, on occasion you can be a bully, slacker, or gossip. None of us is perfect, so we all have qualities that can at times make us difficult to work with. That's okay as long as you know your own weaknesses and actively seek to control and improve them.

Once you've identified your role(s) in the organizational family, reflect on the rest of your group. Who makes up your organizational family tree? How do the different family members positively or negatively impact your work environment? How effectively or ineffectively do you communicate with each type of family member? As a leader, what have you done or what will you do to foster professional excellence within all members of your organizational family? Remember, communication is a process, and even if the other person is behaving in a way that's less than professional, you must still work to maintain professional excellence. Furthermore, as the leader, you must work to develop professional excellence for all your team members, both functional and dysfunctional (see Table 10.4).

**Table 10.4 Making Criticism Constructive**

| | Constructive Criticism (The Dos) | Destructive Criticism (The Don'ts) |
|---|---|---|
| Address issues in a timely fashion. | Talk to the employee within a week of the issue, sooner if the issue is deemed urgent. | Don't wait until the next annual evaluation. |
| Discuss the issue in a private setting. | Schedule a meeting—in a neutral location if possible. | Don't talk to the employee in front of coworkers or customers. |
| Hold the discussion at a time when no one will be rushed or interrupted. | Allow enough time to fully discuss the issue. Turn off cell phones, pagers, etc. | Don't cram a 60-minute meeting into 15 minutes. Don't show disrespect by answering a phone during the meeting. |
| Focus the conversation on one issue. | Keep the meeting focused on the issue at hand. Hold multiple meetings if there are multiple issues. | Don't hit the employee with a laundry list of things he or she is doing wrong. |
| Keep comments focused on behaviors. | State behaviors that can be measured: "You have been late to work six times in the past 4 weeks." | Don't provide commentary on the behavior: "You are obviously not a morning person." |
| Make comments specific, not general. | Both problems and solutions should be specifically and clearly defined: "As stated in our dress code, you cannot wear shorts or T-shirts to work." | Don't give general or vague communication: "You need to dress better for work." |
| Focus on solutions. | State the behavior and then ask, "How can we improve this situation?" | Don't tell an employee what he or she is doing wrong without any discussion of ways to improve. |
| Set clearly defined goals for improvement. | The meeting should end with a measurable goal/solution in place. | Don't end without a plan for improvement. |
| Allow and encourage the employee to participate actively in the problem-solving and goal-setting process. | At every point in the conversation, ask the employee for input and truly listen to that input. | Don't do all the talking. |
| Follow through by providing support when needed. | Identify things the employee needs to improve, such as training or mentoring. | Don't miss opportunities to develop employee skills. |
| Follow up on the progress. | Immediately schedule a follow-up meeting to discuss progress. | Don't forget about the issue until it occurs again. |

## Leader as Parent

If the department or organization is like a family, then, metaphorically speaking, the leader is a parent. Again, this can have both positive and negative ramifications. On the positive side, good parents are understanding, focus on developing their children, and serve as role models. The same holds true for good leaders. A good leader understands employees' duties, workloads, constraints, and goals because he or she is open to giving and receiving feedback. Good leaders also develop their employees. If you have a quality employee in your organization, a star or even a team player, you should work to retain that employee. Clearly, he or she will not stay in the same job forever, so you should coach that employee, helping him or her advance within your organization. A big part of developing employees is giving them proper training and then empowering them to take on assignments and responsibilities. Finally, good leaders serve as **role models**. Telling employees that customer service is important and then failing to display it yourself is the mark of an unprofessional leader. "Do what I say, not what I do" is ineffective with children and adults. A leader with professional excellence makes certain that his or her behavior reflects the values and attitudes he or she wants everyone on the team to emulate.

The leader as parent metaphor also has some negative ramifications. First, leaders may begin treating employees like children. This can result in the leader making excuses when employees don't perform their duties. Second, the leader as parent may make all the decisions for the group and fail to share leadership. *Father Knows Best* was a clever title for a 1950s sitcom, but it is no way to develop a team in the 21st century. Leadership must be shared. The third negative ramification of leader as parent comes when leaders begin to feel as though they cannot fire their employees, since you cannot fire your children. As we will discuss in a moment, learning to reprimand or fire employees is something a leader must do.

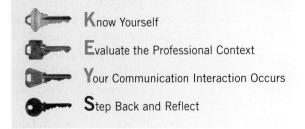

Know Yourself

Evaluate the Professional Context

Your Communication Interaction Occurs

Step Back and Reflect

# Giving Feedback

Can this family/parenting metaphor help in your quest for professional excellence as a leader? The answer is a resounding "yes." Anyone who has watched *Supernanny* knows that many valuable leadership lessons can be learned from good parenting. How can the Super Nanny take a house full of unruly kids and whip them into shape in a week? By being an excellent leader. Unlike the parents, the Super Nanny is not afraid to lay out the expectations, provide feedback, and follow through with consequences. Good behavior is rewarded, and bad behavior results in a trip to the naughty chair. Although putting a naughty chair in your workplace will not work, the underlying principles will. Leaders with professional excellence set expectations; provide feedback for praise, accountability, and motivation; and enact consequences. A leader with professional excellence understands how to use feedback to mentor stars as well as to turn difficult family members into team players.

The good news is, laying out expectations, providing feedback, and following through with consequences works for all types of difficult employees, as well as star employees. You don't need to become a psychologist who analyzes each type of difficult employee and then develops a plan that fits his or her psychological profile. Instead, you must make sure everyone understands what's expected of them in terms of both job performance and professional behavior. You must provide constant feedback, praising those employees who meet expectations and reprimanding those who fail to meet them. You must follow through, which can mean a bonus, a reprimand, or termination. Let's take a closer look at feedback as it relates to each of the principles noted above.

## Setting Expectations

Parenting metaphor or no parenting metaphor, the first thing any leader must do is set clear expectations for performance and professionalism. In today's diverse workplace, you cannot assume that others share your vision of excellence in performance or professionalism. Furthermore, trying to impose a standard on others is almost certain to fail. When you assume a leadership position, hold a meeting in which you discuss performance and professionalism with your team. What are the rules and regulations laid out by the organization? How has the team worked in the past? What should stay? What can be improved? How do they see excellence in performance and professionalism? How do you visualize excellence in performance and professionalism? Through this discussion (or series of discussions), you and your team will collectively develop a vision of excellence in performance and professionalism that meets your expectations as a leader and simultaneously earns the support of the team.

What if you're already in a leadership position? Is it too late to set clear expectations for performance and professionalism? No, of course it isn't. Select a time that marks a new phase for your team, such as after the completion of a big project or at the beginning of the new fiscal year. Then hold a retreat in which you celebrate the team's past successes and begin setting new goals for the future. As part of this discussion, address the questions on professionalism and performance noted above. In the end, you can't expect success from your team if they don't know what success looks like. Excellence in professionalism and performance must be clearly defined.

## Providing Feedback Regularly

Once the expectations for performance and excellence have been clearly defined, you must discuss them on a regular basis. These discussions should become a part of your team meetings. In addition, you must give feedback on performance and professionalism to individuals both publicly and privately.

Poor leaders often fall into the **annual feedback trap**. Because many leaders are extremely busy and/or because they are conflict avoidant, they save all their feedback for the official **performance appraisal**. It is common for organizations to require some type of formal, written evaluation to be conducted with employees once a year. This performance appraisal usually involves an interview and a written summary of the employee's strengths and weaknesses on the job. Annual performance appraisals are a useful communication tool. This tool provides an opportunity for leaders to learn about employees' long-term goals, which can be used for mentoring purposes. In addition, it's an opportunity to praise strengths formally, as well as a time to lay out action plans for improving weaknesses. But the annual performance appraisal is only one of many communication tools used by excellent leaders. Feedback exchanges should be held often between you, as the leader, and your team members. No one should have to wait an entire year to be praised. In addition, no behavior that warrants improvement should go an entire year without being addressed.

The best leaders provide honest feedback that helps employees improve and develop professionally.

## Praising Team Members

In terms of praise, a leader with professional excellence should give praise daily. You must make a habit of letting employees know they are valued. Your team members should be complimented on a job well done every time the job is done well. Major successes or accomplishments should be marked with a celebration of some type. In fact, celebrating successes should be a part of the organizational culture under your leadership. In addition to publicly praising and acknowledging success, take time to privately acknowledge outstanding performance and professionalism. For example, Margie keeps a pack of thank-you cards in her desk. When an employee or coworker goes the extra mile, she then can immediately send that employee a handwritten note thanking him or her for those efforts or congratulating him or her on the recent success. It doesn't take her a lot of time to do this, but the gesture is meaningful and makes Margie stand out as a leader.

## Holding Team Members Accountable

In an ideal workplace, once the expectations are laid out, all you ever need to do is praise employees for meeting and surpassing those expectations. Unfortunately, we have never met anyone who is in an ideal workplace. This means that just as you must learn to praise success on a regular basis, you must also learn to hold others accountable when they fail to meet expectations in performance or professionalism.

Unlike praising, which should be done both publicly and privately, holding someone accountable should be done only privately. There are two reasons why privacy is so important. First, discussing someone's shortcomings or weaknesses privately shows respect for the other person. Rather than embarrassing the other person in front of his or her coworkers—or worse yet, customers—you can create a comfortable environment in which you can talk honestly and work toward a solution. It is really a matter of saving face. **Face-saving behavior** is both verbal and nonverbal communication that honors and maintains the other person's sense of self-respect in a given situation (Clare & Danilovic, 2012; Ting-Toomey, 1990). When you show the other person respect, he or she saves face. This makes that person more open to engaging in improvement. If you disrespect the other person, he or she loses face. As a result, the other person may feel the need to disrespect you or ignore your comments in an attempt to reclaim face, becoming less likely to engage in improvement.

Second, discussing shortcomings or weaknesses one-on-one in a private setting increases the chances that the message is heard. For example, Jane makes a habit of taking long lunches. Her boss, Steve, has noticed this behavior as well as the frustration it is causing among her coworkers. At the next team meeting, Steve states, "I have noticed that our punctuality is becoming a problem and some of you are beginning to make tardiness a habit. Let's all try to make sure we are on time for the start of shifts and after our lunches and breaks." Following the meeting, Steve's star employee, Dana, comes up to Steve and apologizes: "I know I was late for work one day last week when my battery died in my car. I am so sorry." Steve assures her that the comment was not directed at her, but she still seems upset. As for Jane, Steve's comments rolled off her back. In fact, she did not even realize they were directed at her. Had Steve met with Jane one-on-one, she would have realized he was talking to her and Dana would not have become unnecessarily upset.

As you begin to increase the amount of feedback flowing throughout the team, the question "How do I (or we) improve?" will inevitably come up. Telling someone he or she has done something wrong or needs to improve, without discussing how, is the mark of a poor leader. Take your typical toddler as an example. We dare say that all toddlers at some point in time throw a temper tantrum. Why? They throw tantrums because they are angry and they do not know any other way to express that anger. An experienced parent knows that to stop the tantrums you must teach the toddler not only that this behavior is unacceptable but also how to handle anger in a more productive way. Seasoned parents can often be heard saying, "Use your words when you are upset." The same strategy holds true with adults. You must let them know if a behavior is unacceptable, and then you discuss how to improve. For example, if you tell an employee, "You need to take more initiative," the results will most likely be disappointing. The employee needs specific instructions about what your expectations are and what he or she should be doing. You may be thinking, "That's silly. They just need to take more initiative. It is self-explanatory." Actually, it is not self-explanatory. Let's look at Charles's case.

Charles had been "written up" in his last evaluation for not taking initiative. Charles walked out of the performance appraisal completely confused. In the beginning, he tried to take initiative, but every time he tried to do something on his own, he was told it was the wrong thing. After a while, he quit trying and just waited until someone told him what to do; then he did what he was told and did it well. He had no idea what his supervisor wanted or how to improve. Fortunately, Charles's supervisor, Stephanie, realized her mistake and developed a means for improving that was specific and clear. All **performance improvement plans** should be specific and clear (see Table 10.5). So in Charles's case, he was told as soon as he completed one task, he should approach Stephanie for his next task. She did not want him to begin a new task unless she okayed it, nor did she want him to stand around waiting until she noticed he was not busy. For the next few weeks, Charles tried this approach. Stephanie noted a lot of improvement in his performance, and she praised his success. She also held a follow-up meeting to discuss his progress and listen to his feedback. During this discussion, Stephanie learned that Charles felt uncomfortable, as though he was interrupting her, every time he asked for a new task. He also was concerned that when she was busy, he was left without anything to do. Stephanie listened

**Table 10.5 Lessons From Parenting Chart**

- Set clear expectations for performance and professionalism.
- Discuss performance on a regular basis.
- Provide honest feedback with concrete examples.
- Develop means for improving that are specific, clear, and measurable.
- Develop individualized means for motivating.
- Focus on one area of improvement at a time (never more than three).
- Follow through. Make sure consequences to positive and negative behavior are clear and enacted.

to Charles's feedback and used the information to change her communication with all her employees. Instead of giving each person one task at a time, she began assigning multiple tasks at once, trusting the employees to complete their lists and then come to her for more assignments when they were done.

Discussing improvement plans with employees is much more effective than simply telling employees what to do. This two-way communication flow will allow for improvements in your leadership and for individual differences among your team members. No two people are alike, so there is no cookie-cutter, one-size-fits-all strategy for improving and/or motivating others.

## Motivating Through Feedback

Leaders with professional excellence develop individualized means for motivating. Individualizing motivation is part of the KEYS process, which requires you to evaluate your audience. What motivates employees to continue to give outstanding performances and reach high levels of professionalism? What motivates employees to improve their areas of weakness? It depends on the individual person in question. The only way to determine what will motivate the individual is to ask him or her.

Although there are many theories on employee motivation, we have found the **Goal Setting Theory** (Locke & Latham, 1984) to be the most effective. According to this theory, goals are not merely assigned; rather, the leader and the team member develop the goal(s) together. Goals must be clear and specific, allowing both parties to have a shared expectation of what is expected. Goals should also be challenging yet attainable, increasing the likelihood for both growth and success. Finally, feedback must be frequent as team members work to achieve their goals.

Discussing an area that needs improvement or defining a goal should mark the beginning, not the end, of the communication on that subject. Leaders with professional excellence immediately schedule a follow-up meeting in which the employee can discuss his or her progress, questions can be answered, and additional support can be provided. The number of follow-up meetings must be determined on a case-by-case basis, but additional meetings should be called immediately if any signs of poor performance return.

## Enacting Consequences

Part of the feedback process includes discussing consequences to both positive and negative behaviors and then making sure those consequences are enacted. For example, Sally was named "Employee of the Month" for April. For this honor, she was supposed to receive a prime parking spot for a month and $500. She did get her parking spot, but it was now August and she had yet to receive the money, which she had planned to use for a vacation. Her boss's failure to follow through made Sally feel demotivated instead of valued and honored.

Failure to follow through is the major reason why there are so many difficult people in the workplace. Despite repeatedly demonstrating unprofessional behavior, many leaders fail to hold these people accountable. As a result, they continue to act in ways that violate clearly defined standards of professionalism and performance, without consequences. Providing feedback, holding people accountable, and following through with consequences are critical leadership responsibilities, yet many leaders fail in these areas.

Giving someone negative feedback and holding him or her accountable is uncomfortable for most of us, but excellent leaders realize it is a necessity (Kuntz & Gomes, 2012; Patterson, Grenny, McMillan, & Switzler, 2005). Without honest feedback, employees cannot improve. If your team members are to grow and develop, they must come to understand the areas that are holding them back. By providing them with honest feedback, you are providing them with a service. Failure to provide honest feedback is a disservice. Furthermore, if the behavior in question has negatively impacted other team members, the work environment, or customers, then it must be stopped, because it is making everyone uncomfortable. If you ignore it, you will be fostering a negative work environment and you run the risk of losing your star employees.

One tool that can help you give negative feedback and hold others accountable is scripting. **Scripting** is the process of mentally rehearsing what you will say during the discussion. As part of scripting, you will anticipate the responses of the other party and think through what you will say to those responses.

When you are giving negative feedback and hold someone accountable, you should be direct. Don't beat around the bush or make irrelevant chitchat. You also should focus on facts and observations while avoiding judgments. So you should say, "You cut Ross off midsentence," as opposed to saying, "You're rude," or you should say, "You spoke so quietly, it was hard to hear," as opposed to saying, "You're afraid."

Remember, the ultimate goal is to create improvement in the other person's behavior. Therefore, whenever possible, use the unite strategies we discussed in Chapter 7. You and your employee are trying to solve the problem together. State the problem as you see it, and then listen. Together, come up with solutions that meet the expectations of professionalism and performance your team has developed.

### Firing Employees

Unfortunately, even if you lay out the expectations, provide honest feedback, and give support, some people will not meet the expectations of professionalism and performance needed to continue working for your team. If that is the case, then you are responsible for firing that person. For some of you, firing another person will be very difficult, but as a leader, it is your responsibility. There is no reason to feel guilty if you followed all the steps noted above. In the end, it is the other person's choice not to live up to the clearly defined expectations and his or her choice to face the consequences.

Harvard psychologist Dr. Martha Stout (2005) claims that 1 in every 25 people is a **sociopath**. This means that they have no conscience, feelings of guilt, shame, or remorse. If you have someone like this on your team, there's nothing you can do to develop him or her into a productive employee. Don't worry; not every difficult employee on your team is a sociopath. He or she just may be in the wrong job. Nevertheless, as the leader, you must look out for the good of the rest of the team, and sometimes firing that bad apple is what is best for the bunch.

Unprofessional employees with negative attitudes can be especially challenging for employees and customers.

When you step into a leadership role, familiarize yourself with your organization's termination policy. For most organizations, you must have documentation in order to fire a person. In other words, you must document expectations, your feedback, and his or her performance. As a leader with professional excellence, you will already have those things in place if and when someone needs to have his or her future freed up for new opportunities.

## Putting It Together

We have spent much of this chapter discussing types of difficult people, as well as strategies for leading all types of employees—whether they be difficult or outstanding. Still, you may be questioning how defining expectations, providing feedback, and enacting consequences can lead to communication excellence for a diverse workforce. Don't you need a variety of different communication strategies to deal with a variety of personalities? No, not if you apply the KEYS approach to each phase of this process.

Let's say you have a department with many hardworking employees and a few stars, as well as a slacker, a drama queen, and a bully/sniper. Begin by *knowing yourself*. Maybe you are conflict avoidant. As a result, you tend to ignore the problems among coworkers that result in work not getting done due to unprofessional drama and slacking in the workplace. In fact, you may even blame the employees who bring the problems to your attention. During meetings, you avoid topics that will "set off" the bully/sniper, and when his or her negativity overruns a meeting, you say nothing. On the rare occasions when you have tried to provide feedback and constructive criticism, the drama queen declares, "Everyone picks on me," which causes the discussion to go off course and never reach a solution. As for the slackers, they both say they will improve, but that improvement is never clearly defined, you never follow up, and the negative behavior continues. You will never reach communication excellence if you allow this to continue.

Even if you are not conflict avoidant, you must still *know yourself*. If there are problems with your team, then you must take charge and address them. But this requires you to take some time to assess how your communication style has been adding to the problems with your team. Are you too busy to follow through? Have you failed to define expectations clearly? Are you indeed providing feedback? Are you better at communicating with one

# Ethical Connection    Nora's Leadership Dilemma

*Please read the passage below, and answer the questions that follow.*

Nora is a project manager for a large advertising firm. While her team has always performed at a high level, two recent hires in her group are making progress difficult and alienating other coworkers. Nora has tried all the coaching techniques available to her, but her problem employees still show no signs of improvement. Although firing employees has always been a last-ditch effort for Nora, she sees no other option but to let one or both employees go. However, one of the problem employees has been with the company for years and is approaching retirement; if the employee is fired now, she will lose her chance for a company pension and could have financial issues into her old age. Nora needs to find a solution soon, because one of her largest clients is rolling out a massive advertising campaign, and Nora's team needs to be working at their finest.

## Questions to Consider

1. What is the ethical dilemma facing Nora as a leader right now?
2. What other communication skills might Nora employ when dealing with her problem employees?
3. What would you consider to be the most fair to the rest of the advertising team?
4. Outside of termination, what other options could Nora consider?

type of difficult person than with another? For example, do the tears of a drama queen have no effect on you, or do you excuse behavior when the tears come? Does a bully intimidate you, or can you hold your ground? Do you tend to hold slackers accountable, or do you push their work on your stars? You must know your own strengths and weaknesses as a communicator so you can factor those in when dealing with your teammates.

Next, you must *evaluate the professional context*. Think about the types of problems and excuses that occur due to the various personalities in your workplace. As the group is defining professional expectations, be certain that all these situations are discussed. Whatever the issue—gossiping, interrupting, negative attitudes, poor performance—discuss it as a group. Because this process is not focused on any one person, it will be easier to get a lot of issues out in the open. Once you have clearly defined, mutually defined expectations, you can quickly redirect any employee when you get to the providing feedback stage. As noted above, practice scripting prior to *your communication interaction*. Regardless of whether the bully/sniper tries to intimidate you, the slacker makes excuses, or the drama queen cries, you must remain focused on clearly defining the problem, developing a solution, and presenting the consequences. State the behaviors in question. Invite cooperation for solutions by asking, "How can we fix this situation?" And do not end the meeting until there is a clearly defined plan in place. At times, this will not be easy. You may have to make statements such as the following: "As a team, we defined respect as an expectation. I find it disrespectful when you call your coworkers names such as 'Ding Bat,' 'Fatty,' and 'Baldy.' This behavior is unacceptable. How can we fix this situation so that our work environment meets this expectation of respect?"

To help ensure success during the feedback sessions, review the steps for conflict resolution discussed in Chapter 7. When giving feedback, your ability to stay focused and not become defensive or lead everyone on a tangent is critical. Stay focused on behavior, and redirect all conversation to that behavior: "Refusing to speak to a coworker about work is not acceptable. I can see that you two have issues outside work, but at work this lack of communication is unacceptable. Communicating with respect and professionalism is one of our expectations, regardless of personal issues. This cannot continue, so how can we—you and I—solve this problem? And I want our discussion to stay focused on your behavior, not your coworker's." Also, remember to use agendas in meetings, as discussed in Chapter 7. Agendas will help focus your meetings and control overtalkers and undertalkers.

Next, you should *step back and reflect* on all the communication that has occurred. You may find it necessary to discuss past communication interactions as part of the process: "I have noticed that this behavior has continued. In the past, when we have discussed it, I do all the talking and you say nothing. Today, I would like to change that. I would like you to lead the discussion. How can we solve this problem?" This will help you more effectively *know yourself* and *evaluate the context* as you move into the follow-up. But remember, you must follow up to either enact the consequence or praise the improvement.

Leading difficult people isn't that difficult. In fact, the formula is simple. You must define expectations, provide feedback, and follow up. If you as the leader are consistent in these three functions, you will be on your way to leadership excellence regardless of the types of difficult people you encounter.

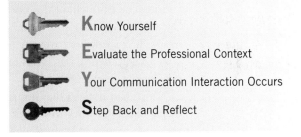

Know Yourself

Evaluate the Professional Context

Your Communication Interaction Occurs

Step Back and Reflect

# Managing Your Public Image

Take a moment and visualize a leader in your mind. What does he or she look like? What does he or she sound like? To excel as a leader with professional excellence, you must take time to reflect on your public image. **Public image** is the impression you give or present to others both verbally and nonverbally. Obviously, the public image you want to present is that of a leader with professional excellence. The way to ensure that this is the image you are actually presenting is through **impression management**—directing the formation of an impression, perception, or view others have of you (Ali & Gulzar, 2012; Goffman, 1971; Harris & Sachau, 2005).

A word of warning is needed here. Impression management is not and should not be about creating a false or deceptive public image. If you want to be viewed as a leader, you must act as a leader and display professional excellence on all levels. Impression management is simply a self-monitoring technique meant to help you put the KEYS process into action.

When it comes to impression management, we often think of clothing. In fact, we would be willing to bet that you have been told at least once in your life to "dress for success." Why are dress and success linked together (besides the fact that they make a cute rhyme)? It is because clothing can convey your status within an organization (Key, 2012; Peluchette, Karl, & Rust, 2006). As noted in Chapter 4, for superiors, conservative, solid-colored, well-fitting, and well-made clothing often communicates power and success.

An old adage states you should dress for the job you want, not the job you have. This is good advice. Let's say your goal is to become a manager. If shorts are permitted on the job but the management team always dresses in business-casual wear, you should put away your shorts and get out your slacks. Dressing for the job you want may not be possible in some organizations. For example, your position may require you to wear a uniform that designates your position. If that is the case, then you should make certain you look like a professional in your designated attire. In fact, regardless of your position or career aspiration, you should always look like a professional. If your position requires a uniform or scrubs, make certain that everything is clean and neatly ironed. If your position requires more casual attire, you should still look professional and be in accordance with the dress code. Hair, makeup, jewelry, and shoes should also be selected with professionalism in mind. You do not have to spend a lot of money to look like a professional—after all, even an Armani suit looks unprofessional if it is dirty or wrinkled. Bottom line, attire is a part of your public image; therefore, dress in a manner that says "professional."

Although it can enhance or deter your public image, clothing in and of itself does not make a leader. It is just one small part of your nonverbal communication that must be considered. Throughout this book, we have talked about verbal and nonverbal communication that conveys professional excellence; all those behaviors contribute to your public image. In a workshop, we once asked a group of leaders to evaluate the impression they were giving their teams. With just a little reflection, several leaders were shocked at the conclusions they reached.

Nancy had noticed that her staff always began their conversations with her with statements like, "I'm sorry to bother you. I know you are busy. I'll just be a minute. I know you have more important things to attend to." She realized she had unintentionally given the impression that communicating with her staff was not a priority. She also realized the potential problems that could stem from this impression, and she began to rethink her impression management.

Rob recalled asking his team to join him for lunch. He was surprised when they all assumed they had done something wrong and he was going to reprimand them. Clearly, he was not communicating enough praise, and the impression he was giving was that of dissatisfaction.

Stephanie noted a very different problem. All day long, her staff would pop in to chit-chat about non-work-related issues. Her office was like a break room. As a result, she had to come to work early, stay late, and work weekends to get her tasks completed. She needed to maintain openness about work-related issues but change the impression that she had nothing to do and/or was there as a friend, not a leader.

By stepping back and reflecting, these leaders were able to more effectively manage the impressions they were giving. Again, impression management is not about creating a false impression but about monitoring your communication so you can present a truthful and professional image.

# KEYS to Excellence in Leadership

Think back to the management of the law firm at the beginning of the chapter. Do you think the management at the law firm showed excellence in leadership in the way they fired their employees? The lack of communication between employees and management cost 14 people their jobs and left a massive workforce depletion at the Florida law firm.

## Know Yourself   Reflections on Leadership Excellence

*The following set of questions will help you gain a better understanding of your own thoughts and values on leadership. Answer each question thoughtfully, and then reflect on the results. How can this knowledge help you be a better leader and a better communicator?*

- Who do you consider an excellent leader?
- How would you describe his or her public image?
- What does an excellent leader look like? Sound like?
- How does an excellent leader behave?
- When you walk into a room, do your associates think you look like a leader?
- What are your positive leadership qualities?
- What leadership qualities do you need to develop?

Think about how using the KEYS approach might have helped matters. The first step, *know yourself*, requires you to understand how you portray yourself as a leader and to assess if you would like working for a boss like yourself. Place yourself in your employees' shoes, and learn what is important and motivating to them.

The second step, *evaluate the professional context*, involves learning more about the environment of your company. Did management at the Florida law firm learn why their employees were wearing orange shirts? According to the fired employees, the orange-shirt theme was common and promoted togetherness; without knowing the context of the orange shirts, managers at the law firm made a drastic and possibly harmful decision.

The third step, *your communication interaction occurs*, appears to be a critical step that the managers ignored. Had management made the effort to talk to their employees about the orange shirts, they could have acquired more information, which might have saved 14 people their jobs. When placed in a leadership position, it is vital that you keep an open line of communication with your employees.

The final step asks you to *step back and reflect* and assess the communication interaction before reaching a decision. Always make sure that you have the most complete and unbiased information as possible before you make decisions that can affect both your and your employees' professional careers. Go over every segment of the interaction, and give considerable thought to how your decision can reflect on your position as a leader in your professional environment.

Do you consider yourself an effective leader? What are your expectations for professional excellence at work? Have you discussed it as a team? Are you comfortable giving feedback? Are you more likely to praise or criticize? *Step back and reflect* on your leadership. What would you most like to improve?

**K**now Yourself

**E**valuate the Professional Context

**Y**our Communication Interaction Occurs

**S**tep Back and Reflect

## Executive Summary

Now that you have finished reading this chapter, you can do the following:

Gain a clear understanding of what constitutes leadership and power:

- *Leadership* is a dynamic relationship based on mutual influence and common purpose between leaders and collaborators, in which both are moved to higher levels of motivation and moral development as they affect real, intended change (p. 236).
- *Legitimate power* is based on a position of authority. The manager has legitimate power over the department budget and employee schedules. While a position/job title may give someone legitimate power, it doesn't mean that person exercises that power (p. 236).
- *Coercive power* refers to the ability to control another person's behavior with negative reinforcement, while *reward power* describes control over another person's behavior with positive reinforcement (p. 237).
- *Expert power* is based on one's superior expertise in a specific field (p. 237).
- You give *referent power* to someone because you want that person to like you (p. 237).
- *Connection power* is based on the old expression, "It's not what you know but who you know." Having a connection to people in positions of power or having a strong support system definitely acts as a source of power (p. 237).

Understand the relationship between leadership theory and communication:

- Just as understanding theories on power can improve your communication as a leader, so, too, can studying leadership theories. Over the past century, scholars have studied leadership-developing theories and models designed to help us understand what effective leadership is and to train us to be better leaders. Implementing the knowledge and insight contained in various leadership theories is a must if you ever plan to excel as a leader (p. 239).

Develop communication strategies for hiring quality employees and leading effective teams:

- Leaders with professional excellence know that hiring is a process that begins long before the first candidate arrives for an interview and lasts long after orientation and training (p. 243).

- When hiring opportunities occur, it's incredibly important that you, as the leader, participate in every stage of the hiring process. It's also important to get the rest of the team involved (p. 243).
- Once the position has been advertised, the interview questions must be drafted. You may or may not be responsible for drafting the questions, but as the leader, you should always review the questions, giving your input and ultimately your approval (p. 244).
- A leader with professional excellence makes certain that new team members feel like part of the team, starting on Day 1. You should make it a point to greet all new employees on the day they arrive (p. 245).
- Excellent leaders involve the team so they, too, can share in the leadership, which will make your job more manageable (p. 246).

Provide feedback as a means to motivate team members and develop difficult people:

- A good leader understands employees' duties, workloads, constraints, and goals, because he or she is open to giving and receiving feedback (p. 251).
- A leader with professional excellence understands how to use feedback to mentor stars as well as to turn difficult family members into team players (p. 251).
- You must provide constant feedback, praising those employees who meet expectations and reprimanding those who fail to meet them. You must follow through, which can mean a bonus, a reprimand, or termination (p. 252).

Use the KEYS process to develop professional excellence as a leader:

- *Know yourself.* Before assessing your team, realize first what you bring to the table (p. 261).
- *Evaluate the professional context.* Realize a participating approach is more likely to succeed. Instead of making the meeting about your goals and your vision, stress the importance of shared leadership and teamwork, asking the team to collectively develop goals and a vision for the department (p. 261).
- *Your communication interaction occurs.* Offer feedback to your team, and give them the opportunity to give you feedback as well (p. 261).
- *Step back and reflect.* Avoid future conflicts. See what is working for you, and hold people accountable for their performance (p. 261).

## Discussion Questions

1. What type(s) of power do you have as a student? How does that source of power impact communication with other students, professors, and administrators?

2. How can you use the information you have learned about leadership theories to develop your leadership skills?

3. Think about the last job interview in which you participated. How effective was the interviewer? What could he or she have done differently to improve the interview process?

4. What goals have you developed for yourself in your career and/or in your workplace? What motivates you to obtain these goals? In what ways does your motivation differ from that of other people you know?

5. Have you ever worked with a difficult person? If so, how did you communicate with this person? Was your communication effective or ineffective? Based on what you have learned in this chapter, how would you change your communication in this situation?

## Terms to Remember

annual feedback trap (p. 252)

authoritative (p. 239)

birthright (p. 235)

bully (p. 248)

charisma (p. 234)

coercive power (p. 237)

connection power (p. 237)

Contingency Theory (p. 242)

democratic (p. 239)

distracter (p. 249)

drama queen (p. 248)

expert power (p. 237)

face-saving behavior (p. 253)

Goal Setting Theory (p. 255)

grump (p. 248)

impression management (p. 259)

job title (p. 235)

laissez-faire (p. 239)

leadership (p. 236)

leadership functions (p. 237)

legitimate power (p. 236)

managerial functions (p. 237)

Managerial Grid (p. 241)

patient (p. 249)

performance appraisal (p. 252)

performance improvement plan (p. 254)

public image (p. 259)

referent power (p. 237)

reward power (p. 237)

roadblock to change (p. 249)

role models (p. 251)

scripting (p. 256)

Situational Leadership Theory (p. 242)

slacker (p. 248)

sniper (p. 248)

sociopath (p. 257)

star (p. 249)

status (p. 236)

subordinate (p. 236)

superior (p. 236)

team player (p. 249)

Theory X (p. 239)

Theory Y (p. 239)

trait (p. 234)

transformational leaders (p. 243)

vampire (p. 248)

Visit the Student Study Site at **www.sagepub.com/keys2e** to access the following resources:

- SAGE journal articles
- Video links
- Web resources

- Web quizzes
- eflashcards

# Presenting in the Workplace

Chapter 11:   Informing and Persuading

Chapter 12:   Speech Design

Chapter 13:   Delivering a Speech With Professional Excellence

## Chapter Outline

**The Importance of Presenting With
  Professional Excellence   269**
**Identifying Presentation Opportunities and
  Purposes   269**
**Speaking to Inform   271**
**Speaking to Persuade   278**
**KEYS to Excellence in Professional
  Presentations   283**
**Executive Summary   286**
**Discussion Questions   287**
**Terms to Remember   287**

## Chapter Objectives

After studying this chapter, you should be able to:

1. Discuss the importance of professional
   excellence in public speaking

2. Identify presenting opportunities

3. Define the purpose of a presentation

4. Design an informative speech

5. Design a persuasive speech

# chapter 11

# Informing and Persuading

**David Henderson, an attorney based out of San Antonio, is no stranger to workplace presentations and public speaking.** Many aspects of his job require him to be an effective communicator and presenter. However, Henderson reached beyond what was expected of him and found himself crowned the world champion of public speaking. Henderson's tale of losing his young cousin to sickle cell disease captured the emotions of the crowd and 14 judges, lifting him past 30,000 contestants from 113 countries and earning him the title of 2010 champion at the Toastmasters World Championship of Public Speaking (Davis, 2010). Henderson joined the Toastmasters to learn to control his emotions during his speeches, as he is required to do so often as a prosecutor for the Bexar County district attorney's office. However, he picked the speech about his cousin's sickle cell disease to strike an emotional chord with his audience. Also, to alleviate the somberness of the subject, Henderson opened his speech with a joke to relax the audience. Henderson noted these (among other) tips for giving him the advantage needed to win the competition.

While many people do not plan on finding themselves in jobs that require them to speak publicly, most employees will be required to give a presentation to others at some point in their careers. Being confident and capable when speaking to your bosses or coworkers is essential to the growth and satisfaction of your job. Especially at the critical job interview phase, being able to present yourself in a positive manner can mean the difference between landing the job and getting passed over. Informing and persuading in the workplace is a daily challenge, but doing so effectively can increase your visibility and desirableness with employers. Henderson offers an excellent (but not the only) example of how to use communication in presentations to your advantage.

Informing and persuading with professional excellence can seem terrifying at first glance, but with practice it can become one of your greatest assets in the workplace. In this chapter, you will learn about the opportunities and purposes of presentations, as well as the tools needed to become an effective presenter. Also, you will learn the differences between informing and persuading, as well as what strategies to use for different types of presentations.

D o you fear giving presentations? For some of you, presenting is indeed a fear. For others of you, it may even be your greatest fear. It's doubtful, however, that any of you would rather die than give a presentation. Even if you don't consider presenting a fear, chances are presenting isn't on your list of favorite activities; of course, there are a few of you who really do enjoy presenting opportunities. The good news is that whether you view presenting as a fear, an annoyance, or a joy, developing presentational skills will help you excel in your career. Our study of business and professional communication is not complete without attention to this type of oral communication. How will you use presentation skills *on the job?* How can presentational excellence enhance your professional excellence? The study and practice of oral communication discussed in the next three chapters will help you overcome your fears and develop presentations with professional excellence.

You will learn the basics, which have been around for more than 2,000 years. These speaking essentials are often connected with **Aristotle**—a Greek philosopher, author of *The Art of Rhetoric,* student of Plato, and teacher of Alexander the Great. Clearly, after 2,000 years, these guidelines have passed the test of time. Yet many people have either failed to learn these basics or fail to implement them. As executive coaches, we have worked with dozens of top leaders in a variety of industries and often find ourselves telling them the same things you'll learn in these chapters. Use this knowledge and the presentation opportunities presented in this course to develop the confidence and abilities needed for professional excellence.

Many of us think of audiences as mean and hostile. As this photo suggests, your audience can turn out to be supportive, interested, and friendly.

# The Importance of Presenting With Professional Excellence

Just as effective communication skills are essential to your professional success, effective oral communication skills are essential if you want to excel in leadership. Presentational excellence is important for the following reasons: (1) Product presentations, team huddles, running meetings, press conferences, special events, and other forms of oral communication reveal something about you as a professional; (2) presentations serve as a tool to motivate employees and communicate effectively about business goals; and (3) presentational excellence is required to achieve professional excellence. To address these important topics, let's take a look at ways to communicate excellence in presentations.

# Identifying Presentation Opportunities and Purposes

The first step in the presentation process is identifying opportunities. Once you have identified the presentation opportunities, you can identify the purpose within them.

## Presentation Opportunities

*Claire:* "I get so tired of the huddle every morning."

*Juan:* "Why do Bill's morning huddles bother you so much?"

*Claire:* "When Jack was doing the huddles, they really got me fired up and ready for the day. I get so bored listening to Bill's morning speech. I can't keep track of what he's saying with all those charts and numbers."

*Juan:* "Poor Bill. Maybe we just need to have an extra cup of coffee so we don't fall asleep."

This brief conversation illustrates that Bill has missed an opportunity to motivate his employees. Instead, he's boring them to death with charts and numbers. Let's explore presentation opportunities in more detail.

There are two types of presentation opportunities available to leaders. One is a **formal presentation,** which occurs in a traditional presentation setting. Presenting a sales pitch to clients and giving a progress report at the district meeting are examples of formal presentations. We have labeled the second type as the **opportunity presentation.** The opportunity presentation is identical in preparation and presentation to the formal presentation, but it occurs in a less traditional setting. For instance,

Bill loves his flip chart and thinks of himself as a good presenter, but his employees have a different view.

How would you approach presenting during a huddle or team meeting similar to the one shown here?

many organizations have **huddles,** during which employees are pulled together to talk. This is not a traditional presentation setting, but it is still an opportunity. Meetings provide another possible setting for opportunity presentations. As a team leader, it will be your job to facilitate meetings. While you may not be required to present at a meeting, the opportunity still exists. Giving a small opening address to kick off a meeting is an example of an opportunity presentation.

As a leader, you must begin identifying presentation opportunities and presenting yourself with professional excellence as you utilize each opportunity. You may consider preparing for presentations, especially opportunity presentations, a waste of time. If you've done okay in the past by giving an **impromptu presentation**—winging it or speaking off the cuff—you may be tempted not to prepare. Remember, professional excellence is not about being "okay." Think back to a presentation you delivered without preparation. How much better would your message have been if you had prepared? Let us reiterate that both formal and opportunity presentations require preparation and practice.

## General Purpose

Once you've identified your presentation opportunity, the next step is to determine your purpose. Presentations can have one of two **general purposes**: to **inform** or to **persuade**. When speaking with an informative purpose, you present the facts. Informative speakers act as teachers relaying information. When speaking with a persuasive purpose, you are acting as an advocate or making an argument. Your role is to advocate for or against something. In some situations, you'll be trying to persuade the audience simply to agree or disagree with an idea—this is known as **passive agreement**. In other situations, you'll be trying to persuade the audience to take some sort of action—this is known as **active agreement** or a **call to action**.

Determining your purpose may seem like a simple enough task, but speakers with professional excellence always think carefully when determining their purpose. For example, you may need to inform employees about a new policy in your organization. Ask yourself, "Am I merely informing them about the policy, or am I persuading them to follow the new policy?" In all likelihood, you will be persuading them. While many presentation opportunities appear informative on the surface, a closer look reveals the need or opportunity to persuade. Let's look at another example: Say you're relaying some information on customer satisfaction scores. Are you simply presenting the information, or is there a secondary purpose? If the scores are low, the secondary purpose may be persuading your team that they need to do a better job the next time around. If the scores are high, it may be to celebrate as a team, acknowledge some outstanding performances, motivate them to keep up the good work, or all the above.

We will explore speaking to inform and speaking to persuade in more detail. But first, it is important to understand the difference between a general purpose and a specific purpose.

## Specific Purpose

Once you've identified the general purpose of your presentation, you'll begin to formulate a **specific purpose**. The specific purpose is to an oral presentation what a thesis statement is to an essay. A specific purpose is a declarative sentence telling the listeners what you want them to understand/know or believe by the end of your presentation.

The following are some examples of specific purposes:

As this photo suggests, the audience and presentation context can sometimes be difficult to predict or can present a challenge.

- I want my employees to understand and follow the new overtime rule.
- I want the executive team to believe our department deserves a 10% budget increase.
- I want Company X to select us as the health care provider for its employees.
- I want my team to feel recognized and appreciated for their hard work.

Designing a presentation is not a linear process in which you move from one step to the next. Instead, designing a presentation is a fluid process. Thus, you may develop a tentative specific purpose and then change it after you have done some analysis and research. In fact, identifying the general and specific purposes for any presentation opportunity will require you to analyze the audience and the context.

# Speaking to Inform

As noted above, when speaking with an informative purpose, your goal is to present the facts. Informative speakers act as teachers relaying information, striving to be **objective** and not influenced or impacted by emotions or their individual point of view.

According to Aristotle, a good persuasive speech includes three **persuasive appeals**: ethos, logos, and pathos. Although Aristotle discussed these appeals in relationship to persuasive presentations, we believe the first two appeals also are important for designing an effective informative presentation.

## Ethos

**Ethos** refers to your **credibility** as a presenter as well as the credibility of the information delivered in your presentation. In order to present with professional excellence, you

## Know Yourself   Credibility

*The following assessment will help you gain a better understanding of how your credibility as a speaker will be assessed. Communication scholar James McCroskey argues that credibility is made up of three basic areas: competence, character, and caring. You can use this measure to assess a speaker's credibility along these three areas. Think about these characteristics of credibility as you build your own persuasive presentation.*

Circle the number that best represents your feelings about the speaker.

| | | | |
|---|---|---|---|
| 1. | Intelligent | 1 2 3 4 5 6 7 | Unintelligent |
| 2. | Ethical | 1 2 3 4 5 6 7 | Unethical |
| 3. | Caring | 1 2 3 4 5 6 7 | Uncaring |
| 4. | Trained | 1 2 3 4 5 6 7 | Untrained |
| 5. | Honest | 1 2 3 4 5 6 7 | Dishonest |
| 6. | Has my interests at heart | 1 2 3 4 5 6 7 | Doesn't have my interests at heart |
| 7. | Expert | 1 2 3 4 5 6 7 | Not an expert |
| 8. | Unselfish | 1 2 3 4 5 6 7 | Selfish |
| 9. | Concerned | 1 2 3 4 5 6 7 | Unconcerned |
| 10. | Informed | 1 2 3 4 5 6 7 | Uninformed |
| 11. | Sympathetic | 1 2 3 4 5 6 7 | Unsympathetic |
| 12. | Understanding | 1 2 3 4 5 6 7 | Not understanding |
| 13. | Competent | 1 2 3 4 5 6 7 | Incompetent |
| 14. | High character | 1 2 3 4 5 6 7 | Low character |
| 15. | Responsive | 1 2 3 4 5 6 7 | Unresponsive |
| 16. | Bright | 1 2 3 4 5 6 7 | Stupid |
| 17. | Trustworthy | 1 2 3 4 5 6 7 | Untrustworthy |
| 18. | Understands how I think | 1 2 3 4 5 6 7 | Doesn't understand how I think |

Now total your scores using the guidelines below.

The scores should range from 6 to 42 for each subscale.
*Competence*: ADD items (1, 4, 7, 10, 13, and 16) for a total score of _____
*Character*: ADD items (2, 5, 8, 11, 14, and 17) for a total score of _____
*Caring*: ADD items (3, 6, 9, 12, 15, and 18) for a total score of _____

Source: Modified from McCroskey and Teven (1999).

must demonstrate credibility and help your audience believe you and the information or argument you are presenting. **Quintilian**, a Roman philosopher and educator, viewed credibility as central to any effective rhetoric, which he defined as "a good man speaking well." The word *good* in Quintilian's quote refers to credibility.

How do you establish credibility? According to Aristotle, presenters must demonstrate ethos or positive character by demonstrating competence, trustworthiness, and goodwill. There are many ways to develop positive character within your presentation, but you must make sure the audience is aware of your expertise and knowledge on the subject matter. In addition, you must conduct research and then cite your sources.

Eileen is the vice president of security for a large resort chain. She's been invited to inform hotel managers about the effectiveness of their new security system at the annual retreat. When Eileen is introduced, both her title and her 15 years with the company are mentioned. This begins to develop her credibility. Within the body of her presentation, Eileen discusses a new security plan that recently was tested at one of the resorts in the chain. When discussing the success of the new plan, she cites improved security scores at that resort and emphasizes that the scores were gathered by an outside agency. By making certain that both she and her data are credible, she has succeeded in establishing ethos.

## Logos

**Logos** is another type of appeal needed in effective presentations. *Logos* is a term that refers to the words of a presentation in the context of organizational structure and the supporting information. When developing an informative presentation, think of yourself as a teacher laying out information about a particular topic. After reviewing your research and analyzing the purpose, audience, and context, you will develop a clear organizational structure for your presentation (we discuss this in the next chapter). However, that structure can't stand without support. The research that you've conducted will become that support. Together, the structure and the information will provide your audience with logical appeal.

What type of research should you include? Obviously, that will depend on the nature of your topic, purpose, audience, and the context. However, any or all of the following may have a place in your presentation: definitions, examples, statistics, and quotations. See Table 11.1 for a more detailed discussion of each.

When it comes to selecting supporting material for your presentations, remember to include a variety. A statistic revealing that your customer base has declined by 25% is powerful, but supporting that stat with an example from a customer who left is stronger because it adds human interest.

### Table 11.1 Supporting Material

| | |
|---|---|
| Definitions | Provide explanations of words or concepts that your listeners need to understand |
| Examples | Provide your listeners with illustrations, parallel cases, or representations of a larger group |
| Statistics | Provide your listeners with numerical data that is used to analyze, interpret, or explain ideas in your speech |
| Quotes | Provide your listeners with insight from experts in the field or people who have had firsthand experience with the subject matter |

## Your Communication Interaction    Stop, Look, and Listen

*Read the passage below, and then answer the questions. As you read, think about ways the KEYS approach could help you improve **your communication interaction** if you were in Sheryl's position.*

*Background Information*

Sheryl Gardner, a senior-level manager, has been asked to speak to a group of management trainees. The speech will take place during one of their training sessions, and Sheryl was told to make it "educational and about communication." Given this information, Sheryl has determined that her general purpose should be to inform; however, *communication* is far too broad to be considered a specific purpose. After analyzing her audience, Sheryl determines that the people in this group will soon be taking over their own departments and should, as a first step, begin developing a communication climate that will foster open communication and teamwork. Since the audience members have already been persuaded that open communication and teamwork are a must in their jobs, Sheryl is simply informing them of the role the communication climate can play in the process.

*Introduction*

In her book *It's Always Something,* Gilda Radner shares the true story of a dog that was involved in a lawn mower accident. Somehow, a poor little dog was hit by a lawn mower, and the blade cut off her back legs. To complicate matters, the dog was pregnant with puppies. The good news is that both the mother and puppies were saved. The bad news is that the mother lost her legs. But the little dog did learn to walk again by taking two steps and then pulling her backside, two steps and then pulling her backside. The most interesting part of the story is that when the puppies learned to walk, they all walked just like her! **[Attention Step]**

As Mr. Ruiz mentioned, my name is Sheryl Gardner, and I have been working for this company for more than 20 years. What began as a part-time job for minimum wage has turned into a career in which I am now a top leader in the management team. **[Establishing Credibility]** Today, I am so grateful to have this opportunity to speak with you about the skill I consider to be one of the most important aspects of managing people and the secret to my success—effective communication. **[Creating a Need]** The material we will be covering is pretty easy to understand but hard to apply. Why is it so hard to apply? It is hard because we learn how to communicate by emulating others. Just as those puppies learned to walk by emulating what they saw their mother do, we learn to communicate by emulating what we see others do. The problem is that many of us have had poor role models in how to communicate effectively. We have formed bad habits, and now that those patterns are established, they are very hard to change. The good news is that we can change. **[Creating a Need]**

We can all become more effective in the art and skill of communication, which is the key to success as a manager. And it all begins with creating a positive communication climate, which is what we will be focusing on today. **[Specific Purpose]** But before you can create a positive communication climate, you need to know what is meant by the term. *Communication climate* refers to an environment in which communication either thrives or languishes. The communication environment in an organization, like the weather, can be sunny and beautiful (a place where people enjoy working), or it can be like a severe thunderstorm or even a hurricane in some instances, where there is consistently unresolved conflict and employees—from management down—don't trust or support one another. As you know, when attempting to drive in a severe thunderstorm, the storm makes it twice as hard to complete the task at hand and get from Point A to Point B. It's the same in an organization with a poor communication climate. Employees are much less focused, cooperative, and productive due to extraneous factors. And they can't move the company from Point A to Point B.

To establish the healthiest communication climate possible, it's important that you, as a manager, stop, look, and listen. Stop and take the time to build relationships with your employees. Look at what your employees are doing for the organization. Listen to your employees' ideas and concerns. **[Preview of Main Points]** Let's start by taking a look at the importance of stopping to build relationships with our employees. **[Transition Statement]**

*Body*

### I. Stop—and take the time to build relationships with your employees

To better understand the process of building relationships, we need to define two communication terms— *impersonal communication* and *interpersonal communication.* Impersonal communication is when we treat people as though they are objects. Unfortunately, this is the type of communication we often engage in with a cashier or server. We will say, "How are you today?" However, if that person really stopped and told us how he or she was, we would think it was quite odd. We all know the standard answer is something like, "Fine, thank you."

If we are engaging in interpersonal communication, thus building a relationship, we should really want to hear the answer when we ask a question. As managers, we must remember that employees are not chess pieces. These are real people we are moving around.

To develop relationships with your employees, you must be genuine. So the way to connect and build relationships with employees will be different for each of you. The way you do it is to play off your own strengths. Some of you may be good at remembering details about people. So when Janice tells you about her kid's broken arm, you remember it. And the next time you talk with Janice, you ask how the arm is doing. Some of you may not be good at that kind of chitchat; so, instead, you can do something else. Maybe you schedule a lunch for the entire team every month and make it a point to sit beside someone different during each luncheon. If that works for you, it is perfect. Maybe you are naturally funny and enjoy joking around with employees. Again, if that is your strength for developing relationships, use it. There is no one right way to do this. You just have to make a commitment to developing relationships and then find a strategy that works for you.

Another vital part of building strong relationships includes the process of looking at or noticing all that our subordinates are doing for the company. **[Transition]**

### II. Look—at what employees are doing for the company, and acknowledge it

Developing relationships will help you become aware of some of the things your team is accomplishing, but to develop a positive communication climate, you must get in the habit of regularly reviewing high performance and success in your team. One way to do this is to develop a habit of asking customers and employees about their experiences with your company. If they had a negative experience, of course work to evaluate the problems. But if they say their experiences are positive, ask them why. Ask them who makes their job easier. Ask them who gave them excellent service. Look at and explore what employees are doing to make this company a success.

*(Continued)*

*(Continued)*

Of course, when you see and hear about employees' outstanding efforts, you will feel a sincere appreciation for that effort, but that is not enough. It's vital that you communicate your appreciation. Acknowledging excellent performance is a central component in developing a positive communication climate.

The obvious ways to show appreciation are by recognizing employees' accomplishments publicly. For example, I give a speech at the beginning of every year titled "The Top 10 Reasons Why We Are Great!" The speech highlights everyone's accomplishments for that year. Of course, a simple pat on the back or thank you can be quite effective as well and should be used all year long.

When researching his book *Whale Done: The Power of Positive Relationships,* Ken Blanchard found that the very same techniques Sea World Trainers used to move 10,000-pound killer whales to action also increase motivation and productivity when managing people. He points out that "accentuating the positive" is the key to success. But you can't accentuate the positive or recognize accomplishments if you fail to look. Looking at what your employees are doing is a must if you want to develop a positive communication climate.

### III. Listen—to their ideas and concerns

Now that we've established the importance of stopping to build relationships with our employees and looking at what they are doing for the company, let's talk about the importance of listening to their ideas and concerns. **[Transition Statement]**

Bob Jicks of COL Management is part of a team that oversees the daily operations of numerous Imaging Centers, and he has been in management for 11 years. He was quoted as saying:

Sometimes I just need to listen to them, talk with them—because no one understands or represents your company like the person answering the phone or greeting patients at the window. If they feel like they are part of the decision process then they are more likely to be part of the implementation process. I had one of our techs when we were building our new building a few years ago suggest that we make the entrance the same level as the street—parking lot—instead of being a curb or bump. That was a little thing but actually made sense—more importantly—gave her ownership or buy-in that she felt like she was part of the team. I used to think it was all about the pay—don't get me wrong it helps—but it is really all about the people. Listening to them—"validating" their issues or complaints—sharing and developing goals together—works better than shoving it down their throat.

## Strategies for Informing With Excellence

When designing an informative speech, or any speech for that matter, you should include all the steps outlined in Chapters 11, 12, and 13. Begin by making certain that the general purpose of this speech should be to inform. Develop a clear specific purpose. Analyze your audience and the context carefully, and be certain that your introductions and conclusions incorporate all the components we discuss in Chapter 12. Develop a clear, easy-to-follow organizational structure with smooth transitions. Follow all the rules for effective supporting aids and delivery with professional excellence (see Chapter 13).

Listening is also one of Steve Covey's "Seven Habits of Highly Effective People." Covey says, "First seek to understand and then to be understood." Highly effective people listen because they know that listening to the other person is the key to building relationships, is the key to understanding what they are doing for the company, and will greatly enhance what you can accomplish as a leader.

We can sometimes unknowingly send messages to our employees that indicate that we aren't listening to them. For example, I was on a committee recently, and our charge was to recommend a speaker to a very important organizational event. The committee spent long hours going over credentials and conducting interviews with potential speakers for the event. When we sent our suggestion to the president of the organization, he ignored the committee and chose someone else. What do you think, through his actions, he communicated to the people on that committee? That he was not listening, perhaps? That he does not value their input, maybe? Things like this hurt the communication climate, motivation, and, ultimately, productivity.

As I stated in the beginning, a lot of this is quite easy to understand but very difficult to apply, because most of us have very well-established communication patterns that do not include listening. If you are preparing your response before the other person stops talking, then you are not listening. If you fail to ask your employees or your clients questions, you are not allowing for listening opportunities. If every idea in the department is yours, you are not listening. Changing bad habits is difficult, but if you make a commitment and stick to it, you can become an effective listener.

### Conclusion

Today we have talked about some ways to create a positive communication climate. **[Signaling the Conclusion]** We do this by stopping to build relationships with employees, looking at what they are doing for the company, and listening to their ideas and concerns. **[Summary]** You now know how to develop a positive communication climate, and by demonstrating these effective communication patterns, you will become a role model for your entire team. Just as those puppies emulated the mother dog, your employees will emulate you. Together, you and your team can make that positive communication climate a reality—you just need to lead the way. **[Memorable Ending]**

## Questions to Consider

1. How would you rate this speech?
2. What features about the speech did you deem effective?
3. What features should have been improved?

Beyond the all-important basics of any successful speech, you need to take into account some additional variables when speaking to inform. First, make certain that you are informing, not persuading. If you begin to incorporate your emotions and your point of view, you have stopped being objective. The range of topics for informative speeches is infinite. You can inform on people, places, things, new products, old products, history, events, process, corporate visions, governmental relations, and concepts from ancient religions to postmodernism. Some of these topics can be controversial. But remember, although your point of view on a controversial issue may be valuable and interesting, it should not be included in an informative speech.

Second, pay careful attention to your audience's level of knowledge and understanding when doing your audience analysis. You do not want to design a speech that informs them about things they already know. It is a waste of your time and their time. On the other hand, if your audience has only a baseline of information about a topic and you design your speech as if they are experts, they will not be able to comprehend the information.

Third, as noted earlier in the chapter, try to incorporate a variety of supporting material, such as examples, quotes, and statistics. This will make certain you appeal to all types of listeners and will make your speech more memorable.

# Speaking to Persuade

When giving a persuasive speech, you are acting an as advocate or making an argument. Your role is to advocate for or against something. As noted above, you will either be trying to persuade the audience simply to agree or disagree with an idea (passive agreement) or to take some sort of action (active agreement or a call to action). Unlike the informative speaker, the persuasive speaker is subjective, influenced or impacted by individual emotions, biases, or point of view.

Aristotle discussed the three persuasive appeals noted earlier in relationship to persuasive presentations. Let's explore each in relationship to your persuasive speeches.

Again, ethos refers to your credibility as a presenter as well as the credibility of the information presented in your presentation. To present with professional excellence, you must demonstrate credibility and help your audience believe you and the information or argument you are presenting. O'Keefe (1990) found that the more credibility you have with an audience, the more you will be able to persuade them. While this may be the case, the sad truth is that most of the messages you hear all day, every day are void of any type of credibility. Advertisements make claims that come from "leading scientists," but the scientists are never named. People running for high-ranking political offices throw facts, quotes, and figures around in debates. The information each side presents often contradicts the other side, yet sources are lacking. To speak with professional excellence, you must rise above this common shortcoming and make sure you establish credibility. Remember to be extremely careful when using the Internet to conduct research. Table 11.2 lists the criteria for evaluating websites.

| Table 11.2 Assessing Internet Sources | |
|---|---|
| Credibility | Are any authors or sources listed? |
| | Is the information linked to other credible sources? |
| Objectivity | Who sponsors or maintains the website? |
| | Are there any hyperlinks or advertisements on the site? If so, what do they reveal about the objectivity of the site? |
| Date | When was this information posted? |
| | Is it current? Is it still valid? |

How do you establish credibility in a persuasive speech? Just as you would in an informative speech, make certain the audience is aware of your expertise and knowledge on the subject matter. Additionally, cite your sources and make certain the sources are credible. When persuading, it is also important to establish **common ground** with your audience. That is, show how you have a shared interest, concern, or background. If your audience believes that you share their attitude toward a topic, it increases your ability to persuade them (McCroskey & Teven, 1999; O'Keefe, 1990; Plantin, 2012).

Logos, as you should recall, refers to the organizational structure and the supporting information found in your speeches. When developing a persuasive presentation, think of yourself as an attorney making an argument. You're building a case with your presentation. In the next chapter, we will discuss ways to organize your persuasive speeches.

## Types of Reasoning

In addition to these organizational patterns, effective persuasive speeches incorporate clear reasoning that guides the listener through the speaker's argument. **Types of reasoning** include inductive, causal, deductive, analogical, and cognitive dissonance.

### Inductive Reasoning

**Inductive reasoning** is building an argument by utilizing individual examples, pieces of information, or cases, and then pulling them together to make a generalization or come to a conclusion. For example, Bob got bad service at Store X. Juan got bad service at Store X. Ming got bad service at Store X. The generalization or conclusion is that Store X gives bad service. The obvious question that you must ask yourself when using inductive reasoning is how many examples or cases are needed to make a generalization? Unfortunately, the answer is that it depends. Each situation must be considered individually. But if your audience does not think you have enough cases to support your generalization, you will not be able to persuade them.

### Causal Reasoning

**Causal reasoning**, more commonly known as the cause–effect relationship, is a type of inductive reasoning. When developing this type of argument, you must demonstrate that certain events or factors (causes) produced, or in some cases prevented, a certain result (the effect). When using causal reasoning, you must be certain that your causes do indeed produce the effect; therefore, your evidence must be credible. Furthermore, you must determine if the cause in your argument is the only cause. In most situations, it will not be the only cause. Therefore, you are wise to make mention of the other causes in your speech and explain why this cause, your cause, should be the focus.

This strategy is known as **inoculation**. Think of it as the vaccination you get to inoculate you from the N1H1 virus. By exposing your body to a bit of the disease, you are not affected by later exposure. In the case of persuasion, when the speaker points out other possible causes in a cause–effect relationship and then explains why they are not as important or relevant, it inoculates the audience from future attempts to persuade them in the other direction.

For example, let's say a hotel manager was trying to persuade her supervisors that the drop in occupancy in her hotel was due to road construction on the highway in front of the hotel. She should mention that tourism is down throughout the United States due to the economy but that the construction is the primary reason for the drop in tourism at her hotel. To build her argument, she could show occupancy drops in other hotels near the highway versus hotels in her town not impacted by the construction.

### Deductive Reasoning

**Deductive reasoning** occurs when the speaker takes general information (premises) and draws a conclusion from that general information. Deductive reasoning is often set up as a syllogism. One famous syllogism is as follows:

Socrates is a man. (Major premise)

All men are mortal. (Minor premise)

Therefore, Socrates is mortal. (Conclusion)

Although the syllogism has been around for a long time, it is still an excellent way to persuade in today's workplace. For example, consider the following persuasive arguments. Americans want to lose weight (major premise). Our new product aids in weight loss (minor premise). Americans will buy our new product (conclusion). Nursing is a highly demanded major (major premise). University W wants to offer highly demanded majors (minor premise). Therefore, University W should offer nursing as a major (conclusion). To use deductive reasoning effectively, you must make certain that both your major and minor premises are accurate and that you convince the audience to accept those premises in the body of your speech.

### Analogical Reasoning

**Analogical reasoning** is simply reasoning from an analogy. In other words, it is making an argument by comparing two cases. When using analogical reasoning, it is important that the cases are comparable. Remember, although two cases or situations may be very similar, they are never identical. To remedy this situation, we once again suggest using inoculation. You should point out the differences and minimize them. Recently, a small-business owner argued in front of the city council that the town should not support a smoking ban in restaurants. He believed that decisions about smoking should be left to the individual business owner. He based his argument on an analogy comparing the limitation of civil liberties when the Nazis first came to power in Germany with the restriction of civil liberties that this ban represented. He stressed that a ban on smoking was among the Nazis' new laws. He also pointed out that he wasn't trying to compare those that supported the ban to Nazis but that the restrictions were similar. His argument was partially persuasive because he was a nonsmoker who had made the choice as a business owner not to allow smoking in his establishment.

### Cognitive Dissonance

**Cognitive dissonance** is another useful tool for persuading an audience. Although it is not one of the standard forms of reasoning, it is well worth mentioning. This theory, developed by researcher Leon Festinger (1957), states that when a person holds two ideas that contradict each other, it creates mental noise or cognitive dissonance in that person's

## Step Back and Reflect    Trust Me: I've Been Here Awhile

*Read the passage about Kevin below, and answer the questions that follow.*

Kevin had been working in the same management position at an insurance company for several years. He had the responsibility of giving a presentation to all the area coordinators. The report was important because the coordinators needed the updated information to help design marketing campaigns in areas where sales had decreased. For months, Kevin had been passing out a one-page sheet that was difficult for the coordinators to read. Rather than discussing specifics, Kevin would say, "I've been here awhile and these sales decreases go away after a while." Instead of preparing a professional presentation, he would tell stories about what had happened at the company years ago. Kevin believed his experience and observation of sales patterns were enough informational support to assure the coordinators that things would turn around.

### Step Back and Reflect

1. What went wrong?
2. What advice would you give Kevin about his presentation?
3. How can the KEYS process help Kevin's situation?

mind. This results in a feeling of discomfort for the person, so he or she looks for ways to reduce the contradiction. If you develop an argument that creates cognitive dissonance and then offer a solution that reduces the contradiction, you are likely to have made a successful persuasive argument.

For example, Paul works for a nonprofit organization that helps disabled veterans. In his speeches, he reminds the audience of the deep gratitude they feel for all veterans, especially those who have been disabled in battle. He then asks them what they have done to show their gratitude. If they have not done anything to show their gratitude, they feel cognitive dissonance. He then provides them with an opportunity to express their gratitude by donating time and/or money to his organization. Most audience members are happy to give because it relieves their discomfort.

## Pathos

The final type of persuasive appeal (after ethos and logos) is **pathos**—a term that refers to emotional appeal. Because informative speeches are objective, emotional appeals should not be present in informative speeches. However, pathos is very powerful, and it does play an important role when persuading with professional excellence. But beware—a presentation that has strong pathos but lacks ethos and/or logos is not effective. Far too many presenters rely solely on emotional appeal. In the moment, they may move an audience, but in the long run, the lack of credibility and logic make for a poor presentation. To achieve professional excellence as a presenter, you must include all three appeals (ethos, logos, and pathos) in your presentations.

## Ethical Connection    A Case of False Information

*Please read the passage below, and answer the questions that follow.*

Travis is a public relations consultant for the local mayor's office. A large part of his job involves advising the mayor's staff on public opinion and assisting in preparing public speeches for the mayor himself. Recently, the city has seen a fierce debate over the state of the city's water system. The majority of the mayor's office (including the mayor) is against appropriating funds to overhaul the city's water system, while many community leaders favor it. Travis and the mayor's office have recently been given an independent study that indicates there will be significant health risks to the population if renovations are not made to the city's antiquated water system; however, the mayor is preparing to deliver a speech that states the exact opposite of the study. Travis faces an ethical dilemma: Should he discredit the mayor's speech and risk losing his job or say nothing and attempt to dissuade the mayor without revealing that the speech contained false information?

### Questions to Consider

1. What ethical rule is the mayor breaking in this example?
2. How could Travis dissuade the mayor from moving forward with this speech?
3. What element of Plato's *ethos, pathos, logos* is being violated here?
4. Is there ever a time when omission of fact would not be unethical in a presentation?

You might be thinking, "How can I incorporate emotional appeal into my presentation?" One way is with the use of language. Selecting words that have a strong emotional **connotation**—or implied meaning—can be very powerful. Incorporating into your presentation research that has strong emotional appeal is another tool.

Pathos also has a place in informative presentations. Selecting language and supporting material with emotional appeal can help an audience relate to the topic and remember an informative message. In the same way, pathos can move an audience to action in a persuasive message.

## Strategies for Persuading With Excellence

When designing a persuasive speech, you should include all the steps outlined in Chapters 11, 12, and 13. Begin by making certain that the general purpose of this speech should be to persuade. Develop a clear specific purpose. Analyze your audience and the context carefully. Be certain that your introductions and conclusions incorporate the appropriate components. Develop a clear, easy-to-follow organizational structure with smooth transitions. Follow all the rules for effective supporting aids and delivery with professional excellence (see Chapter 13).

You may be thinking, "Wait a minute, didn't I just read the above paragraph?" Yes, you did. But the basic components of an effective speech, informative or persuasive, are worth repeating. As we explained earlier, these basics are often overlooked by so-called professionals. You must be certain to include them in all your speeches so you can speak with professional excellence.

Beyond the basics, there are a few additional facts you should be aware of when persuading. First, your entire speech should be persuasive. In other words, an informative speech with a persuasive conclusion does not rise to the level of excellence. If the audience does not know what you are persuading them to do or believe until the end of the speech, you have given a weak persuasive speech, at best. Your speech should be organized as an argument. The use of persuasive appeals should be prevalent throughout the speech and not saved for the end.

Your audience will find it helpful to review statistics presented in a format that's easy to read and understand. Avoid overloading your audience with too much technical information.

Second, although you can and should be subjective in a persuasive speech, your opinion is not enough to persuade an audience. After all, "because I think so" or "because I said so" is not among Aristotle's persuasive appeals. Within your speech, you must develop a clear argument, supported by solid logical appeals and credible evidence, such as statistics, examples, and quotes.

Third, when analyzing your audience, you must assess the target audience. Think of the target audience as the people on the fence. Some people already agree with you or are already engaging in the action you are trying to persuade them toward. They don't need to be persuaded. Another group—we hope a very small one—may never be persuaded. The remaining individuals are whom your speech should be aimed toward. A sample of a fully developed persuasive speech is presented in the next chapter.

# KEYS to Excellence in Professional Presentations

Remember David Henderson, who won the world public speaking contest? Although his job required a great deal of public speaking, he was not a professional speaker by trade. Although many students will not become public orators in their careers, most jobs require some amount of public speaking. Using the KEYS strategy can help you become effective in all your public speaking experiences. The first step, *know yourself*, involves knowing your strengths and weaknesses and how to use them to your advantage. Be aware of your shortcomings and try to minimize them, and pay particularly close attention to your nonverbal communication. Most people don't realize they are using distracting body language because it is unconscious; practice your speaking skills and learn to use positive nonverbal communication.

The second step, *evaluate the professional context*, requires you to understand whom you are presenting to. A presentation given to your superiors will most likely be very formal, but if you are presenting to your coworkers, then you might take a more informal tone to put your audience at ease. Know the culture of your organization, and tailor your presentations to meet the expected standards.

## Evaluate the Professional Context    No Raises

*Read the following passage about Roy, and then answer the questions. As you read, focus on* **evaluating the professional context**.

Roy is a supervisor for Child Protective Services. The new budget was just announced for his department. Last year, the budget was flat and no one got a pay raise, so hopes were high that this year would be different. Unfortunately, additional budget cuts translated to another year without raises. Employee morale was clearly lowered by this news. Roy realized he needed to address this issue. He called his team together and gave the following speech:

We do not have easy jobs. In fact, I would argue that we have one of the toughest jobs there is. It's not easy to see the pain and abuse we witness day after day. It's not easy to go home and relax when your heart has been ripped out at work. And it's sure not easy to endure all this when you feel as though you have been slapped in the face by your employer, who is not even willing to give you the raises you have earned. So today, I don't want to make excuses about budget cuts. I just want to share with you a story that helps me handle my anger and keep my morale up in times such as these.

Almost 20 years ago, I was called in to investigate a case of abuse. The situation was not unique. Both parents had drug problems, and the stepfather was abusing both the mother and the children. At one point, I had to physically pull the three boys away from their mother, who was screaming for her babies, while the oldest boy, Samuel, spit in my face. I had to see the fear in the boys' faces as they were placed with strangers, and I wondered if it was all worth it. About a year later, I ran into Samuel at a movie theater. At first, I did not recognize him. He looked so much healthier. He told me that his mom had gotten away from her abusive spouse, she had gone to rehab, and she had gotten her boys back. And then something I will never forget, he said, "I am so sorry I spit on you that day. I think about that all the time. I was so scared that I didn't realize you were the hero who came in and saved us."

I know that each of you can share a similar story. We all have met a Samuel or two in this job—kids who may hate you in the moment but later see you as the hero. The problem is, it isn't easy being a hero. It's not like in the movies, with superpowers and accolades. It's about a lot of hard work and very little recognition. It's not easy being a hero, but for those kids we save from neglect and abuse, our efforts do make a difference. I wish I could give you all the raises you deserve. But I can't. All I can do is let you know that I'm proud to work with such a fine team. And to me, each and every one of you is a hero. I realize that does not pay your mortgage or put gas in your cars, but to the Samuels of the world, it means a whole lot more. It's okay to be angry about your raises, but don't forget why we are here. None of us took this job for the money. We aren't the kind of people who choose the easy life—we have chosen the lives of heroes. It may not be easy, but I believe, I know you believe, and I am certain the Samuels of the world believe that it's worth the sacrifice.

### Questions to Consider

1. How did Roy use language and examples for emotional appeal? Did Roy evaluate the professional context effectively? Why or why not?

2. Do you think he was successful at raising morale? Why or why not?

The third step, *your communication interaction occurs*, involves taking what you have learned in the first two steps and applying them to your presentation. Be aware of your personal presentation style, and be prepared to alter it if the situation calls for it. Also, try to critique the audience's responses during your presentation and make any necessary adjustments or clarifications if it appears necessary.

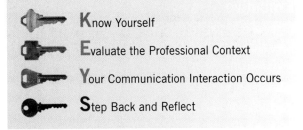

The final step calls for you to *step back and reflect*. Assess your audience's reaction to your presentation, and get feedback to see if your presentation was effective. Think about the verbal and nonverbal communication you used and decide what communication was positive or negative. You must constantly grow as a public speaker, and your presentations will become more effective as you continue to practice.

## Executive Summary

Now that you have finished reading this chapter, you can do the following:

Discuss the importance of professional excellence in public speaking:

- Just as effective communication skills are essential to your professional success, effective oral communication skills are essential if you want to excel in leadership (p. 269).
- Product presentations, team huddles, running meetings, press conferences, special events, and other forms of oral communication reveal something about you as a professional (p. 269).
- Presentations serve as a tool to motivate employees and communicate effectively about business goals (p. 269).
- Presentational excellence is necessary to achieve professional excellence (p. 269).

Identify presenting opportunities:

- The first step in the presentation process is identifying opportunities. Once you have identified the presentation opportunities, you can identify the purpose within them (p. 269).
- There are two types of presentation opportunities available to leaders. One is a *formal presentation*, which occurs in a traditional presentation setting. Presenting a sales pitch to clients and giving a progress report at the district meeting are examples of formal presentations (p. 269).
- The *opportunity presentation* is identical in preparation and presentation to the formal presentation, but it occurs in a less traditional setting. For instance, many organizations have *huddles*, during which employees are pulled together to talk (p. 269).

Define the purpose of a presentation:

- Presentations can have one of two *general purposes*: to *inform* or to *persuade* (p. 270).
- When speaking with an informative purpose, you present the facts (p. 270).
- When speaking with a persuasive purpose, you are acting as an advocate or making an argument. Your role is to advocate for or against something (p. 270).
- Determining your purpose may seem like a simple enough task, but speakers with professional excellence always think carefully when determining their purpose (p. 270).
- Once you've identified the general purpose of your presentation, you'll begin to formulate a *specific purpose*. The specific purpose is to an oral presentation what a thesis statement is to an essay. A specific purpose is a declarative sentence telling the listeners what you want them to understand/know or believe by the end of your presentation (p. 271).

Design an informative speech:

- Begin by making certain that the general purpose of this speech should be to inform. Develop a clear specific purpose. Analyze your audience and the context carefully (p. 276).
- Make certain that you are informing, not persuading. If you begin to incorporate your emotions and your point of view, you have stopped being objective (p. 277).
- Pay careful attention to your audience's level of knowledge and understanding when doing your audience analysis. You do not want to design a speech that informs them about things they already know. It is a waste of your time and their time. On the other hand, if your audience has only a baseline of information about a topic and you design your speech as if they are experts, they will not be able to comprehend the information (p. 278).
- Try to incorporate a variety of supporting material, such as examples, quotes, and statistics. This will make certain you appeal to all types of listeners and will make your speech more memorable (p. 278).

Design a persuasive speech:

- To present with professional excellence, you must demonstrate *credibility* and help your audience believe you and the information or argument you are presenting (p. 278).
- When persuading, it is also important to establish *common ground* with your audience. That is, show how you have a shared interest, concern, or background. If your audience believes that you share their attitude toward a topic, it increases your ability to persuade them (p. 279).
- Begin by making certain that the general purpose of this speech should be to persuade. Develop a clear specific purpose. Analyze your audience and the context carefully (p. 282).
- Develop a clear, easy-to-follow organizational structure with smooth transitions. Follow all the rules for effective supporting aids and delivery with professional excellence (p. 282).

Use the KEYS process to develop professional excellence with informative and persuasive presentations:

- *Know yourself.* Know your strengths and weaknesses and how to use them to your advantage. Be aware of your shortcomings and try to minimize them, and pay particularly close attention to your nonverbal communication (p. 283).
- *Evaluate the professional context.* Understand whom you are presenting to. A presentation given to your superiors will most likely be very formal, but if you are presenting to your coworkers, you might take a more informal tone to put your audience at ease (p. 283).

- *Your communication interaction occurs.* Take what you have learned in the first two steps and apply them to your presentation. Be aware of your personal presentation style and be prepared to alter it if the situation calls for it (p. 285).
- *Step back and reflect.* Assess your audience's reaction to your presentation, and get feedback to see if your presentation was effective (p. 285).

## Discussion Questions

1. Can you think of a time when a presentation would have been a more effective channel for delivering a message than an e-mail or memo? Why do you think it would have been more effective?

2. Take a moment to think about someone whom you view as an excellent presenter. What are the qualities of this person's verbal and nonverbal communication? Does this speaker incorporate Aristotle's appeals (ethos, logos, and pathos)?

3. Take a moment to think about someone whom you view as a bad presenter. What are the qualities of this person's verbal and nonverbal communication while presenting? Does this speaker neglect to incorporate Aristotle's appeals (ethos, logos, and pathos)?

4. Discuss the qualities of an excellent presentation. In your view, what factors make a presentation memorable?

5. Reflect on an occupation that interests you or one in which you are currently working. What are some situations that might require you to give an informative or persuasive presentation?

## Terms to Remember

active agreement (call to action) (p. 270)

analogical reasoning (p. 280)

Aristotle (p. 268)

causal reasoning (p. 279)

cognitive dissonance (p. 280)

common ground (p. 279)

connotation (p. 282)

credibility (p. 271)

deductive reasoning (p. 280)

ethos (p. 271)

formal presentation (p. 269)

general purpose (p. 270)

huddles (p. 270)

impromptu presentation (p. 270)

inductive reasoning (p. 279)

inform (p. 270)

inoculation (p. 279)

logos (p. 273)

objective (p. 271)

opportunity presentation (p. 269)

passive agreement (p. 270)

pathos (p. 281)

persuade (p. 270)

persuasive appeals (p. 271)

Quintilian (p. 272)

specific purpose (p. 271)

types of reasoning (p. 279)

Visit the Student Study Site at **www.sagepub.com/keys2e** to access the following resources:

- SAGE journal articles
- Video links
- Web resources

- Web quizzes
- eflashcards

## Chapter Outline

**Analyzing the Audience** 290

**Analyzing the Context** 291

**Researching** 292

**Organizing Your Presentation** 296

**Introductions** 299

**Conclusions** 301

**Language** 304

**KEYS to Excellence in Designing a
Speech** 305

**Executive Summary** 306

**Discussion Questions** 307

**Terms to Remember** 307

## Chapter Objectives

After studying this chapter, you should be able to:

1. Analyze audience and context

2. Gather research for your speeches

3. Organize the body of a speech and incorporate effective transitions

4. Develop effective introductions and conclusions

5. Understand the role and value of language

# chapter 12

# Speech Design

**Former Illinois governor Rod Blagojevich faced a daunting task in his last public speech before beginning a 14-year prison term in March 2012.** Blagojevich was convicted of charges of corruption for attempting to sell President Barack Obama's vacant Senate seat after the 2008 election. "I certainly made my share of mistakes. I take responsibility, and I'm responsible . . . for the things that I said, the things I talked about doing. The political talk about how to raise campaign funds, the things that we believed were political horse trades and legal . . . I take responsibility for saying those things," Blagojevich said (Jeffreys, 2012). Blagojevich said that he took responsibility for his actions and thanked all his supporters. He ended by reminding people about the positive outcomes during his time as governor, including not raising the income tax rate and providing health care for all children in Illinois. Clearly, this was Blagojevich's final attempt at damage control and an effort to portray himself in the best possible light in the face of such serious charges of corruption.

Most people will never have to give a speech under circumstances like Blagojevich's, but it is important to understand what methods work best to gain your audience's approval. Even though Blagojevich faced an angry audience and was forced to speak about his upcoming incarceration, he still managed to highlight positive outcomes from his time as governor. He emphasized that he took responsibility for his actions and thanked everyone who supported him. All these small details were added so that Blagojevich could accomplish some damage control for his public image. His final public statements also serve as one example of how to design a speech when the speaker can expect to face a hostile audience.

Designing a speech with professional excellence can often make or break a person's professional career. Whether you are discussing a topic that is favorable or negative toward your audience, it is important to be aware of what methods are available to you in order to make your speech a success. In this chapter, you will learn how to gather your research and organize your presentation to give you the greatest chance of success.

# Analyzing the Audience

If you want to present with professional excellence, you must be audience centered. Don't fall into the trap of so many mediocre presenters by focusing all your energy on your nerves or your PowerPoint slides. The best presenters, the best communicators in general, are aware of all the components involved in the communication process, and they pay particular attention to the audience.

What are the most common qualities that contribute to excellent presentations when the audience is seated in a large/open space such as the one shown here?

When you envision an **audience-centered speaker**, what images come to mind? Do you picture a seasoned presenter who can adjust or change the message midsentence to suit the audience's mood? For those of you who are beginners, this may seem like an impossible skill, one that you'll never master. You say to yourself, "There's no way I'm ever going to be able to adjust my presentation in the moment." With enough practice, we are certain you can develop this skill, but being audience centered is about much more than responding to feedback during your actual presentation. There are many things you can and should do proactively to become more audience centered. To become audience centered, start by asking a series of questions designed to answer one all-important larger question, "Who is my audience?" This **audience analysis** will frame your entire presentation, so it must be considered first, last, and during every stage in the design process (see Table 12.1).

| Table 12.1 Who Is My Audience? | |
|---|---|
| Demographic questions | • What is the general demographic information for this audience (i.e., sex, age, race, ethnicity, job title)? |
| | • What is the audience's level of knowledge concerning this topic? |
| Relational questions | • What is my relationship with the audience? |
| | • What is their relationship with one another? |

## Step Back and Reflect — Dr. Jacobs Learns About Audience Analysis

*Read the passage about Connie below, and answer the questions that follow.*

After reviewing enrollment figures, Dr. Jacobs, the vice president of University Effectiveness, discovered a way to generate more funds for his institution with only minor changes in scheduling. Dr. Jacobs identified this as a speaking opportunity to persuade the faculty members, who handled scheduling, to make these changes. He set up a meeting with each of the colleges within the university. Since everyone he would be speaking to was a faculty member, he decided to use the same presentation for each audience.

His first meeting was with the College of Arts and Humanities. He began the presentation with an example. The example came from the College of Science and Technology, but Dr. Jacobs felt that it applied to all colleges. Within the first graph, there was a list of the average salaries for the Science and Technology faculty. The average for the Science and Technology faculty was significantly higher than the average salary of the Arts and Humanities faculty listening to the presentation. The next slide showed the average class size based on college. The class size for the Arts and Humanities faculty was much larger than that of every other college at the university. Dr. Jacobs went on to explain how to make four scheduling changes, stressing the simplicity of making each change. He ended with a graph that showed how much additional funding would be generated by these changes.

At the conclusion of his presentation, Dr. Jacobs opened for questions. He was surprised by the nature of the questions the audience asked. None of them had to do with the changes he had discussed. Instead, they were all about faculty equity in pay and workload. The audience walked out of the meeting visibly upset. Dr. Jacobs was not sure if they had heard a word he said.

### Step Back and Reflect

1. What went wrong?
2. What advice would you give Dr. Jacobs about audience analysis?
3. How can the KEYS process help his situation?

## Analyzing the Context

So far, we have discussed identifying your purpose and analyzing your audience, but you must realize that neither of these steps occurs in a vacuum. They can't be done effectively without including a **context analysis**. After all, the context plays an important role in determining the purpose of the presentation. In addition, the context has a huge impact on the audience. Again, you must ask yourself a series of questions to analyze your context (see Table 12.2).

Once you've answered each of the questions about context, ask yourself, "How can I use this knowledge to improve my presentation?" For example, if you know the audience is required to be at your presentation, you may need to work harder to show them why the information is relevant to them. If the audience is standing, you must keep your remarks

**Table 12.2 What Is the Context?**

| Physical setting | • Is there a stage? |
|---|---|
| | • Will I have a podium or a microphone? |
| | • Is PowerPoint available? |
| | • Is the audience sitting or standing? |
| | • If they are sitting, how comfortable are the chairs? |
| Attitudinal questions | • Why are they here (required or by choice)? |
| | • Is the topic of this presentation seen as positive, negative, neutral, or a mix? |
| | • Will anyone else speak before or after me? If so, what is the nature of his or her topic(s)? |

brief. If you have a large audience, no stage, and flat seating, you may need to rearrange the furniture to help the audience see you or you may need to walk around. Use the information you learn from your analysis to enhance your presentation.

# Researching

*The Internet has made researching so easy. All you have to do is type your topic into Google, and bang, there is everything you need to know. In fact, a quick exploration of Wikipedia is really all anyone needs when it comes to research.*

Obviously, the preceding paragraph is a joke. At least, we hope you see it as an obvious joke. Sadly, many of our students and even some of our executives might miss the sarcastic tone intended for the above paragraph. According to Hamilton (1996), poor presenters often make the mistake of either relying solely on their own knowledge or relying solely on the Internet. Either way, a lack of research results in a poor presentation.

One of the many skills you will learn during your college experience is how to conduct **research**. As we discussed in Chapter 5, research is the central skill used during the explorer phase of the creative process. Research is also a central skill needed to present with professional excellence. Shortchanging the research process by limiting yourself to a quick Google search or the report in hand will result in a poor presentation.

## Gathering Research

The research you need to develop and support your presentation can and should come from a variety of sources. Depending on the topic, you may use internal sources, external sources, or a combination of the two. **Internal sources** include information that

# Evaluate the Professional Context    The Annual Company Barbeque

*Read the following passage, and then answer the questions. As you read, focus on* **evaluating the professional context**.

Laurence, Evan, and Avery were all asked to say a few words at the annual company barbeque. The barbeque is designed to be a fun celebration that includes all employees, their families, and their friends. This year, there was a lot to celebrate since the company had experienced tremendous growth. The physical setting included a small stage, microphone, and a field with no chairs. The audience included employees, family members (many of whom were small children), and friends. The audience was happy to be at the event, but for many of them, the speeches were keeping them from the fun.

Laurence did not prepare his comments, because he didn't see this as a formal speaking opportunity. When handed the microphone, he said, "The annual company barbeque is a longstanding tradition here at Company D. So I encourage all of you to keep the tradition alive and well by having a lot of fun here today."

Evan welcomed this speaking opportunity, and he had prepared some remarks. His speech went as follows:

To the rest of the world, Company D is made up of all the outstanding employees that are here today. Let's give a round of applause to all Company D employees. [Allow time for applause.] What a team!

Now stop for one moment and look around this crowd. Go on, look around. What do you see? I'll tell you what I see. I see our real team, our complete team. The unprecedented success of Company D did not happen simply because we have a great team at work. It happened because we are supported by a great team when we leave work, a team made of our families and our friends, many of whom are here today. It is this at-home team that understood our long hours this year, helped us unwind, served as our sounding boards, and supported us, allowing us to grow as a company.

This barbeque is merely a small token of appreciation for all that you do—you being employees, family, and friends. Congratulations on an amazing year, thank you once again, and enjoy the 45th Annual Company D Barbeque—you've earned it!

Avery was the last one to speak. Like Evan, she had prepared her remarks. Avery had been with the company for many years, so she decided to take this opportunity to discuss the history of the organization over the past 45 years. She thought to herself, "This barbeque is part of our history, and the company has gone through a lot of changes this year, so some reflection would be nice." Her speech was about 25 minutes long.

By the end of the speech, the audience was restless and unhappy.

## Questions to Consider

1. Based on the information provided above, how would you rate each speaker?

2. How did the purpose of the event, the physical setting, and the audience factor into your analysis of each speaker's effectiveness?

3. Using the KEYS process, what advice would you give each speaker?

Research results, statistics, and financial information must be organized with graphics the audience can understand. Avoid information overload when you are presenting on information that involves a variety of sources.

comes from within the organization, such as reports, policies, or interviews with employees and/or customers. **External sources** include information that comes from outside the organization, such as from outside agencies, the competition, the government, and the media.

If you were giving a presentation on improving customer service within your organization, you could find supporting material in a variety of places. You might start with the new policy on customer service that created this presentation opportunity. You might then research past customer satisfaction scores within your organization, as well as data showing how your organization compares to the competition. You might interview some executives about the importance of customer service or ask some employees with outstanding customer service their thoughts on the subject (see Table 12.3). You might find some quotes or examples from organizations or leaders known for their customer service. Remember that you can't begin and end your research with the new policy if you want to present with professional excellence.

| Table 12.3 Conducting an Interview | |
| --- | --- |
| Before the interview | • What is your purpose? Know why you are conducting the interview and what information you wish to gain. This may require conducting background research prior to the interview. |
| | • Who are you interviewing? Based on your purpose, determine whom you need to interview. |
| | • When and where is your interview? Schedule your interview in advance. Dress in a style that enhances your credibility. |
| | • How will you conduct the interview? Decide if you will take notes, record the conversation, or both. Develop an interview schedule. Your interview schedule should include a list of all your questions. |
| During the interview | • Are you presenting yourself as a professional? Be sure to arrive early and dress in a style that enhances your credibility. |
| | • Are you following the rules for good etiquette? These rules include greeting the interviewee, reminding him or her of your purpose, respecting his or her time, and saying thank you. |
| | • Did you ask all your questions? Make sure you ask the questions on your interview schedule and any of the follow-up questions you may have. |
| After the interview | • What information will you use? As soon as the interview is over, review your notes or listen to your tape and decide what information should be included in your speech. |

## Ethical Connection   Debate Team Dilemma

*Please read the passage below, and answer the questions that follow.*

John is a member of his university's debate team, and his school is in the running to win the regional debate competition this year. Unfortunately, John personally disagrees with the side his team has been assigned to debate. The factual information available for the topic favors the opposing team, so John has suggested that the debate team focus on emotional appeals. The speech he has designed is very effective on emotional appeals, but his facts and rhetoric are almost nonexistent. The team feels that they can win with their presentation style but are cautious about presenting the speech while not acknowledging the facts. The debate topic covers a controversial issue that is going to a vote in local elections, and the team does not want to mislead voters into making an uninformed decision about the issue.

### Questions to Consider

1. What is the ethical dilemma facing the debate team?
2. Why is a scarcity of facts damaging to a presentation?
3. What other strategies could John use for his debate besides an emotional appeal?
4. Why are emotional appeals so dangerous when debating a topic?

## Determining What to Include

If you have done your job as a researcher, you will have more information than you need. At this point in the process, you must determine what to include. Ask yourself a few key questions:

- What information does this audience need to know so they understand this topic and/or are persuaded by this argument?
- What information is most relevant to this audience?
- What information would be most interesting (new or different) to this audience?
- What information is needed to support my specific purpose effectively?

Based on your answers to these questions, you can determine which information should be included in your presentation.

Loading a presentation full of data and statistics that have no relevance to the audience and/or the purpose is the mark of a poor speaker. Furthermore, speakers who give examples based on personal experience are deemed more trustworthy by audiences compared with speakers who present other types of support (Collins, 2012;

People connect to appropriate stories about life, such as children, pets, and other topics that reflect human interest.

Koballa, 1989). Put simply, personal examples are more persuasive than statistics (Kazoleas, 1993; Metsämäki, 2012).

When determining what to include, you must also think about ways to provide variety to keep the audience engaged. A few well-placed, relevant statistics coupled with some examples can really help reinforce a message. According to Walter Fisher (1984), we are all storytelling creatures and like to tell and hear stories about people (this is where human interest comes in). Combining these elements could enhance your presentation.

# Organizing Your Presentation

Now that you've conducted your research and decided what to include, the time has come to get organized. Giving a presentation that's well organized increases the likelihood that your audience will pay attention to, understand, and remember your message.

## Organizing the Body

You must develop clear organization within the body of your presentation. Your typical, not-so-memorable speaker will take all the information available and lump it together as three main points. This is simply not acceptable. In the 21st century, it's as easy as the click of a mouse to move information around as you develop the best organizational pattern for your presentation. It takes very little effort to develop a presentation that people can follow and remember. To excel as a speaker with professional excellence, make a commitment to solid organization. This is a relatively easy process—all you need to do is consider the various organizational formats until you find the one that best fits the presentation.

Presenting a message that motivates employees to work hard and get the job done requires professional excellence.

One organizational pattern that's often utilized to persuade in business and professional settings is **Monroe's Motivated Sequence**—a five-step process, developed in 1935 by Purdue University professor Alan H. Monroe, that includes the *attention step*, *need step*, *satisfaction step*, *visualization step*, and *action step*. The sequence begins with an attention step, in which the speaker engages the audience through the use of attention-getting devices (we discuss these devices in the "Introductions" section of this chapter). In the needs step, the speaker establishes the problem and thereby the need for a change. During the satisfaction step, the speaker provides a solution for the problem presented. The visualization step increases the audience's desire for the solution by helping them visualize the benefits it will bring. Finally, the action step reinforces the solution with a specific, clear call to action.

If Monroe's Motivated Sequence is not the right organizational pattern for your presentation, consider other common patterns, which include the following: classification, chronological, spatial, cause–effect, problem–solution, pro–con, and comparison–contrast. Table 12.4 provides a definition and example of each format. Consider each format before making your final selection, and ask yourself two simple questions:

- What is the best way to organize this information so my audience can follow me?
- What is the best way to organize this presentation so my audience will remember my message?

| Table 12.4 Organizational Patterns for Presentations | | |
|---|---|---|
| Classification | Dividing a topic into categories or main points | • Current enrollment<br>• Recruitment strategy<br>• Projected enrollment |
| Chronological | Presenting topics that span a length of time, deal with the development of an idea, or explain the steps in a process | • How to run the new training module<br>• Reviewing the timeline for the new product rollout |
| Spatial | Discussing a subject in terms of spatial structure; discussing the function, arrangement, or description of parts | Introducing the new dress code by describing it from head to toe or toe to head |
| Cause–effect | Communicating a relationship in which one thing is caused by another | Informing the audience how the move to a global market (cause) will change the shipping procedure (effect) |
| Problem–solution | Communicating both a problem that needs to be solved and the solution in the problem–solution structure that is most effective | • Problem: high turnover rate among top employees<br>• Solution: new bonus system and increased internal promotions |
| Pro–con | Discussing both the pros, or positives, and the cons, or negatives, of an idea | Discussing the pros and cons of purchasing Macs versus PCs |
| Comparison–contrast | Showing similarities or differences between things | Discussing a change in insurance carriers by illustrating the similarities between the old and new carriers and then the differences between them |

## Developing Transitions

One mark of an excellent presenter is that he or she provides a clear organizational structure through the use of transitions. What is a transition? A **transition** is any word or phrase that helps guide the listener from one point to the next.

Presenting with professional excellence sometimes requires the use of a microphone.

Let's face it, most audience members are not good listeners. To counter this problem, you must learn to tell them what you are going to say, say it, and then tell them what you said. Why would you want to use so much repetition? Will it bore the audience? We assure you it will not bore them. Instead, it will help them. Bottom line, if you're giving a presentation and you actually want your audience to remember your message, you must repeat yourself. So begin by clearly introducing your topic and specific purpose during the introduction, followed by a preview of your main points. Next, clearly state each main point during the presentation, and state them again in the conclusion. It sounds very mechanical, but it's a formula that works.

Within the body of your presentation, clear transitions must appear between your main points. Let's say you are giving a presentation on hurricane evacuation procedures for your workplace. As you complete your discussion of the first main point and move to the next main point, add an **internal summary** followed by an **internal preview**:

> Now that we have looked at how equipment will be protected during the storm [internal summary], let's examine the ways Company X would protect you if such a disaster were to occur [internal preview].

The use of internal previews and summaries helps the audience follow your organizational structure with ease by providing additional reinforcement of your message.

For presentations with more than three main points, internal previews and summaries between each point can be overkill. Instead, use **signposts**—words or phrases that let the audience know where you are within the presentation. Imagine you're driving down a stretch of unfamiliar road. If you don't see any road signs for a while, you might worry that you have taken a wrong turn. You ask, "Where am I? How much farther do I have to go?" Then a sign appears telling you where you are, and you feel relieved. A signpost does the same thing within a presentation. Signposts are useful both between main points and within main points. Using the hurricane example again, signposts could be used when discussing steps for protecting electronic equipment.

> We will take four steps to protect electronic equipment:
>
> *First,* all data will be backed up on flash drives and taken to a secure location away from the storm. [Discuss this subpoint.]
>
> *Second,* all electronic equipment will be unplugged and wrapped in plastic bags. [Discuss this subpoint.]
>
> *Third,* all electronic equipment in exterior offices with windows will be moved to interior offices. [Discuss this subpoint.]
>
> *Fourth,* all electronic equipment in interior offices will be taken off the floor and placed on desks or shelves. [Discuss this subpoint.]

## Know Yourself    Being Organized in the Body of the Presentation

*The following questions will help you gain a better understanding of your effectiveness when organizing a speech. Answer each question thoughtfully, and then reflect on the results. How can this knowledge help you be a better communicator and a better speech designer?*

1. Did you clearly follow an organizational pattern?
2. Did you use section transitions and nonverbal transitions to signal to the audience that you are changing points?
3. Did you use internal previews to let the audience know what you will be discussing next? These are similar to the presentation previews in the introduction but cover only main body points.
4. Did you use internal summaries to remind the audience of what you just covered?
5. Did you give signposts (*first, second, to clarify*, etc.) as a way to help the audience know where you are in the middle of a main point?

Source: Edwards, Edwards, Wahl, and Myers (2013).

# Introductions

Although an introduction should have a preview and a conclusion should have a summary, remember that a preview does not equal an introduction, nor does a summary equal a conclusion. Well-developed introductions and conclusions are essential components of excellent presentations. Let's begin by looking at what makes a well-developed introduction.

Presentations characterized with professional excellence always include a solid **introduction**—the part of the presentation in which you gain attention, introduce the topic, develop credibility, relate the topic to the audience, and preview your main points. When you stand in front of an audience, you should imagine them sitting there with remote controls in their hands. If you don't immediately capture their attention, they will mentally change the channel. Plus, if you don't immediately pull them in, they will start daydreaming about winning the lotto, running through their to-do lists, or thinking about what they should have for lunch. You can never become an excellent speaker if the audience isn't listening to you, so developing your attention getter is critical.

Presenters must capture audience members' attention and promote listening so the message presented is received.

## Your Communication Interaction    Presentations at Work

*Read the passage below, and then answer the questions. As you read, think about ways the KEYS approach could help you improve **your communication interaction** if you were in Beatrice's position.*

Beatrice is an elementary school principal who is developing a presentation that she will give at an orientation for new teachers. She has written the following introduction:

When you decided to become a teacher, I have no doubt someone shared with you the words of the playwright George Bernard Shaw: "He who can, does. He who cannot, teaches." Today, I would like to counter the words of Mr. Shaw with the words of one of the greatest intellects in the history of the human race, Aristotle. Aristotle said, "All who have mediated on the art of governing mankind have been convinced that the fate of empires depend on the education of youth." If Aristotle is correct, and I believe he is, you accepted an extremely important task when you entered this profession and accepted this job. And I am here today to welcome you to the toughest but most important job there is. Welcome to the world of teaching. This next year will be challenging, but I promise it also will be extremely rewarding. Today, in addition to my welcome, I would like to introduce you to the administrative team and discuss three areas of support we will provide to you throughout the year.

### Questions to Consider

1. Is Beatrice's introduction effective? Why or why not?
2. Did she include all five required components of an introduction?
3. What changes, if any, do you think she needs to make?

How do you gain an audience's attention, and how do you really make yourself stand out as a speaker? First, make certain to eliminate any pre-introductions. Do not begin by saying any of the following or any variation of the following:

- Hi, my name is Tony.
- I am very excited to have this opportunity to talk to you today.
- I am really nervous.
- Today I would like to talk to you about . . . blah . . . blah.

Instead, start off with something that captures the audience's attention. You can start with a story, a quote, a statistic—anything that is going to spark interest. Once you have their attention, then you can introduce yourself and your topic. But in the first few seconds of your presentation, do something that will pull them in so they won't change the channel. We'll say it one more time: All introductions should begin with gaining the audience's attention.

Similarly, introductions should always end with a preview of your main points. This will help the audience transition from the introduction to the body—and it will also reinforce your message. Therefore, in an introduction, gaining attention should occur first and the preview should occur last, but there is no formula for how the other three components should appear. When it comes to introducing the topic, making the topic relevant to the audience, and developing credibility, you have some flexibility. For example, you could begin with a story that gains attention and begins to develop your credibility. Or you might start with a statistic that draws attention and establishes credibility, and then introduce the topic. On the other hand, you could address each of the components separately.

Regardless of how they appear, make certain all five components are present during the introduction. Remember, being audience centered is necessary if you want to speak with professional excellence. By introducing your topic, you help orient the audience. We've heard countless presentations that have failed to achieve the simple task of introducing the topic—the audience was left guessing as to the exact focus of the presentation. By establishing credibility, you help the audience determine why they should trust you and the information you are presenting. Further, by making the topic relevant to the audience, you help them answer some of the following questions: Why is this information important to me? How is it going to impact me? Why should I pay attention and listen?

# Conclusions

The final part of your presentation is your **conclusion**. A well-designed conclusion can elevate a presentation from average to excellent, while a poor conclusion can make an otherwise excellent presentation fall flat.

Sadly, speakers often drop the ball when it comes to conclusions. By keeping a few simple steps in mind, you can easily design an excellent conclusion. These steps include stating that you are concluding, concisely summarizing, and ending with a strong impression.

When you have completed your main points, it's time to move into the conclusion. Keep three things in mind as you move into the conclusion. First, if you have any additional points or information to cover, then you are not ready to conclude. New information belongs in the body of the presentation. Second, you should let the audience know that you are concluding. There are countless ways to mark your move into the conclusion. You can say, "In conclusion," "In summary," "As I close," "I would like to end with," "I would like to close by saying," and so on. Third, once you've verbally moved into the conclusion, you must conclude. Never create a **false close**—when a speaker signals to the audience that the presentation is concluding but keeps going by introducing more information. When you tell the audience you're concluding, you must summarize, drive the point home, and stop talking. If you say "in conclusion" and then continue on with new information and no clear end in sight, the audience will respond negatively. After you signal your conclusion, provide a summary. As noted above, tell them what you're going to say, say it, and tell them what you said. The conclusion is the time for the "tell them what you said." This is critical if you want your audience to remember your message.

Finally, end by leaving a strong impression. End with a quote or story, refer back to something you talked about in the beginning, or use a memorable statistic or something else that people will remember. Never end with a statement such as, "Well, I guess that's it." Never begin packing up before the applause, and even if you'll be taking questions, avoid ending with the statement, "Does anyone have any questions?" Wait for the applause and then move into questions. Following these three simple steps will help you appear polished and will give the presentation a smooth close that will greatly enhance the audience's perception of you as a speaker.

# Persuasive Speech

## Background Information

The following speech will be delivered by a manager, William Orr, to his team. The ABC Company is offering employee training programs on customer service to all employees. The training is not mandatory, but William believes that his team would benefit greatly from taking part in the training. Please review William's speech. Note his use of Monroe's Motivated Sequence, an organizational pattern shown to be effective when attempting to move an audience to action. Also pay attention to his use of transitions and the components of his introduction and conclusion.

## Excellent Customer Service Benefits Us All

*Introduction*

*After being introduced, William moves behind the podium and stands there for 1 minute without saying anything.* **[Attention step]**

Did that seem like a long time? Well in reality, that was only 1 minute—1 little minute. But it probably seemed like a lot longer to you. You have all experienced bad service, haven't you? We know exactly how it feels to be that waiting customer. You know that 1 minute seems like an eternity to you when you are the customer who is standing there, waiting to be acknowledged or served. But have you ever left a customer waiting? Even for a minute? I have to admit it, I have. And I didn't think much about it. In fact, until recently, I did not even make the connection that some of my behaviors were leading to bad customer service. **[Credibility—establishing common ground]**

Today, I'm here to tell you about some workshops that the ABC Company will offer over the next few weeks. The workshops will be on customer service training. I have attended these workshops, and I know firsthand how beneficial they are. In fact, they have improved my customer service skills tenfold. **[Credibility—competence]** It is my hope that you'll see these workshops as both important and beneficial for yourself and the team and sign up to attend. **[Specific purpose]** Let's take a moment and discuss how our customers meet our needs, then we'll discuss some of the problems related to customer service and, finally, how we all benefit when our customers are happy. **[Preview]**

*Body*

### I. Why We Need to Give Excellent Customer Service

To be successful as a company, we must all have good customer relations, because our customers are valuable to us. We need to provide excellent customer service, or we will lose our customers. The bottom line is that without the customer base, we don't have a company. Without the company, none of us—including you—has a job. **[Need/problem step]**

Please don't get me wrong. I am not criticizing your performance. The ABC Company succeeds because of you. You make ABC Company better! But we need our customers to be happy to make it all work. Through these workshops, we are going to learn skills that will aid us in continuing to improve in this area. Even though we are doing a good job, our goal at ABC Company is to strive to get better. It's like in athletics—the champions win by working hard and continually striving to improve for the next game. That doesn't mean they aren't good; it just means they must keep improving to stay at the top. Here, we not only want to be employed, but we want to be successful in what we do. In our game, it is not championship rings; it is bonuses. Strong customer relations will earn each of us, you and me, extra money come bonus time.

Now that we've reviewed how our customers meet our needs, let's look at how these workshops can help us provide better customer service. **[Transition]**

### II. How to Improve Your Customer Service (Solution/Satisfaction)

The skills and strategies taught during the workshops should help us deal with many of the complexities related to people and, we hope, make your job easier and more enjoyable. For example, one of the topics they will cover is nonverbal communication. The 1-minute pause at the beginning is an example of the impact that our nonverbal communication can have on people. According to [SOURCE], 93% of communication effectiveness is determined by our nonverbal cues. So sometimes, we might unintentionally make our customers feel unwelcome in our facility without even meaning to. When is the last time you thought about the way you communicate with customers nonverbally? Could you use some help or insight in this area? Well, these workshops will provide that information.

Another topic the workshops will cover is how our language impacts the listener. Have you ever had a small problem with a customer escalate into a big problem and you were not sure why? It may have been the difference between saying "you" versus saying "I." When there is a potential conflict, you will learn that it's best to start sentences with the word *I*, not *you*, because *you* can put the listener in the defensive mode and increase the likelihood that the problem will escalate. For example, let's pretend a customer needs assistance filing insurance claims. As our receptionist, Jane, attempts to explain how everything works, the customer continues to ask the same questions over and over, in part because she is attempting to answer her texts at the same time. As this is going on, a line is forming and the other customers are getting upset, so Jane MUST address the problem. Jane COULD say, "You need to stop texting and listen because I can't help you much longer because you are holding up the line." Of course, this is likely to put the customer on the defensive and create additional problems. A better approach is for Jane to say something like, "I am having a hard time getting my point across at this time. I would be happy to assist another customer so you can take care of the texting issue. Then we can focus on the forms without the distraction. Which do you prefer to handle first, the texts or the forms?" Of course, there is no perfect solution, but the strategies the workshop teaches will decrease the likelihood of a major conflict.

Another important topic covered in the workshops is how to diffuse an upset customer. Sadly, we have all had and will continue to have angry customers. How can this workshop help with that issue? Well, you all know Mark in the Westside office. Mark was telling me about a woman he helped last October. The woman had moved across the United States from Nevada to Florida because of her husband's career. Three months after this dear woman moved, her husband informed her that he wanted a divorce. When she came to Mark's store, the woman had planned to have her phone fixed and then open an account without her husband's name on it. The problem was that she was at a breaking point. When Mark informed her that the tech people had left for the day, she lost it emotionally. The more Mark tried to help her, the more upset she became. The good news is that Mark handled it beautifully. He knew exactly what to do, and he attributed his ability to excel in this situation to the information he learned in the customer service workshops.

Now we've covered a little bit on how our customers meet our needs and how the workshops can assist us in solving many customer-related problems, so we are ready to focus on how we ALL benefit when our customers are happy. **[Transition statement]**

### III. The Benefits of Improved Customer Service

I was reading on CNN's website that Apple Computers has been rated No. 1 on *Fortune* magazine's list of the Top 20 Most Admired Companies. The former CEO and founder of Apple, Steve Jobs, said that he was not easy on his employees. Before he passed away, Jobs explained that he took already great people and pushed them to be even better by coming up with more aggressive visions of how it could be. That is what the ABC Company wants to do for us—for you. You are being offered the resources that will make us even better.

So take a minute and imagine what it could be like. What if you excelled at giving customer service? Even if you see this as one of your strengths, what if you were better? Your current customers would be happy, which always makes coming to work a lot more pleasant. The number of customers would increase, which means larger bonuses. And when those difficult situations come up, and they will inevitably come up, you would have better tools for handling them.

All these benefits are waiting for you, and all you have to do is come after my presentation and sign up. Literally, all you have to do is write down your name. We will take care of the cost and the scheduling. What could be easier? **[Action step]**

### Conclusion

In conclusion, I have discussed why we need excellent customer service, how you can improve your customer service, and the benefits of improved customer service. **[Summary]** I hope you are as excited about the workshops as I am. And the best part is that I don't have to wait, not even 1 minute, to sign up for this wonderful opportunity. And remember, if we don't care about our customers, they will not care about us! **[Memorable conclusion]**

# Language

As a presenter, you don't want parts of your presentation to have the same qualities you find in a casual conversation. Specifically, your delivery should have a conversational quality to it, while other parts of your presentation, such as the structure/organization, should be more formal than what is found in a typical conversation. So what about language? Should language be formal or informal? When it comes to language as it relates to public speaking, you'll walk a fine line. Your language needs to be more formal than casual conversation but not so formal that you are speaking over your audience's heads.

One easy step you can take to adapt your language to any speaking occasion is to cut out cuss words, slang terms, and colloquialisms. **Cuss words** or curse words, also referred to as swear words, are viewed as obscene expressions. **Slang** terms are either made-up words or words used to express something other than their formal meaning. For example, *snow* is a slang term when used to refer to cocaine. Using **texting language** in your presentations would be considered a type of slang. Texting abbreviations (e.g., OMG, TU, BFF) have no place in a presentation. **Colloquialisms** are like slang terms but are locally or regionally based. As a result, they may be confusing to people from outside the region and/or could make you seem less credible to a national or global audience. For example, if you're from the northeastern part of the United States, you may use "yous" or "yous guys." If you're from the South, you might say "y'all" or "all y'all." Remember to avoid the use of cuss words, slang, texting language, and colloquialisms in your presentations.

This does not mean that when you have a speaking opportunity you should break out the dictionary and thesaurus to find the longest, fanciest words you can. Your expansive vocabulary may make you look smart, but who cares how smart you are if your audience can't understand you? Select words with which your audience is familiar. If you're going to introduce some terms that audience members may not know, define them within your presentation.

Cuss words and profanity can certainly tarnish your presentation.

Excellent presenters pay close attention to language. Not only do they understand the line between too formal and too informal, but they also understand the power of imagery and repetition. When a speaker uses **imagery,** he or she helps the audience paint a picture with words. This can be done with the use of **metaphor** or descriptive terms.

**Repetition** is also a powerful language device. By repeating a phrase or creating a parallel structure within your presentation, you can create a sense of anticipation for audience members. Think about the first time you hear a new song. What do you remember when the song is over? More than likely, you remember the chorus because it's repeated. As you listen to the song, you anticipate the chorus after each verse and it gets stuck in your head. Advertisers use this same technique when trying to get you to remember a product. They repeat a catchphrase or jingle that you will remember. By using repetition and/or a parallel structure, you can unify a presentation and reinforce the message for each member of the audience.

# KEYS to Excellence in Designing a Speech

Remember Rod Blagojevich, the former governor from the beginning of the chapter? Even though he knew he was facing a hostile audience, he designed his speech to highlight the positive outcomes of his governorship and emphasize his apology to the public. Hopefully, your speeches will not be in front of such a hostile crowd, but you can still use the KEYS method to ensure you deliver an effective speech. The first step, *know yourself*, requires that you know both yourself and your topic, and how your audience can relate to that topic. A speech given in front of your peers in a classroom should sound different than would a speech given in a business setting, even if covering the same topic. Research your audience, and tailor your speech to address their expectations.

The next step, *evaluate the professional context*, involves knowing the culture of your audience. Is your audience mostly made up of young college students, or older professional businesspeople? Always ensure that you have a general idea of what the makeup of your audience will look like, and make sure to prepare your speech in a way that can answer almost everybody's concerns about your presentation.

The third step, *your communication interaction occurs*, can be difficult to focus; this step asks you to consistently critique both yourself and the audience. With more practice, this step becomes easier to perform and can help your speeches be more effective with different audiences. While it is important to focus on delivering your speech correctly, you must also be able to gather feedback for the final task, *step back and reflect*. Think about how you presented your speech to the audience, and decide whether it was an effective method or not. Ask yourself if the same delivery method would work just as well with a culturally different audience. The more you learn to adapt your presentations, the easier it will be to deal with unresponsive or hostile audiences.

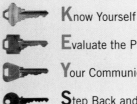

**K**now Yourself

**E**valuate the Professional Context

**Y**our Communication Interaction Occurs

**S**tep Back and Reflect

## Executive Summary

Now that you have finished reading this chapter, you can do the following:

Analyze audience and context:

- If you want to present with professional excellence, you must be audience centered. The best presenters, the best communicators in general, are aware of all the components involved in the communication process, and they pay particular attention to the audience (p. 290).
- To become an *audience-centered speaker*, start by asking a series of questions designed to answer one all-important larger question, "Who is my audience?" (p. 290).
- In addition, the context has a huge impact on the audience. Again, you must ask yourself a series of questions to analyze your context (see Table 12.2) (p. 291).

Gather research for your speeches:

- The *research* you need to develop and support your presentation can and should come from a variety of sources. Depending on the topic, you may use internal sources, external sources, or a combination of the two (p. 292).
- *Internal sources* include information that comes from within the organization, such as reports, policies, or interviews with employees and/or customers (p. 292).
- *External sources* include information that comes from outside the organization, such as from outside agencies, the competition, the government, and the media (p. 294).
- If you have done your job as a researcher, you will have more information than you need. At this point in the process, you must determine what to include (p. 295).

Organize the body of a speech and incorporate effective transitions:

- You must develop clear organization within the body of your presentation. Your typical, not-so-memorable speaker will take all the information available and lump it together as three main points (p. 296).
- One organizational pattern that's often utilized to persuade in business and professional settings is *Monroe's Motivated Sequence*—a five-step process, developed in 1935 by Purdue University professor Alan H. Monroe, that includes the attention step, need step, satisfaction step, visualization step, and action step (p. 296).
- A *transition* is any word or phrase that helps guide the listener from one point to the next. Within the body of your presentation, clear transitions must appear between your main points. As you complete your discussion of the first main point and move to the next main point, add an *internal summary* followed by an *internal preview* (p. 297).
- For presentations with more than three main points, internal previews and summaries between each point can be overkill. Instead, use *signposts*—words or phrases that let the audience know where you are within the presentation (p. 298).

Develop effective introductions and conclusions:

- Although an introduction should have a preview and a conclusion should have a summary, remember that a preview does not equal an introduction, nor does a summary equal a conclusion. Well-developed introductions and conclusions are essential components of excellent presentations (p. 299).
- *Introductions* should always end with a preview of your main points. This will help the audience transition from the introduction to the body—and it will also reinforce your message (p. 300).
- The final part of your presentation is your *conclusion*. A well-designed conclusion can elevate a presentation from average to excellent, while a poor conclusion can make an otherwise excellent presentation fall flat (p. 301).
- Once you've verbally moved into the conclusion, you must conclude. Never create a *false close*—when a speaker signals to the audience that the presentation is concluding but keeps going by introducing more information (p. 301).
- End by leaving a strong impression. End with a quote or story, refer back to something you talked about in the beginning, or use a memorable statistic or something else people will remember (p. 301).

Understand the role and value of language:

- Your language needs to be more formal than casual conversation but not too formal so as to speak over your audience's heads (p. 304).
- Excellent presenters pay close attention to language. Not only do they understand the line between being too formal and too informal, but they also understand the power of imagery and repetition. When a speaker uses *imagery*, he or she helps the audience paint a picture with words. This can be done with the use of metaphor or descriptive terms (p. 304).
- *Repetition* is also a powerful language device. By repeating a phrase or creating a parallel structure within your presentation, you can create a sense of anticipation for audience members (p. 304).

Use the KEYS process to develop professional excellence with speech design:

- *Know yourself.* Know both yourself and your topic, and how your audience can relate to that topic. A speech given in front of your peers in a classroom should sound different than would a speech given in a business setting, even if covering the same topic (p. 305).
- *Evaluate the professional context.* Always ensure that you have a general idea of what the makeup of your audience will look like, and make sure to prepare your speech in a way that can answer almost everybody's concerns about your presentation (p. 305).
- *Your communication interaction occurs.* Consistently critique both yourself and the audience. With more practice, this step becomes easier to perform and can help your speeches be more effective with different audiences (p. 305).
- *Step back and reflect.* Think about how you presented your speech to the audience, and decide whether it was an effective method or not. Ask yourself if the same delivery method would work just as well with a culturally different audience (p. 305).

## Discussion Questions

1. How would you go about taking an inventory of your audience before presenting? What are some examples of ways to retrieve information about an audience before a presentation?

2. Have you ever seen a speaker make an error when analyzing the audience or context? How did it impact the presentation?

3. How do you typically go about gathering research? Is your method effective? Is it thorough? How could it be improved?

4. Think about someone whom you find to be an excellent speaker. What makes this speaker excellent? How does he or she structure introductions and conclusions? Does he or she give attention to language and/or supporting aids? Are they memorable? Why?

5. Review the organizational patterns discussed in this chapter. Considering this information, what preference do you have related to the way you organize information for a presentation?

## Terms to Remember

audience analysis (p. 290)

audience-centered speaker (p. 290)

colloquialisms (p. 304)

conclusion (p. 301)

context analysis (p. 291)

cuss words (p. 304)

external sources (p. 294)

false close (p. 301)

imagery (p. 304)

internal preview (p. 298)

internal sources (p. 292)

internal summary (p. 298)

introduction (p. 299)

metaphor (p. 304)

Monroe's Motivated
Sequence (p. 296)

repetition (p. 304)

research (p. 292)

signposts (p. 298)

slang (p. 304)

texting language
(p. 304)

transition (p. 297)

Visit the Student Study Site at **www.sagepub.com/keys2e** to access the following resources:

- SAGE journal articles
- Video links
- Web resources
- Web quizzes
- eflashcards

## Chapter Outline

**Delivering the Presentation With Professional Excellence** 312

**PowerPoint and Other Supporting Aids** 316

**Practice Makes Perfect** 326

**Team Presentations** 326

**KEYS to Excellence in Delivering a Speech** 328

**Executive Summary** 332

**Discussion Questions** 333

**Terms to Remember** 333

## Chapter Objectives

After studying this chapter, you should be able to:

1. Recognize the positive benefits of the adrenaline rush that comes from speaking in public

2. Understand the role of nonverbal communication in presenting a speech

3. Deliver an extemporaneous speech with professional excellence

4. Understand how to use supporting aids effectively

5. Present an effective team presentation

# chapter 13

# Delivering a Speech With Professional Excellence

**The late Steve Jobs, former CEO of Apple Inc., was known for being one of the most charismatic orators of his time.** He oversaw the massive growth of the Apple brand in the 21st century and also played a major role during the unveiling of new Apple products. During the iPad 2 launch event in March 2011, Jobs gave one of the most memorable speeches of his life. Although he had taken an indefinite medical leave of absence earlier in the year, Jobs discussed the future of Apple in a post-PC world. He emphasized the company's philosophy concerning the marriage of technology and liberal arts, and he insisted that business devices do not necessarily have to be dull and boring. Jobs said: "It's in Apple's DNA that technology alone is not enough. That it's technology married with liberal arts, married with the humanities, that yields us the result that makes our hearts sing" (Slattery, 2011). Fans and experts alike applauded Jobs's words, and even after his death, he is held up as one of the greatest innovators and public speakers of the new millennium.

It might be tempting to think that a company such as Apple can rely on its products alone and does not need good public relations to deliver successful products. However, the presence of Steve Jobs at almost every major Apple unveiling had a significant impact on the success of the product being introduced. Jobs had an established credibility, and the optimistic language he used to tie the company's products into everyday life helped give Apple the household status it has today. It is important to note exactly how visible Jobs was as the company's CEO. Many companies rely on famous actors or characters to sell their products, but Jobs was as identifiable with Apple as Colonel Sanders is with Kentucky Fried Chicken. Jobs was an excellent public speaker and face for the company, and Apple benefited greatly as a result.

Delivering a speech with professional excellence can help you not only influence your audience but succeed in business as well. Creating an excellent public image for your company helps encourage customers to use your products or services. In this chapter, you will learn how to deliver a speech effectively and also what types of supporting aids can be the most effective in enhancing your speech. While there is no concrete method to delivering a memorable speech, you will become familiar with different ways to become an effective speaker.

# Delivering the Presentation With Professional Excellence

Why is public speaking dreaded? Do speakers fear their inability to organize information or design an effective introduction? Do they fear conducting research? The truth of the matter is that people don't really fear public speaking; they fear the unknown. As we discussed in Chapter 1, not knowing what to expect and being concerned about what people think of you as a speaker can trigger communication anxiety. While people have different levels of anxiety when speaking in public, we emphasize that overcoming these fears and honing your skills when delivering a presentation are essential to achieving professional excellence.

## The Adrenaline Rush

When you get up to deliver a presentation, your body will experience an **adrenaline rush**. The **delivery** of the presentation requires you to put yourself "out there" in front of an audience, and in the deep recesses of your mind, your body is signaling, "Danger, danger." Now your body must decide to take flight or fight. Although you may want to take flight and go back to your seat, you know you have to give the presentation. So your body moves into fight mode and releases lots of adrenaline to help you. Yes, you read that correctly—to help you. Believe it or not, this adrenaline rush is a positive thing. As you practice public speaking, you will learn what responses to expect when you have an adrenaline rush—it will no longer be an unknown. Then you can learn how to handle each response. In the end, you'll be able to use the adrenaline to your advantage by presenting with energy and passion.

In delivering presentations, you will get an opportunity to know yourself. After each presentation, step back and reflect on how you respond to the adrenaline in your system. Learning to understand your responses will help you change the way you think about presentations, which is important, because for some speakers, thinking about the presentation creates more apprehension than actually giving it (Daly, Vangelisti, & Weber, 1995; Yen et al., 2012). Let's review some common responses and some practical ways to handle each of them.

### Sweating

What if you sweat? Unfortunately, you can't really control this normal bodily response, so you'll just have to learn how to adjust. To minimize sweating, select clothing that is lightweight and made of natural fibers. Make sure you have access to cold water before and during your presentation. Bring a handkerchief or tissue with you so you can wipe your brow or dab your lip if needed. If you're wearing a jacket, leave it on to avoid revealing damp underarms.

### Blushing

Just like sweating, blushing is something you can't control. For some of you, your cheeks will get red; for others, it will be your ears. Some of the techniques used to handle sweating may help minimize blushing, but like sweating, it's just something you'll have to learn to live with. However, there's some good news. First, by the time your introduction is over, much of the redness may fade. Second, a little blushing will not be noticed by the audience and is irrelevant to the way people perceive your presentation.

### Hands

For some people, the energy created by the adrenaline rush comes out in their hands. If you're lucky, talking with your hands comes naturally. This can be an added benefit for your delivery. Effective hand gestures add visual interest to the speaker and a more dynamic delivery style.

If you do talk with your hands, there are a few things you should do to ensure that this remains a benefit and does not become a distraction. Avoid holding objects such as pens or pointers, and place all beverages beyond the reach of your arms. Nothing is more distracting than accidentally throwing a pen at the audience or knocking a drink all over your notes.

Unfortunately, for some of you, that nervous energy doesn't turn into dynamic hand gestures but, rather, manifests as shaky hands. What should you do if you have shaky hands? Again, don't hold anything. Leave your notes on the podium. If you're not going to use a podium and you need to hold your notes, use index cards. Index paper is thicker and the cards are relatively small, so a little shaking will be far less noticeable.

Preparing, coaching, maintaining a positive attitude, and visualizing success contribute to presenting with professional excellence.

If you're someone who doesn't talk with your hands, there are a few things you should keep in mind. For example, never put your hands in your pockets. Instead, place your hands comfortably on the podium or allow your arms to hang by your sides.

### Feet

For other people, the adrenaline rush will head straight to their feet. You begin your presentation, and suddenly you're overcome by this need to shuffle, bounce, and move. The solution to this problem is simply to walk around. One of the biggest mistakes you can make is boxing yourself into a small space. Squishing yourself behind a podium or in a corner to put the PowerPoint slides center stage is the worst thing you can do to yourself. If you have a lot of nervous energy in your feet and you don't walk around, you will feel like a caged animal. When you're speaking, you have control of the room, so exercise that control while walking around. Slowly and deliberately walk from one side of the room to the other, and maintain eye contact with the entire audience during the presentation.

### Vocal Quality

To develop yourself as a presenter with an outstanding delivery style, you will have to master several vocal qualities, each of which can be impacted by the rush of adrenaline. Sometimes, nervous energy can translate into a shaky or cracking voice. Just like sweating and blushing, there's not a lot you can do about this. Fortunately, chances are the only person that will notice the change in your voice is you. Furthermore, the effects usually lessen or disappear altogether by the end of the introduction.

**Volume** is another factor to consider. For some of you, nervousness will result in a quiet presentation. To overcome this problem, you simply need to set your volume dial and focus on projecting. When you begin speaking, focus on an audience member in the back corner of the room and project your voice to that person—and maintain this volume throughout the presentation.

For many speakers, nervousness will cause an increase in **speaking rate**. The good news is that a rate slightly faster than average may actually be preferred. However, for those of you who are already "fast talkers," this rate increase can make it difficult for the audience to listen to and absorb your presentation. To counter this, take a few deep breaths before beginning your presentation. Deliberate breathing not only will slow your rate of speech but also will help reduce your nervousness in general. Taking sips of water may also be helpful. It will allow you a moment to slow your pace and check your breathing. It will also aid in reducing dry mouth, which can accompany a quick pace.

### Vocal Fillers

One of the most common signs of nervousness is **vocal fillers**. These occur when the speaker should pause but instead fills the silence. Fillers include sounds such as "umm" and "aah." Words such as *and* and *like* are also commonly used as fillers. Becoming aware of the fact that you're using vocal fillers can be all it takes to reduce them. If you suffer from an overuse of vocal fillers, be certain to prepare your presentation at least 1 week in advance of the speaking event. Run through the outline a few times each day to increase your familiarity with the material and your comfort level with pauses.

### Eye Contact

While this might be surprising to you, making **eye contact** with your audience is one of the best ways to reduce nervousness. You may find it difficult to take the standard public speaking advice, which is to imagine the audience members in their underwear. Most speakers never succeed in doing that. Unfortunately, many speakers do succeed at imagining their audience as an angry mob waiting to throw rotten tomatoes. Rest assured, this will not be the case. Most audiences are supportive, friendly, and initially interested. Making eye contact with your audience and working to communicate with them in the same way you would communicate with a friend during a conversation is a quick way to reduce nervousness, increase credibility, and establish a positive rapport.

### Clothing

Your appearance is part of your nonverbal communication, so it's part of your delivery. Presenting yourself in a way that enhances your credibility and professionalism is important if you want the audience to trust the information you're presenting or to be persuaded by your message. Unfortunately, many speakers don't think about their appearance until it's too late. As a result, their choice of clothing increases nervousness instead of adding to their credibility. The trick is to make your clothing work for you. For example, a few pieces of jewelry, such as a watch or small earrings, are fine. On the other hand, wearing dangling bracelets that clank together every time you move your hands is distracting for both you and the audience. As noted above, wear clothing that decreases sweating, but make sure you're still appropriately covered. Brand new shoes may look nice, but if they rub blisters, they will negatively impact your overall performance. Take time to think about the impact your clothing will have on your presentation.

## Sense of Play

After teaching public speaking for a combined 30 years and listening to thousands of speeches, we can say with certainty that the most important thing you can do to handle the anxiety created by public speaking is to treat the experience with a sense of play. Let's look at the reality of the situation. Typically, you'll speak to an audience for between 5 and 30 minutes. Is 30 minutes really worth all that worrying? What if you faint? What if you accidentally flash the audience? What if you spill your drink on your notes? What if you bump the table over and the podium hits you in the head, knocking you to the ground? Chances are none of these things will happen. Instead, any problems you face will be minor.

But truth be told, all these things have happened to us and we still continue to love speaking in public. Why? Are we deranged? No, we have learned to treat public speaking with a sense of play. If something small doesn't go according to plan, we realize that, for the most part, no one but us will notice. If we make a bigger mistake, such as spilling a drink, we acknowledge it, laugh it off, and then move forward. Yes, we are embarrassed, but that's life, and it has little impact on the audience.

Public speaking is an extremely valuable skill and one you should work to master. Prior to giving any speech, you should do your research, design an audience-centered message, and practice. In the moment when you are delivering the speech, you have to learn to roll with it. The adrenaline rush will impact you in some way, shape, or form. Begin to determine your responses to the rush, and develop strategies to overcome or accept those responses. Never give public speaking more power over your life than it deserves. It's okay if it makes you a little nervous, but never let it stand between you and an opportunity to express yourself as a leader.

## Presenting From an Outline

There is no one right way to deliver a presentation. Each of you will have differences in your speaking styles that will add unique elements to your presentations. While delivery styles vary, all speakers should strive for a delivery style that has a **conversational quality,** which includes an extemporaneous speaking style and good eye contact. The ultimate goal is to have your delivery enhance, rather than distract from, the overall impression.

Speaking from an outline is one simple way to increase the conversational quality of your presentation. There are many benefits to using an outline. You will not write a presentation, but you will design your presentation. This means that you should not write your presentation out word-for-word and read it out loud. Speaking from a **manuscript** is very difficult. Only the most skilled speakers can manage to do it and still maintain a conversational style. When speakers try to deliver their presentations from a manuscript, the result is usually a horrible delivery with the speaker reading the presentation to the audience. No one enjoys having a presentation read to them. It's called public speaking and not public reading for a reason. Having an outline, as opposed to a manuscript, eliminates the possibility of reading the presentation.

On the flip side, having no outline often results in speakers committing their presentations to memory, resulting in a **monotone** speaking style that's guaranteed to ruin a well-designed presentation. An outline helps the speaker follow the presentation design while still maintaining the freedom to deliver it in a slightly different fashion each time. This doesn't mean you should get up in front of the audience and wing it. You must practice the presentation so your specific purpose and presentation design remain the same—but your exact choice of words can vary slightly, helping you maintain an extemporaneous speaking style.

What if I lose my place? What if I go blank? Beginning speakers inevitably will ask one or both of these questions when the notion of speaking from an outline is discussed. First, it's far easier to lose your place in a manuscript than in an outline. Second, it's far easier to blank out when trying to recite back a presentation from memory than when speaking from an outline. If you find yourself at a loss for words for a moment, a little water will help. Simply pick up the glass or bottle, take a sip, and simultaneously find your place. No one in the audience will even notice.

As noted above, while you're not writing out a manuscript or memorizing every word, you should still prepare. There are going to be occasions when you have to give an impromptu presentation, but those situations are rare. Begin by preparing a detailed practice outline, known as your speaking notes. As you become more familiar with your presentation, streamline it into a speaking outline. According to Leech (1992), a speaking outline is less detailed than your speaking notes (see Table 13.1).

# PowerPoint and Other Supporting Aids

Let's face it—the world has gone high-tech. As audience members, we've become used to seeing visually stimulating images come at us faster than we can blink and hearing sounds from state-of-the-art audio systems in our theaters, homes, and cars. It is no wonder, then, that a lonely presenter in front of an audience can seem a bit boring. Don't misunderstand;

**Table 13.1 Presentation Outline Template**

**Introduction**
- I. Attention getter
- II. Introduce topic and specific purpose
- III. Establish credibility
- IV. Relate topic directly to the audience
- V. Preview main points

**Body**
- I. Main point
  - A. Definition
  - B. Supporting example

[Transition: Internal summary; internal preview]
- II. Main point
  - A. Supporting graph
  - B. Relevant statistic

**Conclusion**
- I. Restate specific purpose
- II. Summarize main points
- III. Memorable ending

## Evaluate the Professional Context   Orange Juice and Presentations Don't Mix

*Read the following passage about Arianna, and then answer the questions. As you read, focus on **evaluating the professional context**.*

Arianna had just begun her new position as a trainer. She loved presenting and had plenty of experience. One of her first audiences was the assembly-line team. Since their shift started early, her training sessions began at 5 a.m. This was early for Arianna, so she was not hungry when she woke up. Still, she wanted something healthy in her stomach, so she grabbed a big glass of orange juice.

As she began her presentation, some odd things began to happen. First, her lip began to sweat, and then she started to see spots. Neither of these things had ever happened to her before when giving a presentation. She decided to finish her point quickly and then give the group a break. Unfortunately, before she could break, her ears began to ring. Then she heard someone say, "She is turning green." She woke up a few minutes later. She had fainted.

The next day, she went to the doctor and found out she was hypoglycemic. The orange juice, which is pure fruit sugar, on her empty stomach had caused her to faint. She was relieved to learn what was wrong, but she still had a problem: She had to go back and finish the training. She was humiliated. How could she go back? Then she remembered something she had learned in school—treat the situation with a sense of play.

How did her audience respond? Did they "boo" her out of the room? Did they request a new trainer? Of course not; they were very supportive. They were happy that she was fine. They even joked about how they recommended her trainings to all their coworkers because there were extra-long breaks during the fainting spells. Arianna went on to have a long and successful career as a trainer.

### Questions to Consider

1. How would you have responded if you were in the audience?
2. What would you have done if you were in Arianna's position?
3. Have you ever had an embarrassing public speaking moment? How did you handle it?
4. How can the KEYS process help you survive situations like Arianna's?

a speaker with an audience-centered message and a dynamic delivery style can still captivate an audience without **supporting aids** (tools used by a speaker to help support the audience's interest in and understanding of the presentation), but utilizing them can bring many benefits.

When we ask students what they dislike about public speaking, two common responses are "I don't like everyone looking at me" and "I'm afraid I will be boring." Using supporting aids can help with these problems. When a supporting aid is displayed, the audience will split their attention between you and the aid, which can help reduce some of your anxiety. In addition, supporting aids provide another layer to your presentations that can enhance interest. It's boring to hear someone recite the steps for CPR during the annual refresher course. Most people would find it far more interesting to watch someone go through those steps. You may catch your audience's attention if you tell them about the dangers of failing to wash their hands, but you are far more likely to hold their interest if you show them an illustration of some common germs found in restaurants, hospitals, or educational settings.

A well-designed supporting aid also helps the audience by increasing understanding, enhancing retention, and facilitating listening. Telling an audience how to dress for success is helpful, but showing them visuals of how the attire should (or should not) look will further increase their level of understanding. For audience members who are **visual learners,** seeing key points, demonstrations, or other supporting materials is essential for their understanding. In addition, every time you repeat your message, you increase **retention**. It is said that a picture is worth a thousand words. Indeed, this seems to be the case when it comes to public speaking. According to Nickerson (1980), our memory of pictures is extremely accurate, and Hishitani (1991) found that this is especially true when the image is vivid. Further, a well-designed PowerPoint presentation can also facilitate listening.

Think back to a time when you were in class and the professor's organization was difficult to follow—not the professor in this class of course. It may have seemed as though he or she was jumping around from point to point. What did you do? If you were like most students, you simply stopped listening. If your audience can't follow your organizational structure, chances are they will stop listening. However, if you develop a clear organizational structure that is reinforced by an effectively designed PowerPoint presentation, you'll be providing them with a clear guide throughout your presentation. Since supporting aids increase understanding, enhance retention, and facilitate listening, they also help shorten meetings (Antonoff, 1990; Cicala, Smith, & Bush, 2012).

Presentation aids used in business seminars similar to the one shown here can make or break professional excellence.

## Should I Use Supporting Aids?

As stated previously, you can give a quality presentation without supporting aids. In fact, if not used properly, a supporting aid can negatively impact a presentation. To determine whether or not you should use a supporting aid, you need to consider the following questions:

- Will the aid enhance rather than distract from my presentation?
- Will the aid increase the audience's understanding of the material?
- Will the aid increase the audience's interest in the topic?
- Will the aid reinforce my message, thereby increasing retention?
- Will the aid enhance my credibility?
- Does the aid have a professional appearance or sound quality?
- Do I have the time needed to prepare and practice with this aid?

If you answered "yes" to all these questions, you should incorporate the supporting aids.

## Types of Supporting Aids

What supporting aids should you use? Supporting aids you may incorporate include **PowerPoint presentations**, video clips, audio clips, graphs, charts, illustrations, photos, models, and demonstrations.

### PowerPoint Presentations

PowerPoint is a software package that enables us to develop a slide show to go along with the presentation. There are other software programs with similar capabilities, but PowerPoint is the most commonly used software in the development of presentation slides. It is not uncommon to hear PowerPoint discussed in a derogatory way: "Power-Point is evil!" (Tufte, 2003); PowerPoint is "the growing electronic menace" (Jaffe, 2000); PowerPoint is PowerPointless.

What's wrong with PowerPoint? Nothing is wrong with it when it's used correctly. In fact, it's a wonderful tool when used correctly. However, the problem is that most of the time it's used incorrectly. Many speakers make the mistake of using PowerPoint as a crutch. PowerPoint is a supporting aid; it's not the whole presentation. Speakers get so caught up with making their PowerPoint slides that they fail to truly develop their presentations. As a result, the speaker becomes a talking head reading slides to the audience.

Your PowerPoint slides are not your speaking notes. When you use PowerPoint, you still need a **speaking outline**. That outline can be in your hands or on a podium and can even be the computer screen if the laptop is in front of you. Regardless of what you use, your notes need to be in front of you, not behind you. If you turn to read the slides, you will be continually turning your back on the audience. Reading slides and turning your back on the audience are both signs of a poor speaker.

When designing your PowerPoint slides, use the same background on each slide. The presentation should be consistent in color and pattern throughout. Remember that each slide should have a limited amount of text; it's better to have more slides with less text on each slide (see Figure 13.1). Continually remind yourself that this is a supporting aid, not your speaking notes. You don't have to include a whole part of your presentation on the slides. Instead, include key words or phrases. When complete sentences are on the slide, or entire paragraphs, the audience usually doesn't see anything but a bunch of text, because nothing stands out. Follow the KISS acronym when designing your slides: Keep It Simple, Speaker.

In addition to limiting your text, also limit the bells and whistles. You want your Power-Point presentation to have a professional appearance, so avoid bold or wild backgrounds, cute pictures, sound effects, and odd fonts. Also, make sure there's enough contrast between the slide's background color and the font color you use for text.

In most instances, the timing feature (with which slides are set to advance automatically at a certain pace) is not recommended because it doesn't leave the speaker any room for error. The extemporaneous delivery is the best style of delivery, and when the timing feature in the slide show software is used, it almost forces the speaker to memorize the presentation.

If you're using technology, always make sure it's available or bring it with you. That said, make certain you know how to use it properly. You should never use supporting aids of any type if you can't practice with them in advance. A good rule to follow is to arrive at your speaking event early and check to see if everything is working properly. If equipment fails for any reason, you must be prepared to deliver your presentation anyway. Always be ready to speak without your supporting aid. Also, it's important to remember that just

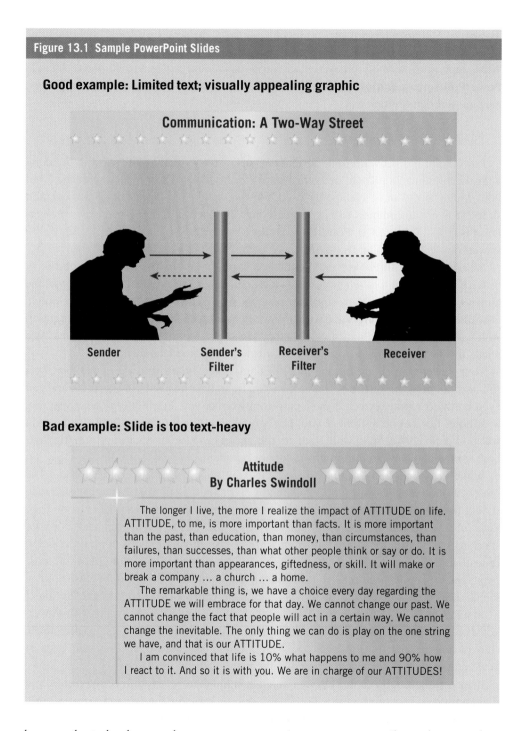

**Figure 13.1 Sample PowerPoint Slides**

**Good example: Limited text; visually appealing graphic**

Communication: A Two-Way Street

Sender     Sender's Filter     Receiver's Filter     Receiver

**Bad example: Slide is too text-heavy**

Attitude
By Charles Swindoll

The longer I live, the more I realize the impact of ATTITUDE on life. ATTITUDE, to me, is more important than facts. It is more important than the past, than education, than money, than circumstances, than failures, than successes, than what other people think or say or do. It is more important than appearances, giftedness, or skill. It will make or break a company ... a church ... a home.

The remarkable thing is, we have a choice every day regarding the ATTITUDE we will embrace for that day. We cannot change our past. We cannot change the fact that people will act in a certain way. We cannot change the inevitable. The only thing we can do is play on the one string we have, and that is our ATTITUDE.

I am convinced that life is 10% what happens to me and 90% how I react to it. And so it is with you. We are in charge of our ATTITUDES!

because the technology works on one computer, it may not necessarily work on another. The technology should be checked on the computer that will be used for the actual presentation. Also, any technology should be checked ahead of time so problems can be resolved before the presentation begins.

The advanced features can, of course, be impressive and add a lot of impact to a presentation, but inserting video and/or audio clips, hyperlinking to websites, etc., increases the likelihood of technical issues. Make sure the video/audio clip(s) are on the hard drive, the desktop, a CD, or a flash drive so they work properly. Another problem is not saving correctly. If, for example, someone has developed a slide show in PowerPoint using Vista and the computer that's being used for the presentation is running an older version of PowerPoint, such as XL, the slide show will not work on that computer unless it's saved as an XL file type.

Just as you practice what you will say during the presentation, it's also recommended that you practice with the technology. Proficiency with technology can enhance credibility, but technical problems can cause an otherwise smooth presentation to lose momentum quickly. Plus, practicing with the technology should help you feel more comfortable and confident in front of the audience, increasing the likelihood that you'll deliver a peak performance. Bottom line, you should be able to deliver your presentation without PowerPoint. It's merely a supporting aid to enhance your presentation; PowerPoint should never and can never replace you.

### Video Clips

Video clips can add some excitement to any presentation. You can use a VCR, DVD player, or a computer with a projector to show clips. If you are using the VCR, make certain the clip is cued prior to the presentation. Cuing DVDs is more difficult. If you have access to a DVD burner, you may want to burn the clip onto a separate DVD so you do not have to worry about cuing it up. If inadequate equipment or copyright laws prohibit you from doing this, find the clip prior to the presentation and then hit "Pause" on the DVD player until it is time to show the clip. If you're going to show a clip from YouTube or some other Internet source, remember to pull it up in advance. If you're planning to incorporate PowerPoint into your presentation, it's always best to save these clips directly in the presentation. If not, save them in a separate file. You should never make your audience wait while you go on the Internet in search of a clip. If you do this, you will offset many of the benefits of using video clips as supporting aids.

### Audio Clips

There are occasions when audio clips may be a necessary part of the presentation. As with video clips, make certain that the CD or tape is cued in advance. Save the clips directly in your PowerPoint presentation if you can. If not, save them on a separate file, but never waste the audience's time searching for them during your presentation. You may also have to provide a CD/cassette player when playing audio clips. When bringing your own equipment, it's advisable to make sure your speakers are adequate for the room size; bring along an extension cord just in case.

### Graphs, Charts, Illustrations, and Photos

You have four options for displaying supporting aids: graphs, charts, illustrations, or photos (see Figures 13.2, 13.3, and 13.4). First, you can copy them directly into your PowerPoint presentation. If you're planning to use PowerPoint, this is by far the easiest method. Second, if you're not using PowerPoint, you can still save the supporting aids in a file or as a PowerPoint slide and then display them at the appropriate time in your presentation. Third, you can use the document camera, or doc cam, to display your supporting aid. Prior to the presentation, adjust the focus of the doc cam and make certain you know where to place the supporting aid on the device (speakers often put the visual on the tray upside down or backward). Finally, you can make a poster that incorporates your graphs, charts, illustrations, or photos—these items can be displayed on a tripod or flip chart.

## Step Back and Reflect    Holly the Corporate Trainer (Comedian)

*Read the passage about Holly below, and answer the questions that follow.*

Holly was asked by the executive office to make the company privacy presentation fun. Holly welcomed the opportunity since she had an interest in adult stand-up comedy. As an attention getter, she showed the training classes a YouTube clip of one of her stand-up routines that included profanity and several lesbian jokes. After all, Holly was openly gay at work, and she didn't think anyone would be offended by her humor. The first two training classes loved the session, but several members of the third class were offended and filed complaints with the main office.

### Step Back and Reflect

1. What went wrong?

2. Have you observed a presentation in which the presenter, like Holly, used a video/audio clip, graph, or image in a professional context that included profanity or content that you viewed as offensive?

3. Can a speaker present sensitive information or "R-rated" content and still be professional?

4. Consider a presenter who believes in the right to express him or herself freely. Is it unethical to judge a presenter who is simply trying to make a point?

5. Does a presenter have an ethical responsibility to warn the audience if profanity or adult content will be presented? Why? Why not?

6. How could the KEYS process help in this situation?

### Objects and Models

Other useful supporting aids for increasing both understanding and interest are objects or models. When incorporating objects into your presentation, make certain they are large enough for the entire audience to see. If not, it's better to photograph the object and then incorporate the photo into your PowerPoint presentation. If you want to pass an object around, think twice. Passing things around while you are speaking can be very distracting for listeners and for you.

Objects can also include models that range from scaled-down versions of oil rigs to miniature buildings to enlarged atoms. As with any object, make sure the models are large enough for the entire audience to see. It's important to note that models can include people who help you conduct demonstrations during your presentation (e.g., dance moves, techniques). Volunteers and assistants are discussed in more detail in the following section on demonstrations.

### Demonstrations

There are many professional occasions that will call for you to give a process presentation (also known as a demonstration or how-to presentation). Effective demonstrations should include supporting aids. In fact, demonstrations often incorporate many of the other types of supporting aids noted above. When used correctly, they result in an entertaining, memorable presentation. In contrast, when done incorrectly, they can result in disaster.

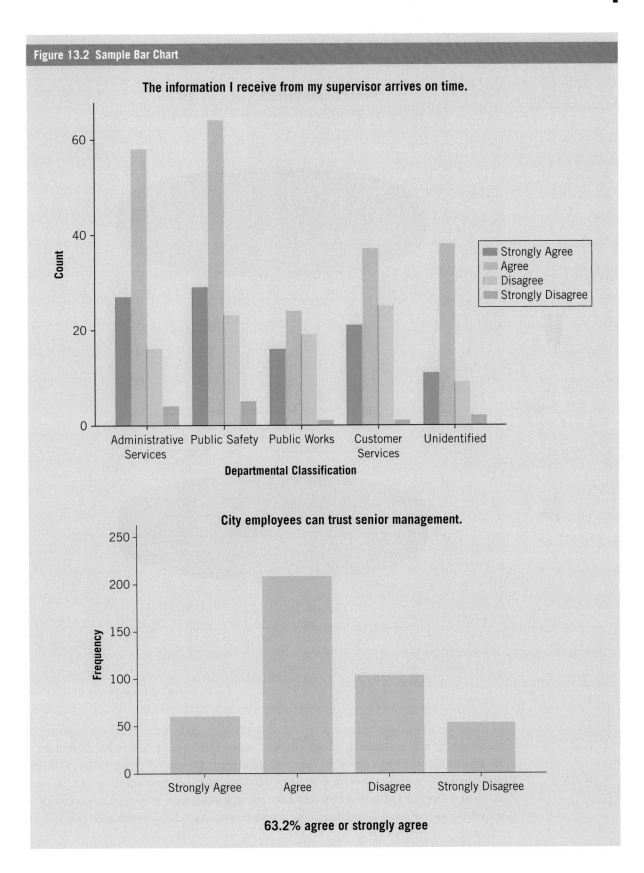

Figure 13.2 Sample Bar Chart

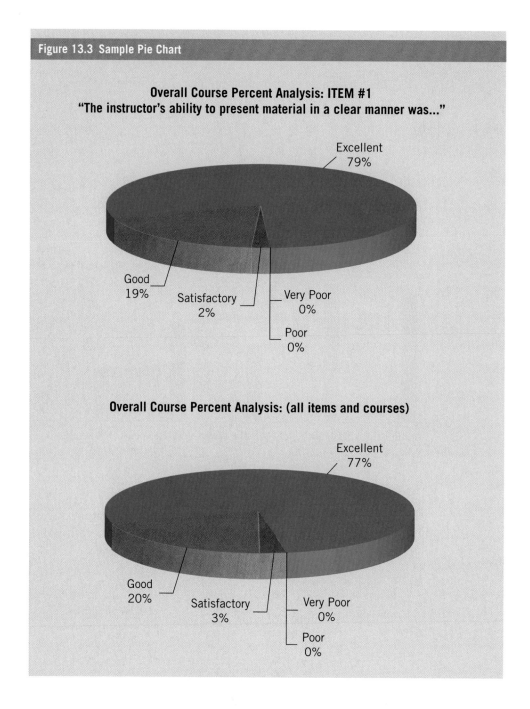

**Figure 13.3 Sample Pie Chart**

**Overall Course Percent Analysis: ITEM #1**
**"The instructor's ability to present material in a clear manner was..."**

Excellent 79%
Good 19%
Satisfactory 2%
Very Poor 0%
Poor 0%

**Overall Course Percent Analysis: (all items and courses)**

Excellent 77%
Good 20%
Satisfactory 3%
Very Poor 0%
Poor 0%

If you plan to use a demonstration, the first step is to determine who should perform the demo. If you're illustrating the steps involved in restraining a violent criminal, it may be difficult for you to perform the demonstration and maintain effective delivery. If the demonstration hinders your eye contact or causes you to become out of breath, use an assistant. Using an assistant is different from using a volunteer. You can't practice with a volunteer, so it's better to use an assistant who can practice the presentation with you in advance.

**Figure 13.4 Sample Illustration for a Presentation Discussing the Thyroid**

**Good example:**

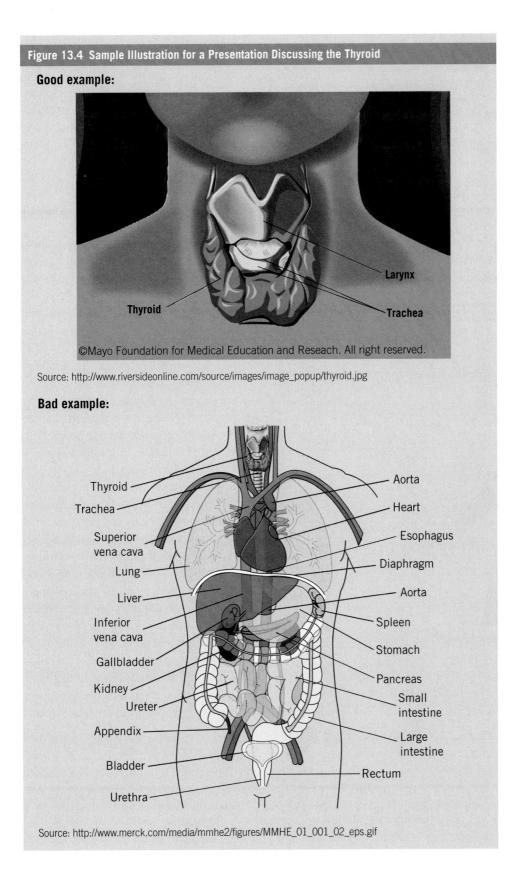

Source: http://www.riversideonline.com/source/images/image_popup/thyroid.jpg

**Bad example:**

Source: http://www.merck.com/media/mmhe2/figures/MMHE_01_001_02_eps.gif

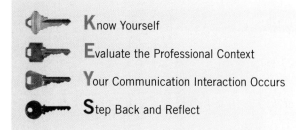

**K**now Yourself

**E**valuate the Professional Context

**Y**our Communication Interaction Occurs

**S**tep Back and Reflect

Remember, when used properly, supporting aids can enhance professional excellence. When used improperly, they can do far more harm than good. Take the time to plan and practice with your supporting aids as you prep for any professional presentation. The KEYS process will help you develop supporting aids with professional excellence.

## Practice Makes Perfect

How do you enter the ranks of excellence? As with any other skill, to excel in presenting, you must practice and hone your technique. Utilize all the information provided in this chapter as you develop your presentation, and then practice.

Flip charts similar to the one shown in this photo are still used in a variety of industries.

There may be times on the job when you have little notice about a speaking opportunity, but most of the time you will have fair warning, which you should use to your advantage.

Once you feel confident in your presentation design, allow others to hear your presentation, request their honest feedback, and listen openly to their comments. When recruiting this practice audience, be selective. Avoid selecting people who are not willing to be critical. You can't improve if all your practice audience says is "good job." An honest practice audience can help you determine if your presentation is effective. Gaining this audience's point of view prior to the presentation is vital. As Keysar and Henley (2002) found, speakers tend to overestimate their effectiveness (determined by whether or not the listener understood the message). Similarly, Campbell, Mothersbaugh, Brammer, and Taylor (2001) found that speakers overestimate the importance of visual aids and underestimate the importance of content and delivery as compared with members of the audience (peers and instructors). Smith and Bainbridge (2006) recommend using a practice audience near in size to your actual audience as a means to increase confidence. If you want to emerge as one of those rare speakers who presents with professional excellence, you must practice.

## Team Presentations

Since many speeches in business and professional settings happen in teams, developing your own skills may not be enough to ensure professional excellence as a public speaker.

## Know Yourself     Quick Guide to Your First Presentation

*The following guide will help you prepare for your presentation. Know the areas in which your speech is strong, and determine the areas that need more work before presenting. Reflect on your assessment before and after you present. This knowledge will help you become a better communicator.*

1. Know your introduction so you can deliver it clearly and passionately.
2. Keep the body of your presentation organized. Writing a clear outline and following it will help you appear credible and stay on task.
3. Be sure to look for a variety of sources to help you inform or persuade your audience.
4. Use transitions to signal changes in thought during your presentation.
5. End the conclusion strong to leave a lasting impression on the audience.
6. Enjoy the presentation experience. Smile when giving your presentation (if it is appropriate for the topic), and your audience will smile back.

Source: Edwards, Edwards, Wahl, and Myers (2013).

Fortunately, the principles for effective individual presentations are the same for group presentations.

Think of the group presentation as one big speech. As such, it should begin like any other effective presentation. For example, it should have a developed introduction, and the introduction should begin with an attention-getting device. The speaker also should establish credibility, relate the topic to the audience, mention the specific purpose for the entire presentation, and preview the main points of the group presentation as a whole.

When it comes to researching and designing the body of the presentation, the group must work together. For a group presentation, having all group members work in conjunction and thoroughly prepare prior to the presentation is vital for success. The key ideas in the presentation should be broken down into main points and discussed in a manner that should be easy to follow. It's important to determine the content, the speaking order, and the amount of time for each speaker. All speakers must work together to avoid significant overlap in content during the presentation. Furthermore, all speakers must work together to guarantee a clearly organized presentation with developed transitions between speakers and their content areas.

When it comes to developing the organization of the presentation, there are several options. The first option is to have one person function as the **organizer**. The organizer will present the introduction, provide the transitions between the other speakers and their content areas, and give the conclusion. In this option, the organizer doesn't give one of the content-area speeches but, rather, remains solely in the organizing role. A second option is to have the organizer give the introduction and the conclusion, while the speakers provide the transitions between each speech. It is perfectly acceptable for each speaker to introduce the next as long as everyone presenting knows how the transitions will work, when they will speak, and generally what they will say prior to the speech. Another option is to have one person give the introduction, each speaker provide the transition into

Poorly designed and delivered presentations are common in the business world. Presentations designed and delivered with professional excellence are much harder to find.

the speaker that follows, and someone else give the conclusion. Regardless of which option your team selects, the entire presentation must have a clearly defined introduction and conclusion with fully developed transitions between speakers.

As each new speaker presents his or her portion of the presentation, he or she must include the components of an effective presentation. Each speaker must have a clear introduction and conclusion. Each speaker must have clear organization. The use of supporting aids must also be handled by the entire group during planning. For example, if PowerPoint is used, all the slides must have the same look, background, and font. They should also be saved as one large file so the audience doesn't have to wait as speakers transition from one PowerPoint presentation to the next.

For the presentation to look professional and polished, both planning and practice must occur as a team. Teams that fail to plan together or don't run through the presentation as a group often stumble and bumble in front of the audience. Team members must also be aware of how they are acting during the entire presentation. Nothing looks worse than a team member who appears distracted or uninterested when the rest of the team is presenting. If you apply everything you've learned about professional excellence to group presentations, you will have all the tools you need for success.

## KEYS to Excellence in Delivering a Speech

In the opening segment of the chapter, we read about Steve Jobs and his success at being one of the greatest public speakers of the 21st century. The skills he used can be tied directly to the KEYS process we have used throughout this text. During the first step, *know yourself*, Jobs had an excellent idea of who he was in relation to his company. He was not only the business head of Apple but, in many ways, the public face of the company as well. He presented himself in a way that spoke not only to consumers but to investors and employees as well. Make sure you know what your role is when delivering a speech.

The next step, *evaluate the professional context*, was also critical to Jobs's success. Jobs knew he was pitching a very advanced piece of technology to a general public that is not always very tech savvy. He tied an expensive piece of technology to everyday life and tailored his speeches so they would appeal to the largest possible number of consumers. He appealed to both the technology buffs and the technology impaired,

## Ethical Connection  Jessica and Shane's Group Presentation Issue

*Please read the passage below, and answer the questions that follow.*

Jessica is a communication student who is working in a group on her class's final presentation. The final project involves a group presentation, with the entire group being graded on the final product. Jessica has discovered that one of her team members, Shane, has been plagiarizing his portion of the project. If Jessica informs her professor, Shane will be kicked out of the class and possibly barred from the university. If the plagiarism is exposed after the group presents, however, Jessica could end up failing the class right before her expected graduation. Shane is close to graduating as well, and Jessica is nervous about getting one of her classmates expelled from school so close to the end of his professional career. However, there are only 2 days left before the project is due, and it is unlikely Shane could completely redo his portion of the paper in that time.

### Questions to Consider

1. What is the ethical issue facing both Jessica and Shane right now?
2. Why is plagiarism in a presentation such a major ethical issue?
3. How would you approach a professor about this issue?
4. Are there any options Jessica could consider that would not involve Shane being removed from the class?

which resulted in widely successful products. Make sure you understand the context of your speech and audience so you can deliver an effective presentation.

During the third step, *your communication interaction occurs*, Jobs was at his finest. He was not just speaking about a product; he was speaking about its potential to change the world. His speeches were not designed simply to persuade people to buy Apple products; they were crafted to inspire people about the possibilities Apple products could create in the future. Whether you are delivering an informative or persuasive speech, your goal should be to keep your audience riveted by your presentation.

The final task, *step back and reflect*, encompasses everything we have discussed about Steve Jobs's success. As we critique his numerous unveilings of Apple products, we see not just what an effective business leader he was but also how great he was at orating. As you reflect on your own speeches, ask yourself if you moved your audience to action; in a business environment, ask if your speech demonstrated professional excellence and motivated the people around you to take action.

Designing a team presentation can be a difficult task. Communicate your expectations up front and try to establish a team vision and overall presentation goal.

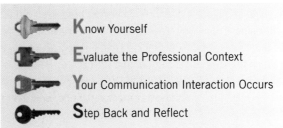

**K**now Yourself

**E**valuate the Professional Context

**Y**our Communication Interaction Occurs

**S**tep Back and Reflect

# Your Communication Interaction    Team Presentation

*Read the passage below, and then answer the questions. As you read, think about ways the KEYS approach could help you improve* **your communication interaction***.*

**Roxanne Huerta:** Holistic Health: Proactively taking care of the whole <u>person</u>. That is our mission. That is what we do for our <u>patients</u>, because Holistic Health is an organization that is dedicated to living out its mission. But let's look at those words again. It does not say "the whole patient"; it says "the whole person." What's the difference? [Dramatic pause] Our mission extends to everyone who walks through our doors, which includes more than our patients. It includes you, our employees.

Good morning, ladies and gentlemen, and welcome to the first day of your healthier life. My name is Roxanne Huerta, and I have worked for Holistic Health for the past 25 years, serving as a human resources executive for the past 9 years. It was in my role as an HR exec to learn about a holistic corporate wellness program, aimed not at patients but at employees. We have tested this program in our California offices, and the results were amazing. So today, I would like to introduce you to our new corporate wellness program. This program is divided into three areas: nutritional, physical, and spiritual. And I have with me today the individuals who will be heading each of these areas. They will be discussing with you the importance of each area to your life, as well as previewing the various tools and resources that will be available to you as part of this program. So without further ado, let me introduce Nicole Boswell, our nutritional expert.

**Nicole Boswell:** Two little words. Two little words are destroying the health of our nation. Two little words jolt us full of energy but then leave us drained and depleted. Two little words make us fat but leave us nutritionally starved. What are these two little words? *Processed foods.*

Sure, we all know that processed food is bad for us, but the temptation to eat it is very powerful. Look around our work environment. In our cafeteria, we served french fries and fish sticks yesterday—two highly processed foods. For snacks, we have vending machines full of processed junk. But not anymore.

Good morning, everyone. My name is Nicole Boswell, and I have worked as a licensed dietician at Holistic Health for 7 years. And I am here to let you know that nutritious can be delicious. But beyond that, it can be just as quick and inexpensive as processed food.

Look at Margaret over there. She is doubting me. Well, Margaret, I don't blame you for doubting me, because most of us lack the tools needed to make delicious, quick, and inexpensive food that is good for us. So over the next 6 months, as part of this wellness program, we are going to do two things.

First, we are going to change all the food served in the cafeteria to meet the criteria of delicious, quick, inexpensive, and nutritious. We are also going to provide you with a shopping list, a cost breakdown, and the recipes for the dishes we serve. We will also be offering cooking classes twice a month to help you further. That way, you can have a healthy meal at work and then make that healthy meal at home. In addition, we will be restocking our vending machines with healthy snacks.

The second thing we are going to do is provide one-on-one nutritional consulting for free to anyone who is interested. We will go over your current diet and lifestyle and help you reach the health goals you set for yourself. The consultations happen during your work day, so you do not have to take time out of your personal life. They are free, they are confidential, and they will be designed to fit you and your life.

So today, I have given you a brief overview of the nutritional part of this program. I look forward to eating nutritional, delicious lunches with you in the cafeteria and talking with you one-on-one during our nutritional consulting sessions. We are going to replace those two little words, *processed foods*, with two very different words, *delicious* and *nutritious*.

**Roxanne:** Thank you, Nicole, for that overview of nutrition. I am going to sign up for my consultation as soon as our presentation is over. Now that we have learned about the nutritional component of this wellness program, let's turn our attention to the physical component. Coach Amy Peoples is here to tell us more.

**Amy Peoples:** [Blows a whistle] Drop and give me 20! Just kidding. Hello, folks. My name is Amy Peoples, and for the past 17 years I have worked as a personal trainer and a fitness coach. In this role, I have learned that most people have a "drop and give me 20" image in their heads when it comes to exercise. They see exercise as work, not as play. The good news is that with this wellness program, we are going to change that image. You are going to learn to reconnect with that kid inside yourself and have some fun by joining the Fun Fit Program. Let me give you an overview.

Here at Holistic Health, we have a state-of-the-art workout facility that you could not use—until now, that is. Starting today, all employees will be able to use our facilities free of charge. In addition, we will be sponsoring a host of fun activities that you can sign up for free of charge. For example, we are going to start an intramural kickball league. We are going to offer beginning dance lessons in ballet, tap, ballroom, and hip-hop. Every day we have a class called "Recess," in which you can take part in a variety of games and activities you loved as a kid. We will be sponsoring a walking club with a host of rewards you can earn. In addition, we have money set aside for activities that you all request. If you want yoga, fencing, or karate, we can do it. The goal is to get you moving while you are having fun.

The best part is that you can do this for 30 minutes every day on company time. Yes, you heard me right, play and get paid. It kind of makes you a professional athlete, right?!

In closing, I just want to reiterate that exercise should be fun, it can be fun, and it will be fun. All you have to do is sign up for something that interests you. Life is too short to miss out on the fun.

**Roxanne:** Thank you, Amy, for informing us about the physical activity and fun that is now available to us. Now I would like to ask our final speaker, Dr. Don Colbert, to talk to us about the spiritual component of this wellness program.

**Don Colbert:** According to Willa Cather, "Happiness is to be dissolved into something completely great." Here at Holistic Health, we have no intention of defining what spirituality means to you. Instead, what we want to do is help you find the time to dissolve into something completely great as a way to feed your spirit. My name is Don Colbert, and I am the founder of Holistic Health. For the past 30 years, I have worked as both a medical doctor and the president of this company. My life is full of abundance and blessings, but nothing has ever made me feel more rewarded than serving others. I love this wellness program for many, many reasons. Like our organization, it is dedicated to holistic health. But the thing that really sold me on this program over others is the spiritual component that centers on serving others. I would like to explain that component to you.

Starting today, you will each be allotted 1 hour per week to volunteer at the organization of your choice. This hour will be part of your 40 work hours, and you will be paid for this hour. The organization you volunteer for is up to you. You can volunteer at your child's school, the local food bank, your church, a nursing home, or the animal shelter. It is completely your choice. All we ask is that you select a location or a cause that is meaningful to you. Select something that you find completely great, a cause into which you can dissolve and find happiness.

By implementing this wellness program, I am hoping to make a difference in your life by allowing you time to make a difference in the lives of others. As Harriet Naylor said, "Volunteering can be an exciting, growing, enjoyable experience. It is truly gratifying to serve a cause, practice your ideals, work with people, solve problems, see benefits, and know you had a hand in them."

**Roxanne:** Thank you, Dr. Colbert. Well today, ladies and gentlemen, you were introduced to our new corporate wellness program. You have been given an overview of each of its components—namely, nutritional, physical, and spiritual. All the speakers will be available to answer additional questions following this presentation, and we hope you have a lot of questions, because we hope you all plan to take part in this program. Holistic Health is not just a name on the door; it is a way of life, for our patients and now for each of us.

## Questions to Consider

1. How are the individual speeches linked to form a cohesive unit? Do the speakers present a unified voice? Why or why not?

2. How are the introductions and conclusions handled in each speech and for the overall team presentation?

3. How does the team incorporate transitions?

## Executive Summary

Now that you have finished reading this chapter, you can do the following:

Recognize the positive benefits of the adrenaline rush that comes from speaking in public:

- When you get up to deliver a presentation, your body will have an *adrenaline rush*. The delivery of the presentation requires you to put yourself "out there" in front of an audience, and in the deep recesses of your mind, your body is signaling, "Danger, danger" (p. 312).
- As you practice public speaking, you will learn what responses to expect when you have an adrenaline rush—they will no longer be an unknown. Then you can learn how to handle each response. In the end, you'll be able to use the adrenaline to your advantage by presenting with energy and passion (p. 312).

Deliver an extemporaneous speech with professional excellence:

- Develop an extemporaneous speaking style and learn that being boxed into a corner behind the computer can increase your nervousness (p. 313).
- Each time your communication interaction occurs, try to improve by taking the time to step back and reflect on how effectively you are communicating with your audience (p. 315).

Understand how to use supporting aids effectively:

- When a *supporting aid* is displayed, the audience will split their attention between you and the aid, which can help reduce some of your anxiety. In addition, supporting aids provide another layer to your presentations that can enhance interest (p. 316).
- A well-designed supporting aid also helps the audience by increasing understanding, enhancing retention, and facilitating listening (p. 317).
- For audience members who are visual learners, seeing key points, demonstrations, or other supporting materials is essential for their understanding. In addition, every time you repeat your message, you increase retention (p. 317).

Present an effective team presentation:

- Think of the group presentation as one big speech. As such, it should begin like any other effective presentation (p. 327).
- When it comes to researching and designing the body of the presentation, the group must work together. For a group presentation, having all group members work in conjunction and thoroughly prepare prior to the presentation is vital for success (p. 327).
- As each new speaker presents his or her portion of the presentation, he or she must include the components of an effective presentation. Each speaker must have a clear introduction and conclusion. Each speaker must have clear organization. The use of supporting aids must also be handled by the entire group during planning (p. 328).
- For the presentation to look professional and polished, both planning and practice must occur as a team. Teams that fail to plan together or don't run through the presentation as a group often stumble and bumble in front of the audience (p. 328).

Use the KEYS process to develop professional excellence when delivering a speech:

- *Know yourself.* Make sure you know what your role is when delivering a speech (p. 328).
- *Evaluate the professional context.* Make sure you understand the context of your speech and audience so you can deliver an effective speech (p. 329).
- *Your communication interaction occurs.* Whether you are delivering an informative or persuasive speech, your goal should be to keep your audience riveted by your presentation (p. 329).
- *Step back and reflect.* As you reflect on your own speeches, ask yourself if you moved your audience to action; in a business environment, ask if your speech demonstrated professional excellence and motivated the people around you to take action (p. 329).

**Discussion Questions**

1. Have you ever seen a speaker reading a speech? What was your impression of that speaker? How did you feel as an audience member?

2. When a professor presents a PowerPoint slide that is loaded with text, how do you, as a listener, respond?

3. Think about the speeches you have given in the past. How much time did you spend practicing the speech? Do you think it was an adequate amount of time? Why or why not?

4. Have you ever given a team presentation? Did the team members develop their presentations as a team or as individuals? Was your overall presentation cohesive?

5. How do you respond to the adrenaline rush that accompanies your public speaking? What can you do to overcome or deal with these responses?

**Terms to Remember**

adrenaline rush (p. 312)
conversational quality (p. 315)
delivery (p. 312)
eye contact (p. 314)
manuscript (p. 315)

monotone (p. 315)
organizer (p. 327)
PowerPoint presentations (p. 319)
retention (p. 318)
speaking outline (p. 319)

speaking rate (p. 314)
supporting aids (p. 317)
visual learners (p. 318)
vocal fillers (p. 314)
volume (p. 314)

Visit the Student Study Site at **www.sagepub.com/keys2e** to access the following resources:

- SAGE journal articles
- Video links
- Web resources

- Web quizzes
- eflashcards

Part V

# Surviving in
the Workplace

Chapter 14:   Résumés, Interviews, and
Negotiation

## Chapter Outline

The Importance of Work–Life Balance    338

Triggers to Imbalance    343

Strategies for Balance    358

KEYS to Excellence With Work–Life
    Balance    368

Executive Summary    370

Discussion Questions    371

Terms to Remember    371

## Chapter Objectives

After studying this chapter, you should be able to:

1. Understand the impact of work–life balance on professional excellence

2. Define work–life balance

3. Discuss the individual and organizational benefits of work–life balance

4. Identify the triggers to imbalance

5. Develop strategies for achieving work–life balance

6. Utilize the KEYS approach to achieve professional excellence regarding work–life balance

# chapter 14

# Work–Life Balance

**Mary Claire Orenic describes herself as one of the happiest women in America, which she attributes to the work–life balance she has achieved.** At 50 years old, Orenic is a senior manager at a global company. She states that although she might put in 45 to 60 hours at her job during the week, she finds time to unwind at the beach on weekends. Orenic also finds other ways to maintain a healthy balance in her life. She tries to work at least two times a week from home and keeps a flexible schedule at her office so she does not find herself commuting in heavy traffic during the workweek. "To drive an hour, sit in an office and do conference calls and email and drive home for another hour, I've lost two hours of productivity," she said (Francis, 2011). Orenic also reported being able to work out arrangements with her CEO to allow time for important family events. By being able to work consistently but still be flexible for private matters, Orenic describes her life as being both satisfying and enjoyable.

In an era of poor economy and increasing workload demands, achieving a healthy work–life balance can be difficult but not impossible. It is important to find a good work–life balance not only for your health but also for your job satisfaction and productivity. Also, with the emergence of new technology, it is possible to take your work away from the office more often now than ever before. Being able to accomplish important tasks away from the office can offer people more time to be with their family and friends. However, if your work requires you to be in a certain place at a given time, good time-management skills can help in cutting down the amount of time you need to spend in the office. The benefits for both yourself and the organization cannot be overstated.

Balancing work and life through communication is an excellent way to better yourself as a member of the professional field and increase your overall job satisfaction. Although a heavy workload can seem daunting, allowing yourself some personal time can mean the difference between doing your work effectively and stressing yourself out to the point of poor performance. In this chapter, you will learn the importance of work–life balance as well as strategies you can use in managing your schedule.

You may have asked yourself, "How do I balance my workload between school, work, and family?" "How can I find the time to meet up with my friends this week?" or "I have an exam in 2 days, but I'm working late tonight and tomorrow night—so when can I squeeze in time to study?" We have some bad news: The same imbalance that many of you are experiencing as you take this course will continue to challenge you as you transition into your career as a professional. The good news is that part of developing professional excellence includes developing strategies for achieving work–life balance.

# The Importance of Work–Life Balance

In previous chapters, we applied the KEYS process to a variety of important aspects of business and professional communication. The topic areas of the text focus on beginning communication principles for *entering the workplace, developing in the workplace,* and *excelling in the workplace.* Welcome to *survival.* This chapter focuses on the importance of work–life balance, the triggers that cause imbalance, as well as the role of corporate health and wellness. Our goal, then, is to invite you to think about things that are important to people beyond work.

Take a moment to reflect on the most important people in your life (we emphasize people, *not* materials or money). You're likely thinking of your family, parents, siblings, spouse, girlfriend, boyfriend, friends, and partners. Now, think about your job getting in the way of your personal relationships and family. What if you didn't have time to spend with your daughter on her birthday because you had to work? What if you felt as though you couldn't take off work, even for one day, because there was simply too much to do? How would you feel if your work life completely dominated your personal life? Many of you have no doubt heard other people say the following: "My job really stinks," "I don't have a life," "All I do is work," or "I'm so behind at work, and the e-mail keeps coming in." Let's face it, sometimes our inbox is simply too full. On top of our world of work, we have bills to pay, sick pets to care for, kids to feed, games to watch, and people to love. Combine the intensity of your personal life with the intensity of work life, and you have one big vacuum draining your energy away! We're not attempting to paint a completely dark picture of your professional life, nor do we want to discourage you from focusing on or developing your career. Instead, our goal is to encourage you to know yourself and to think about the challenges people across industries encounter. Further, be aware of challenges such as stress, burnout, information overload, and difficult clients, which can hinder communication.

Achieving work–life balance is important for the following reasons: (1) Imbalance between your work life and personal life can negatively influence the way you communicate, (2) work–life balance fosters meaningful and successful relationships at home and at work, and (3) work–life balance is necessary to sustain professional excellence. The KEYS process is central to connecting work–life balance with professional excellence, helping you *survive in the workplace*.

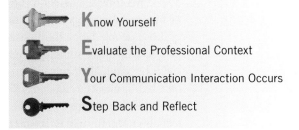

**K**now Yourself

**E**valuate the Professional Context

**Y**our Communication Interaction Occurs

**S**tep Back and Reflect

## Work–Life Balance Defined

Scholars sometimes refer to work–life balance as work–family balance. *Life* is a more general reference to the self outside of work, while *family* refers to a collective group of people (e.g., spouses, children, partners) with whom the professional resides outside of work. We approach the topic of work–life balance by comparing the time people are at the job or completing job-related tasks (work) with the time that people are not working (life).

For many, personal life is connected to family, while others think of it as private experience, leisure time, or downtime separate from work. The line or division between work and life is referred to as a **boundary.** Put simply, there's a boundary or line between work and personal/family time. The assumption is that if professionals have a boundary between work and personal life, then **balance** is the result. However, communication scholar Erika Kirby and her colleagues (Kirby, Golden, Medved, Jorgenson, & Buzzanell, 2003) explain that the problem of "boundaries" in work–life management stems from the concept that there are "separate spheres." This distinction assumes the presence of two different spaces of experience and action (Ba', 2011; Bailyn, 1993; Buzzanell, 1994; Medved & Kirby, 2005; Mumby & Putnam, 1992). But in reality, our lives can't be neatly divided into two parts.

For example, your sick child does not suddenly recover between the hours of 9 and 5 so you can go to work with no concerns about your family. Nor does your family say, "Don't worry about spending the holidays with us; we know Christmas is your busiest season at work. We don't really care if we see you." This boundary metaphor has an additional shortcoming. It tends to favor the organization, placing work first and in the position of "managing" employees' personal lives (Ferguson, Carlson, Zivnuska, & Whitten, 2012; Kirby & Harter, 2001).

To get more of a handle on this interesting topic, let's begin with some definitions. The definition of **family** is highly complex and controversial (Coontz, 2000; Glavin & Schieman, 2012; Wahl, McBride, & Schrodt,

Giving attention to both work and personal life can be challenging for professionals, regardless of industry.

2005). We consider family to be all people in a household, which consists of a minimum of two members related by blood, adoption, marriage, civil union, or partnership—one of those people being the householder, who owns or rents the residence. Family is about people who share something relationally, mentally, physically, psychologically, economically, or spiritually with one another. Families are arranged in various structures (e.g., blended or intact), characteristics (e.g., healthy or dysfunctional), and systems (e.g., open or closed) across the family life cycle (e.g., married with no children, married with three teenagers; Braithwaite & Baxter, 2006). Indeed, families are diverse across populations.

**Work** is defined as an "instrument of activity intended to provide goods and services to support life" (Edwards & Rothbard, 2000, p. 179). Further, as Edwards and Rothbard explain, "work typically entails members in a market or employing organization that compensates the worker for his or her contributions" (p. 179). But for most of us, work is more than merely a means to receive compensation. Work plays an important role in our lives, significantly impacting self-concept and well-being (Martin, 2012; Morris & Madsen, 2007; Schor, 1998).

Another term important to this discussion is **community**—a geographic space identified as a place to work toward a good life (e.g., health, safety, well-being). The term *community* has a number of historical uses—for example, developing a place with boundaries that identifies a neighborhood and thus marks who lives inside and who lives outside, or more ideologically, a coming together in social communion (Bellah, Madsen, Sullivan, Swidler, & Tipton, 1985; Young & Schieman, 2012).

The most common notion seems to be that communities are identified as groups of interdependent people who discuss actions and share practices and have a concern for the common good. As many of you make decisions about where to live and work, the term *community* helps you understand life and leisure outside of work. In order to attract the best candidates, companies often talk up the community where the company is located. For example, "Most of our employees live in The Woodlands—it's just a short commute from Houston with some nice housing options, great shopping, and excellent schools." The term *community* is also informative to ethnic minorities, people with disabilities, and lesbian and gay working professionals. Indeed, people want to work and live in communities where they feel safe and included.

While this topic is inconsistently defined despite vast scholarly inquiry (Drago, 2007; Glavin & Schieman, 2012), **work–life balance** is the "accomplishment of role-related expectations that are negotiated and shared between an individual and his or her role-related partners in the work and family [life] domains" (Grzywacz & Carlson, 2007, p. 458). Now that you have a better understanding of the important terms included in the work–life balance topic, let's take a look at why this is important for you as a professional and for the organization.

Why do you need to understand work–life balance? If you are like the vast majority of American workers, you will struggle to find a functional, productive balance between your work and your life. Let's look at some facts. First of all, a majority of couples with children under the age of 18 are both employed (a number that has continued to grow), 35% of workers provide care for aging parents (the number of professionals providing eldercare to loved ones will continue to grow), and a majority of working professionals in the United States report difficulty balancing work and family life (Drago, 2007; Glavin & Schieman, 2012). Research also suggests that the absence of work–life balance, usually defined in terms of increased family conflict, may be detrimental to personal health and organizational performance (Byrne, 2005; Glavin & Schieman, 2012; Grzywacz & Carlson, 2007). Put simply, work–life balance impacts individual lives *and* the whole organization.

What happens when working professionals feel a sense of balance between their work and personal lives? Does the organization benefit? In fact, indicators of balance have been connected with better employee commitment, job satisfaction, and professional engagement (Allen, Herst, Bruck, & Sutton, 2000; Yuille, Change, Gudmundsson, & Sawang, 2012). On the other hand, when balance is missing, employees are more prone to quit, abuse sick leave, and perform poorly on the job. As a result, work–life balance is at the core of good business practices today, leading organizations to develop a culture that supports the balance of work and individual life (Drago, 2007; Grzywacz & Carlson, 2007; Vidal, Leiva, & Navarro, 2012). Let's take a more detailed look at the individual benefits and then the organizational benefits of work–life balance.

## Individual Benefits

What's in it for you? What are the individual benefits of striving for and achieving this balance? If you fail to develop strategies for achieving balance, work time will attempt to colonize your personal time, leaving you with feelings of imbalance, stress, and burnout (Cameron, 2011; Deetz, 1992; Kirby et al., 2003; Rapoport & Bailyn, 1996; Schor, 1992, 1998;). **Burnout**—chronic exhaustion from persistent workload, decreased motivation, and apathy toward work—has a number of causes (Leiter, Day, Harvie, & Shaughnessy, 2007; Morales, Piero, Rodriguez, & Bliese, 2012). As a professional striving for balance, be aware of the causes of burnout:

- Doing the same type of work with little variation, especially if this work seems meaningless
- Giving a great deal personally and not getting back much in the way of appreciation or other positive responses
- Lacking a sense of accomplishment and meaning in your work
- Being under constant and strong pressure to produce, perform, and meet deadlines— many of which may be unrealistic
- Working with difficult people
- Conflict and tension among staff, an absence of support from colleagues, and an abundance of criticism
- Lack of trust between supervisors and associates, creating conflict rather than team-work toward commonly valued goals
- Not having opportunities for personal expression or for taking initiative in trying new approaches; a situation in which experimentation, change, and innovations not only are not valued but are actively discouraged
- Having unrealistic demands on your time and energy
- Having jobs that are both personally and unprofessionally taxing without much opportunity for supervision, continued education, or other forms of training
- Unresolved personal conflicts beyond the job situation, such as marital tensions, chronic health problems, or financial problems

Stress and burnout impact your mood and attitude at work and at home.

When individuals in any given industry have a sense of work–life balance or feel that their organization at least takes interest in their personal life outside of work, some of the major problems for individuals, such as burnout, can be prevented (Leiter et al., 2007; Snyder, 2012).

Many professionals, including many top business executives, report that finding the right balance between work and personal life is difficult (Golden & Geisler, 2007; Snyder, 2012). In cases where there is a balance, however, a number of individual benefits result (see Table 14.1).

## Organizational Benefits

What's in it for the organization? What are the organizational benefits of having a balanced workforce? Many organizational leaders and human resource professionals are striving to change their work culture by implementing training programs to motivate their workforce and make them feel happy so they'll continue to produce and perform (Morris & Madsen, 2007; Tews, Michel, & Bartlett, 2012). Work–life balance is challenging for organizations due to mergers, downsizing, changes in government regulations/policies, the complex nature of work and family roles, the expansion and use of technology, the increase in dual-income marriages, the increased number of women entering the workforce, and increases in job-related stress and its impact on employee health and wellness (McDonald & Hite, 2008; Tews, Michel, & Bartlett, 2012). As a result of these challenges, many organizations today have a problem with **employee retention**—getting employees to continue working for the same company. Due to **employee attrition**—the loss or

---

**Table 14.1  Individual Benefits of Work–Life Balance**

Employees are happier at work and at home when they

- have greater control of their working lives;
- have the time to focus more on life outside of work;
- don't bring problems from home to work and vice versa;
- are shown loyalty and commitment;
- have improved self-esteem, health, concentration, and confidence;
- have better relations with management;
- feel a greater responsibility and sense of ownership.

Source: Byrne (2005).

turnover of employees to other jobs and industries perceived as having healthier workplace cultures (e.g., employee focused, best places to work)—organizations are focused on the satisfaction of their workforces as much as on the customers and clients they serve, and work–life balance is at the core of this effort (Dex & Bond, 2005; Drago, 2007; Tews, Michel, & Bartlett, 2012). For organizations that foster employee work–life balance, there are a number of benefits (see Table 14.2).

---

**Table 14.2 Organizational Benefits of Work–Life Balance**

For employers, having a more motivated, productive, and less stressed workforce results in

- maximized available labor;
- reduced costs;
- retaining valued employees;
- the reputation of being an employer of choice;
- reduced absenteeism;
- increased productivity;
- attracting a wider range of candidates, such as older, part-time workers; and
- making employees feel valued.

Source: Byrne (2005).

---

# Triggers to Imbalance

What factors contribute to imbalance between work and life? What experiences do professionals have that promote imbalance? We define **imbalance triggers** as experiences (e.g., conflict, aggression, overload, negativity) that cause professionals to feel drained, used, abused, and unhappy. In the sections that follow, we describe the following imbalance triggers: personality types, difficult people in the workplace, technologically blurred lines, and life demands.

## Personality Types

Above, we defined imbalance triggers as experiences. So are we saying that personality type is an experience? No, of course we aren't. However, your personality type can lend itself to many of the experiences that cause imbalance. The categorization of personality types is extensive and varies with insights ranging from Jung to Myers-Briggs. For our purposes, let's keep it simple and focus on the two classic personality types: Type A and Type B.

According to Friedman and Rosenman (1974), who studied the relationship between personality type and heart disease, if you have a Type A personality, you are highly competitive, are often seen as driven, are focused on time and deadlines, can be aggressive,

# Know Yourself    Work Time and Personal Time

A great place to begin striving for balance is by taking an inventory of your work time related to your personal time. While some of the items in the table below refer to work specifically, you should also think about your work as a college student and how you balance your time studying and attending classes with your personal/family life. Just because you're a college student, it doesn't mean you're not working. For those of you who have jobs and attend school, think of them both as work. Take the following quiz to check your level of work–life balance.

*Directions: Beside each statement, place either* A *for "Agree,"* B *for "Sometimes," or* C *for "Disagree" as it relates to your experience.*

_C_ 1. At the moment, because the job demands it, I usually work long hours.
_B_ 2. There isn't much time to socialize/relax with my partner/family in the week.
_C_ 3. I have to take work home most evenings.
_A_ 4. I often work late or on weekends to deal with paperwork without interruptions.
_B_ 5. Relaxing and forgetting about work issues is hard to do.
_B_ 6. I worry about the effect of work stress on my health.
_C_ 7. My relationship with my partner is suffering because of the pressure or long hours of my work.
_A_ 8. My family is missing out on my input, either because I don't see enough of them or because I am too tired.
_B_ 9. Finding time for hobbies, leisure activities, or to maintain friendships and extended family relationships is difficult.
_A_ 10. I would like to reduce my working hours and stress levels but feel I have no control over the current situation.

5B
3A
2C

| Results: | |
|---|---|
| If you checked all or mostly As | You may already be under considerable stress from your lack of work–life balance. Over time, your productivity could suffer, along with relationships, your health, and long-term employability. As an individual, start to address your own needs so you become more effective. At work, try to promote better work–life balance to the advantage of the whole workplace. |
| If you checked all or mostly Bs | You are not entirely happy with your work–life balance but in a good position not to let the situation get out of control. By encouraging your organization to adopt a work–life strategy, you can help create an enhanced working environment that will benefit you, the organization, and colleagues at all levels. |
| If you checked all or mostly Cs | You have set your own priorities in work–life balance, making them work for you. As well as the benefits to you and your family, your organization is getting more from you. Show leadership by encouraging a culture that respects work–life balance for all and takes into account the fact that individuals have differing demands at various stages of the life cycle. When people have a sense of control over their work–life balance, they can be more productive and committed to their work and better prepared to manage the demands of today's rapidly changing workplace. |

How did you do? For true professional excellence, you should strive for mostly Cs. Take some time to explore your sources of imbalance, stress, and burnout.

If you did mark some As, what can you do to eliminate the imbalance in the future?

Source: Daniels and McCarraher (2000).

and find it difficult to relax. Type As can be described as high-achieving, workaholic stress junkies (Evans, Becker, Zahn, Keesee, & Bilotta, 2012; Friedman, 1996). On the other hand, if you're a Type B individual, you are laid-back, easygoing, and don't find it difficult to relax. There are still other individuals, known as Type AB, who are a mix of the two personality types.

Given these definitions, it's not surprising that Type A individuals struggle to find balance between work and life. After all, to maintain the competitive edge and be high-achieving in a world full of people who breathe, eat, and sleep work, you must forget about balance and tip the scale in favor of work, right? Fortunately, this is not the case. As we will discuss in the "Life Demands" section of this chapter, Type As also benefit from work–life balance. Put simply, if you're a Type A personality, you must recognize that you'll have a tendency to live your life out of balance. This does not mean there's something wrong with you. There's nothing wrong with your personality. In fact, most great leaders demonstrate Type A personalities. The workplace and the world need high-achieving individuals—you just need to remember the old proverb, with a 21st century update: "All work and no play makes Jack a dull, stressed, unhappy, and unhealthy boy—and the same applies to Jill." Therefore, you must actively follow the strategies we outline later in this chapter to help avoid living the life of a workaholic stress junkie and to allow yourself to live life with professional excellence.

Competition and high performance demands exist in most professions.

As for you Type Bs, don't think you're safe from imbalance. The Type B trait can lend itself to experiences such as procrastination, which can result in as much imbalance as being a workaholic. The Type A stays at work late because she wants to get ahead or make the report perfect. The Type B stays at work late because he didn't pay attention to deadlines and now he has a project that is far from complete and due in the morning. Either way, both people will be at work late experiencing stress, and neither one has good work–life balance.

## The Impact of Difficult People on Work–Life Balance

Personality type can also impact the way you deal with difficult people in the workplace. For example, the Type A employee may end up doing all the work of departmental slackers because he cannot stand to wait until the last minute. The Type B leader's laid-back personality may cause him to allow a slacker to get away with doing next to nothing, which he and the rest of the team then have to make up for. Either way, failing to address these difficult people creates more work for leaders and functional employees. The resulting workload imbalance can bleed into one's nonwork time. In Chapter 10, we discussed difficult people as related to leadership and building a team. Because this is such an important and common issue in the workplace, we would like to reexamine it as it relates to work–life balance. To do this, we will focus on three specific situations involving difficult people: angry customers and clients, workplace bullying, and workplace mobbing.

### Angry Customers and Clients

As we established in Chapter 6, communicating effectively with customers, clients, or potential business contacts is essential in professional contexts. All organizations have customers or clients, and you must excel in communicating with these individuals. At the same time, customers or clients who expect and demand excellent service can sometimes cross the line by acting rude and uncivil. As the popular phrase goes, "The customer is always right." Do you think this is always true? What about customers who disrespect working professionals in every situation? Working as communication consultants, we have heard professionals across industries tell stories about angry customers and clients. These stories are usually filled with questions about what to do and how to act in these hostile situations. What can professionals do when customers totally lose control? How do you know when the line has been crossed? Indeed, customer service can be extremely difficult where listening, conflict management, and problem-solving skills are ineffective.

Most of the research in this area has focused on how employee communication skills (e.g., politeness, smiling, positive attitude, eye contact) can optimize customer satisfaction (Avey, Wernsing, & Luthans, 2008; Evanschitzky, Sharma, & Prykop, 2012; Pugh, 2001). In addition to performance demands for communication excellence, employees have to help the organization recover from service and product failure, respond to customer complaints, apologize for mistakes, and the like. The emotional and psychological demands, especially when dealing with angry customer outbursts, have a negative impact on employees. Thus, dealing with angry customers can serve as an imbalance trigger, leading to staff absenteeism, lack of commitment, burnout, stress, and turnover (Dallimore, Sparks, & Butcher, 2007; Morales et al., 2012). Not only are employees negatively impacted, but organizations face decreased customer satisfaction, product quality, and profit.

How can organizations address the negative impact of difficult customers on employees? Managers should consider employee development opportunities (e.g., corporate wellness programs, training activities) to help manage the risk (Dallimore et al., 2007; Kelly, Allender, & Calquhoun, 2007; Ritchie, 2012). Now that we've considered the challenges of customer service demands, let's take a look at some sources of imbalance from your fellow employees and coworkers.

### Workplace Bullying

Bullying at work can have both a direct and indirect influence on organizational productivity, as well as a direct impact on your work–life balance. While the notion of bullying in the workplace might sound a bit dramatic, if you encounter a bully in the future (if you haven't already), you'll know what hit you! In fact, bullying in the workplace takes place more than you might think—the frequency and form of bullying in "professional" environments is alarming and often goes unreported or unnoticed or is swept under the rug (Harvey et al., 2007; Harvey, Heames, Richey, & Leopard, 2006). Further, bullying is more devastating and stressful than all other sources of work-related stress combined. **Workplace bullying** is defined as repeated acts and practices that are directed intentionally or unconsciously and that cause embarrassment, humiliation, and stress. Bullying negatively influences job performance, causes an unhealthy work environment, and leads employees to spend their time away from work trying to figure out how to survive or cope with the abuse at work (Harvey et al., 2006, 2007; Sandvik & Tracy, 2012).

What does workplace bullying look like? How can you better understand the types of bullying behavior? Let's take a look at the following seven categories provided by workplace bullying experts (Harvey et al., 2006):

1. "Calling out" a target in public for being different or because he or she is not part of the "in group"

2. Using people as scapegoats to draw attention to the victims or to reduce attention on the bully for a failure of the group; the scapegoat's status seems to face more of a threat than the bully's

3. Someone with more power or a higher position in the organization sexually harassing coworkers

4. Increasing workload and pressure to perform with unrealistic deadlines and the like (i.e., "Get this project done in 2 weeks or you're fired")

5. Targeting an individual, preventing access to opportunities, withholding information, or physically/socially isolating an individual

6. Failing to give credit to individuals who deserve recognition, setting workers up to fail, and overemphasizing failures

7. Inflicting physical abuse on or causing harm to the targeted individual or group

To fully understand the negative impact that bullying has in the workplace and to place this topic in the context of the modern organization, take a look at the workplace bullying facts in Table 14.3.

Indeed, workplace bullying can be a real problem for individual employees and for the organization.

What kind of negative impact does workplace bullying have on employees and the organization? First, workplace bullies can have a huge impact on the day-to-day, task-oriented performance of employees. Factors such as employee motivation, attitude about work, and focus on completing tasks are destroyed by the bully (A. Khan & R. Khan, 2012; Tracy, Lutgen-Sandvik, & Alberts,

Bullying and incivility at work can cause stress and burnout for anyone. How would you handle a bully at work?

### Table 14.3 Workplace Bullying Facts

- Female bullies target other women 84% of the time; male bullies target women 69% of the time.
- Bullies are bosses 81% of the time.
- Bullying is a health hazard to the victim, with 41% of the victims diagnosed with depression and more than 80% reporting that effects of bullying prevent them from being productive at work.
- Support for the victim was not forthcoming from coworkers, superiors, or from human resources personnel.
- Less than 10% of bullies were punished, transferred, or terminated.
- The prognosis for the bullied individual was the opposite of that of the bully in that 82% lost their jobs—44% involuntarily and 38% voluntarily.
- Most victims (94%) suffer from severe anxiety and from obsession over the bully's motives and tactics.
- On a regular basis, 47% of workers have observed bullying in their organizations.
- More than 50% of workers interviewed felt that bullying significantly reduced worker productivity.
- The number of employees feeling secure/safe at work fell from 76% in 1990 to 43% in 2002.
- A majority of victims (89%) frequently or constantly think about past bullying events.

Source: Table adapted and reproduced with permission of the Workplace Bullying and Trauma Institute (www.bullyinginstitute.org) and Harvey et al. (2006).

2006). Second, productive employees who are committed to the organization and have a positive attitude will tend not to go the extra mile out of fear that the bully will sabotage their best efforts. Bullies tend to extinguish the stars and go-to people, preventing them from helping lead the organization toward positive change and excellence goals. Third, organizational change is difficult since the bully is fighting off all the positive agents for change in the organization; the only demands met are those of the bully. Finally, workplace bullies act as organizational cancer, eventually killing the entire business. Does any of the preceding information about workplace bullying ring true in your experience? How would you strive for balance if you encountered a bully in the workplace? What would you do as a leader or manager to prevent bullying (see Table 14.4)?

How victims talk about workplace bullying is important to explore. To get a richer understanding of the impact of workplace bullying, review in Table 14.5 the painful metaphors associated with this behavior.

### Workplace Mobbing

If reading about workplace bullying as an imbalance trigger was not enough, there's more. Another imbalance trigger important to your study of work–life balance is

## Table 14.4 How Can the Negative Consequences of Bullying Be Addressed?

| | |
|---|---|
| Environmental issues | • Objective determination of the present organizational climate and the employees' perspective on bullying activity levels and severity in the organization<br><br>• Assessment of present formal standard operating procedures relative to dysfunctional bullying activities in the organization<br><br>• Identification of the specific location of bullying activities in the organizational cultures across all departments, locations, or managers<br><br>• Development of training specifically directed at countering bullying activities that should be provided to bullies as well as the personnel in the departments/locations that have been identified as having a higher incidence of bullying activities<br><br>• Assessment of management's past actions relative to bullying activities within the organization in a given period of time<br><br>• Continuous monitoring of the bullying policies, processes, and procedures to ensure their successful implementation and updating |
| Issues with existing and potential bullies | • Put selection processes in place to reduce the likelihood of hiring bullies (e.g., behavioral interviewing).<br><br>• Restructure the job requirements of the bully to reduce his/her direct contact with vulnerable groups/individuals in the organization.<br><br>• Assign additional training and awareness coaching to the identified bully based on his/her past behaviors and the resulting impact on the victims and observers of bullying events.<br><br>• Redesign the job to reduce the bully's supervision responsibilities and increase the nonpersonnel dimensions of his/her position.<br><br>• Provide professional counseling for the bully to allow him/her to gain insights into the impact of his/her behaviors as well as the impact on the victim/observers.<br><br>• Have the willingness and authority to terminate chronic bullies from the organization. |
| Issues with bullied individuals | • Complete an assessment of victim's self-esteem dimensions (e.g., cognitive, emotional, achievement, character, and physical) and develop training, counseling, and mentoring to address perceived shortcomings in the victim's self-image.<br><br>• Develop a support mechanism for those in the organization who are potential targets of bullies to help preempt the bully's attacks.<br><br>• Establish a review mechanism that can be used by the victim without fear of retaliation.<br><br>• Provide programs to victims/potential victims that demonstrate the options open to them relative to bullying activities.<br><br>• Have the willingness to support the potential victim before, during, and after a bullying event.<br><br>• Give the victim the opportunity to be relocated in the organization to reduce direct supervision of or contact with the documented bully. |

Source: Table adapted and reproduced with permission of Harvey et al. (2006).

**Table 14.5 What Does Workplace Bullying Feel Like?**

| Category | Themes and Examples |
|---|---|
| Bullying process as . . . | *Game or battle:* Bullies "play dirty" and "make their own rules."<br>*Nightmare:* "It's the Matrix. We live in two different worlds."<br>*Water torture:* It is a "hammering away," "drum beat," or "pressure screw."<br>*Noxious substance:* "It just kind of drips on down, just festers." He would "feed us a whole line of garbage." |
| The bully as . . . | *Narcissistic dictator or royalty:* "You literally have a Hitler running around down there."<br>*Two-faced actor:* Bullies put on "a good show for the boss," or they would "be real sweet one time one day, and the next day . . . very evil, conniving."<br>*Evil or demon:* Bullies are "evil," "devils," "witches," "demons," and "Jekyll and Hyde." |
| The target as . . . | *Slave or animal:* "You're a personal servant to the owner and his will." "He considers you his property."<br>*Prisoner:* "I feel like I'm doing time." "I felt like I had a prison record."<br>*Child:* "I felt like a little girl." It "is like having an abusive father."<br>*Heartbroken lover:* "My heart was broken." I felt "sad, confused, unworthy, and broken-hearted." |

Source: Table adapted and reproduced with permission of Tracy et al. (2006).

**workplace mobbing**—"the nonsexual harassment of a coworker by a group of other workers or other members of an organization designed to secure the removal from the organization of the one who is targeted" (Duffy & Sperry, 2007, p. 398). Duffy and Sperry further explain that mobbing "results in the humiliation, devaluation, discrediting, degradation, loss of professional reputation, and, usually, the removal of the target from the organization" (p. 398).

As with workplace bullying, you might be inclined to think of workplace mobbing as extreme or dramatic. Does this really happen? How often does workplace mobbing occur? Workplace mobbing first received attention in Europe but has emerged as a subject of increasing attention in the United States and Canada (Duffy & Sperry, 2012; Westhues, 2005, 2006). Victims of mobbing are typically accomplished professionals who exemplify commitment, honesty, integrity, intelligence, innovation, and competence (Duffy & Sperry, 2007, 2012). Instances of workplace mobbing continue to grow in the United States. You might be wondering, "How is workplace mobbing different from bullying?" Mobbing is "a group attack on a worker," while bullying is "an attack by a single individual" (Duffy & Sperry, 2007, p. 398).

What does workplace mobbing look like? How can you better understand the types of mobbing behavior? There are, in fact, five phases that usually occur in workplace mobbing. The five phases that follow have been identified by professional counselors who worked with mobbing victims in two clinical cases (Duffy & Sperry, 2007, 2012; Ferris, 2004; Leymann & Gustaffson, 1996).

As this image suggests, mobbing in the workplace can certainly make people feel alone.

**Phase 1: The triggering event.** An event occurs that leads an employee to stand out as different or not part of the in crowd due to high performance or disagreement with status quo.

**Phase 2: Aggressive acts and psychological assaults against the victim.** A mob forms and begins to punish the target by cutting him or her out of professional decisions. The victim is given low-ranking assignments and a difficult work schedule. The mob begins to gossip and spread rumors that the victim is a problem.

**Phase 3: Active involvement of the administration.** Leaders are alerted of the target and of the situation. The administration comes in and raises questions about the victim. They tend to side with the mob because a majority of distrust and dissatisfaction with the victim is expressed. The mob is asked questions about the victim, such as "Is he collegial?" "Do you trust her?" "Is he disgruntled?"

**Phase 4: Labeling of the victim.** The victim is given an official label (e.g., noncollegial, difficult to work with, not a team player) by the administration and the mob.

**Phase 5: Expulsion.** The victim has it so bad that she or he quits or is eventually fired.

Regardless of whether you must deal with angry customers, bullies, mobs, or the array of difficult people discussed previously in this book (e.g., slackers, drama queens, sexual harassers), dealing with a difficult person in the workplace is a trigger for work–life imbalance.

## Technologically Blurred Boundaries

*Pam:* My boss is driving me crazy.

*Julie:* What did she do now?

*Pam:* She is completely overloading me with projects, and she has no boundaries.

*Julie:* What do you mean?

*Pam:* There's nothing I can do since she's my boss! Since she gave us all new smartphones and laptops to start the new quarter, she sends text messages constantly and expects us to reply to work-related e-mail late at night. The other night, she sent numerous e-mails starting at 11:00 p.m. and continuing until 4:30 a.m.!"

Working late or at home on professional projects can open the door for your personal life to take a hit.

What does this brief conversation between Pam and Julie reveal? Clearly, Pam is having a problem dealing with a difficult boss who does not understand work–life boundaries. Unfortunately, Pam is not alone. New mobile **information and communications technologies (ICTs)** such as personal digital assistants (PDAs) and smartphones (e.g., iPhone, BlackBerry) harm work–life boundaries and also serve as tools for managing them (Eikhof, 2012; Golden & Geisler, 2007). Indeed, technology helps professionals be more productive and stay connected with clients, respond quickly, accomplish tasks despite geographic distance, travel with tons of data, maintain electronic calendars, organizers, and more. Yet some people believe that e-mail systems and other forms of communication technology—created to help us manage our time more efficiently—have actually increased our work-related tasks and maintenance (Ballard, 2008; Eikhof, 2012). Take a moment to think about your own use of technology. Does your use of technology help or hinder work–life boundary management?

## Life Demands

The term *work–life* is a bit misleading. After all, your work is a part of your life, and your life away from the job is full of non-employment-related work. The term *work–life* is really meant to capture the competing demands that are placed on the 21st century employee. This book provides you with a host of skills and strategies that will help you handle work demands with professional excellence. So it seems only fair that we turn our attention for a moment to some life demands, such as household and family responsibilities, as well as health responsibilities.

### Household and Family Responsibilities

Whether you live alone or with a houseful of people and pets, your household must be maintained. This requires keeping up with housework, yardwork, grocery shopping, paying the bills, and more. If you have a cleaning person and a personal assistant, consider yourself lucky. But if you are like the overwhelming majority of workers, you must be responsible for some or all of these duties.

As noted earlier in the chapter, a majority of couples with children under the age of 18 are both employed, and 35% of workers provide care for aging parents (Drago, 2007; Glavin & Schieman, 2012). This means that on top of the duties noted above, you'll probably need to find time to take your elderly parents to the grocery store and medical appointments. You'll have to use your time away from the office to coach soccer and chauffeur your children to and from ballet, piano, and karate lessons. Of course, your dog will also need to go for a walk. If you live in an apartment, make that two or three walks.

## Evaluate the Professional Context    Elisabeth's Experience With Telecommuting

*Read the following passage about Elisabeth, and then answer the questions. As you read, focus on* **evaluating the professional context**.

Elisabeth thought that her use of technology was going to help her work–life balance. Elisabeth had three children ranging in age from 4 to 10. When she was given the option to telecommute, she was thrilled—her dream had come true. She would no longer have to drive back and forth through rush-hour traffic. Her children would no longer have to go to the Latchkey program after school. She could set her own hours—as long as everything was completed by the preset deadlines. Yet Elisabeth's dream quickly turned into a nightmare. For example, because she was "home" all day, her husband and mother would ask her to run errands for them because they had to be at work, her neighbor would drop by to chat, and her friends would insist that she meet them for lunch since she was "free." As for her children, they had a difficult time understanding that mommy was working even though she was in the house. When they arrived home at 3:00 p.m., there was a constant demand for her help and/or attention. As a result, Elisabeth found herself working until the wee hours of the morning trying to get her projects completed. Work life and home life had blurred into one big blob, which included absolutely no downtime for Elisabeth.

### Questions to Consider

1. What advice would you give Elisabeth?
2. Do you think her situation is common?
3. Would you have difficulty working from home? Why or why not?
4. Is the professional context different for employees working from home? Why or why not?
5. How could the KEYS process help her situation?

While caring for your home, children, parents, and pets may be a labor of love, it's still very demanding and stressful, with the majority of the stress falling on women. In fact, when women entered the workforce, all their former duties in the home and for the family didn't disappear. Instead, they were moved into a second shift of work (Hochschild, 1989). When women increased their financial contribution, men didn't necessarily increase their domestic contribution (Goldstein, 2000; Greenstein, 1996; Risman & Godwin, 2001; Wood, 2003). In fact, some professional women report that husbands not only fail to do their fair share of housework, but they actually add to the amount of housework that needs to be done!

Establishing activities such as spending time with friends or your pets can help manage stress and provide some sense of leisure time away from work.

## Step Back and Reflect    Jarrett and Kim's Story

*Read the passage below, and answer the questions that follow.*

Six weeks ago, Jarrett and Kim had twins. It was a time of great joy and great stress. Jarrett, a medical resident, had been sleep-deprived from working long hours, even before the twins arrived. Now he was so tired that he began to fear he might make a mistake. He felt his only recourse was to sleep in the break room between shifts so his sleep would not be interrupted by the twins' crying. Kim's maternity leave was over, and she had to return to work. Physically, she was in no shape to serve as the superstar employee she had been. A difficult pregnancy and an emergency C-section had left her drained. Trying to care for and nurse twins with little help from her spouse had depleted what little reserves she had left. But the physical issues were nothing compared with the emotional issues. Kim had always considered herself a career woman. She wanted kids, but predelivery, she was certain that by 6 weeks she would be dying to get back to work. That did not prove to be the case. The thought of placing her twins in day care left her in tears. She wanted to be at home with her babies. She did not want to go back to work. But they could not afford their house, their cars, and Jarrett's student loan payments without her income.

### Step Back and Reflect

1. What went wrong?
2. Do you think that working moms and working dads share the workload on the home front? What impact does this balance or imbalance have on each party?
3. How could Kim and Jarrett utilize the KEYS approach to improve their communication interaction?

When it comes to caring for elderly parents, that responsibility also tends to fall on daughters more often than sons. According to Wood (1994), the responsibility of caring for aging parents and aging in-laws falls predominantly on women. Since wives take on more than husbands, and daughters take on more than sons, it is not surprising to learn that mothers tend to take on more of the parenting duties than fathers. Some of it is necessary. After all, fathers can't get pregnant or nurse. Nevertheless, fathers are indeed very important, and the demands on working fathers are intense—but the demands placed on working mothers can be downright exhausting.

Due to the lack of work–life balance experienced by working mothers, "in the span of the past decade, full-time work outside the home has lost some of its appeal to mothers. This trend holds both for mothers who have such jobs and those who don't" (PEW Research Center, 2007). (See Table 14.6 for exact figures.) As for fathers, the data are quite different. In fact, 72% of the fathers surveyed reported a full-time position outside of the home as their ideal (PEW Research Center, 2007).

Given this data, you might ask yourself, "Why are so many women with children working?" Certainly, some women work outside of the home because they find their jobs fulfilling and rewarding, while some women work to achieve a higher standard of living for themselves and their families. However, it's also important to note that not all women have a choice when it comes to working outside of the home. Increased divorce rate and

**Table 14.6 Work Grows Less Attractive to Moms**

From 1997 to 2007:
Full-Time Work Grows Less Attractive to Moms

Considering everything, what would be the ideal situation for you—working full-time, part-time, or not at all outside the home?

| | Working mothers | | | At-home mothers | | |
|---|---|---|---|---|---|---|
| | 1997 | 2007 | Change '97 to '07 | 1997 | 2007 | Change '97 to '07 |
| | % | % | | % | % | |
| **What's ideal for you?** | | | | | | |
| Full-time work | 32 | 21 | −11 | 24 | 16 | −8 |
| Part-time work | 48 | 60 | +12 | 37 | 33 | −4 |
| Not working | 20 | 19 | −1 | 39 | 48 | −9 |
| Don't know | * | * | | * | 3 | |
| | 100 | 100 | | 100 | 100 | |
| Number of respondents | 317 | 259 | | 140 | 153 | |

Note: Based on mothers with children under age 18.        Pew Research Center

Source: PEW Research Center (2007).

economic necessity due to higher cost of living are also cited as reasons mothers work outside of the home (PEW Research Center, 2007).

If you're a man reading this book, you may be feeling pretty lucky right about now, but don't begin celebrating quite yet. Household and family demands impact you as well. The stories of Jackson, Joel, and Wesley capture some of the demands and pressures placed on men.

Jackson was a successful partner in a law firm. His firm was profitable, and everyone earned a good salary. But for some of the partners, good was not good enough. There was a move to increase the number of clients and the profile of the firm to increase revenue. Jackson opposed the change because it would mean more time in the office and less time with his family. When Jackson voiced his concerns, the other partners accused him of not being a team player.

When Joel's son was born, he and his wife decided that one of them should stay home with the child. Joel was thrilled for the opportunity and enjoyed every moment he spent caring for his son and his home. Yet, when Joel's son entered kindergarten and he decided to go back to work, he was shocked at the negative response he got from potential employers when they learned he had "wasted 5 years playing Mr. Mom."

Wesley is a teacher. He loves teaching, and he's very good at it. The problem is that he doesn't earn the same high-level salaries as his male friends and family members.

Wesley often feels like a poor provider because he can't afford an expensive house or expensive gifts for his wife and children. Although his family has never complained, he feels as though it's his job to provide, and he's concerned that he's not providing enough.

While the demands vary in type and intensity, both women and men have to juggle household demands, family demands, and work demands. Unfortunately, living demanding lives takes a toll on your health.

*Health Responsibilities*

For men, work-related stress and the negative habits that accompany a stressful lifestyle have long been known to have a detrimental impact on health. As the number of women in the workplace has increased, so too have the health risks that accompany work-related stress and a life lived out of balance.

Do you really need to worry about the impact of work and work–life balance on your health? Should your employer worry about your health and your stress level? After all, what's wrong with a little stress? A little stress every once in a while may not be harmful, but prolonged stress and daily stress is very dangerous. Stress is commonly linked to headaches, stomachaches, short temper, depression, and anxiety. See Table 14.7 for a more extensive list of stress-related problems.

### Table 14.7 Health Problems Linked With Stress

| | | |
|---|---|---|
| Trouble sleeping | Tension | Weight gain or loss |
| Headaches | Increased asthma flare-ups | Heart disease |
| Constipation | Stomach cramping | High blood pressure |
| Diarrhea | Stomach bloating | Irritable bowel syndrome |
| Irritability | Increased arthritis flare-ups | Diabetes |
| Lack of energy | Depression | Neck and/or back pain |
| Anger | Anxiety | Less sexual desire |
| Sadness | Skin problems (such as hives) | Sexual dysfunction |
| Lack of concentration | Hyperthyroidism | Difficulty getting pregnant |
| Hair loss | Obesity | Obsessive-compulsive |
| Tooth and gum disease | Ulcers | disorder |
| Cancer (possibly) | | Anxiety disorder |

Source: Adapted from the Office of Women's Health (2010) and Scott (2007).

The link between work–life balance, stress, and health can be a vicious cycle. Let's look at obesity as an illustration of how this works. Obesity is one of the health problems linked to stress and is a growing problem in the United States. Drake was very active and fit in high school, but as his 10-year class reunion approached, he became aware of the negative impact his work had had on his health. During law school, Drake had to study all the time. As a result, he stopped playing sports for fun and rarely made it to the gym. Now Drake is a successful attorney, which requires long hours and weekends. This leaves no time for exercise, and his hectic schedule often allows him little time to prepare or eat a healthy meal. Instead, Drake grabs a burger or hits the vending machine for his meals. Because of the stress on the job and the lack of downtime needed to unwind, Drake often has headaches, backaches, and sleepless nights. All this has resulted in the 50-pound tire Drake is carrying around his middle. Drake knows that his weight increases his chances of a heart attack (see Figure 14.1 on page 358). He also knows that all the stress negatively impacts his performance on the job. But he does not know how to change his current lifestyle. What can he do? Drake is like millions of other Americans. He has no work–life balance, and he lacks the communication strategies that can help him obtain that balance.

Lunch breaks are often rushed, and many of today's professionals are pressured to accomplish numerous tasks in a short amount of time. As this photo suggests, fast-food diets and skipping meals can become the norm.

# Strategies for Balance

We recognize that balancing the challenges of work with your personal and family life will not be easy. However, striving for balance will promote better communication at work and at home. Remember, part of professional excellence is getting to know yourself to understand how the sources of imbalance are influencing your communication and well-being. Furthermore, many of the strategies that can help you obtain balance are communication strategies. It is through effective communication that we find work–life balance, and once we have found that balance, it will improve our communication.

In the sections that follow, we review some strategies for developing work–life balance: knowing yourself, developing emotional intelligence, learning time-management skills, using the PDA as a tool for balance, and taking a vacation.

## Knowing Yourself

The first step in developing work–life balance is determining the priorities in your life and then assessing how much time you devote to each priority. Take inventory of how many hours you spend on various tasks and responsibilities each day. How do you manage your life? Many of you may realize that there is too much going on. Even if you're coping, you still may not have work–life balance. Where do you spend most of your time? Is this where you want to spend most of your time? No doubt, friends and family are important to you, but how much time do they get? What about your health? How much time do you spend exercising so you can unwind and relieve your stress? Knowing yourself means evaluating where you

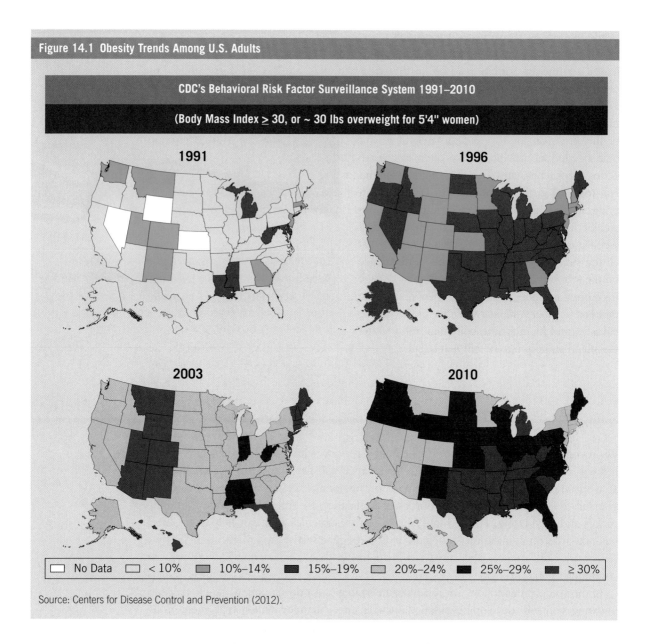

Figure 14.1 Obesity Trends Among U.S. Adults

CDC's Behavioral Risk Factor Surveillance System 1991–2010

(Body Mass Index ≥ 30, or ~ 30 lbs overweight for 5'4" women)

1991    1996

2003    2010

No Data    < 10%    10%–14%    15%–19%    20%–24%    25%–29%    ≥ 30%

Source: Centers for Disease Control and Prevention (2012).

want to spend your time (priorities) as compared with where you actually spend your time (reality). For true work–life balance, your priorities and your reality should line up.

To do this, you must also know your personality type. So are you a Type A or a Type B? If you are a Type A, you must learn the art of saying no. If you are a Type B, you need to become a proactive communicator versus a reactive communicator.

One of the first words you learned to say was "no." At age 2, it was probably your favorite word, but as adults, it is a difficult word for Type As to say. You may have trouble giving up control, you may think you can do it better, the task may sound appealing to you, or you may believe you can indeed do it all. Regardless of the reason you fail to say no, by repeatedly saying yes, you fill your plate so full that you become overworked, overstressed, angry, ill, or all the above. If saying no is difficult for you, reframe your thinking. Learn to say yes to your priorities, which means you must turn down nonpriorities. Make a list of your priorities and your future goals. When you are asked to take on another task, buy yourself some time to think by saying something like, "I will need to check my calendar," "Let me confer with my team," or "I will need to discuss this with my boss." If the task lines up with your priorities and if you have time to complete the task during your regular work hours, then accept. If not, learn to say no tactfully but firmly. You might say, "I am afraid that will not be possible," "Thank you for considering me, but I must pass," or "Although it's a wonderful opportunity, I cannot accept at this time." Then stop talking. Do not allow the other party to pull you into a debate about how much time you have or how much you are needed. Just repeat your answer again: "As I said, it's a wonderful opportunity, but I cannot accept at this time."

Type B individuals must learn to function as proactive communicators, not reactive communicators. Since Type B individuals tend to be more laid-back and less time/deadline focused, they may have a tendency to ignore small problems until they become big problems or allow poor time management to affect the quality of their work. As a proactive communicator, you must implement many of the strategies discussed earlier in the text. For example, as a leader, develop agendas for all meetings to keep yourself on task, set up meetings to lay out expectations for employee performance before there's a problem, hold regular meetings to give and receive feedback, hold employees accountable, confront difficult employees, and develop your time-management skills (which we discuss later in this chapter). All these strategies will help you stay on task, decrease stress in the workplace, and achieve professional excellence.

In actuality, learning to say no and learning to be proactive benefit everyone, regardless of personality type. The important thing to remember is that if you're going to achieve work–life balance, you must begin by knowing yourself.

## Developing Emotional Intelligence

To achieve work–life balance, you also must develop **emotional intelligence**—your ability to monitor your own and others' feelings and emotions, to discriminate among them, and to use this information to guide your thinking and actions (Angelidis & Ibrahim, 2012; Engelberg & Sjoberg, 2004; O'Sullivan, 2005; Salovey & Mayer, 1990). The concept of emotional intelligence was initiated in the psychology discipline and clearly informs business and professional communication (Angelidis & Ibrahim, 2012; Morand, 2001). People striving for work–life balance and professional excellence consult popular books on the topic (Bradberry & Greaves, 2005; Chang, Sy, & Choi, 2012; Goleman, 1995).

Professionals who exercise emotional intelligence are more balanced in that they know their own emotions and attempt to understand the emotions of others. In addition, emotional intelligence encourages you to utilize your emotions for flexible planning, creative thinking, and motivating you to accomplish goals and problem (Chang et al., 2012; Mayer & Salovey, 1993; Morand, 2001). By learning to manage your emotions when you're

## Ethical Connection  Too Much Work

*Please read the passage below, and answer the questions that follow.*

Jason is the vice president of a large petrochemical company. While he enjoys his work and the position he has, the demands on his time are quite severe. Jason typically works 60 hours a week, and with a new business merger looming, it looks as though he will be working even more now. Jason's wife has voiced her concern about his work schedule, and she expects to give birth to their first child within the month. Jason is worried that with his new work demands he will not be able to give his wife and baby the attention they need. His company has already indicated that he will need to work long hours for the foreseeable future, and his position is in jeopardy if he takes a personal leave of absence. John has other job options available, but he could not expect the same high-ranking position (and pay) that he enjoys at his current job.

### Questions to Consider

1. What is the ethical dilemma facing John?
2. What impact do John's family obligations have on his professional career?
3. Why is achieving work–life balance a critical factor when entering a professional field?
4. Are there any other options John could explore before finding new employment?

dealing with stress caused by difficult people, deadlines, information overload, or a whole host of other triggers, you'll be able to address the issue at hand and then move on. The stress, worry, and so on won't bleed into other areas of either your work or your life. Do you have a grasp on your own emotions and how they influence your communication? How perceptive are you of emotions in other people? As a means to better understand emotional intelligence, let's explore one emotion in more detail—anger.

*Understanding Anger*

Many, if not all, of the imbalance triggers in the previous sections of this chapter can cause any professional to experience anger. **Anger** is defined as an emotional state that varies in intensity from mild irritation to intense fury and rage, a feeling of keen displeasure for what we regard as a wrong toward ourselves or others (Parlamis, 2012; Thomas, 1998). Anger is known as a secondary emotion. In other words, anger occurs as a response to a situation or another emotion. Maybe a coworker embarrasses you, which in turn causes you to feel anger. For many, anger is viewed as something that shouldn't be expressed or felt, but it's important to realize that anger is a normal human emotion.

In general, people become angry when they encounter a *real* or *perceived* threat to themselves (e.g., bullies, mobs, difficult customers). Similar to our discussion of the causes of or triggers to imbalance, there are also triggers to anger. **External triggers** to anger are things going on in your environment at work and at home, usually stimulated by others. **Internal triggers** to anger are concerns and frustrations you have about past, current, and future events or a general negativity toward yourself (i.e., "I'm really angry at myself for not making that change sooner").

Something at some point in time is going to cause you to experience anger in a business and professional setting. The trigger source may very well be directly from a coworker or client. Perhaps your anger will be triggered by something going on in your personal life. No matter the source, it's critical for you to avoid the following counterproductive expressions of anger (Callahan, 1999):

1. Repressing (stuffing) or denying your anger

2. Displacing anger by projecting it onto the wrong target

3. Using alcohol, drugs, or other potentially harmful distractions for understanding and expressing your feelings

4. Treating depression—which may be anger turned inward—solely as depression

5. Confusing anger with the desire for revenge

### Releasing Anger in Healthy Ways

Does Eugene's experience resonate with you? Have you ever felt as though it was impossible to manage all the responsibilities between school, friends, family, and work? Notice how the questions on the anger worksheet tap into both your feeling and your actions or behaviors. Take a moment to make a list or reflect on activities or best practices for managing anger, especially in business and professional situations. Below is a list of strategies for releasing anger in healthy ways:

- Admit that you're angry. Honesty is crucial. You also need to be free of judgmental reactions to your anger. Remember, anger is a normal feeling. Swallowing or repressing anger can be dangerous.
- Identify the reason for your anger. Ask, "What situation or event is making me angry?" Clarify your position. What is the problem? What is the real issue behind your angry feelings?
- Ask what you want to accomplish with your anger. Anger tells us that something is bothering us. What needs to be done to correct the problem?
- Talk it out. Discuss the problem with a trusted friend or qualified professional. This helps you see if your emotion is "current" anger or "old" anger. If you think you have a lot of unexpressed anger from the past, begin to explore the issue gently.
- Practice relaxation techniques. Deep breathing and other relaxation techniques can help you release anger and tension from the body.
- Use physical exercise to get your anger out. You can often alleviate angry emotions through physical activity, such as a long walk, yardwork, or whatever outlet you choose.
- Speak up when you feel angry or shortly afterward. If possible, express your anger to the person with whom you are concerned. Using "I" statements can help you express anger in a reasonable manner when an issue or concern is important to you (e.g., "I feel angry when you fail to complete your part of the project by the assigned deadline"). Then let go of the anger. Don't dwell on hurt feelings.

## Your Communication Interaction    Eugene's Anger Inventory

*Read the passage below, and then answer the questions. As you read, think about ways the KEYS approach could help you improve* **your communication interaction** *if you were in Eugene's position.*

Eugene's imbalance between work, school, service, and his personal life continued. He realized that he wasn't feeling like himself. In fact, he started lashing out at people and had developed a negative attitude about every aspect of his life. Eugene's lack of work–life balance got so out of control that he started to have a difficult time managing his anger. For example, when he got behind on his duties at the fraternity, his brothers offered to help. Instead of saying thanks, he yelled at them for doubting his ability. When he got a low score on his exam, he ripped the paper up and threw it in the trash in front of his professor and his classmates. When his girlfriend offered to make him dinner, he accused her of pressuring him and stormed off.

Fortunately, Eugene was required to attend a workshop for the bar and grill at which he was working part-time. The company had a corporate training policy for all employees to complete a customer service workshop—and part of the program included a worksheet on dealing with anger. Take a moment to respond to some of the questions below that were helpful to Eugene.

1. When I am angry, I usually feel . . .

   _____

2. When I am angry, I usually (do what?) . . .

   _____

3. When someone gets angry with me, I usually feel . . .

   _____

4. When someone gets angry, I usually (do what?) . . .

   _____

5. Three things that make me angry are . . .

   _____

6. Two things I can do to express anger more constructively are . . .

   _____

### Questions to Consider

1. Respond to the questions above. What did you learn about yourself?
2. Is anger management a problem for you?
3. Do you exhibit stress in other ways?
4. Have you ever felt overwhelmed and overloaded as Eugene did? How did you handle it?

You'll no doubt have to deal with anger, as well as a host of other emotions, in the workplace. It's up to you to know yourself so you can recognize those emotions and assess how they are influencing your communication. Part of communicating with professional excellence requires you to lay out expectations and standards of professionalism and hold people accountable when they fail to maintain those expectations and standards. It's best to confront the difficult people and/or situations that are creating anger and stress in your workplace. Use "I" statements to express your emotions, develop healthy strategies for releasing emotions, and fire people if you must. If you don't have the power to fire a bully, say no to unrealistic demands, or refuse service to an out-of-control customer, find a new place to work.

## Developing Time-Management Skills

Part of striving for balance is taking control of how you manage your time. In fact, management and business scholars have found that many working professionals have such a difficult time managing the work–life boundary that some give up and are prone to misbehave by engaging in personal activities at work (Bull & Brown, 2012; D'Abate, 2005). To avoid the unprofessional practice, let's take a serious look at how to manage time effectively. You must identify the **external time wasters**—things you don't feel as though you have any control over (e.g., things we are required to attend, such as meetings, or people to whom we're required to talk). In addition, identify **internal time wasters**—more personal internal things brought on by mind-set, motivation, and bad habits. Business consultant Una Byrne (2008) offers a comprehensive list of both external and internal time wasters (see Table 14.8), similar to the work of Steven Covey (2003).

### Table 14.8 Time Wasters

| External Time Wasters | Internal Time Wasters |
| --- | --- |
| • Telephone interruptions | • Procrastination |
| • E-mail | • Failure to delegate |
| • Meetings | • Unclear objectives |
| • Visitors | • Failure to set priorities |
| • Socializing | • Crisis management |
| • Excessive paperwork | • Failure to plan |
| • Lack of communication and information | • Poor scheduling |
| • Lack of policies and procedures | • Lack of self-discipline |
| • Lack of competent personnel | • Attempting to do too much at once |
| • Red tape | • Lack of relevant skills |

Source: Adapted from Byrne (2008).

Review the listings of external and internal time wasters. Where do you stand? Part of striving for balance and professional excellence is identifying your strengths and weaknesses. Do you have a problem with time management? Take a look at Table 14.9 and think about some time-management strategies that can alleviate both internal and external time wasters. Perhaps technology is the answer. As you reflect on time management, let's transition into the final section of this chapter, which explores the influence of technology on work–life boundary management.

## Using the PDA to Maintain Balance

As noted earlier, new mobile information and communications technologies (ICTs) such as PDAs and smartphones (e.g., iPhone, BlackBerry) harm work–life boundaries and serve as tools for managing them (Eikhof, 2012; Golden & Geisler, 2007). Previously, we discussed the harm technology can have on work–life balance, but as communication scholars Golden and Geisler explain,

| Table 14.9 Prioritizing Your Time | |
|---|---|
| Important and urgent | Things for which you have to make time. What's important now? Constantly asking this will lead to a manageable number of tasks. Everything you have to do should not go in this box. Remember, this is your high-priority box. |
| Important and not urgent | Tasks in this category are typically "preventative" in nature. For example, spending time with your staff ensures that things are going well and that they're happy. They can also be tasks where things that will become important and urgent get planned and organized and started. |
| Not important and urgent | Usually, interruptions, some phone calls, and e-mails fall into this category. They need to be dealt with in an "urgent" way to establish their significance and make a decision on how they need to be dealt with. This category is usually associated with someone else's priorities. |
| Not important and not urgent | These are tasks that should be done in "slack" periods. Some e-mails, some phone calls, filing, and other busy work. This may also be time when you catch up with colleagues and engage in work-related reading or professional development. |

Source: Table adapted and reproduced with permission of Byrne (2008) and Covey (2003).

While PDAs have not achieved the level of penetration in the consumer market that cell phones have, their design and functionality gives them heuristic value as we consider the impact of ICTs on work–life relationships generally and boundary management in particular. . . . The personal digital assistant is one of several mobile technologies that promise organizational members resources for managing work–life boundaries. (pp. 520–521)

So studying the way professionals use PDAs to manage their work–life boundaries taps into the influence of technology on the dynamics of work–life boundary management. To explore PDAs' influence on work–life boundaries, Golden and Geisler (2007) asked the following questions: "What practices do PDA users engage in that are implicated in work–life boundary management? What sense do PDA users make of their practices, and what interpretive resources do PDA users draw on in the accounts of these practices? In what ways do PDA users' practices and discourse (the way users talk about their technology use) reflect the spirit of the PDA's design?" Take a look at the results from this research to get a sense of how people talk about PDAs in relation to work–life boundary management (see Table 14.10).

### Table 14.10  PDA-Mediated Work–Life Boundary Management

| Interpretive Repertoires | Discursive Moves | PDA Use | Forms of Boundary |
|---|---|---|---|
| Containing work | 1. Setting limits<br>2. Controlling chaos<br>3. Keeping a lid on it | • Calendaring<br>• Calendaring, task list, notes, etc.<br>• Segregating use, turning it off | Boundary placement/ segregating work and personal life |
| Integrating the self | 1. Domain altering<br>2. The constant companion<br>3. Enhancing life | • Notes<br>• Carrying the PDA everywhere<br>• PDA as focal point for social interaction | Boundary transcending/ integrating work and personal life |
| Transitioning work | 1. Working in the home space<br>2. Making work mobile | • Notes (e-mail)<br>• Notes, calendar, task list (e-mail) | Boundary transcending/ moving work across the work–life boundary |
| Protecting the private | 1. Life calendaring<br>2. Keeping the PDA private | • Calendaring<br>• Segregating use, synchronizing with networked computers | Boundary placement/ segregating work and personal life |

Source: Table adapted and reproduced with permission of Golden and Geisler (2007).

Professionals who are out of balance or burned out may find it difficult to relax. In our consulting practice, we have heard many professionals talk about how they feel guilty if they take any time away from work-related projects.

## Taking a Vacation

Vacation may not seem like a relevant topic in a text on communication, but let us assure you that taking vacation time will make you a better communicator, and you will need to utilize several communication strategies if you plan to enjoy a true vacation. Culturally, people in the United States are not very good at taking vacations. In fact, when compared with other nations, U.S. employees take the least amount of vacation time (see Table 14.11).

When looking at these vacation statistics, your first instinct may be to blame employers. Surely, the reason people in the United States take fewer vacation days is because they *have* fewer vacations days, right? Wrong. According to a survey conducted by Harris Interactive (2008) for Expedia.com, about one third of employed U.S. adults (35%) reported that they did not take all their vacation days that year. The reasons included

- the need to schedule vacation time in advance (13%),
- getting money back for unused vacation days (12%), and
- work is life, making it too hard to get away (10%).

A 2012 survey shows that this lack-of-vacation trend is getting worse, not better. The American work ethic, coupled with ambition and the fear of losing one's job during a recession, resulted in more than 40% of those surveyed reporting that they took no vacation in the previous year (Jones & Trejos, 2012). This same article cited a survey conducted by JetBlue in September 2012 that showed 57% of employee respondents claiming they would end the year with unused vacation time. Carroll Rheem, a senior research director at PhoCusWright, a travel industry research firm, stated, "Sometimes they forget to take care of their work–life balance" (Jones & Trejos, 2012, p. 1).

Given the problems resulting from stress, discussed earlier in this chapter, the need to unwind seems clear. In fact, many nations require employees to take a minimum amount of vacation time. In other words, taking a vacation is required (see Table 14.12). Unfortunately, the United States is not one of those nations, even though 40% of U.S. adults reported working more than 40 hours a week (Harris Interactive, 2008).

Why would employers require a minimum amount of vacation time? Maybe it's because vacation time increases job satisfaction, morale, and productivity (Harris Interactive, 2008). As we discussed earlier, it also helps reduce stress and burnout.

Whether you're looking for an entry-level position or a position as the CEO, be aware of the organization's attitude about vacation time. If you're offered a position with a company that allows or encourages its employees to work to the point of burnout, then you should pass and wait for a better offer. If you're in a leadership position in your organization, you must work to develop an organizational culture that encourages employees to take vacations. Talk to employees about when they plan to take time off. This will allow you to keep the organization running smoothly even when key players are gone. This will also help prevent employees from failing to schedule time in advance and then losing the time as a result. If you notice an employee is stressed, encourage him or her to take some time off to recharge. Most important, you need to be a role model. Take your vacation time so employees know it's okay for them to do the same.

When you or any member of your team goes on vacation, set a "Do Not Disturb" policy. Taking calls, checking e-mails, and conducting meetings via teleconference while in a tropical paradise is not a vacation. You are still plugged in, so you cannot truly relax

| Table 14.11 Minimum Required Vacation Time | |
|---|---|
| Germany and Finland | 6 weeks |
| Norway, Sweden, and France | 5 weeks |
| Most of Europe and Australia | 4 weeks |
| Colombia and New Zealand | 3 weeks |
| Canada and Japan | 2 weeks |
| United States and China | 0 weeks |

Source: DeLossy (2007).

and rejuvenate. You must completely unplug. This will be difficult, as the technological boundaries between work and vacation are increasingly becoming blurred. For example, 83% of BlackBerry users reported checking e-mail while on vacation (Carrasco, 2007). If you're taking a vacation, tell everyone that you will not be taking your cell phone (even if you do take it along, leave it turned off). If an emergency occurs, they can track you down through the hotel. This will reduce the number of so-called "emergencies." The same goes for your laptop. Tell your team that you will not be checking your voice mails or e-mails. Change your voice message and set up an e-mail auto-reply message to tell people you are gone and when you will return. Then stick to your word and don't check in.

# KEYS to Excellence With Work–Life Balance

At the beginning of the chapter, we read about Mary Claire Orenic and her success in achieving work–like balance. As with other cases that have appeared throughout the text, the KEYS approach to professional excellence was useful for Orenic. First, she made some adjustments and realized that taking on too many responsibilities could affect her communication decisions. When examining the first key, *know yourself*, Orenic determined that she wanted to achieve professional excellence, and part of that entailed improving her work–life balance. She realized that her effectiveness as a senior manager could be compromised by too much stress or burnout, and she took several steps to achieve a healthy balance between work and personal life. When you find yourself becoming overwhelmed by work, think critically about steps you can take to create more personal time for yourself.

The second step, *evaluate the professional context*, asked Orenic to learn how creating work–life balance would work in her company. Orenic was fortunate that her company allowed her to work from home a few times per week, but chances are many of you will not have that luxury with your job. If it is possible, working from home can be very effective in achieving work–life balance, but make sure you understand the culture of your company before approaching such an idea.

The third step, *your communication interaction occurs*, offers several innovative ideas to be productive in your personal time. New technology allows many people to meet, brainstorm, and work from across the globe, eliminating the need for lengthy business trips and time away from home. Find out if some of your collaborative work can take place away from the office via a smartphone, tablet, or personal computer.

The final task, *step back and reflect*, asks you to determine if both you and your employer are happy with your work–life balance. If your company is flexible and you are creative, you shouldn't have too much trouble creating a system that keeps both your personal life and professional career in a healthy state.

Do you ever feel completely overwhelmed by all the demands on your time? How do you handle the stress? What have you learned in this chapter that could help you better manage work–life balance?

**K**now Yourself

**E**valuate the Professional Context

**Y**our Communication Interaction Occurs

**S**tep Back and Reflect

## Executive Summary

Now that you have finished reading this chapter, you can do the following:

Understand the impact of work–life balance on professional excellence:

- Achieving work–life balance is important for the following reasons: (1) Imbalance between your work life and personal life can negatively influence the way you communicate, (2) work–life balance fosters meaningful and successful relationships at home and at work, and (3) work–life balance must be present to sustain professional excellence (p. 339).

Define work–life balance:

- Scholars sometimes refer to work–life balance as work-family balance. *Life* is a more general reference to the self outside of work, while *family* refers to a collective group of people (e.g., spouses, children, partners) with whom the professional resides outside of work (p. 339).
- *Work–life balance* is the "accomplishment of role-related expectations that are negotiated and shared between an individual and his or her role-related partners in the work and family [life] domains" (Grzywacz & Carlson, 2007, p. 458) (p. 340).

Discuss the individual and organizational benefits of work–life balance:

- If you fail to develop strategies for achieving balance, work time will attempt to colonize your personal time, leaving you with feelings of imbalance, stress, and *burnout* (p. 341).
- Employees are happier at work and at home when they have greater control of their working lives; have the time to focus more on life outside of work; don't bring problems from home to work and vice versa; are shown loyalty and commitment; have improved self-esteem, health, concentration, and confidence; have better relations with management; and feel a greater responsibility and sense of ownership (p. 341).
- For employers, having a more motivated, productive, and less stressed workforce results in maximized available labor; reduced costs; retaining valued employees; the reputation of being an employer

of choice; reduced absenteeism; increased productivity; attracting a wider range of candidates, such as older, part-time workers; and making employees feel valued (p. 343).

Identify the triggers to imbalance:

- *Imbalance triggers* are experiences (e.g., conflict, aggression, overload, negativity) that cause professionals to feel drained, used, abused, and unhappy (p. 343).
- *External triggers* to anger are things going on in your environment at work and at home, usually stimulated by others (p. 361).
- *Internal triggers* to anger are concerns and frustrations you have about past, current, and future events or a general negativity toward yourself (p. 361).

Develop strategies for achieving work–life balance:

- Striving for balance will promote better communication at work and at home. Part of professional excellence is getting to know yourself to understand how the sources of imbalance are influencing your communication and well-being (p. 358).
- The first step in developing work–life balance is determining the priorities in your life and then assessing how much time you devote to each one (p. 358).
- You also must develop emotional intelligence—your ability to monitor your own and others' feelings and emotions, to discriminate among them, and to use this information to guide your thinking and actions (p. 360).
- Part of striving for balance is taking control of how you manage your time. In fact, management and business scholars have found that many working professionals have such a difficult time managing the work–life boundary that some give up and are prone to misbehave by engaging in personal activities at work (p. 363).

Utilize the KEYS approach to achieve professional excellence regarding work–life balance:

- *Know yourself.* Determine if you want to achieve professional excellence, and know that part of that entails improving your work–life balance (p. 368).
- *Evaluate the professional context.* Become more audience centered and aware of how

you come across to other people when you experience stress and burnout. Become more mindful of how your communication can be influenced by your anger (p. 368).

- *Your communication interaction occurs.* Be a more professional communicator in that you manage your emotions and make better choices even when you are stressed out due to managing numerous challenges in your life. Start to think before reacting, and be much more mindful of how your overload can negatively impact your communication (p. 368).

- *Step back and reflect.* Become more reflective of your workload and how it influences communication in your personal and professional life and your overall health (p. 368).

## Discussion Questions

1. Discuss an example of a time when you felt burned out or overloaded. How did you respond? How did burnout impact your communication with other people?

2. Have you ever experienced or observed bullying? How did you respond to the bullying? As a professional, what steps would you take to address workplace bullying?

3. How do you manage stress and emotions such as anger? What strategies do you have, if any, that work for you?

4. Can the risks and health consequences (for individuals and organizations) associated with difficult customers and coworkers be alleviated with employee education and training? What experiences have you had, if any, concerning training or education related to uncivil workplace behavior?

5. Do you use ICTs such as PDAs to manage time between your school, work, and family life? Do these devices help you achieve balance? If so, what technologies work for you? If not, what traditional life organizers do you recommend?

## Terms to Remember

anger (p. 360)

balance (p. 339)

boundary (p. 339)

burnout (p. 341)

community (p. 340)

emotional intelligence (p. 359)

employee attrition (p. 342)

employee retention (p. 342)

external time wasters (p. 363)

external triggers (p. 361)

family (p. 339)

imbalance triggers (p. 343)

information and communications technologies (ICTs) (p. 352)

internal time wasters (p. 363)

internal triggers (p. 361)

work (p. 340)

work–life balance (p. 340)

workplace bullying (p. 347)

workplace mobbing (p. 350)

Visit the Student Study Site at **www.sagepub.com/keys2e** to access the following resources:

- SAGE journal articles
- Video links
- Web resources
- Web quizzes
- eflashcards

# Epilogue

## *Communication Is Work*

> *Communication in commuter-marriages had several characteristics that made it a form of work, including being effortful, structured, frequent, high quality, and frustrating.*
>
> —Bergen, Kirby, and McBride (2007, p. 300)

In November 2001, we became friends and colleagues who share a passion for applying communication research and competencies across contexts. Our careers have been spent teaching communication in higher education, working as communication consultants in corporate environments, and communicating professionally as department chairs or as college deans. In many ways, communication defines our lives. Still, we too must continually remind ourselves that *communication is work*. No matter how many successes we have or challenges we overcome in our own *professional* and *personal* lives, we must work to maintain communication excellence.

We both believe that communication is a foundation of business and professional excellence—and that is the driving theme of this text, which we hope resonates with you in whatever professional and personal stage you're currently experiencing. As you look back on the topics you studied in this course and look into the future, it's natural for you to think, "What do I do now? Will I know when I've arrived? Am I still doing a good job?" While most of your time spent reading this book, studying for exams, and completing projects is integral to striving for business and professional excellence, we must emphasize that much more is left on the horizon that goes beyond what we have presented in this textbook.

We want to emphasize that communication is a constant process, something that must be at the center of both your *professional* and *personal* life. Thus, as you move forward, remember that communication is not a destination you reach, leading you to cheer, "I'm done and have arrived." The focus must be more of constant energy from moment to moment, not just at work but also at home. This constant presence of communication in your life may make you feel as though you are continually trying to become something or someone else—but the good news is that constant communication presence and self-awareness is what excellence is all about. As our friends and colleagues remind us, communication can be a form of labor (work) that takes effort, structure, persistence, quality, and frustration (Bergen et al., 2007).

Beyond our view of communication as work, we want to emphasize that, just like your personal family, your professional family can be both functional and dysfunctional. Many of our own professional experiences have been filled with joy, civility, dignity, and respect—and these are ideal in human relationships. In contrast, we also have experienced firsthand and working as consultants across professional contexts situations in which front-line employees, shift leaders, general managers, and corporate executives suffered from utter chaos, uncivil communication, uncertainty, information overload, and burnout in the workplace. Our former client Mitch, president and CEO of a large health care system in the United States, said, "Everything professionally [at work] is going well, but I'm losing my family. The stress and work demands have taken over my family. . . . I think Stacey and I are moving toward divorce." Another professional, Robert, who works in the petrochemical industry, describes the stress of company downsizing: "We [the employees] don't know what to expect here at the plant on a day-to-day basis. . . . There are so many people losing their jobs, and the folks in the executive office don't communicate with us. . . . We are completely in the dark . . . and don't know if we will have jobs tomorrow or the next day." Throughout this text, we have provided you with the tools to overcome the challenges faced by Mitch and Robert—to move beyond dysfunctional environments and excel with professional excellence.

We hope that the KEYS process presented in this text will serve as a constant reminder that evaluating your own communication across professional contexts should be at the core of everything—and remember that excellence should feel never-ending, like a journey without a finish line. The conversation about the quality, ethicality, and emotionality of communication across contexts has started. What goals will you set for yourself? How will you respond in good times and in bad? What will be your role? The journey (the work) continues . . .

# References

Adams, S. (2010, October 7). The new rules of business etiquette. *Forbes*. Retrieved from http://finance.yahoo.com/news/pf_article_110944.html

Adler, R. B., & Proctor, R. F., II. (2007). *Looking out/looking in* (12th ed.). Belmont, CA: Thompson & Wadsworth.

Albrecht, K. (1992). *The only thing that matters: Bringing the power of the customer into the center of your business*. New York: HarperBusiness.

Ali, A., & Gulzar, A. (2012). Impact of emotional intelligence competencies on impression creation: Exploring the mediating role of impression management skills. *International Journal of Economics and Management Sciences, 1*(6), 29–34.

Allen, G. (2002). *Supervision: A hyperlink book*. Retrieved July 18, 2008, from telecollege.dccd.edu/mgmt1374/book

Allen, T. D., Herst, D. E., Bruck, C. S., & Sutton, M. (2000). Consequences associated with work-to-family conflict: A review and agenda for future research. *Journal of Occupational Health Psychology, 5,* 278–308.

Andersen, P. A., Guerrero, L. K., & Jones, S. M. (2006). Nonverbal behavior in intimate interactions and intimate relationships. In V. Manusov & M. L. Patterson (Eds.), *The SAGE handbook of nonverbal communication* (pp. 259–277). Thousand Oaks, CA: Sage.

Angelidis, J., & Ibrahim, N. A. (2012). The impact of emotional intelligence on the ethical judgment of managers. *Journal of Business Ethics, 99*(1), 111–119.

Antonoff, M. (1990, July 27). Presentations that persuade. *Personal Computing, 14,* 62–68.

Argyle, M. (1988). *Bodily communication*. London: Methuen.

Arlat, J., Kalbarczyk, Z., & Nanya, T. (2012). Nanocomputing: Small devices, large dependability challenges. *Security and Privacy, 10*(1), 69–72.

Armour, S. (2005, July 19). Your appearance can affect the size of your paycheck. *USA Today*. Retrieved from http://www.usatoday.com/money/workplace/2005-07-19-bias-usat_x.htm

Avey, J. B., Wernsing, T. A., & Luthans, F. (2008). Can positive employees help positive organizational change? Impact of psychological capital and emotions on relevant attitudes and behaviors. *Journal of Applied Behavioral Science, 44,* 48–70.

Ba', S. (2011). Symbolic boundaries: Integration and separation of work and family life. *Community, Work and Family, 14*(3), 317–334.

Babad, E., Avni-Babad, D., & Rosenthal, R. (2003). Teachers' brief nonverbal behaviors in defined instructional situations can predict students' evaluations. *Journal of Educational Psychology, 95,* 553–563.

Bailyn, L. (1993). *Breaking the mold: Women, men, and time in the new corporate world*. New York: Free Press.

Ballard, D. I. (2008). The experience of time at work. In L. K. Guerrero & M. L. Hecht (Eds.), *The nonverbal communication reader: Classic and contemporary readings* (3rd ed., pp. 258–269). Prospect Heights, IL: Waveland.

Barbuto, J. E., & Gifford, G. T. (2012). Motivation and leader-member exchange: Evidence counter to similarity attraction theory. *International Journal of Leadership Studies, 7*(1), 18–28.

Barker, L., & Watson, K. (2000). *Listen up*. New York: St. Martin's Press.

Barley, S. R., Meyerson, D. E., & Grodal, S. (2011). E-mail as a source and symbol of stress. *Journal of Organization Science, 22*(4), 897–906.

Barrett, C. (2008, May). Talking Southwest culture. *Spirit: Southwest Airlines*, p. 12.

Bass, A. N. (2010). From business dining to public speaking: Tips for acquiring professional presence and its role in the business curricula. *American Journal of Business Education, 3*(2), 57–64.

Beatty, M. J. (1988). Situational and predispositional correlates of public speaking anxiety. *Communication Education, 37,* 28–38.

Beebe, S. A., Beebe, S. J., & Ivy, D. K. (2007). *Communication: Principles for a lifetime* (3rd ed.). Boston: Allyn & Bacon.

Bell, M. P., Özbilgin, M. F., Beauregard, T. A., & Sürgevil, O. (2011). Voice, silence, and diversity in 21st century organizations: Strategies for inclusion of gay, lesbian, bisexual, and transgender employees. *Human Resource Management, 50*(1), 131–146.

Bellah, R., Madsen, R., Sullivan, W. M., Swidler, A., & Tipton, S. M. (1985). *Habits of the heart: Individualism and commitment in American life*. Berkeley: University of California Press.

Benne, K., & Sheats, P. (1948). Functional roles of group members. *Journal of Social Issues, 4,* 41–49.

Bergman, M. E., Watrous-Rodriguez, K. M., & Chalkley, K. M. (2008). Identity and language: Contributions to and consequences of speaking Spanish in the workplace. *Hispanic Journal of Behavioral Science, 30,* 40–68.

Bernstein, A. J. (2001). *Emotional vampires: Dealing with people who drain you dry*. New York: McGraw Hill.

Bhunia, A., & Das, S. A. (2012). Explore the impact of workplace spirituality on motivations for earnings management—an empirical analysis. *International Journal of Scientific and Research Publications, 2*(2), 194–201.

Biggiero, L., Sammarra, A., & Dandi, R. (2012). The effect of e-mail use and adoption on organizational participation: The case of a public administration. *Human Systems Management, 29*(1), 27–39.

Bingham, S. G. (1991). Communication strategies for managing sexual harassment in organizations: Understanding message options and their effects. *Journal of Applied Communication Research, 19,* 88–115.

Birdwhistell, R. L. (1970). *Kinesics and context.* Philadelphia: University of Pennsylvania Press.

Blake, R. R., & Mouton, J. S. (1964). *The managerial grid.* Houston, TX: Gulf.

Blake, R. R., & Mouton, J. S. (1978). *The new managerial grid.* Houston, TX: Gulf.

Bly, R. W. (1999). *The encyclopedia of business letters, fax memos, and e-mail.* Franklin Lakes, NJ: Career Press.

Boerner, S., Schäffner, M., & Gebert, D. (2012). The complementarity of team meetings and cross-functional communication: Empirical evidence from new services development teams. *Journal of Leadership & Organizational Studies, 19*(2), 1–11.

Bok, S. (1989). *Secrets: On the ethics of concealment and revelation.* New York: Vintage Books.

Bok, S. (1999). *Lying: Moral choice in public and private life.* New York: Vintage.

Bolman, L. G., & Deal, T. E. (1997). *Reframing organizations: Artistry, choice and leadership* (2nd ed.). San Francisco: Jossey-Bass.

Bradberry, T., & Greaves, J. (2005). *The emotional intelligence quick book.* New York: Simon & Schuster.

Braithwaite, D. O. (1990). From majority to minority: An analysis of cultural change from ablebodied to disabled. *International Journal of Intercultural Relations, 14,* 465–483.

Braithwaite, D. O. (1996). "I am a person first": Different perspectives on the communication of persons with disabilities. In E. B. Ray (Ed.), *Communication and disenfranchisement: Social health issues and implications* (pp. 257–272). Mahwah, NJ: Erlbaum.

Braithwaite, D. O., & Baxter, L. A. (Eds.). (2006). *Engaging theories in family communication: Multiple perspectives.* Thousand Oaks, CA: Sage.

Braithwaite, D. O., & Braithwaite, C. A. (2009). "Which is my good leg?" Cultural communication of persons with disabilities. In L. W. Samovar, R. Porter, & E. R. McDaniel (Eds.), *Intercultural*

*communication: A reader* (9th ed., pp. 207–218). Belmont, CA: Wadsworth.

Braithwaite, D. O., & Thompson, T. L. (2000). *Handbook of communication and people with disabilities: Research and application.* Mahwah, NJ: Erlbaum.

Bremner, S. (2012). Socialization and the acquisition of professional discourse: A case study in the PR industry. *Written Communication, 29*(1), 7–32.

Briody, E., Pester, T. M., & Trotter, R. (2012). A story's impact on organizational-culture change. *Journal of Organizational Change Management, 25*(1), 67–87.

Brownell, J. (1994). Teaching listening: Some thoughts on behavioral approaches. *Business Communication Quarterly, 57,* 19–24.

Brownell, J. (1996). *Listening: Attitudes, principles, and skills.* Boston: Allyn & Bacon.

Bruneau, T. (2012). Chronemics: Time-binding and the construction of personal time. *A Review of General Semantics, 69*(1), 72–92.

Bull, M., & Brown, T. (2012). Change communication: The impact on satisfaction with alternative workplace strategies. *Facilities, 30*(3), 135–151.

Burgoon, J. K., & Jones, S. B. (1976). Toward a theory of personal space expectations and their violations. *Human Communication Research, 2,* 131–146.

Burkard, A. W., Boticki, M. A., & Madson, M. B. (2002). Workplace discrimination, prejudice, and diversity measurement: A review of instrumentation. *Journal of Career Assessment, 10,* 343–361.

Buzzanell, P. M. (1994). Gaining a voice: Feminist organizational communication theorizing. *Management Communication Quarterly, 7,* 339–389.

Buzzanell, P. M. (1999). Tensions and burdens in employment interviewing processes: Perspectives of nondominant group applicants. *Journal of Business Communication, 36,* 134–162.

By, R. T., Burnes, B., & Oswick, C. (2012). Change management: Leadership, values and ethics. *Journal of Change Management, 12*(1), 1–5.

Byrne, U. (2005). Work–life balance: Why are we all talking about it? *Business Information Review, 22,* 53–59.

Byrne, U. (2008). If you want something done, ask a busy person. *Business Information Review, 25,* 190–196.

Byron, K., & Baldridge, D. C. (2007). E-mail recipients' impressions of senders' likeability: The interactive effect of nonverbal cues and recipients' personality. *Journal of Business Communication, 44,* 137–160.

Callahan, B. N. (1999). *Grief counseling: A manual for social workers.* Denver, CO: Love.

Cameron, S. (2011). *Handbook on the economics of leisure.* Northampton, MA: Edward Elgar.

Campbell, K. S., Mothersbaugh, D. L., Brammer, C., & Taylor, T. (2001). Peer versus self assessment of oral business presentation performance. *Business Communication Quarterly, 64,* 23–43.

Carrasco, M. (2007, July 31). *Fun BlackBerry statistics.* Retrieved from http://www.realsoftwaredevelopment.com/fun-blackberry-statistics/

Carter, S. (1996). *Integrity.* New York: Basic.

Cavico, F. J., Muffler, S. C., & Mujtaba, B. G. (2012). Sexual orientation and gender identity discrimination in the American workplace: Legal and ethical considerations. *International Journal of Humanities and Social Science, 2*(1), 1–20.

Centers for Disease Control and Prevention. (2004). *Obesity trends among US adults: CDC's behavioral risk factor surveillance system 1991–2003.* Retrieved October 27, 2008, from http://www.obesityinamerica.org/trends/html

Centers for Disease Control and Prevention. (2012). *Overweight and obesity: Data and statistics.* Retrieved from http://www.cdc.gov/obesity/data/index.html

Chang, J. W., Sy, T., & Choi, J. N. (2012). Team emotional intelligence and performance interactive dynamics between leaders and members. *Small Group Research, 43*(1), 75–104.

Chapman, B., & Monahan, R. (2011, December 6). Ex-city educrat fined $6,500 for email misuse. *New York Daily News.* Retrieved from http://articles.nydailynews.com/2011-12-06/news/30483603_1_real-estate-holdings-private-firm-bear-stearns

Chen, C. Y., Pedersen, S., & Murphy, K. L. (2012). The influence of perceived information overload on student participation and knowledge construction in computer-mediated communication. *Instructional Science, 40*(2), 325–349.

Chen, X. H., Zhao, K., Liu, X., & Wu, D. (2012). Improve employees' job satisfaction and innovation performance using conflict management. *International Journal of Conflict Management, 23*(2), 23–33.

Chesebro, J. D., & McCroskey, J. C. (2001). The relationship of teacher clarity and immediacy with student state receiver apprehension, affect, and cognitive learning. *Communication Education, 50,* 59–68.

Cho, V., & Hung, H. (2011). The effectiveness of short message service for communication with concerns of privacy protection and conflict avoidance. *Journal of Computer-Mediated Communication, 16*(2), 250–270.

Cicala, J. E., Smith, R. K., & Bush, A. J. (2012). What makes sales presentations effective—a buyer-seller perspective. *Journal of Business and Industrial Marketing, 27*(2), 78–88.

Clare, J., & Danilovic, V. (2012). Reputation for resolve, interests, and conflict. *Conflict Management and Peace Science, 29*(1), 3–27.

Couch, D., & Liamputtong, P. (2008). Online dating and mating: The use of the Internet to meet sexual partners. *Qualitative Health Research, 18,* 269–279.

Cozzetto, D. A., & Pedeliski, T. B. (1996). Privacy and the workplace. *Review of Public Personnel Administration, 16,* 21–31.

Choy, S. C., & Oo, P. S. (2012). Reflective thinking and teaching practices: A precursor for incorporating critical thinking into the classroom? *International Journal of Instruction, 5*(1), 167–182.

Christian, J., Porter, L. W., & Moffit, G. (2006). Workplace diversity and group relations: An overview. *Group Process and Intergroup Relations, 9,* 459–466.

Clarke, J. T. (1989). Lawyer-client relations. *Journal of Professional Services Marketing, 5,* 101–104.

Collins, P. (2012). *The art of speeches and presentations*. West Sussex, UK: John Wiley.

Conrad, D., & Newberry, R. (2011). 24 business communication skills: Attitudes of human resource managers versus business educators. *American Communication Journal, 13*(1), 4–23.

Coontz, S. (2000). Historical perspectives on family studies. *Journal of Marriage and the Family, 62,* 283–297.

Covey, S. R. (2003). *The 7 habits of highly effective people personal workbook*. New York: Fireside.

Crockett, R. (2011, March 14). Listening is critical in today's multicultural workplace. *Harvard Business Review Blog Network*. Retrieved from http://blogs .hbr.org/cs/2011/03/shhh_listening_is_ critical_in.html

Crosby, O. (2000). Employment interviewing: Seizing the opportunity and the job. *Occupational Outlook Quarterly, 44,* 14–21.

D'Abate, C. P. (2005). Working hard or hardly working: A study of individuals engaging in personal business on the job. *Human Relations, 58,* 1009–1032.

Dallas, M. E. (2011, September 30). Doctors consider nonverbal cues in medical decisions. *HealthDay*. Retrieved from http://news.health.com/2011/09/30/ doctors-consider-nonverbal-cues-in-medical-decisions/

Dallimore, K. S., Sparks, B. A., & Butcher, K. (2007). The influence of angry customer outbursts on service providers' facial displays and affective states. *Journal of Service Research, 10,* 78–92.

Daly, J. A., Vangelisti, A. L., & Weber, D. J. (1995). Speech anxiety affects how people prepare speeches: A protocol analysis of the preparation process of speakers. *Communication Monographs, 62,* 383–397.

Daniels, L., & McCarraher, L. (2000). *The work–life manual*. London: Industrial Society.

Davis, V. T. (2010, September 22). Local attorney crowned world champion of public speaking. *San Antonio Express-News*. Retrieved from http://www.mysanantonio.com/news/local_news/article/ Local-attorney-crowned-world-champion-of-public-670371.php

Deetz, S. A. (1992). *Democracy in an age of colonization*. Albany: State University of New York Press.

DeGroot, M. G., & Motowidlo, S. J. (1999). Why visual and vocal interview cues can affect interviewers' judgments and predict job performance. *Journal of Applied Psychology, 84,* 986–993.

DeLossy, D. (2007). Minimum required vacation time around the world. *Marie Claire*. Retrieved November 15, 2008, from http://www.marieclaire. com/life/career/successful/vacation-bulletin?click=main_sr

Den Hartog, D. N., & Belschak, F. D. (2012). When does transformational leadership enhance employee proactive behavior? The role of autonomy and role breadth self-efficacy. *Journal of Applied Psychology, 97*(1), 194–202.

Deshpande, A. (2012). Workplace spirituality, organizational learning capabilities and mass customization: An integrated framework. *International Journal of Business and Management, 7*(5), 3–18.

Dewey, J. (1910). *How we think*. Boston: D. C. Heath.

Dex, S., & Bond, S. (2005). Measuring work–life balance and its covariates. *Work, Employment, and Society, 19,* 627–637.

Diaz, I., Chiaburu, D. S., Zimmerman, R. D., & Boswell, W. R. (2012). Communication technology: Pros and cons of constant connection to work. *Journal of Vocational Behavior, 80,* 500–508.

Diffle, W., & Landau, S. (2007). *Privacy on the line: The politics of wiretapping and encryption*. Boston: MIT Press.

Dillard, J., & Segrin, C. (1987). *Intimate relationships in organizations: Relational types, illicitness, and power*. Paper presented at the annual conference of the International Communication Association, Montreal, Canada.

Dillard, J. P., Solomon, D. H., & Palmer, M. T. (1999). Structuring the concept of relational communication. *Communication Monographs, 66,* 49–65.

Dipboye, R. L. (1992). *Selection interviews: Process perspective*. Cincinnati, OH: South-Western.

Dorio, M., & Axelrod, A. (2000). *The complete idiots guide to the perfect interview*. Indianapolis, IN: Alpha.

Dougherty, D. S. (2001). Sexual harassment as [dys]functional process: A feminist standpoint analysis. *Journal of Applied Communication Research, 29,* 372–402.

Doyle, T. A. (1998). *Allyn & Bacon quick guide to the Internet for speech communication.* Boston: Allyn & Bacon.

Drago, R. (2007). *Striking a balance: Work, family, and life.* Boston: Dollars & Sense.

Driscoll, K., & Wiebe, E. (2007). Technical spirituality at work: Jacques Ellul on workplace spirituality. *Journal of Management Inquiry, 16,* 333–348.

Duck, S. W. (1994). *Meaningful relationships.* Thousand Oaks, CA: Sage.

Duck, S. W. (2007). *Human relationships* (4th ed.). Thousand Oaks, CA: Sage.

Duffy, M., & Sperry, L. (2007). Workplace mobbing: Individual and family health consequences. *Family Journal: Counseling and Therapy for Couples and Families, 15,* 398–404.

Duffy, M., & Sperry, L. (2012). *Mobbing: Causes, consequences and solutions.* New York: Oxford University Press.

Eadie, W. F. (2009). In plain sight: Gay and lesbian communication and culture. In L. W. Samovar, R. Porter, & E. R. McDaniel (Eds.), *Intercultural communication: A reader* (9th ed., pp. 219–231). Belmont, CA: Wadsworth.

Edwards, A., Edwards, C., Wahl, S. T., & Myers, S. (2013). *The communication age: Connecting and engaging.* Thousand Oaks, CA: Sage.

Edwards, C., Edwards, A., Qing, Q., & Wahl, S. T. (2007). The influence of computer-mediated word-of-mouth communication on student perceptions of instructors and attitudes toward learning course content. *Communication Education, 56,* 255–277.

Edwards, J. R., & Rothbard, N. P. (2000). Mechanisms linking work and family: Clarifying the relationship between work and family constructs. *Academy of Management Review, 25,* 178–199.

Eikhof, D. R. (2012). A double-edged sword: Twenty-first century workplace trends and gender equality. *Gender in Management: An International Journal, 27*(1), 7–22.

Eisenberg, E., Goodall, H. L., Jr., & Trethewey, A. (2007). *Organizational communication: Balancing creativity and constraint* (5th ed.). Boston: Bedford/St Martin's.

Eisenberg, E., Monge, P., & Farace, R. V. (1984). Co-orientation on communication rules in managerial dyads. *Human Communication Research, 11,* 261–271.

Ekman, P. (1965). Communication through nonverbal behavior: A source of information about an interpersonal relationship. In S. S. Tomkins & C. E. Izard (Eds.), *Affect, cognition, and personality* (pp. 390–442). New York: Springer.

Ekman, P., & Friesen, W. V. (1969a). Nonverbal leakage and clues to deception. *Psychiatry, 32,* 88–106.

Ekman, P., & Friesen, W. V. (1969b). The repertoire of nonverbal behavior: Categories, origins, usage, and coding. *Semiotica, 1,* 49–98.

Engelberg, E., & Sjoberg, L. (2004). Emotional intelligence, affect intensity, and social adjustment. *Personality and Individual Differences, 37,* 533–542.

Equal Employment Opportunity Commission. (1980). Guidelines on discrimination because of sex. *Federal Register, 45,* 74676–74677.

Evans, G. W., Becker, F. D., Zahn, A., Keesee, A. M., & Bilotta, E. (2012). Capturing the ecology of workplace stress with cumulative risk assessment. *Environment and Behavior, 44*(1), 136–154.

Evanschitzky, H., Sharma, A., & Prykop, C. (2012). The role of the sales employee in securing customer satisfaction. *European Journal of Marketing, 46*(3), 489–508.

Farnham, A. (2012, March 19). Florida law firm fires workers for wearing orange. *ABC News.* Retrieved from http://abcnews.go.com/blogs/business/2012/03/law-firm-fires-workers-for-wearing-orange/

Ferguson, M., Carlson, D., Zivnuska, S., & Whitten, D. (2012). Support at work and home: The path to satisfaction through balance. *Journal of Vocational Behavior, 80*(2), 299–307.

Ferris, P. (2004). A preliminary typology of organizational response to allegations of workplace bullying: See no evil, hear no evil, speak no evil. *British* *Journal of Guidance and Counseling, 32,* 389–395.

Festinger, L. (1957). *A theory of cognitive dissonance.* Stanford, CA: Stanford University Press.

Fiedler, F. E. (1997). Situational control and a dynamic theory of leadership. In K. Grint (Ed.), *Leadership: Classical, contemporary, and critical approaches.* Oxford, UK: Oxford University Press.

Fiedler, F. E., & Garcia, J. E. (1987). *New approaches to effective leadership.* New York: John Wiley.

Finder, A. (June, 2006). For some online persona undermines a resume. *New York Times,* p. 11.

Fine, M. G. (1996). Cultural diversity in the workplace: The state of the field. *Journal of Business Communication, 33,* 485–502.

Fisher, R., Ury, W., & Patton, B. (1991). *Getting to yes: Negotiating agreement without giving in* (2nd ed.). New York: Penguin Books.

Fisher, W. R. (1984). Narration as human communication paradigm: The case of public moral argument. *Communication Monographs, 51,* 1–22.

Fleming, P. (2007). Sexuality, power, and resistance in the workplace. *Organization Studies, 28,* 230–256.

Flynn, N. (2006a). *Blog rules: A business guide to managing policy, public relations, and legal issues.* New York: AMACOM.

Flynn, N. (2006b). *E-mail management: 50 tips for keeping your inbox under control.* Boston: Thomson Course Technology.

Flynn, N. (2009). *The e-policy handbook: Rules and best practices to safely manage your company's email, blogs, social networking, and other electronic communication tools* (2nd ed.). New York: AMACOM.

Flynn, N., & Flynn, T. (2003). *Writing effective e-mail: Improving your electronic communication.* Boston: Thomson Course Technology.

Foley, G. N., & Gentile, J. P. (2010). Nonverbal communication in psychotherapy. *Psychiatry (Edgmont), 7*(6), 38–44.

Ford, C. E., & Stickle, T. (2012). Securing recipiency in workplace meetings: Multimodal practices. *Discourse Studies, 14*(1), 11–30.

Foste, E. A., & Botero, I. C. (2012). Personal reputation: Effects of upward communication on impressions about new employees. *Management Communication Quarterly, 26*(1), 48–73.

Francis, E. (2011, November 1). 'Happiest woman' succeeds in finding work–life balance. *ABCNews Blogs: Medical Unit.* Retrieved from http://abcnews.go.com/blogs/health/2011/11/01/happiest-woman-succeeds-in-finding-work-life-balance/

Freiberg, K., & Freiberg, J. (1996). *NUTS! Southwest Airlines' crazy recipe for business and personal success.* Austin, TX: Bard.

French, R., & Raven, B. (1968). The bases of power. In D. Cartwright & A. Zander (Eds.), *Group dynamics* (pp. 601–623). New York: Harper & Row.

Friedman, M. (1996). *Type A behavior: Its diagnosis and treatment.* New York: Plenum.

Friedman, M., & Rosenman, R. H. (1974). *Type A behavior and your heart.* New York: Knopf.

Fryer, B. (2009, November 5). Is listening an endangered skill? *Harvard Business Review Blog Network.* Retrieved from http://blogs.hbr.org/hbr/hbreditors/2009/11/is_listening_an_endangered_ski.html

Fulk, J., & Mani, S. (1986). Distortion of communication in hierarchical relationships. In M. L. McLaughlin (Ed.), *Communication yearbook* (Vol. 9, pp. 483–510). Newbury, CA: Sage.

Gabbott, M., & Hogg, G. (2000). An empirical investigation of the impact of nonverbal communication on service evaluation. *European Journal of Marketing, 34*, 384–399.

Galliard, B. M., Myers, K. K., & Seibold, D. R. (2010). Organizational assimilation: A multidimensional reconceptualization and measure. *Management Communication Quarterly, 24*, 552–578.

Genova, G. L. (2009). No place to play: Current employee privacy rights in social networking sites. *Business Communication Quarterly, 72*, 97–101.

Gibbs, M., Hewing, P., Hulbert, J., Ramsey, D., & Smith, A. (1985). How to teach effective listening skills in a basic communication class: Teaching methodology and concepts committee.

*Business Communication Quarterly, 48*, 30–33.

Gilbert, J., Carr-Ruffino, N., Ivancevich, J. M., & Konopaske, R. (2012). Toxic versus cooperative behaviors at work: The role of organizational culture and leadership in creating community-centered organizations. *International Journal of Leadership Studies, 7*(1), 29–47.

Glavin, P., & Schieman, S. (2012). Work–family role blurring and work–family conflict: The moderating influence of job resources and job demands. *Work and Occupations, 39*(1), 71–98.

Goffman, E. (1971). *Relations in public: Microstudies of the public order.* New York: Harper Colophon.

Golden, A. G., & Geisler, C. (2007). Work–life boundary management and the personal digital assistant. *Human Relations, 60*, 519–551.

Goldstein, A. (2000, February 27). Breadwinning wives alter marriage equation. *Washington Post,* p. A1.

Goleman, D. (1995). *Emotional intelligence.* New York: Bantam.

Goodall, H. L. (1991). *Living in the rock n roll mystery.* Carbondale: Southern Illinois University Press.

Gosselin, P., Gilles, K., & Dore, F. Y. (1995). Components and recognition of facial expression in the communication of emotion by actors. *Journal of Personality and Social Psychology, 68*, 83–96.

Gouran, D. S. (1990). *Making decisions in groups: Choices and consequences.* Prospectus Heights, IL: Waveland. (Original work published in 1982)

Gouran, D. S., & Hirokawa, R. Y. (1996). Functional theory and communication in decision-making and problem-solving groups. In R. Y. Hirokawa & M. S. Poole (Eds.), *Communication and group decision-making* (2nd ed., pp. 55–80). Thousand Oaks, CA: Sage.

Graham, S., Santos, D., & Vanderplank, R. (2008). Listening comprehension and strategy use: A longitudinal exploration. *System, 36*, 52–68.

Gray, F. E. (2010). Specific oral communication skills desired in new accountancy graduates. *Business Communication Quarterly, 73*(1), 40–67.

Gray, K. (2011). You're hired! Practical tips and techniques for the confident interview.

*Legal Information Management, 11*(1), 69–71.

Greenstein, T. (1996). Husband's participation in domestic labor: The interactive effect of wives' and husbands' domestic ideologies. *Journal of Marriage and the Family, 58*, 585–595.

Grzywacz, J. G., & Carlson, D. S. (2007). Conceptualizing work–family balance: Implications for practice and research. *Advances in Developing Human Resources, 9*, 455–471.

Gudykunst, W. B. (2004). *Bridging differences* (4th ed.). Thousand Oaks, CA: Sage.

Gueguen, N., & Jacob, C. (2002). Direct look versus evasive glance and compliance with a request. *Journal of Social Psychology, 142*, 393–397.

Haas, J. W., & Arnold, C. (1995). An examination of the role of listening in judgments of communication competence in co-workers. *Journal of Business Communication, 32*, 123–139.

Hackman, J. R. (2012). From causes to conditions in group research. *Journal of Organizational Behavior, 33*(3), 428–444.

**Hall, E.T. (1959).** *The silent language.* Garden City, NY: Doubleday.

Hall, E. T. (1963). A system for the notation of proxemic behavior. *American Anthropology, 65*, 1003–1026.

Hall, E. T. (1966). *The hidden dimension.* Garden City, NY: Doubleday.

Hamilton, C. (1996). *Essentials of public speaking.* Belmont, CA: Wadsworth.

Hancock, S. (1999). How to learn more by studying less. *Management Services, 43*, 20–22.

Hansen, R. (n.d.). Salary negotiation do's and don'ts. Retrieved May 1, 2012 from http://www.quintcareers.com/salary-dos-donts.html

Harris Interactive. (2008). *Expedia.com: 2007 International Vacation Deprivation Survey Results.* Retrieved November 16, 2008, from http://media.expedia.com/media/content/expus/graphics/promos/vacations/Expedia_International_Vacation_Deprivation_Survey_Results_2007.pdf

Harris, P., & Sachau, D. (2005). Is cleanliness next to godliness? The role of housekeeping in impression formation. *Environment and Behavior, 37*, 81–99.

Harrison, R. P., & Crouch, W. W. (1975). Nonverbal communication: Theory and research. In G. J. Hanneman & W. J. McEwen (Eds.), *Communication and behavior* (pp. 76–97). Reading, MA: Addison-Wesley.

Harrison, T. (1985). Communication and participative decision-making: An exploratory study. *Personnel Psychology, 38,* 93–116.

Harvey, M. G., Buckley, M. R., Heames, J. T., Zinko, R., Brouer, R. L., & Ferris, G. R. (2007). A bully as an archetypal destructive leader. *Journal of Leadership and Organizational Studies, 14,* 117–129.

Harvey, M. G., Heames, J. T., Richey, R. G., & Leopard, M. (2006). Bullying: From the playground to the boardroom [Electronic version]. *Journal of Leadership and Organizational Studies, 12,* 1–11.

Hellweg, S. (1987). Organizational grapevine: A state of the art review. In B. Dervin & M. Voight (Eds.), *Progress in the communication sciences* (Vol. 8, pp. 213–230). Norwood, NJ: Ablex.

Hermes, J. J. (2008, April 25). Colleges create Facebook-style social networks to reach alumni. *Chronicle of Higher Education,* p. A18.

Hersey, P., & Blanchard, K. H. (1977). *The management of organizational behavior: Utilizing human resources* (3rd ed.). Englewood Cliffs, NJ: Prentice Hall.

Heslin, R. (1974, May). *Steps toward a taxonomy of touching.* Paper presented at the meeting of the Midwestern Psychological Association, Chicago.

Hewett, B., & Robidoux, C. (2010). *Virtual collaborative writing in the workplace: Computer-mediated communication technologies and processes.* Hershey, PA: IGI Global.

Highet, G. (1989). *The art of teaching.* New York: Random House.

Hill, C. J., & Garner, S. J. (1991). Factors influencing physician choice. *Hospital and Health Services Administration, 36,* 491–504.

Hinkle, L. L. (2001). Perceptions of supervisor nonverbal immediacy, vocalics, and subordinate liking. *Communication Research Reports, 18,* 128–136.

Hishitani, S. (1991). Vividness of image and retrieval time. *Perceptions and Motor Skills, 73,* 115–123.

Hlemstra, K. M. (1999). Shake my hand: Making the right first impression in business with nonverbal communications. *Business Communication Quarterly, 62,* 71–74.

Hochschild, A. (with Machung, A.). (1989). *The second shift: Working parents and the revolution at home.* New York: Viking/Penguin.

Houtenville, A., & Kalargyrou, V. (2012). People with disabilities: Employers' perspectives on recruitment practices, strategies, and challenges in leisure and hospitality. *Cornell Hospitality Quarterly, 53*(1), 40–52.

Huffcutt, A. I. (2010). From science to practice: Seven principles for conducting employment interviews. *Applied H.R.M. Research, 12*(1), 121–136.

Hult, C. A., & Huckin, T. N. (1999). *The new century handbook.* Boston: Allyn & Bacon.

Ivy, D. K., & Wahl, S. T. (2009). *The nonverbal self: Communication for a lifetime.* Boston: Allyn & Bacon.

Jablin, F. (1979). Superior-subordinate communication: The state of the art. *Psychological Bulletin, 86,* 1201–1222.

Jablin, F. (1987). Organizational entry, assimilation, and exit. In F. Jablin, L. Putnam, K. Roberts, & L. Porter (Eds.), *Handbook of organizational communication* (pp. 679–740). Newbury Park, CA: Sage.

Jackson, H. (2005). Sitting comfortably? Then let's talk! *Psychologist, 18,* 691.

Jafari, J., & Way, W. (1994). Multicultural strategies in tourism. *Cornell Hotel and Restaurant Administration Quarterly, 35,* 72–80.

Jaffe, G. (2000, April 26). What's your point, Lieutenant? Just cut to the pie charts: The Pentagon declares war on electronic slide shows that make briefings a pain. *Wall Street Journal,* p. A1.

Jalongo, M. R. (2008). *Learning to listen, listening to learn.* Washington, DC: National Association for the Education of Young Children.

Jang, C. Y., & Stefanone, M. A. (2011). Non-directed self-disclosure in the blogosphere. *Information, Communication and Society, 14*(7), 1039–1059.

Janis, I. L. (1982). *Groupthink* (Rev. ed.). Boston: Houghton Mifflin.

Janis, I. L. (1989). *Crucial decisions: Leadership in policymaking and crisis management.* New York: Free Press.

Japp, P. M., Meister, M., & Japp, D. K. (2005). *Communication ethics, media, and popular culture.* New York: Peter Lang.

Jeffreys, S. (2012, March 14). Blagojevich gives final public speech before prison term. *WREX News 13.* Retrieved from http://www.wrex.com/story/17160904/blagojevich-gives-final-public-speech-before-prison-term

Johannesen, R. L., Valde, K. S., & Whedbee, K. E. (2008). *Ethics in human communication* (6th ed.). Prospect Heights, IL: Waveland.

Johnson, T. (2012). Negotiating salary 101: Tactics for better compensation. Retrieved August 18, 2012 from http://womenforhire.com/advice/negotiating_salary_benefits/negotiating_salary_101_tactics_for_better_compensation/

Johnston, S. (2011, October 20). Landing a job through LinkedIn: 4 success stories. *AOL Jobs.* Retrieved from http://jobs.aol.com/articles/2011/10/20/landing-a-job-through-linkedin-4-success-stories/

Jones, C., & Trejos, N. (2012, May 24). Summer travel outlook. *USA Today,* p. 1.

Jones, S. E., & LeBaron, C. D. (2002). Research on the relationship between verbal and nonverbal communication: Emerging integrations. *Journal of Communication, 52,* 499–523.

Jovin, E. (2007). *E-mail etiquette for business professionals.* New York: Syntaxis.

Judge, T. A., Higgins, C. A., & Cable, D. M. (2000). The employment interview: A review of recent research and recommendations for future research. *Human Resource Management Review, 10,* 383–406.

Kals, E., & Jiranek, P. (2012). Organizational justice. *Justice and Conflicts, 4,* 219–235.

Karl, K., & Peluchette, J. (2006). How does workplace fun impact employee perceptions of customer service quality? *Journal of Leadership and Organizational Studies, 13,* 1–13.

Katzenbach, J. R., & Smith, D. K. (1993). *The wisdom of teams: Creating the high performance organization.* Boston: Harvard Business School Press.

Kauffeld, S., & Lehmann-Willenbrock, N. (2011). Meetings matter: Effects of team meetings on team and organizational success. *Small Group Research, 43*(2), 130–158.

Kazoleas, D. C. (1993, Winter). A comparison of persuasive effectiveness of qualitative versus quantitative evidence: A test of explanatory hypothesis. *Communication Quarterly, 41,* 40–50.

Kelleher, Z., & Hall, H. (2005). Response to risk: Experts and end-user perspectives on email security, and the role of the business information professional in policy development. *Business Information Review, 22,* 46–52.

Kelly, P., Allender, S., & Calquhoun, D. (2007). New work ethics? The corporate athlete's back end index and organizational performance. *Organization, 14,* 267–285.

Kerr, D. (2012, February 2). Apple CEO Tim Cook donates $100 million to charity. *CNET News.* Retrieved from http://news.cnet.com/8301-13579_3-57370922-37/apple-ceo-tim-cook-donates-$100-million-to-charity/

Key, J. (2012). *Journey towards professionalism: Straight talk for today's generation.* Bloomington, IN: Universe.

Keysar, B., & Henley, A. S. (2002). Speakers' overestimation of their effectiveness. *Psychological Science, 13,* 207–213.

Keyton, J., & Beck, S. J. (2010). Examining emotional communication: Laughter in jury deliberations. *Small Group Research, 41,* 386–407.

Khan, A., & Khan, R. (2012). Understanding and managing workplace bullying. *Industrial and Commercial Training, 44*(2), 85–89.

Khan, F., & Khan, M. E. (2012). Achieving success through effective business communication. *Information and Knowledge Management, 2,* 46–50.

Kibby, M. D. (2005). Email forwardables: Folklore in the age of the Internet. *New Media and Society, 7,* 770–790.

Kinlaw, D. C. (1991). *Developing superior work teams: Building quality and the competitive edge.* Lexington, MA: Lexington Books.

Kirby, E. L., Golden, A. G., Medved, C. E., Jorgenson, J., & Buzzanell, P. M. (2003). An organizational communication challenge to the discourse of work and family research: From problematics to empowerment. In P. J. Kalbfleisch (Ed.), *Communication yearbook 27* (pp. 1–44). Mahwah, NJ: Lawrence Erlbaum.

Kirby, E. L., & Harter, L. M. (2001). Discourses of diversity and the quality of work life: The character and costs of the managerial metaphor. *Management Communication Quarterly, 15,* 121–127.

Kirkhaug, R. (2010). Charisma or group belonging as antecedents of employee work effort? *Journal of Business Ethics, 96*(4), 647–656.

Kleinke, C. L. (1986). Gaze and eye contact: A research review. *Psychological Bulletin, 100,* 78–100.

Knapp, M. L., & Hall, J. A. (2006). *Nonverbal communication in human interaction* (6th ed.). Belmont, CA: Thomson/Wadsworth.

Knapp, M. L., & Hall, J. A. (2009). *Nonverbal communication in human interaction.* Boston: Wadsworth.

Knowles, D. (2010, February 26). Store fires woman for wearing Muslim head scarf. *AOL News.* Retrieved from http://www.aolnews.com/2010/02/26/store-fires-woman-for-wearing-muslim-head-scarf/

Koballa, T. R., Jr. (1989). Persuading teachers to reexamine the innovative elementary science programs of yesterday: The effect of anecdotal versus data-summary communications. *Journal of Research in Science Teaching, 23,* 437–449.

Konrad, A. M., Moore, M. E., Doherty, A. J., Ng, E. S. W., & Breward, K. (2012). Vocational status and perceived well-being of workers with disabilities. *Equality, Diversity and Inclusion: An International Journal, 31*(2), 100–123.

Krapels, R. H. (2000). Communication training in two companies. *Business Communication Quarterly, 63,* 104–110.

Kress, G. L., & Schar, M. (2012). Teamology—the art and science of design team formation. In H. Plattner, C. Meinel, & L. Leifer (Eds.), *Design thinking research: Studying co-creation in practice* (pp. 189–209). Berlin: Springer.

Kuntz, J. R. C., & Gomes, J. F. S. (2012). Transformational change in organizations: A self-regulation approach. *Journal of Organizational Change Management, 25*(1), 143–162.

Kupritz, V., & Hillsman, T. (2011). The impact of the physical environment on supervisory communication skills transfer. *Journal of Business Communication, 48*(2), 148–185.

Langan, K. (2012). Training Millennials: A practical and theoretical approach. *References Services Review, 40*(1), 24–48.

Laplante, D., & Ambady, N. (2003). On how things are said: Voice tone, voice intensity, verbal content, and perceptions of politeness. *Journal of Language and Social Psychology, 22,* 434–442.

Lavan, I. (2002). NLP in business—Or more than a trip to the zoo. *Industrial and Commercial Training, 34,* 182–188.

Lawson, H. M., & Leck, K. (2006). Dynamics of Internet dating. *Social Science Computer Review, 24,* 189–208.

Leech, T. (1992). *How to prepare, stage, and deliver winning presentations* (2nd ed.). New York: AMACOM.

Lehrer, V. (1998). Vital speeches of the day. *Journalism, 57,* 139–143.

Leigh, T. W., & Summers, J. O. (2002). An initial evaluation of industrial buyers' impressions of salespersons' nonverbal cues. *Journal of Personal Selling and Sales Management, 22,* 41–54.

Leiter, M. P., Day, A. L., Harvie, P., & Shaughnessy, K. (2007). Personal and organizational knowledge transfer: Implications for worklife engagement. *Human Relations, 60,* 259–283.

Levi, D. (2011). *Group dynamics for teams.* Thousand Oaks, CA: Sage.

Lewis, J. S., & Geroy, G. D. (2000). Employee spirituality in the workplace: A cross-cultural view for the management of spiritual employees. *Journal of Management Education, 24,* 682–694.

Leymann, H., & Gustaffson, A. (1996). Mobbing at work and the development of post traumatic stress disorders. *European Journal of Work and Organizational Psychology, 5,* 251–275.

Li, N., Jackson, M. H., & Trees, A. R. (2008). Relating online: Managing dialectical contradictions in massively multiplayer online role-playing game relationships. *Games and Culture, 3,* 76–97.

Lindsell-Roberts, S. (2004). *Strategic business letters and e-mail.* Boston: Houghton Mifflin.

Locher, M. A. (2010). Introduction: Politeness and impoliteness in computer-mediated communication. *Journal of Politeness Research, 6*(1), 1–5.

Locke, E., & Latham, G. (1984). *Goal setting: A motivational technique that really works!* Englewood Cliffs, NJ: Prentice Hall.

Lohmann, A., Arriaga, X. B., & Goodfriend, W. (2003). Close relationships and placemaking: Do objects in a couple's home reflect couplehood? *Personal Relationships, 10,* 437–449.

Louet, S. (2012, January 27). Your voice: Your passport to authority. *Science.* Retrieved from http://sciencecareers.sciencemag.org/career_magazine/previous_issues/articles/2012_01_27/caredit.a1200010

Lucas, S. E. (2007). *The art of public speaking* (9th ed.). New York: Random House.

Lumsden, G., & Lumsden, D. (1997). *Communicating in groups and teams: Sharing leadership* (2nd ed.). Belmont, CA: Wadsworth.

Mallard, J., & Quintanilla, K. (2007, November). *Does videotaped feedback for speeches impact student learning?* Student self-assessment of public speaking presented at the National Communication Association annual convention, Chicago.

Mann, R. D. (1959). A review of the relationship between personality and performance in small groups. *Psychological Bulletin, 66*(4), 241–270.

Manning, G. L., & Reece, B. (1989). *Selling today: An extension of the marketing concept.* Boston: Allyn & Bacon.

Martin, M. (2012). *Happiness and the good life.* New York: Oxford University Press.

Martin, W. B. (1986). Defining what quality service is for you. *Cornell Hotel and Restaurant Administration Quarterly, 26,* 32–39.

Marulanda-Carter, L., & Jackson, T. W. (2012). Effects of e-mail addiction and interruptions on employees. *Journal of Systems and Information Technology, 14*(1), 82–94.

Maslow, A. (1965). *Eupsychian management.* Homewood, IL: R. D. Irwin.

Mathenge, G. D. (2011). Ethical considerations in human resource management in Kenya: Theory and practice. *Public Policy and Administration Research, 1*(4), 8–20.

Mathews, M. M. (1951). *A dictionary of Americanisms on historical principles.* Chicago: University of Chicago Press.

Mayer, J., & Salovey, P. (1993). The intelligence of emotional intelligence. *Intelligence, 17,* 433–442.

McCaskey, M. B. (1979). The hidden messages managers send. *Harvard Business Review, 57,* 135–140.

McCroskey, J. (1982). Oral communication apprehension: A reconceptualization. In M. Burgoon (Ed.), *Communication yearbook 6* (pp. 136–170). Beverly Hills, CA: Sage.

McCroskey, J. C. (1984). The communication apprehension perspective. In J. A. Daly & J. C. McCroskey (Eds.), *Avoiding communication: Shyness, reticence, and communication apprehension* (pp. 13–38). Beverly Hills, CA: Sage.

McCroskey, J. C., & Teven, J. (1999). Goodwill: A reexamination of the construct and its measurement. *Communication Monographs, 66,* 90–103.

McDaniel, E. R., Samovar, L. A., & Porter, R. E. (2009). Understanding intercultural communication: The working principles. In L. W. Samovar, R. Porter, & E. R. McDaniel (Eds.), *Intercultural communication: A reader* (9th ed., pp. 6–17). Belmont, CA: Wadsworth.

McDermott, E. (2006). Surviving in dangerous places: Lesbian identity performances in the workplace, social class, and psychological health. *Feminism and Psychology, 16,* 193–211.

McDonald, K. S., & Hite, L. M. (2008). The next generation of career success: Implications for HRD. *Advances in Developing Human Resources, 10,* 86–103.

McGregor, D. (1960). *The human side of enterprise.* New York: McGraw Hill.

McKnight, M. R. (1995). The nature of people skills. *Journal of Management Education, 19,* 190–204.

Medved, C. E., & Kirby, E. L. (2005). Family CEOs: A feminist analysis of corporate mothering discourses. *Management Communication Quarterly, 18,* 435–478.

Mehrabian, A. (1981). *Silent messages: Implicit communication of emotions and attitudes.* Belmont, CA: Wadsworth.

Metsämäki, M. (2012). Persuasive discourse in EFL debate. *Theory and Practice in Language Studies, 2*(2), 205–213.

Miller, S. (2008). Workforce diversity. *Broadcasting and Cable, 138*(36), 19–20.

Mitroff, I., & Kilmann, R. (1975). Stories managers tell: A new tool for organizational problem solving. *Management Review, 64,* 18–28.

Moe, N. B., Dingsøyr, T., & Dybå, T. (2010). A teamwork model for understanding an agile team: A case study of a scrum project. *Information and Software Technology, 52*(5), 480–491.

Molloy, J. T. (1988). *New dress for success.* New York: Warner Books Edition.

Molloy, J. T. (1996). *New women's dress for success.* New York: Warner Books Edition.

Morales, M., Piero, J. M., Rodriguez, I., & Bliese, P. D. (2012). Perceived collective burnout: A multilevel explanation of burnout. *Anxiety, Stress and Coping: An International Journal, 25*(1), 43–61.

Morand, D. A. (2001). The emotional intelligence of managers: Assessing the construct of validity of a nonverbal measure of "people skills." *Journal of Business and Psychology, 16,* 21–33.

Morasch, L. J. (2004). *I hear you talking, but I don't understand you: Medical jargon and clear communication.* Molina Healthcare and California Academy of Family Physicians. Retrieved from http://www.medicalleadership.org/downloads/Medical-Jargon.pdf

Morris, D. (1985). *Body watching.* New York: Crown.

Morris, M. L., & Madsen, S. R. (2007). Advancing work–life integration in individuals, organizations, and communities. *Advances in Developing Human Resources, 9,* 439–454.

Muir, C. (1996). Workplace readiness for communicating diversity. *Journal of Business Communication, 33,* 475–484.

Mumby, D. K., & Putnam, L. L. (1992). The politics of emotion: A feminist reading of bounded rationality. *Academy of Management Review, 17,* 465–486.

Musgrove, M. (2011, November 8). Corporate tenants adopting revolutionary workplace technologies [Press release]. Retrieved from http://newsroom.cisco.com/press-release-content?type=webcontent&articleId=533335

Myers, K. K., & McPhee, R. D. (2006). Influences on member assimilation in workgroups in high-reliability organizations: A multilevel analysis. *Human Communication Research, 32,* 440–468.

Myers, S. A., & Anderson, C. M. (2008). *The fundamentals of small group communication.* Thousand Oaks, CA: Sage.

Negotiation Strategies. (n.d.). Retrieved August 18, 2012, from http://www.grad.illinois.edu/careerservices/negotiationstrategies

Nelson, D., & Heeney, W. (1984). Directed listening: A model for administrative communication. *National Association of Secondary School Principals, 68,* 124–129.

Nichols, S., & Stevens, L. (1957, September). Listening to people. *Harvard Business Review.* Retrieved from http://hbr.org/1957/09/listening-to-people/ar/1

Nickerson, R. S. (1980). Short-term memory for complex meaningful visual configurations: Demonstration of capacity. *Canadian Journal of Psychology, 19,* 155–160.

Nitin, A. B., Shamra, S. M., Kumar, K., Aggarwal, A., Goyal, S., Choudhary, K., et al. (2012). Classification of flames in computer-mediated communications. *International Journal of Computer Applications, 14*(6), 1–6.

Nixon, J., & West, J. (1989). Listening: Vital to communication. *Business Communication Quarterly, 52,* 15–18.

Nolan, M. J. (1975). The relationship between verbal and nonverbal communication. In G. J. Hanneman & W. J. McEwen (Eds.), *Communication and behavior* (pp. 98–119). Reading, MA: Addison-Wesley.

O'Connor, E. S. (1993). People skills as a discipline, pedagogy, and set of standard practices. *Journal of Management Education, 17,* 218–227.

Office of Women's Health. (2010). *Stress and your health fact sheet.* Retrieved from http://www.womenshealth.gov/publications/our-publications/fact-sheet/stress-your-health.cfm#a

The office romance: Why office romance is on the wane. (2010, September 16). *Bloomberg Businessweek.* Retrieved from http://www.businessweek.com/magazine/content/10_39/b4196073729941.htm#p1

O'Keefe, D. J. (1990). *Persuasion: Theory and research.* Newbury Park, CA: Sage.

Okoro, E., & Washington, M. (2011). Communicating in a multicultural classroom: A study of students' nonverbal behavior and attitudes toward faculty attire. *Journal of College Teaching and Learning, 8*(7), 27–38.

Okoro, E. A., & Washington, M. C. (2012). Workforce diversity and organizational communication: Analysis of human capital performance and productivity. *Journal of Diversity Management, 7*(1), 57–62.

O'Sullivan, M. (2005). Emotional intelligence and deception detection: Why most people can't "read" others, but a few can. In R. E. Riggio & R. S. Feldman (Eds.), *Applications of nonverbal communication* (pp. 215–253). Mahwah, NJ: Erlbaum.

Parlamis, J. D. (2012). Venting as emotion regulation: The influence of venting responses and respondent identity on anger and emotional tone. *International Journal of Conflict Management, 23*(1), 77–96.

Patterson, K., Grenny, J., McMillan, R., & Switzler, A. (2005). *Crucial confrontations: Tools for resolving broken promises, violated expectations, and bad behavior.* New York: McGraw Hill.

Pearce, W. B., Cronen, V. E., & Conklin, F. (1979). On what to look at when analyzing communication: A hierarchical model of actors' meanings. *Communication, 4,* 195–220.

Peluchette, J. V., Karl, K., & Rust, K. (2006). Dressing to impress: Beliefs and attitudes regarding workplace attire. *Journal of Business and Psychology, 21,* 45–63.

Peters, T. (1987). *Thriving on chaos.* New York: Knopf.

Peterson, D. R. (1992). Interpersonal relationships as a link between person and environment. In W. B. Walsh, K. H. Craik, & R. H. Price (Eds.), *Person-environment psychology: Models and perspectives* (pp. 127–155). Hillsdale, NJ: Erlbaum.

Petronio, S. (2000). *Balancing the secrets of private disclosures.* Mahwah, NJ: Erlbaum.

Petronio, S. (2002). *Boundaries of privacy: Dialectics of disclosure.* New York: State University of New York Press.

Petronio, S. (2007). Translational research endeavors and the practices of communication privacy management. *Journal of Applied Communication Research, 35,* 218–222.

PEW Research Center. (2007, July 12). *From 1997–2007: Full-time work grows less attractive to moms.* Retrieved from http://pewresearch.org/pubs/536/working-women

Pickholz, M. G., & Zimmerman, P. (2002). Litigation in the current environment. *CPA Journal, 72,* 62–63.

Plantin, C. (2012). Persuasion or alignment? *Argumentation, 26*(1), 83–97.

Pomerleau, R. (1994). A desideratum for managing the diverse workplace. *Review of Public Personnel Administration, 14,* 85–100.

Posthuma, R. A. (2012). Conflict management and emotions. *International Journal of Conflict Management, 23*(1), 4–5.

Powell, G. (2012). Six ways of seeing the elephant: The intersection of sex, gender, and leadership. *Gender in Management: An International Journal, 27*(2), 119–141.

Pugh, D. (2001). Service with a smile: Emotional contagion in the service encounter. *Academy of Management Journal, 44,* 1018–1027.

Quintanilla, K., & Mallard, J. (2008). Understanding the role of communication bravado: An important issue for trainers/teachers. *Texas Speech Communication Journal, 33,* 44–49.

Rapoport, R., & Bailyn, L. (1996). *Rethinking life and work: Toward a better future*. New York: Ford Foundation.

Redfield, R. (1953). *The primitive world and its transformation*. Ithaca, NY: Cornell University Press.

Regenbogen, C., Schneider, D. A., Gur, R. E., Schneider, F., Habel, U., & Kellermann, T. (2012). Multimodal human communication-targeting facial expressions, speech content and prosody. *Neuro-Image, 60*, 2346–2356.

Rhoads, M. (2010). Face-to-face and computer-mediated communication: What does theory tell us and what have we learned so far? *Journal of Planning Literature, 25*(2), 111–122.

Richmond, V. P., McCroskey, J. C., & Johnson, A. E. (2003). Development of the Nonverbal Immediacy Scale (NIS): Measures of self- and other-perceived nonverbal immediacy. *Communication Quarterly, 51*, 502–515.

Riggio, R. E. (2005). Business applications of nonverbal communication. In R. E. Riggio & R. S. Feldman (Eds.), *Applications of nonverbal communication* (pp. 119–138). Mahwah, NJ: Erlbaum.

Riley, P., & Eisenberg, E. (1992). *The ACE model of management*. Unpublished working paper, University of Southern California, Los Angeles.

Risman, B., & Godwin, S. (2001). Twentieth-century changes in economic work and family. In D. Vannoy (Ed.), *Gender mosaics* (pp. 134–144). Los Angeles: Roxbury.

Ritchie, L. (2012). Negotiating power through communication: Using an employee participation intervention to construct a discursive space for debate. *Journal of Communication Management, 16*(1), 95–107.

Roach, K. D. (1997). Effects of graduate teaching assistant attire on student learning, misbehaviors, and ratings of instruction. *Communication Quarterly, 45*, 125–141.

Roberts, J. A., & Wasieleski, D. M. (2012). Moral reasoning in computer-based task environments: Exploring the interplay between cognitive and technological factors on individuals' propensity to break rules. *Journal of Business Ethics, 106*, 1–22.

Roberts, S. J., & Roach, T. (2009). Social networking web sites and human resource personnel: Suggestions for job searches. *Business Communication Quarterly, 72*, 110–114.

Robinson, E. J., & Robinson, W. P. (1982). The advancement of children's verbal referential communication skills: The role of metacognitive guidance. *International Journal of Behavioral Development, 5*, 329–355.

Rosener, J. B. (1997). Sexual static. In K. Grint (Ed.), *Leadership: Classical, contemporary, and critical approaches*. Oxford, UK: Oxford University Press.

Ruetzler, T., Taylor, J., Reynolds, D., Baker, W., & Killen, C. (2012). What is professional attire today? A conjoint analysis of personal presentation attributes. *International Journal of Hospitality Management, 31*(3), 937–943.

Rule, J. B. (2007). *Privacy in peril: How we are sacrificing a fundamental right in exchange for security and convenience*. New York: Oxford University Press.

Sadler, P. (1997). *Leadership*. London: Kogan.

Salovey, P., & Mayer, J. (1990). Emotional intelligence. *Imagination, Cognition, and Personality, 9*, 185–211.

Samovar, L., Porter, R. E., & McDaniel, E. R. (2007). *Communication between cultures* (6th ed.). Belmont, CA: Wadsworth.

Sampson, E. (1995). First impressions: The power of personal style. *Library Management, 16*, 25–29.

Sandvik, P. L., & Tracy, S. J. (2012). Answering five key questions about workplace bullying: How communication scholarship provides thought leadership for transforming abuse at work. *Management Communication Quarterly, 26*(1), 3–47.

Savolainen, R. (2007). Filtering and withdrawing: Strategies for coping with information overload in everyday contexts. *Journal of Information Science, 33*, 611–621.

Scarduzio, J. A., & Geist-Martin, P. (2010). Accounting for victimization: Male professors' ideological positioning in stories of sexual harassment. *Management Communication Quarterly, 24*(3), 419–445.

Schein, E. (1992). *Organizational culture and leadership* (2nd ed.). San Francisco: Jossey Bass.

Schiller, S. Z., & Mandviwalla, M. (2007). Virtual team research: An analysis of theory use and framework for theory appropriation. *Small Group Research, 38*, 12–59.

Schor, J. B. (1992). *The overworked American: The unexpected decline of leisure*. New York: Basic.

Schor, J. B. (1998). *The overspent American: Why we buy what we don't need*. New York: Basic.

Scott, E. (2007). *Stress: How it affects your body and how you can stay healthier*. Retrieved from http://stress.about.com/od/stresshealth/a/stresshealth.htm

Shaw, M. E. (1981). *Group dynamics: The psychology of small group behavior* (3rd ed.). New York: McGraw-Hill.

Sheriff, A., & Ravishankar, G. (2012). The techniques and rationale of e-surveillance practices in organizations. *International Journal of Multidisciplinary Research, 2*(2), 281–290.

Shipley, D., & Schwalbe, W. (2008). *Send: Why people email so badly and how to do it better*. New York: Knopf.

Shirey, M. R. (2012). Group think, organizational strategy, and change. *Journal of Nursing Administration, 42*(2), 67–71.

Simon, L. S., Judge, T. A., & Halvorsen-Ganepola, M. D. (2010). In good company? A multi-study, multi-level investigation of the effects of coworker relationships on employee well-being. *Journal of Vocational Behavior, 76*, 534–546.

Slattery, B. (2011, August 26). Top three Steve Jobs speeches. *Today @ PCWorld*. Retrieved from http://www.pcworld.com/article/238905/top_three_steve_jobs_speeches.html

Slovensky, R., & Ross, W. H. (2012). Should human resource managers use social media to screen job applicants? Managerial and legal issues in the USA. *Info, 14*(1), 55–69.

Slutsky, I. (2010). Why LinkedIn is the social network that will never die. *Advertising Age, 81*(43), 2–23.

Smith, T. E., & Bainbridge, A. (2006). Get real: Does practicing speeches before an audience improve performance? *Communication Quarterly, 54*, 111–125.

Snyder, J. (2012). Extending the empathic communication model of burnout: Incorporating individual differences to learn more about workplace emotion, communicative responsiveness, and burnout. *Communication Quarterly, 60*(1), 122–142.

Solove, D. J. (2008). *Understanding privacy.* Boston: Harvard University Press.

Spitzberg, B. H. (2006). Preliminary development of a model and measure of computer-mediated communication (CMC) competence. *Journal of Computer-Mediated Communication, 11*(2), 629–666.

Stamou, A. G., Maroniti, K. S., & Dinas, K. D. (2012). Representing "traditional" and "progressive" women in Greek television: The role of "feminine"/"masculine" speech styles in the mediation of gender identity construction. *Women's Studies International Forum, 35,* 38–52.

Staples, S. D., & Webster, J. (2007). Exploring traditional and virtual team members' "best practices": A social cognitive theory perspective. *Small Group Research, 38,* 60–97.

Stengel, J. R., Dixon, A., & Allen, C. (2003, November). Listening begins at home. *Harvard Business Review.* Retrieved from http://hbr.org/2003/11/listening-begins-at-home/ar/1

Stogdill, R. M. (1948). Personal factors associated with leadership: A survey of the literature. *Journal of Psychology, 25,* 35–71.

Stout, M. (2005). *The sociopath next door.* New York: Broadway.

Sypher, B., Bostrom, R., & Seibert, J. (1989). Listening, communication abilities, and success at work. *Journal of Business Communication, 26,* 293–303.

Tamaki, J. (1991, October 10). Sexual harassment in the workplace. *Los Angeles Times,* p. D2.

Tannen, D. (1990). *You just don't understand: Women and men in conversation.* New York: HarperCollins.

Tannen, D. (1998). *The argument culture: Stopping America's war of words.* New York: Ballentine.

Taylor, B., & Conrad, C. (1992). Narratives of sexual harassment: Organizational dimensions. *Journal of Applied Communication Research, 20,* 401–418.

Teece, D. J. (2010). Business models, business strategy and innovation. *Long Range Planning, 43,* 172–194.

Tews, M., Michel, J. W., & Bartlett, A. (2012). The fundamental role of workplace fun in applicant attraction. *Journal of Leadership and Organizational Studies, 19*(1), 105–114.

Thomas, S. P. (1998). *Transforming nurses' anger and pain.* New York: Springer.

Thompson, B. (2008). Characteristics of parent-teacher e-mail communication. *Communication Education, 57,* 201–223.

Ting-Toomey, S. (1990). *A face negotiation perspective communicating for peace.* Newbury Park, CA: Sage.

Tracy, S. J., Lutgen-Sandvik, P., & Alberts, J. K. (2006). Nightmares, demons, and slaves: Exploring the painful metaphors of workplace bullying. *Management Communication Quarterly, 20,* 148–185.

Travers, N. L. (2012). Academic perspectives on college-level learning: Implications for workplace learning. *Journal of Workplace Learning, 24*(2), 105–118.

Trenerry, B., & Paradies, Y. (2012). Organizational assessment: An overlooked approach to managing diversity and addressing racism in the workplace. *Journal of Diversity Management, 7*(1), 11–26.

Tuckman, B. W., & Jensen, M. C. (1977). Stages of small group development revisited. *Group and Organizational Studies, 2,* 419–427.

Tufte, E. (2003, September). PowerPoint is evil! *Wired,* Issue 11.09. Retrieved from http://www.wired.com/wired/archive/11.09/ppt2.html

U.S. Bureau of Labor Statistics. (2010). *Occupational outlook handbook.* Washington, DC: U.S. Department of Labor. Retrieved from http://www.bls.gov/oco

Vanevenhoven, J., Delaney-Klinger, K., Winkel, D., & Wagner, R. (2011). How to get in the "first pile." *American Journal of Business Education, 4*(8), 19–24.

Varlander, S. (2012). Individual flexibility in the workplace: A spatial perspective. *Journal of Applied Behavioral Science, 48*(1), 33–61.

Vidal, M. E., Leiva, D. C., & Navarro, J. G. (2012). Gaps between managers. *International Journal of Human Resource Management, 23*(4), 645–661.

Von Oech, R. (1983). *A whack on the side of the head.* New York: Warner.

Von Oech, R. (1986). *A kick in the seat of the pants.* New York: Harper Perennial.

Vorakulpipat, C., Visoottiviseth, V., & Siwamogsatham, S. (2012). Polite sender: A resource-saving spam e-mail countermeasure based on sender responsibilities and recipient justifications. *Computers and Security, 31*(3), 286–298.

Wahl, S. T., McBride, M. C., & Schrodt, P. (2005). Becoming "point and click" parents: A case study of communication and online adoption. *Journal of Family Communication, 5,* 279–294.

Waldeck, J., Seibold, D., & Flanagin, A. (2005). Organizational assimilation and technology use. *Communication Monographs, 72,* 161–183.

Walther, J. B., Loh, T., & Granka, L. (2005). Let me count the ways: The interchange of verbal and nonverbal cues in computer-mediated and face-to-face affinity. *Journal of Language and Social Psychology, 24,* 36–65.

Wang, Z., David, P., Srivastava, J., Powers, S., Brady, C., D'Angelo, J., et al. (2012). Behavioral performance and visual attention in communication multitasking: A comparison between instant messaging and online voice chat. *Computers in Human Behavior, 28*(3), 968–975.

Watkins-Allen, M., Coopman, S. J., Hart, J. L., & Walker, K. L. (2007). Workplace surveillance and managing privacy boundaries. *Management Communication Quarterly, 21,* 172–200.

Watson, K., & Barker, L. (1995). *Listening styles profile.* Amsterdam: Pfeiffer.

Watson-Manheim, M. B., Chudoba, K. M., & Crowston, K. (2012). Perceived discontinuities and constructed continuities in virtual work. *Info Systems, 22*(1), 29–52.

Watzlawick, P., Beavin, J., & Jackson, D. (1967). *Pragmatics of human communication.* New York: Norton.

Welch, M. (2012). Appropriateness and acceptability: Employee perspectives of internal communication. *Public Relations Review, 38*(2), 246–254.

West, M. A. (2012). *Effective teamwork*. West Sussex, UK: John Wiley.

Westhues, K. (2005). *Workplace mobbing in the academe: Reports from twenty universities*. Lewiston, NY: Edwin Mellen.

Westhues, K. (2006). *The envy of excellence: Administrative mobbing of high achieving professors*. Lewiston, NY: Edwin Mellen.

Wheeless, L. R. (1975). An investigation of receiver apprehension and social context dimensions of communication apprehension. *Speech Teacher, 24*, 261–268.

Wheeless, L. R., Preiss, R. W., & Gayle, B. M. (1997). Receiver apprehension, informational receptivity, and cognitive processing. In J. A. Daly, J. C. McCroskey, J. Ayres, T. Hopf, & D. M. Ayres (Eds.), *Avoiding communication: Shyness, reticence, and communication apprehension* (pp. 151–187). Cresskill, NJ: Hampton Press.

Williams, C. J. (2012, March 2). California physician assistant wins $168 million in harassment suit. *Los Angeles Times*. Retrieved from http://www.workplacebullying.org/2012/03/02/168mil/

Wisse, B., & Rus, D. (2012). Leader self-concept and self-interested behavior. *Journal of Personnel Psychology, 11*(1), 40–48.

Wollman, D. (2008, March). Get ahead: Don't be an email ass. *Laptop*, pp. 120–121.

Wood, J. T. (1994). *Who cares: Women, care, and culture*. Carbondale: Southern Illinois University Press.

Wood, J. T. (2003). *Gendered lives: Communication, gender, and culture* (5th ed.). Belmont, CA: Wadsworth/Thomson Learning.

Wood, J. T. (2008). *Gendered lives: Communication, gender, and culture* (8th ed.). Boston: Wadsworth.

Wood, J. T. (2009). *Communication in our lives* (5th ed.). Boston: Wadsworth.

Wright, B., Moynihan, D., & Pandey, S. (2012). Pulling the levers: Transformational leadership, public service motivation, and mission valence. *Public Administration Review, 72*(2), 206–215.

Wright, K. (2004). On-line relational maintenance strategies and perceptions of partners with exclusively Internet-based and primarily Internet-based relationships. *Communication Studies, 55*, 239–253.

Wright, P. (1996). *Managerial leadership*. London: Routledge.

Yee, N., Bailenson, J. N., Urbanek, M., Chang, F., & Merget, D. (2008). The unbearable likeness of being digital: The persistence of nonverbal social norms in online virtual environments. In L. K. Guerrero & M. L. Hecht (Eds.), *The nonverbal communication reader: Classic and contemporary readings* (3rd ed., pp. 203–208). Prospect Heights, IL: Waveland.

Yen, J. Y., Yen, C. F., Chen, C. S., Wang, P. W., Chang, Y. H., & Ko, C. H. (2012). Social anxiety in online and real-life interaction and their associated factors. *Cyberpsychology, Behavior, and Social Networking, 15*(1), 7–12.

Young, M., & Schieman, S. (2012). When hard times take a toll: The distressing consequences of economic hardship and life events within the family-work interface. *Journal of Health and Social Behavior, 53*(1), 84–98.

Young, S., Kelsey, D., & Lancaster, A. (2011). Predicted outcome value of e-mail communication: Factors that foster professional relational development between students and teachers. *Communication Education, 60*(4), 371–388.

Yuille, C., Change, A., Gudmundsson, A., & Sawang, S. (2012). The role of life friendly policies on employees. *Journal of Management and Organization, 18*(1), 53–63.

Zhou, Q., Hirst, G., & Shipton, H. (2011). Context matters: Combined influence of participation and intellectual stimulation on the promotion focus–employee creativity relationship. *Journal of Organizational Behavior*. doi:10.1002/job.779

Zhu, C. (2012). Student satisfaction, performance, and knowledge construction in online collaborative learning. *Educational Technology and Society, 15*(1), 127–136.

# Glossary

**accent:** Refers to a person's pronunciation of various words in a language

**action-oriented listeners:** Characterized by direct, concise, error-free communication that is used to negotiate and accomplish a goal

**active agreement (call to action):** Persuading the audience to take some sort of action

**active listener:** One who is fully engaged in the role of listener, making sense of the message and then verifying the accuracy of sense making

**adapters:** Gestures we use to release tension

**adrenaline rush:** A physiological process that occurs when adrenaline enters the body; often results in nervous behavior and anxiety for a speaker

**advocacy:** A strategy for communicating with a supervisor in which the employee evaluates the supervisor's needs and preferences and then develops a message, argument, or proposal that lines up with those needs and preferences

**affect displays:** Facial expressions and gestures that display emotion

**agenda:** A guide or an overview of the topics that will be covered during the meeting

**analogical reasoning:** Reasoning from an analogy; making an argument by comparing two cases

**anger:** An emotional state that varies in intensity from mild irritation to intense fury and rage; a feeling of keen displeasure for what we regard as a wrong toward ourselves or others

**annual feedback trap:** Saving all feedback, both positive and negative, for discussion during an employee's annual performance appraisal

**Aristotle:** A Greek philosopher, author of *The Art of Rhetoric*, student of Plato, and teacher of Alexander the Great

**artifacts:** Temporary embellishments (e.g., jewelry, sunglasses, perfume) or objects characteristic of a particular culture or institution (e.g., furniture, buildings, technology, artwork, logos) that provide information—both good and bad—about personalities, attitudes, group affiliation, and organizational membership

**artist:** One of the four roles in innovative problem solving; puts ideas together in new ways

**assimilation process:** The adjustment period and "settling in" that's common for anyone starting a new job

**asynchronous time:** When messages are posted at one time and read at another time

**audience analysis:** Asking a series of questions designed to enhance the speaker's understanding of the listeners

**audience-based communication apprehension:** Explains a person's fear of speaking to certain people or groups

**audience-centered speaker:** A speaker who thinks about the audience during every step of the presentation design and delivery process

**authoritative:** A leadership style in which the leader makes all the decisions with little input from the team

**awards and honors:** A résumé section that lists relevant awards and honors received by the job seeker

**balance:** When there's equal time divided between work and personal life

**behavioral questions:** A type of interviewing question that asks job seekers to explain how they have handled past situations as well as how they would handle hypothetical situations

**bias:** Any assumption we make or attitude we have about the person, issue, or topic before we have heard all the facts

**birthright:** A position of power passed on from parent to child; monarchies are based on birthright

**boundary:** The line or division between work and life

**bully:** A type of difficult person characterized by a bad temper; uses aggression and anger to get his or her way

**burnout:** Chronic exhaustion from persistent workload, decreased motivation, and apathy toward work

**business letter:** Used to communicate formal matters in business, jurisprudence, or otherwise

**career exploration:** A part of the exploring stage of the job-seeking process; requires job seekers to research opportunities/careers in their majors that correspond with their desires, goals, and priorities

**career planning centers:** A student services department located on most college and university campuses whose mission is to help students identify careers, find internships, and prepare for employment; may also be referred to as career services, career placements, career development, or career counseling

**causal reasoning:** A type of inductive reasoning, more commonly known as the cause–effect relationship

**channel:** The means by which messages are sent

**charisma:** Includes characteristics such as magnetic charm, allure, and an almost supernatural or magical ability to appeal to followers

**chronemics:** The study of time as communication

**classified/help-wanted ads:** A section of the newspaper that lists job openings

**coach:** The role of the team member with the designated leadership title; duties include calling the meetings, setting the agenda, and facilitating the discussion

**codes:** Categories of nonverbal communication

**coercive power:** Derived from one's ability to control another person's behavior with negative reinforcement

**cognitive dissonance:** A theory, developed by Leon Festinger (1957), positing that when a person has two ideas that contradict each other, it creates mental noise or cognitive dissonance; a useful persuasive strategy

**colloquialisms:** Slang terms that are locally or regionally based

**common ground:** Showing the audience how you have a shared interest, concern, or background

**communication apprehension:** An individual's level of fear or anxiety associated with either real or anticipated communication with another person or persons

**communication bravado:** Having a positive view of one's own communication when, in reality, it is bad, leading to conflict and hurt feelings in others

**communication network:** A group of individuals who regularly share a line of communication; can be either formal or informal

**Communication Privacy Management:** Theory developed by Sandra Petronio that describes how people establish rules about privacy and manage privacy using spatial metaphors

**communication rules:** Shared understanding of what communication means and what constitutes appropriate communication given the context

**community:** A geographic space identified as a place to work toward a good life (e.g., health, safety, well-being)

**compromise:** A lose–lose approach to decision making in which parties blend and concede parts of their individual solutions

**computer-mediated communication (CMC):** Human communication that occurs through some form of technology

**conclusion:** The end of a presentation; should include a concluding statement, a summary of the specific purpose and main points, and a strong final impression

**conflict:** A necessary part of team problem solving and innovative thinking; can be productive and positive if handled properly

**connection power:** Based on one's connection to people in positions of power or access to a strong support system

**connotation:** The feelings or emotions that a word implies

**consensus:** A win–win approach to decision making that occurs when a solution or agreement that all team members can support is reached

**constitutive rules:** Define what communication means by prompting us to count certain kinds of communication

**contact information:** Includes job seeker's name, mailing address, phone number, and e-mail address

**content layer:** The information being discussed; descriptive information such as the time of a meeting, project due date, or the names of coworkers assigned to a team

**content-oriented listeners:** Characterized by an interest in intellectual challenge, complex information, and a desire to evaluate information carefully before forming judgments and opinions

**context:** The location, space, and occasion where communication occurs

**context analysis:** Asking a series of questions designed to enhance the speaker's understanding of the speaking situation

**context-based communication apprehension:** Describes a fear of communicating in certain contexts, for example, a fear of public speaking

**Contingency Theory:** A situational leadership theory developed by Fiedler; requires leaders to assess the situation by examining three factors: the leader–follower relationship, the task structure, and the position power

**conversational listening:** Listening exemplified by the speaking role shifting from one person to another with some degree of frequency

**conversational quality:** Presenting in a style similar to that used in casual conversation; known as an extemporaneous speaking style

**corporate blog:** A web log used to improve internal communication at work or for external marketing and public relations

**cover letters:** One-page letters that accompany the résumé; include the job seeker's interest in a specific position, overview of qualifications, and desire for an interview

**credibility:** The believability of the speaker and/or the information being presented

**criteria:** The standard used to make a decision

**critical listening:** Requires the listener to evaluate the information being sent; may also require some sort of oral or written feedback

**cultural competence:** Refers to the level of knowledge a person has about others who are different in some way in comparison with himself or herself

**cultural diversity awareness:** Being aware of diversity that's present in any working or social environment

**cultural rituals:** Practices, behaviors, celebrations, and traditions common to people, organizations, and institutions

**culture:** The rules of living and functioning in society

**cuss words:** Also referred to as curse or swear words; viewed as obscene expressions; should not appear in a presentation

**customer relations:** The interaction between employees or representatives of an organization or business and the people the organization sells to or serves; also known as customer service

**customized résumé:** A résumé tailored to each position to which the job seeker applies; a concise, audience-centered version of the generic résumé

**decision by the leader:** Decision-making approach in which members advise the leader, who then makes the ultimate decision

**decision making:** A step in the problem-solving process in which the team chooses among a set of alternatives

**decode:** When we make meaning out of verbal and nonverbal cues others send

**deductive reasoning:** Occurs when the speaker takes general information (premises) and draws a conclusion from that general information

**deintensification:** When we reduce the intensity of a facial expression connected to a certain emotion

**delivery:** The nonverbal component of public speaking; ideally consists of good eye contact and a conversational speaking style

**democratic:** Leadership style in which the leader follows the will of the people, or at least the majority of the people, with decisions often made through voting

**devil's advocate:** The functional team role that ensures dissenting points of view are discussed

**dialect:** Refers to pronunciation, vocabulary, and syntax variations in a language

**discrimination:** The act of excluding or denying people of products, rights, and services based on their race, ethnicity, religion, gender, age, sexual orientation, or disability

**disguising conversation:** Making statements about something to see how other people react

**distracter:** A type of difficult person characterized by a communication style full of tangents

**downsizing letter:** Used to inform other businesses about skilled employees available for employment due to company downsizing (e.g., layoffs, fired employees)

**drama queen:** A type of difficult person characterized by the need to create drama in the workplace by starting arguments, gossiping, holding grudges, and the like

**dyads:** Two people communicating

**education:** A résumé section that highlights a job seeker's educational background; should not include high school information

**electronic aggression:** A form of aggressive communication in which people interacting on professional topics are filled with emotionality

**electronic bulletin board:** An online service to which anyone, not just a subscriber, can obtain access to read postings

**electronic résumés:** Résumés that will be submitted to employers electronically via the Internet; formatting is extremely important when designing electronic résumés

**e-mail dialogues:** Exchanges of messages about a particular topic using e-mail, professional blog space, and other electronic tools to encourage participation that will ideally lead to new ideas, strategic planning, and sound decision making

**e-mail flame:** A hostile message that is blunt, rude, insensitive, or obscene

**e-mail forwards:** Consist of virus alerts, chain letters, stories disguised as warnings, petitions or calls for help, jokes, pictures, and the like

**emblems:** Specific, widely understood meanings in a given culture that can actually substitute for a word or phrase

**emotional intelligence:** Our ability to monitor our own and others' feelings and emotions, to discriminate among them, and to use this information to guide our thinking and actions

**empathetic listening:** The ability to pay full attention to another person, void of critique, and to express sensitivity to the sender's nonverbal behavior

**employee attrition:** The loss or turnover of employees to other jobs and industries perceived as having healthier workplace culture

**employee retention:** Getting employees to continue working for the same company

**employee reviews:** A form of written communication used in business and professional settings to provide feedback to employees about how they are performing on the job

**employment experience:** A résumé section that includes information on past employment positions, such as name of organization, dates of employment, location of organization, and possibly duties; also can be titled "Work History" or "Work/Employment History"

**encode:** Use of verbal and nonverbal cues to help others understand what we mean

**environment:** Constructed or natural surroundings that influence your communicative decisions, attitude, and mood

**ethical considerations:** The variety of factors important for us to consider in any scenario in which we're making a decision, conducting an evaluation, or making a selection

**ethical dilemmas:** Situations that do not seem to present clear choices between right and wrong or good and evil

**ethics:** The discussion, determination, and deliberation processes that attempt to decide what is right or wrong, what others should or should not do, and what is considered appropriate in our individual, communal, and professional lives

**ethnicity:** A social group that may be joined together by factors such as shared history, shared identity, shared geography, or shared culture

**ethos:** The credibility of the speaker and the information presented in the presentation; one of Aristotle's three forms of rhetoric

**evaluating:** The logical assessment of the value of the message

**expert power:** Derived from one's superior expertise in a specific field

**explorer:** One of the four roles in innovative problem solving; seeks out new information

**exploring stage:** The first stage of the job-seeking process, which includes self-exploration and career exploration

**external communication plan:** A plan that focuses on communicating information about the organization or business to citizens or employee families outside any given business

**external customers:** The people or entities that an organization serves or provides products to and that are external to the company

**external noise:** Outside distractions that interfere with the message, such as audible talking during a meeting, ruffling of papers, or a cell phone going off in the next cubicle

**external sources:** Include information that comes from outside the organization

**external time wasters:** Things you don't feel as though you have any control over (e.g., things we are required to attend, such as meetings, or people to whom we're required to talk)

**external triggers:** Things going on in your environment at work and at home, usually stimulated by others

**eye contact:** When a speaker looks at the audience while speaking; effective means for reducing nervousness

**face-saving behavior:** Verbal and nonverbal communication that honors and maintains the other person's sense of self-respect in a given situation

**face-to-face interviews:** An interview format in which all parties are in the same room

**false close:** When speakers tell the audience they are concluding and then present new information

**false empowerment:** Occurs when a leader acts as if he or she plans to involve the group in the decision-making process and then makes his or her own decision regardless of the input received from the group

**family:** People in a household, which consists of a minimum of two members related by blood, adoption, marriage, civil union, or partnership—one of them being the householder, who owns or rents the residence

**feedback:** Information or messages communicated between sender and receiver

**fight:** One of three modes of conflict resolution; requires you to engage in some type of confrontation; a win–lose approach to problem solving

**flight:** One of three modes of conflict resolution; occurs when you choose not to engage or deal with a conflict; a lose–lose approach to problem solving

**formal communication network:** The official lines of communication and reporting structure prescribed by the organizational chart

**formal presentation:** A public speaking opportunity that occurs in a traditional speaking setting, such as presenting a sales pitch to clients or a progress report at the district meeting

**friendship/warmth touch:** The type of touch people use to show platonic affection toward each other

**functional/professional touch:** Touch that normally takes place within the context of a professional relationship and is low in intimacy

**gatekeeping:** When subordinates pass some, but not all, of the information on to the supervisor

**general distortion:** When a superior is given a message that the subordinate has changed or altered to serve his or her own purposes

**general language:** Characterized by vague descriptions that can be interpreted in a variety of ways by the recipient

**general purpose:** The overall goal of a presentation, to either inform or persuade

**generic résumé:** A list of all the information a job seeker may wish to include in a customized résumé

**globalization:** A process that brings each of us into greater contact with the rest of the world and gives our daily lives an increasingly international orientation

**Goal Setting Theory:** A motivational theory in which a leader and a team member develop the goal(s) for the team member together

**grammar:** Attention to the rules of language, such as appropriate use of complete sentences, punctuation, transitions, organization, spacing, paragraphs, and format

**grapevine:** Regularly occurring lines of communication that exist within an organization but are not prescribed by the organizational chart; also known as the informal communication network

**group:** Three or more individuals who are working toward a common goal or share a common purpose

**groupthink:** The tendency of highly cohesive groups to suspend critical thinking and make faulty decisions

**grump:** A type of difficult person characterized by a negative attitude

**haptics:** The study of touch and human contact

**hearing:** Your physical ability to detect sounds

**hobbies and interests:** A section that appears on some job seekers' résumés; not recommended

**huddles:** Short meetings in which employees are pulled together to share information; often occur at the beginning or end of the day

**human communication:** The process of making sense of the world and sharing that sense with others by creating meaning through the use of verbal and nonverbal messages

**HURIER model:** A six-step listening process: **H**earing, **U**nderstanding, **R**emembering, **I**nterpreting, **E**valuating, and **R**esponding

**illegal questions:** Interview questions that violate the Civil Rights Act of 1964, Title VII, by asking questions regarding race, color, religion, sex, national origin, disability, or age when hiring or promoting employees

**illustrators:** Gestures that complement, enhance, or substitute for the verbal message

**imagery:** Painting a picture or image with one's words

**imbalance triggers:** Experiences (e.g., conflict, aggression, overload, negativity) that cause professionals to feel drained, used, abused, and unhappy

**impression management:** Directing the formation of an impression, perception, or view others have of you

**impromptu presentation:** Delivering a presentation with very limited, if any, preparation

**indirect questioning:** Asking questions in a roundabout way to retrieve information that will make you more competitive, help you make better choices, and help you survive in an organization

**inductive reasoning:** Building an argument by utilizing individual examples, pieces of information, or cases, and pulling them together to make a generalization or conclusion

**inform:** The general purpose of presentations in which the speaker presents the facts, acting as a teacher relaying information

**informal communication network:** Regularly occurring lines of communication that exist within an organization but are not prescribed by the organizational chart; also known as the grapevine

**information and communications technologies (ICTs):** mobile digital devices such as personal digital assistants and smartphones (e.g., iPhone, Blackberry) that may both harm work–life boundaries and serve as tools for managing them

**information overload:** When information, requests for feedback, taking on new projects, responding to questions, answering the phone, and taking required online classes for work, on top of attending to loved ones, children, pets, and other family matters, leave us stressed and feeling as though things are spinning out of control

**informational listening:** Allows you to focus on the content of the message in order to acquire knowledge

**ingratiation:** A strategy for communicating with a supervisor in which the employee acts warm and friendly toward him or her

**inoculation:** When a speaker points out information that could hurt a persuasive argument and explains why it is not important or relevant, in an attempt to minimize its impact in the future

**intensification:** Expression that exaggerates how we feel about something

**interests:** The needs and concerns underlying each position

**internal communication plan:** A plan that focuses on communication taking place inside the daily operations of any given business

**internal customer:** An employee who needs services or products from other parts of the organization to complete his or her work

**internal noise:** Internal conditions or distractions that interfere with the message

**internal preview:** The preview of an idea or main point found within the body of a presentation

**internal sources:** Include information that comes from within the organization, such as reports, policies, or interviews with employees and/or customers

**internal summary:** The summary of an idea or a main point found within the body of a presentation

**internal time wasters:** More personal internal things brought on by mind-set, motivation, and bad habits

**internal triggers:** Concerns and frustrations you have about past, current, and future events or a general negativity toward yourself (i.e., "I'm really angry at myself for not making that change sooner")

**Internet:** An excellent tool for locating employment opportunities and researching potential employers

**internship:** An on-the-job learning opportunity for students; can be paid, unpaid, or for college credit

**interpersonal communication:** The cocreation of meaning as people interact

**interpreting:** Making sense of verbal and nonverbal codes to assign meaning to the information received

**intimacy:** Characterized by feelings of closeness and trust that you share with other people

**introduction:** The start of a presentation; should include five components: gain attention, introduce the topic, develop credibility, relate the topic to the audience, and preview the main points

**jargon:** The terminology or language of a given field or profession

**job fairs:** Events in which multiple employers come together to recruit potential employees; held both on college campuses and in the community

**job seeker:** Any person trying to gain employment (although job seekers are commonly referred to as interviewees, the job-seeking process includes much more than the interviewing stage)

**job-seeking process:** Six stages involved in finding employment: exploring, researching, applying, interviewing, following up, and accepting

**job title:** The name associated with each position in an organization; intended to designate duties and status

**judge:** One of the four roles in innovative problem solving; evaluates possible solutions and then selects one solution for implementation

**kinesics:** General term for the study of human movement, gestures, and posture

**laissez-faire:** Leadership style in which the team makes the decisions with little input from the leader; French expression meaning "allow to do"

**language barriers:** When people trying to communicate do not share a common language

**lead:** The person who is accountable for a given task

**leadership:** A dynamic relationship based on mutual influence and common purpose between leaders and collaborators, in which both are moved to higher levels of motivation and moral development as they affect real, intended change

**leadership functions:** Include influencing and guiding followers, as well as being innovative and creating a vision for future direction

**legitimate power:** Derived from one's position of authority

**listening:** Receiving verbal and nonverbal messages and then determining meaning from those messages

**listserv:** A computer service that facilitates discussions by connecting people who share common interests

**logos:** The logic of the presentation; established through both the organizational structure and the supporting information; one of Aristotle's three forms of rhetoric

**love/intimacy touch:** Highly personal and intimate touch used to communicate affection

**managerial functions:** Include being in charge of and responsible for various goals and functions in an organization, as well as supervising subordinates

**Managerial Grid:** A situational leadership theory developed by Robert Blake and Jane Mouton; includes five managerial styles: impoverished, country club, authoritative, middle-of-the road, and team

**manuscript:** A speaking text written out word-for-word; speakers should avoid using manuscripts

**masking:** Hiding an expression connected to a felt emotion and replacing it with an expression more appropriate to the situation

**meeting environment:** Includes both the time and place a meeting is held; considered a part of the communication

**meetingthink:** The suspension of critical thinking due to common variables such as false empowerment, overload, or poorly run meetings

**memo:** Short for *memorandum*; typically a short note or update distributed in business

**message:** The information or feedback that is communicated

**message overload:** Receiving too much information at once, making it difficult to stay focused on the primary message being communicated

**metaphor:** A literary device in which the speaker uses comparison

**misspellings:** Mistakes in spelling

**mock interviews:** A practice run done prior to an interview to help job seekers anticipate questions, script answers, and lessen nervousness

**monotone:** A vocal quality that has only one pitch; a lack of vocal variety in a speaker's voice

**Monroe's Motivated Sequence:** A five-step organizational format; steps include attention, need, satisfaction, visualization, and action

**mutual respect:** People seeking understanding through the vehicle of open dialogue; attempting to understand others with an open mind leads them to respond with mutual respect and understanding

**narratives:** Stories we use to come to understand the organizational culture and one another

**negotiation:** A strategy used by a job seeker if he or she does not believe the salary, working conditions, and/or benefits are satisfactory; involves providing a counter offer to the initial terms of employment presented by a potential employer

**networking notes:** A form of thank-you letter used to remind employers of your interview and to convince them that you're the right person for the job

**neutralization:** The process of using facial expressions to hide how we really feel

**noise:** External or internal disruption to the context

**nonverbal communication:** Communication other than written or spoken language that creates meaning for someone

**norm:** An unwritten rule of behavior

**objective:** A one- or two-sentence declarative statement about a job seeker's career goals; also, relaying information without being influenced or impacted by emotions or individual point of view, necessary in informative presentations

**oculesics:** The study of eye behavior

**one-on-one interview:** A face-to-face interview can consist of one interviewer and one interviewee; job seekers may undergo a series of one-on-one interviews

**online application:** An electronic form used by employers to standardize the information gathered from job seekers; commonly requests information found on a traditional résumé

**opportunity presentation:** A public speaking opportunity that occurs in a less traditional speaking setting, such as during huddles or at the start of meetings

**organizational chart:** Visual representation of the supervision and reporting structure of a company; outlines the formal communication network

**organizational culture:** The way an organization operates, the attitudes the employees have, and the overall tone and approach to any given business

**organizational values:** Specific principles or guidelines such as safety, teamwork, integrity, or ownership that are typically outlined in support of any given organizational mission or goal

**organizer:** Member of a team presentation who provides the introduction, conclusion, and transitions to the presentation

**overload:** Occurs when group members have so much on their plates that they cannot truly concentrate on and engage in a meeting

**overt questioning:** The practice of asking a direct question about what you want to know

**overtalker:** Group member who dominates conversations, occasionally leading the discussion on irrelevant tangents

**panel interview:** An interviewing format that includes more than one interviewer, multiple interviewees, or both

**paraphrase:** Restating or summarizing what is communicated to clarify meaning and check understanding

**passive agreement:** Persuading the audience simply to agree or disagree with an idea

**passive listener:** One who simply receives a message without giving feedback or verifying understanding of the message

**pathos:** The emotional appeal; one of Aristotle's three forms of rhetoric

**patient:** A type of difficult person who treats coworkers and sometimes even supervisors as counselors; brings personal problems to work and discusses them on company time

**people-oriented listeners:** Characterized by demonstrating concern for others' emotions and interests, finding common ground, and responding to the emotional states of human behavior

**perception checking:** Asking others if one's perceptions or sense of understanding is correct or incorrect

**performance appraisal:** Formal evaluation that often involves an interview and a written summary of the employee's strengths and weaknesses on the job

**performance improvement plan:** A specific and clear strategy for improving employee performance; should be derived from two-way communication

**persuade:** The general purpose of presentations in which the speaker advocates for something or against something

**persuasive appeals:** Developed by Aristotle—ethos, logos, and pathos

**phishing:** Sending authentic-looking but fraudulent e-mails designed to steal sensitive personal information

**physical appearance:** The ways our bodies and overall appearance nonverbally communicate to others and impact our view of ourselves in everyday life

**planning documents:** Forms of written communication usually presented with maps and other visual designs to lay out a broader vision of where the company is going and what specific strategies will be utilized in the near future

**position:** A demand that includes each person's solution to the problem

**PowerPoint presentations:** A Microsoft software package used to develop computer-generated supporting aids

**presentational listening:** A type of listening that takes place in situations where a clear role of speaking and listening functions is prescribed

**press releases:** Forms of written communication used to send messages to a variety of media organizations, including newspaper, radio, television, and Internet

**private employment agencies:** For-profit organizations, also known as head hunters, that help job seekers find jobs and help employers find qualified workers for a fee

**proactive media writing:** A form of written communication similar to a press release that emphasizes an organization's commitment to safety and compliance

**problem solving:** Generating quality alternatives from which to select, selecting the best alternative, and then working to implement that choice

**process directives:** Descriptions of new policies/procedures and changes to those already in place

**professional associations:** Organizations designed to facilitate networking and educational opportunities for professionals in a given field or industry by sponsoring meetings and conferences

**professional etiquette:** Displaying the behaviors of social etiquette and good manners in a professional setting

**professional excellence:** Being recognized for your skills as a communicator, serving as a role model to those around you, recognizing your strengths and developing your weaknesses, being audience centered, understanding the context, and possessing the ability to adapt and continually improve

**proposals:** Forms of written communication utilized in many business and professional settings to propose products and services to potential clients

**proxemics:** How people create and use space and distance, as well as how they behave to protect and defend that space

**public image:** The impression you give or present to others both verbally and nonverbally

**qualitative data:** Characterized by actual words, phrases, responses to open-ended questions, and interviews

**quantitative data:** Characterized by numbers, percentages, statistics, and surveys

**questions:** Requests made to learn information or clarify understanding

**Quintilian:** A Roman philosopher and educator

**race:** The categorization of people based on physical characteristics such as skin color, dimensions of the human face, and hair

**receiver:** The listener who interprets the message

**receiver apprehension:** The fear of misinterpreting, inadequately processing, and/or not being able to adjust psychologically to messages sent by others

**recommendation letter:** A form of written communication used to provide a documented reference for students and professionals

**references:** Persons who can tell potential employers about a job seeker's experience, knowledge, work ethic, and character

**referent power:** Given to someone because you want that person to like you

**reflection:** Listening technique characterized by observing and interpreting verbal and nonverbal cues in order to summarize and restate back to the speaker to clarify content and meaning

**Reflective Thinking Process:** Problem-solving process developed by John Dewey that includes describing and analyzing the problem, generating possible solutions, evaluating all solutions, deciding on the solution, and planning how to implement the solution

**regulative rules:** Describe when, how, where, and with whom to talk about certain things; also dictate appropriateness

**regulators:** Gestures used to control turn-taking in conversations

**relational layer:** Communication that reveals how you feel about the receiver

**relationship roles:** Functional roles that help the team maintain positive relationships among members

**relevant experience:** A résumé section that includes relevant employment history as well as internships, relevant class projects, relevant work with student organizations, or volunteering; often used in place of the "Employment Experience" section by recent college graduates

**remembering:** Recalling the message so it can be acted on

**repetition:** A powerful language device that creates a parallel structure within a presentation and creates a sense of anticipation for audience members

**reports:** Written communication used to summarize research or assessment findings to inform managers about important issues related to business (e.g., customer service, employee satisfaction, employee morale)

**research:** Gathering information (definitions, examples, statistics, testimonies, etc.) that aids in the design of the presentation and supports the specific purpose

**researching stage:** The second stage of the job-seeking process, which comprises two components: researching openings and researching potential employers; requires job seekers to find the right fit as opposed to merely searching for vacancies and applying to anything and everything that is available

**responding:** Giving some form of a *response* to the message, either verbally or nonverbally

**résumé:** A snapshot of the job seeker as an employee; highlights skill sets to provide a picture of how the job seeker fits this position and this organization

**retention:** To remember over a long period of time

**reward power:** Derived from one's ability to control another person's behavior with positive reinforcement

**roadblock to change:** A type of difficult person characterized by a dislike and even refusal to carry out changes in his or her duties

**role models:** People who display behaviors and attitudes that are replicated by others

**round robin technique:** A communication technique in which team members go around the circle, allowing everyone to share his or her perceptions of the issue; requires members to listen and not interrupt while other team members are speaking

**scannable résumés:** A résumé that will be submitted to an employer and/or transmitted by the employer via fax or computer scanning; formatting is extremely important when designing scannable résumés

**scripting:** The process of mentally rehearsing what you will say during the discussion

**scripting answers:** Answering interview questions using a three-part formula: directly answer the question, back up the answer with a specific example, and tie the answer back to this company and/or this position

**self-centered roles:** Dysfunctional roles that can interfere with a team's functioning

**self-disclose:** To share information that people cannot learn about us unless we reveal it to them

**self-exploration:** Part of the exploring stage of the job-seeking process; requires a job seeker to identify his/her desires, goals, and priorities

**semantic information distance:** A difference in perception that exists between employees and supervisors over fundamental areas such as organizational issues or basic job duties

**sender:** Person initiating the exchange

**sexual arousal:** Touches that are extremely intimate

**sexual orientation:** Term referring to the sex of a person with whom we wish to engage in sexual activity

**shadowing:** A learning opportunity for job seekers in which they watch/follow a professional to learn what is involved in a given position and/or profession

**signposts:** Words or phrases that indicate the speaker's place in the organizational structure; for example, *step one*, *step two*, etc.

**situational communication apprehension:** Refers to apprehension

to communicate in specific sets of circumstances

**Situational Leadership Theory:** Developed by Hersey and Blanchard; requires leaders to examine task behavior, relationship behavior, and level of maturity/readiness of the followers to select the most effective communication style

**skills:** Information that must be highlighted on the job seeker's résumé either as a separate section or as part of his or her experiences; may include information about computer knowledge, leadership, communication abilities, language fluency, and more

**slacker:** A type of difficult person characterized by lack of productivity; finds any excuse not to work

**slang:** Words that are either made-up or used to express something other than their formal meaning; should not appear in a presentation

**sniper:** A type of difficult person characterized by sarcastic and inappropriate comments meant to wound those at which they are aimed

**socialization:** The experiences that shape our attitudes, perceptions, emotions, and communication choices

**social/polite touch:** Touch connected to cultural norms, such as hugs or pats on the back; convey relatively low intimacy within a relationship

**sociopath:** A type of difficult person characterized by a lack of conscience and guilt; it is estimated that 1 out of every 25 people is a sociopath

**spam:** The use of a user's e-mail address for a purpose to which the user didn't agree; junk e-mail sent by "spammers" who obtain e-mail addresses by buying company

customer lists or using programs to produce e-mail addresses randomly

**speaking outline:** A tool used by the speaker when delivering a presentation; more concise and less detailed than the practice outline

**speaking rate:** The rate of speed at which a speaker talks

**specific language:** Specific with facts, percentages, conclusions, and recommendations

**specific purpose:** Declarative sentence telling the listeners what the speaker wants them to understand/know or believe by the end of the presentation; the equivalent of a thesis statement in an essay

**stages of team development:** Forming, storming, norming, performing, and adjourning

**star:** An employee who possesses all the qualities of a team player but also wants to take on extra duties, learn more, and advance his or her career

**State employment service:** A not-for-profit government agency, sometimes called the Job Service, that helps job seekers find jobs and employers find qualified workers, at no cost to either

**status:** A person's rank or position in an organization

**stereotypes:** The way humans use their minds to perceive others as belonging to a social group

**strategic planning:** The development of a plan that emphasizes goals, initiatives, strategies, and targets utilized to help employees strive for a shared vision and commitment to the core values in an organization

**subordinate:** Employee, typically a lower-status person

**summarization:** Occurs when an employee summarizes a message in such a way that emphasis is placed on certain aspects of the message

**summary:** A résumé section that includes an overview of the job seeker's qualifications relevant to the position to which he or she is applying

**superior:** Supervisor or employee, typically a higher-status person

**supporting aids:** Tools used by a speaker to help support the audience's interest in and understanding of the presentation; visual or audio aids used to enhance a presentation

**surveillance:** Using observational skills to take stock of any given situation

**synchronous time:** Communication with little lag time between comments

**task roles:** Functional roles that help the team complete its tasks and achieve its goals

**team:** A group in which members share leadership responsibility for creating a team identity, achieving mutually defined goals, and fostering innovative thinking

**team player:** An employee who completes tasks, gets along with coworkers, and serves customers with a positive attitude; hardworking and dependable

**telephone interviews:** A type of interview conducted over the phone; often used during the early screening phases of the interview process

**testing limits:** Cutting corners or choosing to avoid a behavior or practice to see how it will influence the outcome

**texting language:** Expressions or acronyms used when sending instant messages and text messages—for example, LOL (laugh out loud) or TU (thank you); should not be used

**thank-you letters:** Written communication used to express appreciation to coworkers and clients

**Theory X:** Management theory based on the underlying assumption that employees are inherently lazy and will avoid work whenever possible; therefore, workers must be closely supervised and communication should be top down; developed by McGregor

**Theory Y:** Management theory based on the underlying assumption that employees can be ambitious and self-motivated and that, therefore, supervisors should seek to empower employees and two-way communication is needed; developed by McGregor

**third-party questioning:** Asking direct questions of people who have had the same experiences as you at a different time

**time-oriented listeners:** Characterized by an awareness of or desire to be in control of the time constraints of interactions

**traditional questions:** A type of interviewing question that asks for basic information about the job seeker, such as "Tell me about your strengths and weaknesses"

**trait:** A distinguishing characteristic or quality that is part of a person's character; traits are often seen as inborn or genetically based

**trait communication apprehension:** Means that one possesses a "shy trait," for example, tending not to raise a hand in class, avoiding certain social situations, and feeling extremely anxious about giving a professional presentation

**transformational leaders:** Leaders who articulate a goal or vision to an organization and then inspire followers to make this vision a reality; a change agent

**transition:** Any word or phrase that helps guide the listener from one point to the next

**translation services:** Interpretation systems available to assist with language barriers and other communication-related concerns

**types of reasoning:** Include inductive reasoning, causal reasoning, deductive reasoning, analogical reasoning, and cognitive dissonance

**typos:** Mistakes in typing

**understanding:** The process of attaching meaning to the verbal communication, or comprehending the literal meaning of the message

**undertalker:** Group member who tends to sit silently during meetings, failing to participate or give input

**unite:** One of three modes of conflict resolution; defines team members as joint problem solvers as opposed to adversaries; a win–win approach to problem solving

**unplugged:** Referring to the avoidance of checking e-mail, sending text messages, watching television, or answering the phone

**upward distortion:** The alteration of messages sent from subordinates to supervisors

**values:** Moral principles or rules that determine ethical behaviors

**vampire:** A type of difficult person characterized by an appealing personality and a lack of productivity; a type of slacker

**verbal communication:** Includes both our words and our verbal fillers (e.g., *um*, *like*)

**videoconference:** A type of interview conducted via live video

**virtual work team:** Tasks and professional projects traditionally accomplished face-to-face that are computer mediated to save on time and travel

**visual learners:** Audience members who more easily comprehend and remember information presented to them through visual as opposed to audio channels

**vocal fillers:** Also known as vocalized pauses; occur when the speaker should pause but instead fills the silence; common fillers include umm, aah, *and*, and *like*

**vocalics:** Sometimes referred to as paralanguage; refers to how people use their voices to communicate and express themselves

**volume:** The loudness or softness of a speaker's voice

**voting:** A decision-making approach in which team members cast a vote for the solution they find meritorious; the solution that receives the most votes is implemented

**warrior:** One of the four roles in innovative problem solving; develops and carries out the plan

**white space:** The portion of the résumé that is void of text; balancing text and white space creates visual appeal; also, the unprescribed portions of the organizational chart where the informal communication network develops

**withholding:** Subordinates fail to pass information on to supervisors

**word of mouth:** A useful tool in the job-seeking process; involves telling everyone the job seeker knows that he or she is job seeking; most effective when the job seeker is specific about the kind of job he or she is seeking

**work:** Instrument of activity intended to provide goods and services to support life

**workforce communication assessment:** An inventory or evaluation of the communication practices of an organization (also known as a communication audit)

**work–life balance:** "Accomplishment of role-related expectations that are negotiated and shared between an individual and his or her role-related partners in the work and family [life] domains" (Grzywacz & Carlson, 2007, p. 458)

**workplace bullying:** Defined as repeated acts and practices that are directed intentionally or unconsciously and that cause embarrassment, humiliation, and stress

**workplace mobbing:** The nonsexual harassment of a coworker by a group of other workers or other members of an organization, designed to secure removal from the organization of the one who is targeted

**workplace surveillance systems:** Efforts to monitor and track employee behavior in terms of the information they access or communicate while at work

**worldview:** Culture's orientation to supernatural, human, and natural entities in the cosmological universe and other philosophical issues influencing how its members see the world

**writing startup sheet:** List of questions that encourage the writer to think about audience, purpose, key issues, and delivery

# Photo Credits

## Part I

Part I Photo   © Jupiterimages/liquidlibrary/Thinkstock

## Chapter 1

Chapter Opener Photo   © Thinkstock/Comstock/ Thinkstock
Photo 1.1   © Brand X Pictures/Brand X Pictures
Photo 1.2   © Pixland/Jupiterimages/Thinkstock
Photo 1.3   © iStockphoto.com/skynesher
Photo 1.4   © iStockphoto.com/aprott
Photo 1.5   © iStockphoto.com/webphotographeer
Photo 1.6   © Jupiterimages/Goodshoot/Thinkstock
Photo 1.7   © Creatas Images/Creatas/Thinkstock

## Chapter 2

Chapter Opener Photo   © iStockphoto.com/fstop123
Photo 2.1   © Jupiterimages/Comstock/Thinkstock
Photo 2.2   © Comstock Images/Comstock/Thinkstock
Photo 2.3   © Goodshoot/Goodshoot/Thinkstock
Photo 2.4   © Stockbyte/Stockbyte/Thinkstock
Photo 2.5   © Creatas/Creatas/Thinkstock
Photo 2.6   © Jupiterimages/Brand X Pictures/Thinkstock
Photo 2.7   © Jupiterimages/BananaStock/Thinkstock
Photo 2.8   © Digital Vision./Digital Vision/Thinkstock

## Chapter 3

Chapter Opener Photo   © Digital Vision/Digital Vision/ Thinkstock
Photo 3.1   © Jupiterimages/Comstock/Thinkstock
Photo 3.2   © Creatas/Creatas/Thinkstock
Photo 3.3   © Jupiterimages/liquidlibrary/Thinkstock
Photo 3.4   © Christopher Robbins/Photodisc/Thinkstock
Photo 3.5   © Noel Hendrickson/Lifesize/Thinkstock
Photo 3.6   © Digital Vision./Photodisc/Thinkstock
Photo 3.7   © iStockphoto.com/bowdenimages

## Part II

Part II Photo   © iStockphoto.com/AdamGregor

## Chapter 4

Chapter Opener Photo   © AP Photo/Tim Post
Photo 4.1   © iStockphoto.com/YinYang
Photo 4.2   © iStockphoto.com/alexsl
Photo 4.3   © iStockphoto.com/Pixsooz
Photo 4.4   © Brand X Pictures/Brand X Pictures/ Thinkstock
Photo 4.5   © Stockbyte/Stockbyte/Thinkstock
Photo 4.6   © Photodisc/Photodisc/Thinkstock
Photo 4.7   © Comstock/Comstock/Thinkstock

## Chapter 5

Chapter Opener Photo   © iStockphoto.com/Juanmonino
Photo 5.1   © Digital Vision./Digital Vision/Thinkstock
Photo 5.2   © Jack Hollingsworth/Photodisc/Thinkstock
Photo 5.3   © George Doyle/Stockbyte/Thinkstock
Photo 5.4   © iStockphoto.com/calvinng
Photo 5.5   © Digital Vision./Digital Vision/Thinkstock

## Part III

Part III Photo   © iStockphoto.com/Yuri_Arcurs

## Chapter 6

Chapter Opener Photo   © iStockphoto.com/shaunl
Photo 6.1   © Jupiterimages/Photos.com/Thinkstock
Photo 6.2   © iStockphoto.com/mediaphotos
Photo 6.3   © iStockphoto.com/alexsl
Photo 6.4   © Jack Hollingsworth/Photodisc/Thinkstock
Photo 6.5   © Pinnacle Pictures/Photodisc/Thinkstock
Photo 6.6   © Hemera Technologies/AbleStock.com/ Thinkstock
Photo 6.7   © iStockphoto.com/MivPiv
Photo 6.8   © iStockphoto.com/SamBurt

## Chapter 7

Chapter Opener Photo   © Jupiterimages/Polka Dot/ Thinkstock
Photo 7.1   © Dennis Wise/Digital Vision/Thinkstock
Photo 7.2   © Jupiterimages/Photos.com/Thinkstock
Photo 7.3   © Jupiterimages/Comstock/Thinkstock
Photo 7.4   © AbleStock/AbleStock.com/Thinkstock
Photo 7.5   © Jupiterimages/Creatas/Thinkstock
Photo 7.6   © Jupiterimages/Creatas/Thinkstock
Photo 7.7   © Comstock/Comstock/Thinkstock
Photo 7.8   © BananaStock/BananaStock/Thinkstock

## Part IV

Part IV Photo   © iStockphoto.com/Vasko

## Chapter 8

Chapter Opener Photo   © iStockphoto.com/courtneyk
Photo 8.1   © Creatas/Creatas/Thinkstock
Photo 8.2   © Ryan McVay/Photodisc/Thinkstock
Photo 8.3   © iStockphoto.com/fazon1
Photo 8.4   © iStockphoto.com/cglade
Photo 8.5   © iStockphoto.com/RushOnPhotography
Photo 8.6   © iStockphoto.com/robas
Photo 8.7   © iStockphoto.com/stevecoleimages
Photo 8.8   © iStockphoto.com/twohumans
Photo 8.9   © Jupiterimages/Pixland/Thinkstock

## Chapter 9

Chapter Opener Photo   © iStockphoto.com/ymgerman
Photo 9.1   © Creatas Images/Creatas/Thinkstock
Photo 9.2   © iStockphoto.com/DNY59
Photo 9.3   © Jupiterimages/Comstock/Thinkstock
Photo 9.4   © iStockphoto.com/hocus-focus
Photo 9.5   © Jack Hollingsworth/Stockbyte/Thinkstock
Photo 9.6   © iStockphoto.com/myshotz

## Chapter 10

Chapter Opener Photo   © Comstock/Comstock/ Thinkstock
Photo 10.1   © iStockphoto.com/MichaelDeLeon

Photo 10.2   © Thinkstock/Comstock/Thinkstock
Photo 10.3   © Mike Powell/Digital Vision/Thinkstock
Photo 10.4   © Digital Vision./Photodisc/Thinkstock
Photo 10.5   © Jupiterimages/Comstock/Thinkstock
Photo 10.6   © iStockphoto.com/jeangill
Photo 10.7   © iStockphoto.com/teekid
Photo 10.8   © iStockphoto.com/sjlocke

## Part V

Part V Photo   © iStockphoto.com/Thomas_EyeDesign

## Chapter 11

Chapter Opener Photo   © iStockphoto.com/mbbirdy
Photo 11.1   © Comstock/Comstock/Thinkstock
Photo 11.2   © John Rowley/Photodisc/Thinkstock
Photo 11.3   © iStockphoto.com/Leontura
Photo 11.4   © Digital Vision./Photodisc/Thinkstock
Photo 11.5   © Jupiterimages/Goodshoot/Thinkstock

## Chapter 12

Chapter Opener Photo   © EPA/Alamy
Photo 12.1   © Comstock/Comstock/Thinkstock
Photo 12.2   © Jupiterimages/Comstock/Thinkstock
Photo 12.3   © iStockphoto.com/dosecreative
Photo 12.4   © Comstock Images/Comstock/Thinkstock
Photo 12.5   © Digital Vision./Digital Vision/Thinkstock
Photo 12.6   © Digital Vision./Digital Vision/Thinkstock
Photo 12.7   © iStockphoto.com/Alina555

## Chapter 13

Chapter Opener Photo   © iStockphoto.com/EdStock
Photo 13.1   © iStockphoto.com/goldenKB
Photo 13.2   © Creatas/Creatas/Thinkstock
Photo 13.3   © Stockbyte/Stockbyte/Thinkstock
Photo 13.4   © Jupiterimages/Goodshoot/Thinkstock
Photo 13.5   © iStockphoto.com/Yuri_Arcurs

## Part VI

Part VI Photo   © iStockphoto.com/PeskyMonkey

## Chapter 14

Chapter Opener Photo   © Comstock Images/Comstock/ Thinkstock
Photo 14.1   © Jupiterimages/Polka Dot/Thinkstock
Photo 14.2   © Jupiterimages/Comstock/Thinkstock
Photo 14.3   © Comstock Images/Comstock/Thinkstock
Photo 14.4   © iStockphoto.com/joakimbkk
Photo 14.5   © iStockphoto.com/DoxaDigital
Photo 14.6   © Andrea Chu/Digital Vision/Thinkstock
Photo 14.7   © Jupiterimages/Brand X Pictures/Thinkstock
Photo 14.8   © iStockphoto.com/Olga_Danylenko
Photo 14.9   © altrendo images/Stockbyte/Thinkstock

## All Chapters

Executive Summary Background Photo   © Comstock/ Comstock/Thinkstock

# Index

Accent, 116
Action-oriented listeners, 59
Active agreement, 270
Active listener
definition, 58
failing to be, 57–59
Adapters, 39
Adjourning stage, of team
development, 172
Adrenaline rush, 312–315
Advocacy, 131
Affect displays, 38–39
Agenda, 154. *See also* Meetings
Alexander the Great, 268
Analogical reasoning, 280
Anger, and emotional intelligence,
360–363
Angry customers and clients, 346
Annual feedback trap, 252
Appearance
job interviews and, 92–95
physical, 37
Applying stage, and the job-seeking
process, 77–88
cover letters, developing, 84–88
résumés, customizing, 82–83, 84
résumés, developing, 77–81
résumés, electronic and scannable,
83–84
online applications, developing,
83–84
*See also* Job-seeking process
Apprehension, communication,
15–17
Aristotle, 268
Artifacts, 37, 108
Artist, role in team
communication,167
*Art of Rhetoric, The* (Aristotle), 268
Assimilation, of college students,
107–112
Assimilation process, 105
Asynchronous time, 193
Attitude, 217, 240 (table)

Audience analysis, in speech design,
290–291
Audience-based communication
apprehension, 15
Audience-centered speaker, 290
Audio clips, 321
Authoritative, 239
Awards and honors, in résumés, 81

Balance, 339, 357–358. *See also*
Work-life balance
Bar chart, 323 (figure)
Barrett, Colleen, 105 (figure)
Bay of Pigs, 170
Behavioral questions, 89
Behavioral leadership theories,
239–240
Bias, 56
Birthright, 235
Blagojevich, Rod, 289
Blair, Jayson, 50
Blake, Robert, 241
Body language. *See* Nonverbal
communication
Body movement, 38–39
Boundaries, technologically blurred,
and work-life balance, 351–352
Boundary, 339
Bully, 248
Burnout, causes of, 341
Business and professional
communication. *See*
Communication; KEYS process;
Workplace, the
Business and professional writing.
*See* Written communication
Business letters, 207–208,
208 (figure), 209 (figure)

Call to action, 270
Career
exploration, 74–75
planning centers, 75
Castro, Fidel, 169

Causal reasoning, 279–280
Channel, 13
Charisma, 234
Charts, 321
Chopourian, Ani, 147, 174
Chronemics, 193
Chronological résumé, 78
Classified/help-wanted ads, 75
Clients, angry, 346
CMC. *See* Computer-mediated
communication
Coach, 156
Codes, 33
Coercive power, 237
Cognitive dissonance, 280–281
College students, assimilating,
107–112
Colloquialisms, 304
Combination résumé, 79
Common ground, 279
Communication
apprehension, 15–17
as work, 373–374
bravado, 10
competencies list, 11 (table)
defining, 10
ethics, 17–19
importance of, 10–11
Keys process, understanding,
8–10
model, 12 (figure)
process of, 11–14
*See also* Interpersonal
communication; KEYS
process; Leadership; Listening;
Nonverbal communication;
Professional presentations;
Team communication;
Technology; Verbal
communication; Workplace,
the; Written communication
Communication interaction,
14 (exercise), 54 (exercise),
78 (exercise), 108 (exercise),

130 (exercise), 159 (exercise), 165 (exercise), 188 (exercise), 210–211 (exercise), 247 (exercise), 274–277 (exercise), 300 (exercise), 330–331 (exercise), 362 (exercise)
Communication network, 132–133
Communication privacy management
    at work, 137–139
    theory, 138
Community, 340
Compromise, 164
Computer-mediated communication (CMC), 182, 187 (exercise). See also Technology
Conclusions, in speech design, 301
Conflict, in team meetings, 169–174
    definition, 169
    groupthink and, 169–170
    meetingthink and, 170–172
    need for, 169–172
    productive conflict, 172
    unite approach, 173–174
    See also Team meetings
Conflict management. See Leadership
Connection power, 237
Connotation, 282
Consensus, 164
Constitutive rules, 28
Contact information, in résumés, 79
Content layer, 41
Content-oriented listeners, 59
Context, 13
Context analysis, in speech design, 291–292
Context-based communication apprehension, 15
Contingency Theory, 242
Conversational listening, 59
Conversational quality, 315–316
Cook, Tim, 49, 62
Corporate blog, 196
Corporate trainer, 322 (exercise)
Cover letters
    definition, 84
    developing, 84–88
Coworker relationships, 132–134
Credibility, 271, 272 (exercise)
Criteria, 162
Critical listening, 58
Criticism, making it constructive, 250 (table)
Cultural competence, 113–114

Cultural diversity awareness and worldview, 112
Cultural rituals, 110
Culture, 104. See also Organizational culture
Cussing Jar, 159 (exercise)
Cuss words, 304
Customer-client relationships, 134–135
Customer relations, 134
Customers, angry, 346
Customer service experience, 130 (exercise)
Customized cover letter and résumé, 87–88 (figure)
Customized résumé, 78

Data, qualitative and quantitative, 220
Debate team dilemma, 295 (exercise)
Decision by the leader approach, 163
Decision making, 159–160
Decode, 12
Deductive reasoning, 280
Deintensification, 39
Delivery, 312
Democratic leadership, 239
Demonstrations, 322–326
Devil's advocate, 163
Dewey, John, 160
Dialect, 116
Difficult people
    dealing with, 248–251
    impact of, on work-life balance, 345–351
Disabilities, people with, in professional contexts, 119–120
Discrimination, 114
Disguising conversation, 107
Distracter, 249
Distractions, limiting, 53–55
Diverse workplace, 6–7, 103–123
    college students and, 107–112
    concepts, 112–114
    culture and, 104–107
    examples of, in professional contexts, 114–120
    KEYS to excellence in, 120–121
Downsizing, business letter for, 208, 209 (figure)
Drama queen, 248
Dyads, 128

Education, in résumés, 79–80
Electronic aggression, 196
Electronic bulletin board, 196
Electronic communication, 184–190. See also E-mail
Electronic résumés, 83
E-mail, 228
    affection in, 191 (exercise)
    being aware of, 186 (table)
    checklist for appropriate content, 189 (table)
    clutter, managing, 193 (table)
    dialogues, 196
    flame, 196
    forwards, 194–195
    inappropriate content, 190 (exercise)
    inappropriate use of, 195 (exercise)
    security issues, 192 (table)
    writing with professional excellence, 228 (table)
    See also Electronic communication
Emblems, 38
Emotional intelligence, 359–363
Empathetic listening, 58
Employee
    attrition, 342
    downsizing, business letter for, 208, 209 (figure)
    firing, 256–257
    profile, 243–244
    retention, 342
    reviews, 208–209, 210–211
    surveillance, and technology, 191–193
Employment experience, in résumés, 80–81
Encode, 12
Environment, perceptions of, 36–37
Ethical connection, 20 (exercise), 56 (exercise), 80 (exercise), 113 (exercise), 155 (exercise), 190 (exercise), 212 (exercise), 258 (exercise), 282 (exercise), 295 (exercise), 329 (exercise), 360 (exercise)
Ethical considerations, 17–18, 19 (exercise)
Ethical dilemmas, 18
Ethics, 17
Ethnicity, in professional contexts, 115
Ethos, 271–273

Evaluating, and listening, 60
Evaluation
   guidelines for, 163 (table)
   tools for, 162 (table)
Excellence. *See* KEYS process
Expectations, setting, 252
Experience, listed in résumés, 80
Expert power, 237
Explorer, role in team
      communication, 166–167
Exploring stage, and the
      job-seeking process, 73–75
   career exploration, 74–75
   self-exploration, 73
   *See also* Job-seeking process
External communication plan, 221
External customers, 134
External noise, 14, 53
External sources, 294
External time wasters, 363
External triggers, 360
Eye contact, 314

Facebook, 185 (table)
Face-saving behavior, 253
Face-to-face interviews, 92
Facial behavior, 39
Facial management techniques, 39
False close, 301
False empowerment, 170
False information, case of,
      282 (exercise)
Family, 339
Feedback, 13, 251–259
   enacting consequences, 256–257
   holding team members
      accountable, 253–255
   motivating through, 255
   praising team members, 253
   providing regularly, 252–253
   putting it all together, 257–259
   setting expectations, 252
Festinger, Leon, 280
Fight, 172
Fisher, Walter, 112
Flight, 172
Fluke, Sandra, 28
Focus group report and
      recommendation, 221–224
      (figure)
Followers, 234
Formal communication network, 133
Formal presentation, 269
Forming stage, of team
      development, 172

Friendship/warmth touch, 40
Functional (skill based) résumé, 78
Functional/professional touch, 40

Gatekeeping, 130–131
Gender, in professional
      contexts, 114
General distortion, 131
General language, 206
Generic résumé, 78, 85–86 (figure)
Globalization, 116
Goal Setting Theory, 255
Grammar, and written
      communication, 207
Grapevine, 133
Graphs, and speech delivery, 321
Group behavior, understanding,
      150 (exercise)
Group presentation, 329 (exercise)
Groups, versus teams, 148–149
Groupthink, 169–170
Grump, 248

Hall, Edward T., 34
Haptics, 40. *See also* Touch
Health problems, linked to stress,
      356 (table)
Hearing, and listening, 51–53, 60
Henderson, David, 267, 283
Henry, Stephen, 25
Hilton, Conrad, 235
Hilton, Paris, 235
Hobbies and interests, listed in
      résumés, 81
Huddles, 270
Human communication, 10
HURIER model, 60

ICTs (information and
      communications technologies),
      352. *See also* Technology
Illegal questions, in an interview, 96
Illustrations, in speech delivery,
      321, 325 (figure)
Illustrators, 38
Imagery, in speech design, 304
Imbalance triggers, 343–357
   difficult people, impact of,
      345–351
   life demands, 352–357
   personality types, 343–345
   technologically blurred
      boundaries, 351–352
   *See also* Work-life balance
Impression management, 259

Impromptu presentation, 270
Indirect questioning, 107
Individual benefits, of work-life
      balance, 341–342, 342 (table)
Inductive reasoning, 279
Inform, 270. *See also* Presentations,
      professional
Informal communication
      network, 133
Information, communicating,
      129–131
Informational listening, 57–58
Information and communications
      technologies (ICTs), 352.
      *See also* Technology
Information overload, 194–195
Informing and persuading. *See*
      Presentations, professional
Ingratiation, 131
Innovation, tools for, 161 (table)
Innovative thinking, in team
      communication, 166–169
   artist role, 167
   explorer role, 166–167
   judge role, 167–168
   warrior role, 168
Inoculation, 279
Intensification, 39
Interests, 173
Internal communication plan, 221
Internal customers, 134
Internal noise, 14, 53
Internal preview, 298
Internal sources, 292
Internal summary, 298
Internal time wasters, 363
Internal triggers, 360–361
Internet, 76
Internship, 75
Interpersonal communication, 7,
      127–145
   KEYS to excellence in, 142–143
   line between professional and
      personal, 135–139
   professional etiquette, 139–142
   relationship types, 129–135
Interpreting, 60
Interview, 6
   conducting, 294 (table)
   panel, 92
Interviewing stage, and the job-
      seeking process, 88–96,
      244–245
   after the interview, 245
   before the interview, 89–94

during the interview, 95–96, 244
*See also* Job-seeking process
Intimacy, 135
Intimate zone, 34
Introductions, in speech design, 299–301
*It's Always Something* (Radner), 274
Ivy, Diana K., 188

Janis, Irving, 170
Jargon, 55, 110
Job
    fairs, 75
    seeker, 73
    title, 235
Jobs, Steve, 49, 62, 311
Job-seeking process, 6, 71–101
    applying (stage three), 77–88
    exploring (stage one), 73–75
    following up (stage five), 96–97
    interviewing (stage four), 88–96
    KEYS to excellence in, 99
    negotiations (stage six), 97–98
    researching (stage two), 75–77
Judge, role in team communication, 167–168

Kennedy, John F., 169
KEYS Process, xiv, xv
    diverse workplace, excellence in, 120–121
    interpersonal communication, excellence in, 142–143
    job-seeking process, excellence in, 99
    leadership, excellence in, 260–261
    listening excellence, 62–63
    nonverbal communication, excellence in, 44–45
    professional presentations, excellence in, 283–285
    speech, delivering a, excellence in, 328–329
    speech design, excellence in, 305
    team communication, excellence in, 174–175
    technology and communication, excellence in, 198–199
    understanding, 8–10
    verbal communication, excellence in, 44–45
    work-life balance, excellence in, 368–369
    workplace, excellence in the, 19–21

written communication, excellence in, 229
*See also* Communication; Workplace, the
Khan, Hani, 103, 120
Kinesics, 38

Laissez-faire, 239
Language
    barriers, 116
    differences, in professional contexts, 116–118
    speech design and, 304–305
Lead, 165
Leadership, 8, 233–263
    definition, 236
    difficult people and, 248–251
    dilemma, 258 (exercise)
    excellence, reflections on, 261 (exercise)
    feedback and, 251–259
    functions, 237
    KEYS to excellence in, 260–261
    power and, 236–238
    public image and, 259–260
    teams and, 243–247
    theories, and improving communication, 239–243
    traits, 235 (table)
Legitimate power, 236
Lesbian, gay, bisexual, and transgender (LGBT), 139
Life demands, and work-life imbalance, 352–357
    health responsibilities, 356–357
    household and family responsibilities, 352–356
Limbaugh, Rush, 28
Listeners
    action-oriented, 59
    active, 57–59
    content-oriented, 59
    passive, 58
    people-oriented, 59
    reflective, 58–59
    time-oriented, 59
Listening, 6, 49–66
    anxiety, 61 (exercise)
    barriers to, 53–59
    conversational, 59
    critical, 58
    empathetic, 58
    hearing and, 51–53
    improving, 60–62
    informational, 57–58

KEYS to excellence in, 62–63
    presentational, 60
    styles and categories of, 59–60
Listserv, 196
Logos, 273
Love/intimacy touch, 40
Lynn, James, 127

Majority rule, 164
Manager, 237
Managerial functions, 237
Managerial Grid, 241, 241 (figure)
Manuscript, and speech delivery, 315–316
Masking, 39
McCroskey, James C., 15
McGregor, Douglas, 239
Media writing. *See* Proactive media writing
Meetings, 149–155
    environment, 150–153
    participants, 155
    topics (agenda), 154
    *See also* Team meetings
Meetingthink, 170–172
    avoiding, 171–172
    false empowerment and, 170
    overload and, 170–171
    poorly run meetings and, 171
    *See also* Team meetings
Memos, 212–219
Message, 13
    clarity, 205–206
    focusing on the, 55–57
    overload, 55
    presentation, 206–207
    structure, 205
Metaphor, 304
Miscovich, Peter, 181, 198
Mission statement, Starbucks Coffee, 106 (figure)
Misspellings, 207
Mock interviews, 91
Models, 322
Monotone, 315–316
Monroe's Motivated Sequence, 296
Mothers, and attractiveness of work, 355 (table)
Motivating, through feedback, 255
Mouton, Jane, 241
Mutual respect, 114

Narratives, 112
Negotiations, 6, 97. *See also* Job-seeking process

Nervousness, reducing, 94
Networking notes, 212
Neutralization, 39
Noise, 14
Nonverbal communication, 6, 25, 29–47
  behaviors associated with, 30–31
  codes of, 33–41, 33 (table)
  dimensions of use, 32
  forming relationships with, 41–44
  impact of, on professions, 42–44
  KEYS to excellence in, 44–45
  *See also* Verbal communication
Norm, 158
Norming stage, of team development, 172

Obama, Barack, 289
Obesity trends, among U.S. adults, 358 (figure)
Objective, 271
Objects, 322
Oculesics, 39
Oliver, Vicky, 3–4, 19
One-on-one interview, 92
Online applications, 83
Online postings, and professional life, 185 (table)
Online social-networking sites, 185 (table)
Orenic, Mary Claire, 337
Organizational Assimilation Index, 109–110 (exercise)
Organizational benefits, of work-life balance, 341–342, 343 (table)
Organizational chart, 133
Organizational culture, 104–105
  shift in, 108 (exercise)
  tactics to learn about, 107
Organizational family, 248–249
Organizational patterns, for presentations, 297 (table)
Organizational values, 18
Organizer, 327
Outline, presenting from an, 315–316
Overload, 170–171
Overtalker, 155
Overt questioning, 107

Panel interviews, 92
Paralanguage. *See* Vocalics
Paraphrase, 58
Parent, the leader as, 251

Parenting chart, lessons from, 255 (table)
Passive agreement, 270
Passive listener, 58
Pathos, 281–282
Patient, 249
PDAs, and work-life balance, 364–365, 365 (table)
People-oriented listeners, 59
Perception checking, 113–114
Performance appraisal, 252
Performance improvement plan, 254
Performance review, 238 (exercise)
Performing stage, of team development, 172
Personality types, and work-life balance, 343–345
Personal zone, 34
Persuade, 270. *See also* Presentations, professional
Persuasive appeals, 271
Persuasive speech, example of, 302–303
Petronio, Sandra, 137
Phishing, 194–195
Photos, 321
Physical appearance, 37–38
Pie chart, 324 (figure)
Plagiarism, 212 (exercise)
Plan, implementing, 166 (table)
Planning documents, 220–221
Play, sense of, and presentations, 315, 317 (exercise)
Pomerleau, Raymond, 104
Position, 173
Power, utilizing, 236–238
PowerPoint and other supporting aids in presentations, 316–326
Practice, and delivering a speech, 326
Presentational listening, 60
Presentations, professional, 8, 267–287
  identifying opportunities and purposes, 269–271
  importance of professional excellence in, 269
  KEYS to excellence in, 283–285
  outline template, 316 (table)
  organizing, 296–298
  quick guide to first, 327
  speaking to inform, 271–278, 274–277 (exercise)
  speaking to persuade, 278–283

supporting aids in, 316–326
  *See also* Speech, delivering a; Speech design
Press releases, 221–226
Price quote, business letter for, 207, 208 (figure)
Privacy. *See* Communication privacy management
Private employment agencies, 76
Proactive media writing, 227–228
Problem solving, and team communication, 158–166
Process directives, 215, 218 (figure)
Productive conflict, 172
Professional associations, 76
Professional context, 18 (exercise), 29 (exercise), 30 (exercise), 57 (exercise), 111 (exercise), 140 (exercise), 165 (exercise), 191 (exercise), 216 (exercise), 245 (exercise), 284 (exercise), 293 (exercise), 317 (exercise), 353 (exercise)
Professional etiquette, 139–142, 184, 197–198
Professional handshake, 40
Professional life, and online postings, 185 (table)
Professional presentations. *See* Presentations, professional
Professions, impact of verbal and nonverbal communication on, 42–44
  accounting and finance, 44
  customer service and sales, 42–43
  hospitality management, 43
  journalism and television broadcasting, 43
  legal, 44
  management, private and public, 44
  medical, 43
  public service, 43
  teaching, 43
Proposals, for services, 219, 219–220 (figure)
Proxemics, 34
Public image, 259–260
Public zone, 34

Qualitative data, 220
Quantitative data, 220
Questions, 59
  anticipating, 89–90
  self-monitoring, 131 (table)
Quintilian, 272

Race, in professional contexts, 115
Radner, Gilda, 274
Rapport talk, 115
Reasoning, types of, 279–281
Receiver, 12
Receiver apprehension, 55
Recommendation letters, 209–211, 213–214 (table), 215 (figure), 216 (exercise)
References, listed in résumés, 81
Referent power, 237
Reflection, 58, 118 (exercise), 137 (exercise), 153 (exercise), 195 (exercise), 217 (exercise), 238 (exercise), 281 (exercise), 291 (exercise), 322 (exercise), 354 (exercise)
Reflective listener, 58–59
Reflective Thinking Process, 160
Regulative rules, 27
Regulators, 39
Relational layer, 41, 129
Relationship roles, 156
Relationships, forming with verbal and nonverbal communication, 41–44
Relationship types, at work, 129–135
    coworker, 132–134
    customer-client, 134–135
    superior-subordinate, 129–132
Relaxation time, by country, 366 (table)
Relevant experience, listed in résumés 80
Religion, in professional contexts, 118–119
Remembering, 60
Repetition, 304
Reports, 219
Report talk, 115
Researching, in speech design, 292–296
Researching stage, and the job-seeking process, 75
    openings, 75–76
    potential employers, 76–77
    See also Job-seeking process
Responding, 60
Résumé, 6, 77–88
    action words, 83 (figure)
    cover letters for, 84–88
    customizing, 82–83, 84
    developing, 77–81
    electronic and scannable, 83–84

sections of, 79–81
    See also Job-seeking process
Retention, 318
Reward power, 237
Rheem, Carroll, 367
Roach, Terry, 185
Roadblock to change, 249
Roberts, Sherry, 185
Rockne, Knute, 167
Role models, 251
Romance, in the workplace, 135
Round robin technique, 174

Salary questions, in an interview, 96
Scannable résumés, 83
Scripting, 256
Scripting answers, 90–91
Self-centered roles, 156
Self-disclose, 138
Self-exploration, 73
Self-monitoring questions, 131 (table)
Semantic information distance, 129
Sender, 12
Sense of play, and presentations, 315, 317 (exercise)
Sexual arousal, 41
Sexual harassment, 136
Sexual orientation, 139, 139 (table)
Shadowing, 75
Signposts, 298
Situational communication apprehension, 15
Situational leadership styles (Hersey and Blanchard), 242 (table)
Situational leadership theories, 241–242
Situational Leadership Theory, 242
Skills, listed in résumés, 80
Slacker, 248
Slang, 304
Sniper, 248
Socialization, 104
Social/polite touch, 40
Social zone, 34
Sociopath, 257
Solutions, in team communication, 162–165
Southwest Airlines, and workplace culture, 105 (figure)
Space, 34
Spam, 194–195
Speaking to inform, 271–278
    ethos, 271–273
    informing with excellence, strategies for, 276–278

logos, 273
    See also Presentations, professional
Speaking to persuade, 278–283
    pathos, 281–282
    persuading with excellence, strategies for, 282–283
    reasoning, types of, 279–281
    See also Presentations, professional
Speaking outline, 319
Speaking rate, 314
Specific language, 206
Speech, delivering a, 311–333
    KEYS to excellence in, 328–329
    PowerPoint and other supporting aids, 316–326
    practice and, 326
    professional excellence and, 312–315
    team presentations, 326–328
    See also Presentations, professional; Speech design
Speech design, 289–308
    audience analysis, 290
    conclusions, 301
    context analysis, 291–292, 292 (table)
    introductions, 299–301
    KEYS to excellence in, 305
    language, 304–305
    organizing, 296–299
    researching, 292–296
    See also Presentations, professional; Speech, delivering a
Spirituality, in professional contexts, 118–119
Stages of team development, 172
Star, 249
Starbucks Coffee mission statement, 106 (figure), 249
State employment service, 76
Status, 236
Stereotypes, 116
Storming stage, of team development, 172
Stout, Martha, 257
Strategic communication plan
    external, 225 (figure)
    internal, 225 (figure)
Strategic planning, 220
Strengthening teams and conducting meetings, 7

Stress, health problems linked to, 356 (table)
Subordinate, 129, 236
Superior-subordinate relationships, 129–132
Supervisor, communicating with, 131–132
Supporting aids, 317, 319–326
  audio clips, 321
  demonstrations, 322–326
  graphs, charts, illustrations, and photos, 321
  objects and models, 322
  PowerPoint presentations, 319–321
  video clips, 321
Surveillance, 107, 191–192
Synchronous time, 193

Tannen, Deborah, 115
Task roles, 156
Team, 148
  communicating about, 246–247
  hiring the right, 243–245
  members, 253–255
  player, 249
  presentations, 326–328, 330–331
  See also Team communication; Team meetings
Team communication, 7, 147–177
  groups versus teams, 148–149
  innovative thinking, cultivating, 166–169
  KEYS to excellence in, 174–175
  problem solving and, 158–166
  meetings, 149–155, 169–174
  team norms, 156–158
  team roles, 156, 157 (table)
  See also Team
Team meetings
  conducting, 149–155
  conflict in, 169–174
  following up and following through, 246
  See also Team communication
Technology, 7, 181–201, 352
  communication and, 182–190
  drawbacks of, 190–196
  KEYS to excellence with, 198
  professional etiquette with, 197–198

Technologically blurred boundaries, and work-life balance, 351–352
Telecommuting, 353 (exercise)
Telephone interviews, 92
Testing limits, 107
Texting language, 304
Thank-you letters, 212, 216 (figure)
Theory X, 239
Theory Y, 239
Third-party questioning, 107
Time, prioritizing, 364 (table)
Time management, 193–194, 363–364, 364 (table)
Time-oriented listeners, 59
Time wasters, 363 (table)
Tools for evaluation, 162 (table)
Tools for innovation, 161 (table)
Touch, 40–41
Traditional questions, 89
Trait, 234
Trait communication apprehension, 15
Transformational leaders, 243
Transformational leadership, 243
Translation services, 117
Truman, Harry S., 247
Typos, 207

Understanding, 60
Undertalker, 155
Unite approach, for conflict resolution, 173–174
Unplugged, 194
Upward distortion, 130

Vacations, and work-life balance, 366–368
Values, 18
Vampire, 248
Verbal communication, 6, 25–29, 41–47
  forming relationships with, 41–44
  impact of, on professions, 42–44
  KEYS to excellence in, 44–45
  See also Nonverbal communication
Video clips, 321
Videoconference, 92
Virtual work team, 182
Visual learners, 318
Vocal expression, 33–34

Vocal fillers, 314
Vocalics, 33
Volume, 314
Voting, 164

Wahl, Shawn T., 188
Warrior, role in team communication, 168, 168 (table)
White space, 82, 133
Withholding, 131
Wood, Julia, 115
Word of mouth, 76
Work, 340
  attitude about, 240 (table)
  attractiveness of, to mothers, 355 (table)
  excess, 360 (exercise)
  interpersonal communication at, 127–145
Workforce communication assessment, 219
Work-life balance, 8, 337–372
  defined, 339–341
  imbalance, triggers to, 343–357
  importance of, 338–343
  KEYS to excellence in, 368–369
  strategies for, 357–358
Workplace, the, 3–23
  bullying, 346–348, 348 (table), 349 (table), 350 (table)
  business and professional excellence in, 5–8
  culture, 104–107
  diversity, 112–114
  KEYS to excellence in, 19–21
  mobbing, 348–351
  romance in, 135
  surveillance systems, 192
  See also Communication; Diverse workplace; Job-seeking process; Work-life balance
Worldview, 112
Writing, business and professional. See Written communication
Writing startup sheet, 206 (exercise), 207
Written communication 7–8, 203–231
  importance of, 204–207
  KEYS to excellence in, 229
  types of, 207–228

# About the Authors

**Kelly M. Quintanilla** is the dean of the College of Liberal Arts and director of the School of Arts, Media, and Communication at Texas A&M University–Corpus Christi. She earned her PhD in communication from Pennsylvania State University in 1994, joining the A&M–CC faculty that same year. She was a professor of communication for 16 years, teaching courses in business and professional communication, teamwork and leadership, organizational communication, public relations, and public speaking. Additionally, she served as department chair/program coordinator in communication from 2000 to 2009. Over the years, Dr. Quintanilla has received awards for her teaching, service, advising, and scholarship. She has also worked as an executive coach and an organizational communication consultant for a variety of industries. Although she loves her career, her greatest love is spending time with her husband, Anthony, and daughter, Logan, on the sunny beaches of South Texas.

**Shawn T. Wahl** (PhD, University of Nebraska, Lincoln) is a professor of communication and head of the Department of Communication in the School of Communication Studies at Missouri State University (MSU). Prior to MSU, he served as head of the Department of Communication, Mass Media, and Theatre at Angelo State University and as the director of graduate studies at Texas A&M University, Corpus Christi. He is coauthor of *The Nonverbal Self: Communication for a Lifetime, Business and Professional Communication: KEYS for Workplace Excellence,* and *Persuasion in Your Life,* and has published articles in *Communication Education, Communication Research Reports, Communication Teacher, Journal of Family Communication,* and *Basic Communication Course Annual.* Shawn served as editor of the *Texas Speech Communication Journal* and is an active member of the National Communication Association, the Central States Communication Association, and the Texas Speech Communication Association. In addition, Shawn has worked across the nation as a corporate trainer, communication consultant, and leadership coach in a variety of industries. Outside of his professional work, he enjoys spending time with his family and two Chinese pugs (Mia and Jake).